...TERATURE
...GY

AFTER the turbulent years of the Civil War and republic, English society and its culture moved in new directions when the monarchy was restored in 1660. New literary forms and styles were developed, and both poetry and drama reached out to wider audiences. The present anthology gathers a wide range of writing from this confident and creative period—a literature which is by turns refined, poignant, and brash. The book is divided into five thematic sections which illustrate the richness and diversity of Restoration culture. In the first, writers shape the renewed national identity, and engage in the emergence of party politics, handling public figures (including the monarch) with a freedom almost unparalleled in earlier literature. The second section, on the town and the country, shows how Restoration literature delighted in satirical observation of London life, while seeing the countryside as a haven of peace. Much Restoration writing takes poetry and the theatre as its subject matter, and the third section reprints satires, elegies, theatrical prologues, and criticism to compose a picture of the literary scene—writers, actresses, audiences, and coffee-house wits. Love and friendship form the focus of the fourth section, which assembles lyrics, satires, dramatic extracts, and autobiographical writings; here one encounters the period's concern with sexual freedom and its characteristically uninhibited vocabulary. The final section gathers writing on religion and philosophy which ranges from mystical devotion to vigorous scepticism. Restoration literature is wide-ranging not only in its subjects but also in its forms, and alongside major canonical literature by writers such as Dryden and Rochester this collection prints scurrilous satires and pamphlets—usually anonymous—which lampooned the period's politicians, along with diaries, theatrical prologues, translations, and several poems newly recovered from manuscript sources.

PAUL HAMMOND is Professor of Seventeenth-Century English Literature at the University of Leeds. He has published extensively on Restoration literature, and his books include *John Oldham and the Renewal of Classical Culture* (1983), *John Dryden: A Literary Life* (1991), *Love between Men in English Literature* (1996), and *Dryden and the Traces of Classical Rome* (1999). He is the editor of *The Poems of John Dryden*, 5 vols. (1995– , in progress) and of *Selected Poems of John Wilmot, Earl of Rochester* (1982). In 2000 he co-edited *John Dryden: Tercentenary Essays* with David Hopkins.

OXFORD WORLD'S CLASSICS

*For over 100 years Oxford World's Classics have brought
readers closer to the world's great literature. Now with over 700
titles—from the 4,000-year-old myths of Mesopotamia to the
twentieth century's greatest novels—the series makes available
lesser-known as well as celebrated writing.*

*The pocket-sized hardbacks of the early years contained
introductions by Virginia Woolf, T. S. Eliot, Graham Greene,
and other literary figures which enriched the experience of reading.
Today the series is recognized for its fine scholarship and
reliability in texts that span world literature, drama and poetry,
religion, philosophy and politics. Each edition includes perceptive
commentary and essential background information to meet the
changing needs of readers.*

OXFORD WORLD'S CLASSICS

Restoration Literature

An Anthology

Edited with an Introduction and Notes by
PAUL HAMMOND

OXFORD
UNIVERSITY PRESS

OXFORD

UNIVERSITY PRESS

Great Clarendon Street, Oxford OX2 6DP

Oxford University Press is a department of the University of Oxford.
It furthers the University's objective of excellence in research, scholarship,
and education by publishing worldwide in

Oxford New York

Athens Auckland Bangkok Bogotá Buenos Aires Cape Town
Chennai Dar es Salaam Delhi Florence Hong Kong Istanbul Karachi
Kolkata Kuala Lumpur Madrid Melbourne Mexico City Mumbai Nairobi
Paris São Paulo Shanghai Singapore Taipei Tokyo Toronto Warsaw

with associated companies in Berlin Ibadan

Oxford is a registered trade mark of Oxford University Press
in the UK and in certain other countries

Published in the United States
by Oxford University Press Inc., New York

British Library Cataloguing in Publication Data

Data available

Library of Congress Cataloging in Publication Data

Restoration literature: an anthology/edited with an introduction and notes
by Paul Hammond.
p. cm.—(Oxford world's classics)
Includes bibliographical references.
1. English literature—Early modern, 1500–1700. 2. Great Britain—History—Restoration,
1660–1688—Literary collections. I. Hammond, Paul, 1953–.
II. Oxford world's classics (Oxford University Press)
PR1131.R47 2002 820.8'004—dc21 2001036908

ISBN 0–19–283331–6

1 3 5 7 9 10 8 6 4 2

Typeset in Ehrhardt
by RefineCatch Limited, Bungay, Suffolk
Printed in Great Britain by
Cox & Wyman Ltd.
Reading, Berkshire

ACKNOWLEDGEMENTS

THE extracts from Pepys's diary are taken from *The Diary of Samuel Pepys*, edited by Robert Latham and William Matthews, 11 vols. (London, 1970–83), copyright © 1972–1986 The Master, Fellows and Scholars of Magdalen College, Cambridge, Robert Latham, and the Executors of William Matthews, and reproduced by kind permission of HarperCollins and the University of California Press. The extract from Lucy Hutchinson's memoir 'To My Children' is taken from *Memoirs of the Life of Colonel Hutchinson with a Fragment of Autobiography*, edited by N. H. Keeble (London, 1995), copyright J. M. Dent, and reproduced by kind permission of the publisher. Poems from manuscripts in the Brotherton Collection, Leeds University Library, are reproduced by kind permission of the Librarian. Item 44h is printed by permission of The Huntington Library, San Marino, California.

I am grateful to Professor David Hopkins for his kindness in reading and commenting on this anthology in typescript.

CONTENTS

LOVE AND FRIENDSHIP

RELIGION AND PHILOSOPHY

INTRODUCTION

Restoration Literature

When our great monarch into exile went,
Wit and religion suffered banishment:
Thus once when Troy was wrapped in fire and smoke,
The helpless gods their burning shrines forsook;
They with the vanquished prince and party go,
And leave their temples empty to the foe:
At length the Muses stand restored again
To that great charge which Nature did ordain.
(JOHN DRYDEN, *To My Lord Chancellor*
(1662), ll. 17–24)

In these lines, part of a poem offered as a New Year's gift to the Earl
of Clarendon, Dryden represents the restoration of the monarchy in
1660 as the restoration, too, of literary culture. 'Wit', apparently, had
been banished along with the exiled Charles. If a single word could
encapsulate the characteristic tenor of Restoration literature, 'wit'
would be a good choice. The word had a wider range of meanings in
the 1660s than it commonly has today: intelligence, mental agility,
penetrating insight, pointed verbal expression, sharp repartee. It
connotes a self-conscious, stylish, civilized panache. It applies
equally to thoughtful philosophical insight and to comic devilment.
It is the hallmark of an intelligent, confident culture. Implicitly, in
Dryden's lines and elsewhere, it defines the gap between Restoration
culture and the preceding decades. The Civil War and Interregnum
were simply a period of destruction, of 'burning shrines', exemplified in miniature by the visit of the Parliamentarian soldiery to
Winchester Cathedral, where they tipped the bones of the Saxon
kings from their mortuary chests, and threw them through the great
west window. To this day, the window is a mosaic of fragments,
where one can pick out occasional heads of kings or saints, but no
pattern. Order and coherence have gone.

This, of course, is a wilfully selective view of English culture in
the 1640s and 1650s, for Dryden is constructing a version of the past
which throws into sharper relief the style and values of his new age.

In fact, poetry had flourished: Cowley, Davenant, Marvell, Milton, and Waller were writing verse which embraced a wide range of subjects, from pastoral to epic, and a variety of political stances from royalist to republican. The playhouses may have been closed, but drama continued to be written, to be read, and to be performed privately. There was prose fiction, in the form of long romances, some of which carried covert royalist messages. Newsbooks and political pamphlets included vigorous topical satire. Religious writing was by no means restricted to rebarbative puritan sermons, for the 1650s were the years of the Cambridge Platonists and the first Quakers, groups which in their different imaginative idioms sought the illumination of the Spirit. If that is what a dark age looks like, what was achieved when the world was 'wrapped in fire and smoke', one might well prefer it to our modern version of enlightenment.

But by choosing that word 'wit' to epitomize the ethos of the new, Restoration culture, Dryden was nevertheless pointing to something real and distinctive. In many of the media which flourished in the period 1660–1700 there is a distinctive poise, clarity, and bite—one might say a self-consciously adult attitude. The theatre exemplifies this. When the playhouses reopened, the two theatrical companies headed by Thomas Killigrew and Sir William Davenant found themselves reinventing the stage. To begin with, the repertoire consisted of Jacobean and Caroline drama, material from the days of Shakespeare and his successors, some of it adapted and refurbished for modern tastes. But soon a new generation of playwrights was providing material more in tune with the aspirations and anxieties of the age: heroic drama, with its longing for transcendence, its fear of life constrained by fate, its troubled attention to the limitations of human freedom; and social comedy, at once enjoying and satirizing the modern pursuit of fashion and of sexual liberty. And the drama moves away from the language of Shakespeare and his age, reflecting a new distaste for extravagant imagery and a relish for the idioms of contemporary metropolitan speech.

The audiences who gathered in the new, intimate, indoor playhouses—no longer in spaces which doubled as bear-baiting arenas—were socially diverse but culturally knowledgeable. Literacy was increasing, publishing was flourishing, commerce was generating wealth which could be used to finance civilized leisure. Royalist writers who had spent the 1650s abroad returned with new ideas about how drama, poetry, and philosophy might be conducted. Translations and adaptations brought literature in the modern and the classical languages within the grasp of readers for whom the originals were inaccessible, and contributed to an evolving sense of neo-classical style and decorum. In Dryden's critical essays from the 1660s and 1670s one hears repeatedly the notion that English culture is more civilized, more refined, more polite than that of Shakespeare's day. This is one aspect of 'wit'. At the same time, Restoration 'wit' is sometimes notoriously bawdy, unbuttoned, ranging beyond the boundaries of good taste and polite manners—but always with panache.

The characteristic verse form of the period is the rhyming couplet, a medium which permits a range of different kinds of wit. It can sound grave and tragic, as in Dryden's elegy on Oldham:

> Once more, hail and farewell; farewell thou young,
> But ah too short, Marcellus of our tongue;
> Thy brows with ivy, and with laurels bound;
> But fate and gloomy night encompass thee around. [33]

Here the movement of the verse is checked by interruption and repetition which evoke the emotion of mourning. The idiom is classical. By contrast, Oldham himself can use the couplet to catch the tone of the drunken bully threatening the innocent passer-by:

> 'Who's there', he cries, and takes you by the throat.
> 'Dog, are you dumb? Speak quickly, else my foot
> Shall march about your buttocks.'   [15]

Here the verse moves with colloquial ease, and the phrasing neatly catches the thug's unsteady mixture of brutal and elevated language. Many writers take advantage of the couplet's epigrammatic possibilities:

> Stiff in opinions, always in the wrong,
> Was everything by starts, and nothing long. [8]

> Man differs more from man, than man from beast.   [83]

Clarity, panache, precision, these are hallmarks of Restoration wit, appealing to a wider audience than the difficult extended imagery of Jacobean poetry.

To illustrate the wide range of wit in Restoration literature, the present anthology is arranged thematically, allowing readers to explore a variety of styles and attitudes in five areas of life. The first is that of national identity and the emergence of party politics, where writers handle public figures (including the King) with a freedom almost unparalleled in earlier literature, at least in print. Then we turn to images of the town and the country, mixing contemporary observation with reflections on what constitutes the good life. Literature and the theatre prove to be rich topics in themselves, as writers handle one another (and their readers) with scorn, envy, and even praise. Love and friendship form the focus of the fourth section, where one hears the distinctively Restoration combination of idealization and disenchantment. And finally, a group of writings on religion and philosophy show that this period was capable of poignant and profound reflection, as well as vigorous scepticism.

Politics and Nation

The term 'Restoration' is conventionally applied not only to the restoration of the monarchy in 1660, but to the whole reign of Charles II (1660–85), and even to the subsequent years up to the end of the seventeenth century. And this forty-year time-span is, in fact, the period covered by the present anthology. But like many cultural and political labels (such as 'Romantic', 'Victorian', 'Postmodern') the term 'Restoration' is convenient but treacherous, obscuring more than it illuminates. Contemporaries might more aptly have called this period 'the age of revolutions', taking the word 'revolution' in its seventeenth-century sense of 'turning around' or 'drastic alteration'. When Charles II, returning from his exile, landed at Dover on 25 May 1660, it seemed to many observers that the old order—the natural order—had been restored. Government of the state by King, Lords, and Commons, and of the Church by bishops and priests, would soon be in place again, and the rule of bourgeois republicans and puritan ministers consigned to oblivion. Pepys, Evelyn, and Dryden [3–5] saw the King's return as the result of both human and divine agency, for alongside the manœuvres of General George Monck, who had summoned Parliament and encouraged it to recall the King, the hand of Providence seemed to be at work. Charles was a second King David, chosen by God; a second Augustus who would bring to Britain the peace, strength, and culture which Rome had enjoyed under the first of its emperors. Apart from Clarendon [2a], writers do not see the reign of Charles I as a lost paradise; rather, the golden age which is being restored in 1660 is a mythic state. As Dryden saw it, the new reign was inaugurating a new epoch, not restoring an old [5]. And indeed, the years 1660–1700 would turn out to be a period of turbulent political change and cultural innovation.

Though the monarchy was restored in 1660, along with much of the visual and verbal imagery which had pertained before the Civil War, there could not be a straightforward resumption of Stuart rule: the monarchy had to be reinvented. Charles I had governed in too personal and autocratic a way for many men's liking, and his execution on that wintry morning of 30 January 1649 had shown irreparably that kings were ultimately accountable to their people, not to God alone, as Stuart ideology had claimed [2b]. Charles II had fewer and easier principles than his father; he was determined not to have to 'go on his travels again', and often preferred the company of his mistresses to that of his ministers. His sexual promiscuity became notorious, and made it harder to see the person of the monarch as sacred, a dilemma which Dryden explores in *Absalom and Achitophel* [8]. Both satirists and moralists disapproved of Charles's behaviour [7, 10]. But there is something to be said for a ruler who is unwilling either to be a martyr himself or to force others into martyrdom. Under Charles II the country was reasonably safe (albeit no longer the respected military power it had been under Cromwell [2c, 6]); Parliament sat frequently and exercised significant influence; and those who would not conform to the Church of England were able to practise their religion in private, albeit at the cost of occasional harassment.

But there was a profound fear which ran like an undertow through English politics, and undermined the peace and stability which Charles tried rather lazily to promote. Hobbes in *Leviathan* (1651) had identified fear as the strongest motivation for the creation of a state: in his view, society is formed in order to counter the fear of anarchy and the consequent loss of personal property. For many people in Restoration England the primal fear was rather of a return to Roman Catholic rule, last experienced more than a century earlier under Mary I. This was no chimera. The principle *cuius regio, eius religio* ('the people must follow their ruler's religion') was common in Europe. Since the time of Elizabeth I, Protestantism and English-ness had been intertwined in the national mythology, and many Protestants thought that rule by a Catholic monarch would mean rule by the Pope and Inquisition—by Antichrist—who would once again burn Protestants at the stake for the good of their souls. Charles I had married a Catholic wife and had made the Church of England more authoritarian and ritualistic, leading some to suspect him of favouring a return to Catholicism. Charles II was also mar-ried to a Catholic, and was suspected of harbouring Catholic sym-pathies himself—rightly suspected, as it turned out, for he was received into the Roman Church on his deathbed. Moreover, his heir was his openly Catholic brother James, Duke of York, and the pro-spect of his accession cast a shadow over the 1670s and early 1680s. In 1678 Titus Oates [9] alleged that there was a Popish Plot to overthrow the government and establish Roman Catholicism; in the panic which resulted from this charge—partly true, mostly invented—many Catholics were tried for treason, and some executed [74]. The atmosphere of paranoia which this generated helped to inflame fears about the succession, and the Whigs, led by the Earl of Shaftesbury, campaigned for James's powers to be transferred to a Protestant regent, or for him to be excluded altogether from the succession in favour of Charles's illegitimate son the Duke of Monmouth [8]. The move failed, and James succeeded on his brother's death in 1685; but he began to promote Catholicism with such blatant disregard for law and public harmony that prominent nobles secretly invited his Dutch Protestant son-in-law William of Orange to take over. It was conveniently unclear whether James II had abdicated or had been abdicated (in seventeenth-century English 'abdicate' is both a transitive and an intransitive verb); at any rate, he fled to France, and William and Mary became joint sovereigns at the invitation of Parliament. Whatever one's view of the legality of this constitutional move, the monarchy had obviously been reinvented once again. Some remained loyal to James as king *de jure*, refused to recognize William's legality [11], and formed a Jacobite faction to restore James. Dryden, Catholic and Jacobite by principle, grew to accept Williamite rule *de facto*, and turned to translation to ponder the tragedy of the destruction of human hopes [12].

One reason why the Civil War in the 1640s had led to an upsurge of radical political ideas is that printing was easy and cheap. New social and religious groups gained access to the medium for the first time, and this did not stop at the Restoration. The political and religious debate was conducted not only in Parliament and in the streets of London, but through print. Political satire developed as a powerful genre, mocking venal and incompetent government ministers, and ambitious, rabble-rousing opposition leaders [8, 9]. Some works were too dangerous to print, however, and manuscript circulation came to be the favoured medium for outspoken oppositional works [6, 7, 11], which were copied by professional scribes or ordinary readers and passed from hand to hand in coffee-houses [36] by those sitting at what became known as the 'treason table'. Such writing pulls no punches, and Restoration satire developed an idiom of caustic, epigrammatic rudeness. But the most rewarding topical poems today are those which transcend their moment by constructing or deconstructing a mythology of political life, by attending thoughtfully to the language through which public affairs are imagined. Terms crucial to the language of Restoration politics, such as 'liberty', 'patriot', 'people', and 'arbitrary government', are defined and redefined from poem to poem. Above all, it is Dryden who achieves this, whether in his optimistic vision of a new age [5], or his dexterous translation of contemporary politics into a quasibiblical tale [8], or his tragic vision of the fall of the city of Troy, and the shadows which gather round the future of Rome [12].

Town and Country

The city was not only an image, a synecdoche for the political identity of the nation, it was the stage where much of its political life was played out, and where its cultural life was fashioned. London was by far the largest city in the kingdom, a predominantly Whig stronghold where Parliament was often pressurized by demonstrations, a flourishing commercial centre, and the arbiter of style. Restoration culture was (or typically represented itself to be) a self-consciously metropolitan culture. London was where modernity was fashioned. London was where the theatres staged the new heroic drama and city comedies, and where the King's court provided its own kinds of spectacular performance and low intrigue. Writers recognized that London comprised distinct constituencies: the City or financial centre, the town with its flourishing bourgeoisie, and the royal court—each had its tastes, and each even had its favourite area of seating in the playhouse. London society seemed obsessively fashionable, *à-la-mode*, conscious of what's in and what's out, of who's in and who's out—and acutely aware of who's in and out of whose bedroom [16, 19]. Lampoons on court ladies proliferated. The Mall, St James's Park, the Royal Exchange, and St Paul's churchyard provided public spaces where people could promenade, gossip, and make assignations [14]. The coffee-houses gave men the opportunity to meet in informal clubs, talk politics, read poems, plan business ventures, escape their wives. The social geography (indeed, the sexual geography) of London became an important element in Restoration poetry and drama. In the 1670s a libertine ethos was cultivated by rakes on the fringes of the court, notably by the Earl of Rochester, who became a myth in his own lifetime, a byword for debauchery and atheism before his equally mythologized deathbed repentance [17, 18]. The city too became a moralized space, seen by Mr Pinchwife as a place where his wife might all too easily lose her innocence [14], and by Bunyan as Vanity Fair, where Christian endangers his soul [20]. The fire which devastated a large tract of London in 1666 [21, 22] was seized upon by Puritan preachers as God's vengeance on an immoral city and court. For Dryden, it was both a human tragedy and a potential new beginning for a rebuilt, modern city.

A long tradition of writing had associated towns with corruption and danger, and the countryside with innocence and health. Oldham's imitation of Juvenal [15] enjoys applying the Roman satirist's overheated denunciations of Rome to the conditions of modern London. Indeed, many of the texts in this section of the anthology are translations, as writers frequently turned to classical Latin and Greek literature when defining the moral and mythic elements of town and country. The landscape of England is often imagined via Roman landscapes, and so it becomes not only a geographical but a conceptual space, the terrain where 'the happy man' (as the tradition calls him) can become truly himself, free from the pressures of life at court or in town. Cowley's charming but pointed rendering of a satire from Horace contrasts country simplicity with courtly corruption: the country life may be unsophisticated, but at least it is safe [25]. It is in the country that Dryden's kinsman has room to hunt, time to be neighbourly, and the opportunity to cultivate true values; hence, when he ventures onto the public stage, he is a true patriot

[29]. Katherine Philips, writing from darkest Wales, sees country life as 'sacred' and 'innocent', for the country is a form of Eden, a place where a prelapsarian golden age can be recreated [23]. Marvell finds in his garden a space where he can lose himself in reverie, even in spiritual ecstasy [26]. But lest this all sound too abstract, there are poets who relish the actual physical pleasures of the countryside. Congreve's version of Horace's *Odes* I. ix is written by a man whose response to cold weather is the rallying cry, 'Let's drink till our own faces shine, | Till we like suns appear' [27]. Horace also provides Dryden with a poem, *Epode* II, which celebrates the practicalities of a farmer's life [24]. This epode had long been a favourite amongst seventeenth-century writers extolling the virtues of the retired life, but Dryden does not over-moralize the text; rather, his vision of the richness of the simple life keeps returning us to the pleasures of honey, pears, turbots, and olives. And (unlike some translators) Dryden preserves the original's ironic ending, where we discover that this praise of rural life is actually spoken by the money-lender Morecraft, who was on the point of selling up and moving to the country, but found the prospect of making big money in the City just irresistible. Ironies attend these ideals, for this is an adult, unillusioned (and sometimes disillusioned) literature. But ideals retain their power, nevertheless, and when Dryden translates Virgil's *Georgics* we see how the rhythms of the agricultural year enable the countryman to live in accordance with nature and the gods [28].

Literature and Theatre

When the nation began again in 1660, so too did its literature, its theatre, and its publishing trade. Poetry could not in itself be a career: no poet before Alexander Pope earned enough from his writing to survive on that alone. Professional writers such as Dryden, Shadwell, and Behn relied on their work for the theatre and on the patronage of rich aristocrats; other writers enjoyed independent means or government posts. But there was a growing market for polite literature, for poetry, playtexts, novels, and translations. Women were an increasingly significant constituency as readers, as patrons whose taste influenced the drama, and as writers: Katherine Philips was much complimented as 'the matchless Orinda', while

Aphra Behn was the first professional woman playwright. Innovatory publishing ventures included Tonson's series of verse miscellanies, and his projects to publish *Paradise Lost* and Dryden's Virgil by public subscription. The metropolitan origin, subject matter, and readership of much Restoration literature helped to produce a relatively small circle of poets and playwrights who were well known to one another and to their audiences. In these circumstances literature itself becomes a subject for literature: Oldham laments that poetry brings no rewards [32], poets praise and vilify other poets [31, 33–5, 42–3], theatrical prologues and epilogues discuss the merits of plays and the talents of the actresses [44].

This may sound parochial and incestuous, but literature's fascination with itself is also part of a loftier aspiration, a self-conscious search for a role and a style. What does it mean to be modern, to do something different from those pre-war poets and dramatists? What does it mean to be English, to write in a way which will stand comparison with the self-confident French? What does it mean to be classical, so that England might become a second Augustan Rome, culturally if not politically? In the literary criticism of the period there is both a confidence in the abilities of the new generation of writers, and a knot of anxieties. We can see this particularly clearly in the reflections on Shakespeare [37–9, 43]. In 1660 the dominant literary regimen was neo-classicism. Europe's literary élite had tired of extravagant plots and far-fetched metaphors, and was requiring classical decorum, simplicity, purity, morality. French drama, epitomized by Racine, seemed to be establishing a new standard here. But Shakespeare, seen as the founder of the English stage, was gloriously incorrect. Should he be imitated? Could he be bettered? Dryden and his contemporaries argued that their culture was more civilized, their language more refined than in the days of Shakespeare and Jonson, so one ought to be able to write better than they had. Yet the English language remained an unstable, mongrel medium. There was as yet no English equivalent to the Académie française to refine and stabilize the language, as Sprat hoped the Royal Society might do [45]. And perhaps Shakespeare and Jonson were inimitable, perhaps they had exhausted the available subjects and left nothing for their successors. What if the heirs have nothing to inherit? Imitation and inheritance become important concerns for these Restoration writers [41, 43]. Congreve, Dryden, Oldham,

Rochester, Shadwell, and a host of lesser figures translate and imitate the Greek and Latin classics, often transposing the originals into contemporary English settings, and shaping an English classicism in a variety of styles. Dryden's eloquent elegy for Oldham uses a Roman idiom throughout [33], while Rochester's *An Allusion to Horace* [34] exploits one of Horace's satires as the springboard for his critique of Dryden and his promotion of his own clique. Dryden matches himself against Shakespeare in plays such as *All for Love* [67] and *Troilus and Cressida*; Shadwell claims to be the heir of Jonson in writing morally improving comedies [40]. And it is this latter claim which generates *Mac Flecknoe* [41], the poem in which Dryden explodes Shadwell's pretensions to be the heir to the classical heritage by casting him instead as the successor to the tedious poetaster Flecknoe. Shadwell's coronation procession as King of Dullness winds through insalubrious quarters of London, greeted with acclaim from Pissing Alley and the Nonconformist graveyard at Bunhill.

This is a kind of street theatre, and *Mac Flecknoe* is full of allusions to contemporary drama which would have been recognized by those privileged enough to find a copy of the poem as it circulated in manuscript. (Oldham copied it into his notebook in 1678.) London audiences enjoyed a lively if not always very subtle theatre. The rival companies—the King's and the Duke's—competed with each other through sensations and gimmicks: all-female casts, flying witches, a prologue spoken by an actor on a donkey, a stage set decorated with mutilated bodies. And the audience provided their own shows: beaux stood on benches preening themselves, wits exchanged repartee, prostitutes plied their trade, and hotheads lost their temper in armed brawls. Competing with this stylish mayhem and meretricious spectacle there were some serious plays. The witty and perceptive comedies of Etherege, Wycherley, and Congreve held a mirror up to the audience's amorous intrigues and social ambitions in a self-consciously materialistic milieu. The heroic drama and tragedies of Dryden, Otway, and Lee—for all their bombastic posturing—dramatized man confronting the constraints of fate and circumstance and articulated a desire for transcendence [67, 80]. Both comedy and tragedy have philosophical interests, especially in the limits to human free-will and autonomy.

Love and Friendship

There is also a philosophical dimension to much of the period's writing on love and friendship, though this is no longer the dazzling metaphysical wit which characterized the poetry of Donne and his contemporaries, now fading from public esteem. Rochester's lyrics [53–63] often evoke the precariousness of emotional and sexual relationships, the elusiveness of fidelity, the unreliability of the body, the inability even of the poem's speaker to know or to act on his feelings. Not only are love and pleasure transient, the 'I' of the poem too seems evanescent. The poetry seems haunted by Hobbes's perception that 'there is no such thing as perpetual tranquillity of mind while we live here, because life itself is but motion, and can never be without desire, nor without fear, no more than without sense' (*Leviathan* (1651), ch. 6). Rochester at his best is wry and poignant; Rochester at his most notorious dares us to be shocked by his cynical poses and obscene language. For all their evocations of sexual encounters, Rochester's poems often seem lonely, even solipsistic, whereas for Katherine Philips poetry was a way of maintaining friendship [48–50], as she consolidated her circle of female associates by writing and exchanging verses. This was semi-private poetry, copied into handsome manuscript volumes for the chosen few. She expressed extreme displeasure (which may or may not have been genuine) when her poems were printed without her consent. Rochester's erotic poems, by contrast, circulated very widely in small manuscript bundles, and were transcribed both into private notebooks and into scribally produced anthologies for sale to wealthy connoisseurs.

Male friendship is given powerful expression in the drama, for example in the bond between Pierre and Jaffeir in Otway's *Venice Preserv'd* (1682), between Antony and Ventidius in Dryden's *All for Love* (1678), or the eponymous hero and Dorax in his *Don Sebastian* (1690). The bond between Nisus and Euryalus, celebrated by Virgil in his *Aeneid*, emerges in Dryden's translation as a deep, self-sacrificing love [51]. It is implicitly, but not overtly, homosexual; indeed, Restoration literature says little about homosexual love, finding no place for the lyrical eroticism of Marlowe and Barnfield, or the passionate devotion of Shakespeare, and providing instead a series of stereotyped roles: the omnivorous rake [18, 59], the diabolical sodomite [9], the effete fop encountered from time to time in Restoration comedy.

In its handling of heterosexual relationships, Restoration literature seems specially interested in figures who take control of their sexuality and their domestic arrangements. So the tragicomedy *Secret Love* ends with the lovers negotiating the terms on which they are prepared to live together after marriage [52]. Antony and Cleopatra retell the story of their mutual passion in a profoundly moving scene which culminates in them accepting each other once again, and taking responsibility for the consequences [67]. Sigismonda asserts her freedom to choose her sexual partner, and boldly redefines the concepts such as 'honour' through which her tyrannical father seeks to constrain her choice and impose his will [66]. And an anonymous poem recovered from a manuscript records the tragic consequences of a sexual affair, as a woman addresses the unborn child which she is about to abort [68]. We also overhear Pepys, in the half-secret language invented for his diary, recording his sexual adventures and the domestic havoc which they caused [65]. Autonomy—an individualism sometimes idealizing, sometimes materialistic—seems at the heart of so much of this writing, and yet we should not overlook the quiet celebrations of mutual, domestic love exemplified by Lucy Hutchinson's memoir of her marriage [69], and Dryden's rendering of Ovid's story of Baucis and Philemon [70], the elderly couple whose final prayer is that they might die together.

Religion and Philosophy

The Church of England had been re-established at the Restoration, but this was not one of its finer periods. Calvinism—the vicious and immoral doctrine that one was irretrievably predestined by God, before one's birth, for eternal salvation or damnation—was no longer the dominant orthodoxy within Anglicanism, and was largely confined to the Nonconformist sects. Anglicanism lost the terror which had inspired Donne's sermons and sonnets, and replaced it with an increasing respect for reason, as the Latitudinarian movement sought to make doctrine amenable to, or at least not too offensive to, reason. The most eloquent expressions of religious faith seem to come in this period from outside the establishment. There is the mystical Traherne—an Anglican priest, indeed, but one who is entirely idiosyncratic in his ecstatic vision of his childhood innocence, the glorious world which he had once inhabited and was seeking to recover [72]. There is Bunyan, creating his stout-hearted pilgrim while in prison for preaching without a licence [73]. There is Langhorne, admitting his sinfulness on the eve of being executed for his supposed complicity in a supposed Catholic plot [74]. There is Robert James, quietly meditating on his transitory life and his hopes of resurrection, using the composition of poetry as a form of private prayer [75]. There is Dryden, now a Catholic, repenting his ideologically wayward youth in biblical and mystical imagery at the outset of his bizarre but brilliant allegorical poem in which a hind and a panther debate transubstantiation and papal infallibility. Religious feeling finds idiosyncratic, individual expression. And no text here is more individual than Hannah Allen's narrative of her religious melancholy, telling of the years during which she was possessed by the conviction that she was damned and about to die, an obsession from which she was gradually weaned by the attentive care of her relations and friends [76]. Some of these—Langhorne, James, Allen—are not specially gifted writers, but the biblical language which they had absorbed since childhood helps them to produce quietly eloquent autobiographical writing.

If an increasing respect for reason leads towards the Enlightenment which the next century would bring, so too do various forms of scepticism. In *The Indian Emperor* [78] Dryden dramatizes a clash of cultures which is also a clash of religions, as the American Indian king Montezuma bravely stands by his ancestral religion in the face of the Spanish invaders' demands that he convert to Christianity— or, more importantly, that he hand over his gold, which is what the priests are really interested in. Rarely has the venal hypocrisy of religious imperialism been so economically exposed. Though a faithful Christian himself, Dryden always loved staging religious and philosophical debates, and in his translations from Horace and Lucretius [79, 81] he is in effect debating with himself by putting into English the philosophies of Stoics and Epicureans, testing them on the pulses of the language and thinking beyond the limits of Christian orthodoxy. What would it be like, he seems to be asking, really to believe that death simply ends us, and that after death we just dissolve into our constituent atoms? What would it be like to recognize that the world is controlled not by divine Providence but by the capricious goddess Fortune: and how could one live in such a way that one is not her slave? Other voices sceptical of Christianity also demand to be heard. Rochester's *Satire against Reason and Mankind* proffers a libertine scepticism, elevating the senses and mocking the very reason which the Latitudinarian churchmen were so proud of. This nihilistic satire is extended in *Upon Nothing* and his translation from Seneca [83–5]. But some voices assimilated classical writings to a kind of Christian providentialism: Wodehouse finds consolation in Claudian [82], while Dryden ends *Palamon and Arcite* [86]—and this anthology—with his Boethian vision of a world in which one struggles to believe in harmony and order.

The Present Anthology

No anthology can wholly satisfy either its compiler or its readers. There can never be enough space to include every work which merits admission, or to accommodate every voice which deserves to be heard. The present volume attempts to provide the reader with annotated texts of some major works, some representative works, and a few surprises. It is inevitably selective, prejudiced even, in its favouring of Dryden and Rochester, and its promotion of little discoveries from manuscript collections. Drama as a genre does not lend itself to anthologizing, and the inclusion of a few extracts and a dozen prologues and epilogues is a way of reminding readers of the rich variety of material which awaits them beyond the limits of this volume. But there is obviously one serious and unavoidable absence in this collection, and that is Milton. *Paradise Lost* is at once the greatest and the least characteristic work of the Restoration period, the most profound critique of its values, desires, and aspirations. It is impossible to include it whole, and crass to abridge it, but it cannot be ignored completely. I have therefore prefaced each of the five sections of this anthology with a short passage from *Paradise Lost* which stands as a Miltonic commentary on what follows. Milton lived a retired life after 1660, fortunate to have escaped execution for his public defence of the regicide, and devoted himself to three extended meditations on the ways of God to man—*Paradise Lost* (1667), *Paradise Regained* (1671), and *Samson Agonistes* (1671)—which were also reflections upon contemporary society. In the five brief extracts from *Paradise Lost* which I have provided here, we have Milton's view of diabolical government; his Eden, the archetypally pure countryside, which is always already lost; his invocation of the Holy Spirit to make him God's poet doing God's work; his praise of the married, fully sexual love of Adam and Eve; and, finally, his hope that man—exiled from Eden—might nevertheless attain the happiness of a paradise within. And that, perhaps, is enough for one volume.

NOTE ON THE TEXTS

EXCEPT where stated otherwise, texts are taken from the first printed editions. Spelling, punctuation, capitals, and italics have been modernized. Omissions within excerpts are marked by a row of spaced points. Editorial interpolations, including editorially devised titles, are enclosed within square brackets. An asterisk in the text directs the reader to the explanatory notes, which deal with allusions and obscurities. Further information on sources can also be found in the notes. Lexical annotation is provided by the glossary. Words explained in the glossary are not marked in the text, as this would disfigure the page excessively.

SELECT BIBLIOGRAPHY

Editions, biographies, and critical studies relating to the authors represented in this anthology are listed in the biographical notes on pp. 414–19.

Primary texts

The requirements of an anthology mean that some writers, and some genres, cannot properly be represented. It has only been possible to gesture at the importance of Restoration drama in the present collection: readers wishing to explore the comedy might start with Etherege (esp. *The Man of Mode*), Wycherley (esp. *The Country Wife* and *The Plain Dealer*) and Congreve (esp. *The Double-Dealer* and *Love for Love*). Recently Aphra Behn's standing has increased. The tragic and heroic drama is best represented by Dryden's *Aureng-Zebe*, *All for Love*, and *Don Sebastian*, and Otway's *Venice Preserv'd*. These plays are available in a variety of modern editions. The extensive topical poetry of the period is anthologized in the collection *Poems on Affairs of State* (listed below). Milton has been accorded only token representation in the present collection, so that his voice is at least heard; but of course *Paradise Lost* is the period's greatest work. His *Paradise Regained* and *Samson Agonistes* are likewise major achievements. Readers wishing to explore more of Dryden's varied and extensive work might turn to his *Heroic Stanzas* on Cromwell, his religious poems *Religio Laici* and *The Hind and the Panther*, and his ode *Alexander's Feast*; but much of his finest poetry is to be found in his translations, notably the versions of Horace and Lucretius in *Sylvae*, his complete Virgil, and the magnificent *Fables Ancient and Modern*, perhaps his most rewarding work for the modern reader. Rochester and Oldham wrote vigorous satires in addition to the ones included in this volume. In prose, Bunyan's *The Pilgrim's Progress* is the period's most enduring work, and is available in countless editions.

Cordner, Michael, *et al.* (eds.), *Four Restoration Marriage Plays* (Oxford, 1995).

Danchin, Pierre (ed.), *The Prologues and Epilogues of the Restoration 1660–1700*, 7 vols. (Nancy, 1981–8).

Lord, George DeF., *et al.* (eds.), *Poems on Affairs of State*, 7 vols. (New Haven, 1963–75). [cited in the notes as 'Yale POAS']

Love, Harold (ed.), *The Penguin Book of Restoration Verse*, 2nd edn. (Harmondsworth, 1997).

Mish, Charles C. (ed.), *Restoration Prose Fiction 1666–1700* (Lincoln, Nebr., 1970).

Salzman, Paul (ed.), *An Anthology of Seventeenth-Century Fiction* (Oxford, 1991).

Spingarn, J. E. (ed.), *Critical Essays of the Seventeenth Century*, 3 vols. (Oxford, 1908).

Vickers, Brian (ed.), *Shakespeare: The Critical Heritage*, 6 vols. (London, 1974–81).

Wilson, John Harold (ed.), *Court Satires of the Restoration* (Columbus, Ohio, 1976).

Womersley, David (ed.), *Restoration Drama: An Anthology* (Oxford, 2000).

Secondary works

This list suggests a variety of historical and critical works. The journals *Restoration* and *The Scriblerian* and the annual *The Year's Work in English Studies* provide a regular bibliography of secondary work in the period.

Ashcraft, Richard, *Revolutionary Politics and Locke's 'Two Treatises of Government'* (Princeton, 1986).

Baxter, Stephen B., *William III* (London, 1966).

Bell, Walter George, *The Great Fire in London in 1666* (London, 1923).

Erskine-Hill, Howard, *The Augustan Idea in English Literature* (London, 1983).

—— *Poetry and the Realm of Politics: Shakespeare to Dryden* (Oxford, 1996).

—— *Poetry of Opposition and Revolution: Dryden to Wordsworth* (Oxford, 1996).

Fisk, Deborah C. Payne (ed.), *The Cambridge Companion to English Restoration Theatre* (Cambridge, 2000).

Griffin, Dustin H., *Literary Patronage in England, 1650–1800* (Cambridge, 1996).

Hammond, Paul, *Love between Men in English Literature* (Basingstoke, 1996).

Harris, Tim, *Politics under the Later Stuarts* (London, 1993).

Howe, Elizabeth, *The First English Actresses* (Cambridge, 1992).

Hughes, Derek, *English Drama 1660–1700* (Oxford, 1996).

Hume, Robert D., *The Development of English Drama in the Late Seventeenth Century* (Oxford, 1976).

Hutton, Ronald, *Charles the Second: King of England, Scotland, and Ireland* (Oxford, 1989).

—— *The Restoration: A Political and Religious History of England and Wales 1658–1667* (Oxford, 1985).

Jones, J. R. (ed.), *The Restored Monarchy 1660–1688* (London, 1979).

Keeble, N. H., *The Literary Culture of Nonconformity in Later Seventeenth-Century England* (Leicester, 1987).

Kenyon, J. P., *The Popish Plot* (London, 1972).

Kewes, Paulina, *Authorship and Appropriation: Writing for the Stage in England, 1660–1710* (Oxford, 1998).

Kroll, Richard W. F., *The Material Word: Literate Culture in the Restoration and Early Eighteenth Century* (Baltimore, 1991).

Love, Harold (ed.), *Restoration Literature: Critical Approaches* (London, 1972).

—— *Scribal Publication in Seventeenth-Century England* (Oxford, 1993).

Maclean, Gerald (ed.), *Culture and Society in the Stuart Restoration* (Cambridge, 1995).

Miller, John, *Popery and Politics in England 1660–1688* (Cambridge, 1973).

—— *James II: A Study in Kingship* (London, 1978).

Monod, Paul Kléber, *Jacobitism and the English People, 1688–1788* (Cambridge, 1989).

Muccubbin, Robert P., and Hamilton-Phillips, Martha (eds.), *The Age of William and Mary: Power, Politics, and Patronage, 1688–1702* (Williamsburg, Va., 1989).

Ogg, David, *England in the Reign of Charles II*, 2nd edn. (Oxford, 1956).

—— *England in the Reigns of James II and William III* (Oxford, 1955).

Owen, Susan J., *Restoration Theatre and Crisis* (Oxford, 1996).

Picard, Liza, *Restoration London* (London, 1997).

Powell, Jocelyn, *Restoration Theatre Production* (London, 1984).

Røstvig, Maren-Sofie, *The Happy Man: Studies in the Metamorphoses of a Classical Ideal, 1600–1700*, 2nd edn. (Oslo, 1962).

Salzman, Paul, *English Prose Fiction 1558–1700* (Oxford, 1985).

Schwoerer, Lois G. (ed.), *The Revolution of 1688–1689* (Cambridge, 1992).

Spurr, John, *The Restoration Church of England* (New Haven, 1991).

Staves, Susan, *Players' Scepters: Fictions of Authority in the Restoration* (Lincoln, Nebr., 1979).

van Lennep, William, *The London Stage 1660–1800: Part I: 1660–1700* (Carbondale, Ill., 1965).

Vieth, David M., *Attribution in Restoration Poetry* (New Haven, 1963).

Zwicker, Steven N. (ed.), *The Cambridge Companion to English Literature 1650–1740* (Cambridge, 1998).

—— *Lines of Authority: Politics and English Literary Culture, 1649–1689* (Ithaca, NY, 1993).

CHRONOLOGY

Dates refer to the appearance of works in print, unless manuscript circulation is specified.

1660   Restoration of the monarchy and return of Charles II

Royal Society founded (receives charter 1662)

Dryden, *Astraea Redux*

Milton, *The Ready and Easy Way to Establish a Free Commonwealth*

Pepys begins his *Diary*

Bunyan imprisoned (to 1672)

1662   Book of Common Prayer

Butler, *Hudibras* Pt. I (Pt. II 1663, Pt. III 1678)

1663   Shakespeare Third Folio (Fourth 1685)

1664   Death of Philips

Flecknoe, *Love's Kingdom*

1665   Plague in London

1666   Great Fire of London

Bunyan, *Grace Abounding*

1667   Death of Cowley

Dryden, *Annus Mirabilis*

Dryden, *Essay of Dramatic Poesy*

Marvell, *Last Instructions* (in MS)

Milton, *Paradise Lost*

Philips, *Works*

Sprat, *History of the Royal Society*

1668   Cowley, *Works*

Shadwell, *The Sullen Lovers*

1669   Pepys stops his *Diary*

Rochester, *Artemisa to Chloe* (?) (in MS) (printed 1679)

1670   Milton, *History of Britain*

Birth of Congreve

RESTORATION LITERATURE

POLITICS AND NATION

1	From *Paradise Lost*, Book II

JOHN MILTON

First published 1667. After the expulsion of the rebel angels from heaven, Satan addresses his followers. In the second extract, he proposes to undertake alone a scheme to seduce the newly created Adam and Eve. The passage is informed by Milton's detestation of Stuart kingship, his experience of the increasingly monarchical government of Cromwell, the failure (as he saw it) of the English people to embrace godly republican liberty, and their servile preference for a Stuart monarchy. In *The Ready and Easy Way to Establish a Free Commonwealth* (February 1660) he warned against 'this noxious humour of returning to bondage', and feared that (unlike the Israelites escaping to the Promised Land) Englishmen were 'now choosing them a captain back for Egypt' (*Complete Prose Works*, vii. 408, 463). The rhetoric of Milton's Satan informs Dryden's presentation of his opponents in *Absalom and Achitophel* (8) and *Mac Flecknoe* (41).

> High on a throne of a royal state, which far
> Outshone the wealth of Ormus and of Ind,
> Or where the gorgeous East with richest hand
> Showers on her kings barbaric pearl and gold,
> Satan exalted sat, by merit raised
> To that bad eminence; and from despair
> Thus high uplifted beyond hope, aspires
> Beyond thus high, insatiate to pursue
> Vain war with heaven; and by success untaught
> His proud imaginations thus displayed: 10
>   'Powers and dominions, deities of heaven,
> For since no deep within her gulf can hold
> Immortal vigour, though oppressed and fallen,

I give not heaven for lost. From this descent
Celestial virtues rising will appear
More glorious and more dread than from no fall,
And trust themselves to fear no second fate:
Me though just right, and the fixed laws of heaven
Did first create your leader, next free choice,
With what besides, in counsel or in fight,   20
Hath been achieved of merit, yet this loss
Thus far at least recovered, hath much more
Established in a safe unenvied throne
Yielded with full consent. The happier state
In heaven, which follows dignity, might draw
Envy from each inferior; but who here
Will envy whom the highest place exposes
Foremost to stand against the thunderer's aim
Your bulwark, and condemns to greatest share
Of endless pain? Where there is then no good   30
For which to strive, no strife can grow up there
From faction; for none sure will claim in hell
Precedence; none, whose portion is so small
Of present pain, that with ambitious mind
Will covet more. With this advantage then
To union, and firm faith, and firm accord,
More than can be in heaven, we now return
To claim our just inheritance of old,
Surer to prosper than prosperity
Could have assured us; and by what best way,   40
Whether of open war or covert guile,
We now debate: who can advise, may speak.'

     .   .   .   .

Satan, whom now transcendent glory raised
Above his fellows, with monarchal pride
Conscious of highest worth, unmoved thus spake:
    'O progeny of heaven, empyreal thrones,   430
With reason hath deep silence and demur
Seized us, though undismayed: long is the way
And hard, that out of hell leads up to light;
Our prison strong, this huge convèx of fire,
Outrageous to devour, immures us round

Ninefold, and gates of burning adamant
Barred over us prohibit all egress.
These passed, if any pass, the void profound
Of unessential night receives him next,
Wide gaping, and with utter loss of being   440
Threatens him, plunged in that abortive gulf.
If thence he scape into whatever world,
Or unknown region, what remains him less
Than unknown dangers and as hard escape.
But I should ill become this throne, O peers,
And this imperial sovereignty, adorned
With splendour, armed with power, if aught proposed
And judged of public moment, in the shape
Of difficulty or danger could deter
Me from attempting. Wherefore do I assume   450
These royalties, and not refuse to reign,
Refusing to accept as great a share
Of hazard as of honour, due alike
To him who reigns, and so much to him due
Of hazard more, as he above the rest
High honoured sits? Go therefore, mighty powers,
Terror of heaven, though fallen; intend at home,
While here shall be our home, what best may ease
The present misery, and render hell
More tolerable; if there be cure or charm   460
To respite or deceive, or slack the pain
Of this ill mansion: intermit no watch
Against a wakeful foe, while I abroad
Through all the coasts of dark destruction seek
Deliverance for us all: this enterprise
None shall partake with me.' Thus saying rose
The monarch, and prevented all reply,
Prudent, lest from his resolution raised
Others among the chief might offer now
(Certain to be refused) what erst they feared;   470
And so refused might in opinion stand
His rivals, winning cheap the high repute
Which he through hazard huge must earn. But they
Dreaded not more the adventure than his voice

Forbidding; and at once with him they rose;
Their rising all at once was as the sound
Of thunder heard remote. Towards him they bend
With awful reverence prone, and as a god
Extol him equal to the highest in heaven:
Nor failed they to express how much they praised,   480
That for the general safety he despised
His own: for neither do the spirits damned
Lose all their virtue; lest bad men should boast
Their specious deeds on earth, which glory excites,
Or close ambition varnished o'er with zeal.
Thus they their doubtful consultations dark
Ended rejoicing in their matchless chief:
As when from mountain tops the dusky clouds
Ascending, while the north wind sleeps, o'erspread
Heaven's cheerful face, the louring element   490
Scowls o'er the darkened landscape snow, or shower;
If chance the radiant sun with farewell sweet
Extend his evening beam, the fields revive,
The birds their notes renew, and bleating herds
Attest their joy, that hill and valley rings.
O shame to men! Devil with devil damned
Firm concord holds, men only disagree
Of creatures rational, though under hope
Of heavenly grace, and God proclaiming peace;
Yet live in hatred, enmity, and strife   500
Among themselves, and levy cruel wars,
Wasting the earth, each other to destroy:
As if (which might induce us to accord)
Man had not hellish foes enow besides,
That day and night for his destruction wait.
     The Stygian council thus dissolved; and forth
In order came the grand infernal peers;
Midst came their mighty paramount, and seemed
Alone the antagonist of heaven, nor less
Than hell's dread emperor with pomp supreme,   510
And Godlike imitated state; him round
A globe of fiery seraphim enclosed
With bright emblazonry, and horrent arms.

Then of their session ended they bid cry
With trumpets' regal sound the great result:
Toward the four winds four speedy cherubim
Put to their mouths the sounding alchemy
By herald's voice explained: the hollow abyss
Heard far and wide, and all the host of hell
With deafening shout returned them loud acclaim.   520
Thence more at ease their minds and somewhat raised
By false presumptuous hope, the rangèd powers
Disband, and wandering, each his several way
Pursues, as inclination or sad choice
Leads him perplexed, where he may likeliest find
Truce to his restless thoughts, and entertain
The irksome hours, till his great chief return.

2 From *The History of the Rebellion and Civil Wars in England* and *The Life of Edward, Earl of Clarendon*

EDWARD HYDE, EARL OF CLARENDON

The *History* was begun in 1646–8, completed in 1668–70, and printed in 1702–4. Historiographical and autobiographical writings not used for the *History* were published as the *Life* in 1759. Clarendon's historical analysis is enriched by character-studies of the protagonists which emphasize their psychological complexity, their moral responsibility for their actions, and the ways in which great results may follow from small decisions or failures.

(a) [*The State of the Nation on the Eve of the Civil War*]

The happiness of the times I mentioned was enviously set off by this, that every other kingdom, every other province were engaged, some entangled, and some almost destroyed, by the rage and fury of arms; those which were ambitiously in contention with their neighbours having the view and apprehensions of the miseries and desolation which they saw other states suffer by a civil war; whilst the kingdoms we now lament were alone looked upon as the garden of the world; Scotland (which was but the wilderness of that garden) in a full, entire, undisturbed peace, which they had never seen; the rage and barbarism (that the blood, for of the charity we speak not) of their private feuds being composed to the reverence, or to the awe, of public justice; in a competency, if not in an excess of plenty, which they had never hope to see, and in a temper (which was the utmost we desired and hoped to see) free from rebellion: Ireland, which had been a sponge to draw, and a gulf to swallow all that could be spared, and all that could be got from England, merely to keep the reputation of a kingdom, reduced to that good degree of husbandry and government, that it not only subsisted of itself, and gave this kingdom all that it might have expected from it; but really increased the revenue of the crown forty or fifty thousand pounds a year, besides much more to the people in the traffic and trade from thence; arts and sciences fruitfully planted there; and the whole nation beginning to be so civilized, that it was a jewel of great lustre in the royal diadem.

When these outworks were thus fortified and adorned, it was no wonder if England was generally thought secure, with the advantages of its own climate; the court in great plenty, or rather (which is the discredit of plenty) excess and luxury; the country rich, and which is more, fully enjoying the pleasure of its own wealth, and so the easier corrupted with the pride and wantonness of it; the church flourishing with learned and extraordinary men, and (which other good times wanted) supplied with oil to feed those lamps; and the protestant religion more advanced against the church of Rome by writing, (without prejudice to other useful and godly labours) especially by those two books of the late lord archbishop of Canterbury his grace, and of Mr Chillingworth,* than it had been from the reformation; trade increased to that degree, that we were the exchange of Christendom, (the revenue thereof to the crown being almost double to what it had been in the best times) and the bullion of all other kingdoms brought to receive a stamp from the mint of England; all foreign merchants looking upon nothing as their own, but what they had laid up in the warehouses of this kingdom; the royal navy, in number and equipage much above former times, very formidable at sea; and the reputation of the greatness and power of the king much more with foreign princes than any of his progenitors; for those rough courses, which made him haply less loved at home, made him more feared abroad; by how much the power of kingdoms is more reverenced than their justice by their neighbours: and it may be, this consideration might not be the least motive, and may not be the worst excuse for those counsels. Lastly, for a complement of all these blessings, they were enjoyed by, and under the protection of, a king, of the most harmless disposition, and the most exemplary piety, the greatest example of sobriety, chastity, and mercy, that any prince hath been endowed with, (and God forgive those that have not been sensible of, and thankful for, those endowments) and who might have said that which Pericles* was proud of, upon his death-bed, 'that no Englishman had ever worn a black gown through his occasion'. In a word, many wise men thought it a time wherein those two miserable adjuncts, which Nerva* was deified for uniting, *imperium et libertas*, were as well reconciled as is possible.

But all these blessings could but enable, not compel us to be happy: we wanted that sense, acknowledgment, and value of our own happiness, which all but we had; and took pains to make, when we could not find, ourselves miserable. There was in truth a strange absence of understanding in most, and a strange perverseness of understanding in the rest: the court full of excess, idleness, and luxury; and the country full of pride, mutiny, and discontent; every man more troubled and perplexed at that they called the violation of one law, than delighted or pleased with the observation of all the rest of the charter: never imputing the increase of their receipts, revenue, and plenty, to the wisdom, virtue, and merit of the crown, but object-ing every small imposition to the exorbitancy and tyranny of the government; the growth of knowledge and learning being dis-relished, for the infirmities of some learned men, and the increase of grace and favour upon the church more repined and murmured at, than the increase of piety and devotion in the church, which was as visible, acknowledged, or taken notice of; whilst the indiscretion and folly of one sermon at Whitehall was more bruited abroad, and commented upon, than the wisdom, sobriety, and devotion of a hundred.

. . . It was about the year 1639, when he was little more than thirty years of age, and when England enjoyed the greatest measure of felicity, that it had ever known; the two crowns of France and Spain worrying each other, by their mutual incursions and invasions of each other, whilst they had both a civil war in their own bowels; the former by frequent rebellions from their own factions and ani-mosities the latter, by the defection of Portugal; and both laboured more to ransack and burn each other's dominions, than to extinguish

their own fire. All Germany weltering in its own blood, and contrib-
uting to each other's destruction, that the poor crown of Sweden
might grow great out of their ruins, and at their charge: Denmark
and Poland being adventurers in the same destructive enterprises.
Holland and the United Provinces wearied and tired with their long
and chargeable war, how prosperous soever they were in it; and
beginning to be more afraid of France their ally, than of Spain their
enemy. Italy every year infested by the arms of Spain and France,
which divided the princes thereof into the several factions.

Of all the princes of Europe, the king of England alone seemed to
be seated upon that pleasant promontory, that might safely view the
tragic sufferings of all his neighbours about him, without any other
concernment than what arose from his own princely heart and
Christian compassion, to see such desolation wrought by the pride,
and passion, and ambition of private persons, supported by princes
who knew not what themselves would have. His three kingdoms
flourishing in entire peace and universal plenty, in danger of nothing
but their own surfeits; and his dominions every day enlarged by
sending out colonies upon large and fruitful plantations; his strong
fleets commanding all seas; and the numerous shipping of the nation
bringing the trade of the world into his ports; nor could it with
unquestionable security be carried any whither else; and all these
blessings enjoyed under a prince of the greatest clemency and justice, and of the greatest piety and devotion, and the most indulgent to
his subjects, and most solicitous for their happiness and prosperity.

O fortunati nimium, bona si sua norint!*

In this blessed conjuncture, when no other prince thought he
wanted any thing to compass what he most desired to be possessed
of, but the affection and friendship of the king of England, a small,
scarce discernible cloud arose in the north, which was shortly after
attended with such a storm, that never gave over raging till it had
shaken, and even rooted up, the greatest and tallest cedars of the
three nations; blasted all its beauty and fruitfulness; brought its
strength to decay, and its glory to reproach, and almost to desolation;
by such a career and deluge of wickedness and rebellion, as by
not being enough foreseen, or in truth suspected, could not be
prevented.

(b) [*The Character of Charles I*]

It will not be unnecessary to add a short character of his person, that posterity may know the inestimable loss which the nation then underwent, in being deprived of a prince whose example would have had a greater influence upon the manners and piety of the nation than the most strict laws can have. To speak first of his private qualifications as a man, before the mention of his princely and royal virtues; he was, if ever any, the most worthy of the title of an honest man; so great a lover of justice, that no temptation could dispose him to a wrongful action, except it was so disguised to him that he believed it to be just. He had a tenderness and compassion of nature, which restrained him from ever doing a hard-hearted thing: and therefore he was so apt to grant pardon to malefactors, that the judges of the land represented to him the damage and insecurity to the public that flowed from such his indulgence. And then he restrained himself from pardoning either murders or highway robberies, and quickly discerned the fruits of his severity by a wonderful reformation of those enormities. He was very punctual and regular in his devotions; he was never known to enter upon his recreations or sports, though never so early in the morning, before he had been at public prayers; so that on hunting days his chaplains were bound to a very early attendance. He was likewise very strict in observing the hours of his private cabinet devotions; and was so severe an exactor of gravity and reverence in all mention of religion, that he could never endure any light or profane word, with what sharpness of wit soever it was covered: and though he was well pleased and delighted with reading verses made upon any occasion, no man durst bring before him any thing that was profane or unclean. That kind of wit had never any countenance then. He was so great an example of conjugal affection, that they who did not imitate him in that particular did not brag of their liberty; and he did not only permit but direct his bishops to prosecute those scandalous vices in the ecclesiastical courts, against persons of eminence and near relation to his service.

His kingly virtues had some mixture and allay, that hindered them from shining in full lustre, and from producing those fruits they should have been attended with. He was not in his nature very bountiful, though he gave very much. This appeared more after the duke of Buckingham's death, after which those showers fell very rarely; and he paused too long in giving, which made those to whom he gave less sensible of the benefit. He kept state to the full, which made his court very orderly; no man presuming to be seen in a place where he had no pretence to be. He saw and observed men long, before he received them about his person; and did not love strangers; nor very confident men. He was a patient hearer of causes; which he frequently accustomed himself to at the council board; and judged very well, and was dexterous in the mediating part: so that he often put an end to causes by persuasion, which the stubbornness of men's humours made dilatory in courts of justice.

He was very fearless in his person, but not very enterprising. He had an excellent understanding, but was not confident enough of it; which made him oftentimes change his own opinion for a worse, and follow the advice of men that did not judge so well as himself. This made him more irresolute than the conjecture of his affairs would admit: if he had been of a rougher and more imperious nature he would have found more respect and duty. And his not applying some severe cures to approaching evils proceeded from the lenity of his nature, and the tenderness of his conscience, which, in all cases of blood, made him choose the softer way, and not hearken to severe counsels, how reasonably soever urged. This only restrained him from pursuing his advantage in the first Scottish expedition, when, humanly speaking, he might have reduced that nation to the most slavish obedience that could have been wished. But no man can say he had then many who advised him to it, but the contrary, by a wonderful indisposition all his council had to fighting, or any other fatigue. He was always an immoderate lover of the Scottish nation, having not only been born there, but educated by that people, and besieged by them always, having few English about him till he was king; and the major number of his servants being still of that nation, who he thought could never fail him. And among these, no man had such an ascendant over him, by the humblest insinuations, as duke Hamilton had.

As he excelled in all other virtues, so in temperance he was so strict that he abhorred all debauchery to that degree that, at a great festival solemnity where he once was, when very many of the nobility of the English and Scots were entertained, being told by one who withdrew from thence what vast draughts of wine they drank, and 'that there was one earl, who had drank most of the rest down, and was not himself moved or altered', the king said, 'that he deserved to be hanged'; and that earl coming shortly after into the room where his majesty was, in some gaiety, to show how unhurt he was from the battle, the king sent one to bid him withdraw from his majesty's presence; nor did he in some days after appear before him.

So many miraculous circumstances contributed to his ruin, that men might well think that heaven and earth and the stars designed it. Though he was, from the first declension of his power, so much betrayed by his own servants, that there were very few who remained faithful to him, yet that treachery proceeded not from any treasonable purpose to do him any harm, but from particular and personal animosities against other men. And, afterwards, the terror all men were under of the parliament, and the guilt they were conscious of themselves, made them watch all opportunities to make themselves gracious to those who could do them good; and so they became spies upon their master, and from one piece of knavery were hardened and confirmed to undertake another; till at last they had no hope of preservation but by the destruction of their master. And after all this, when a man might reasonably believe that less than a universal defection of three nations could not have reduced a great king to so ugly a fate, it is most certain, that, in that very hour when he was thus wickedly murdered in the sight of the sun, he had as great a share in the hearts and affections of his subjects in general, was as much beloved, esteemed, and longed for by the people in general of the three nations, as any of his predecessors had ever been. To conclude, he was the worthiest gentleman, the best master, the best friend, the best husband, the best father, and the best Christian, that the age in which he lived produced. And if he were not the best king, if he were without some parts and qualities which have made some kings great and happy, no other prince was ever unhappy who was possessed of half his virtues and endowments, and so much without any kind of vice.

(c) [*The Death and Character of Oliver Cromwell*]

It had been observed in England, that, though from the dissolution of the last parliament, all things seemed to succeed, at home and abroad, to the protector's wish, and his power and greatness to be better established than ever it had been, yet he never had the same serenity of mind he had been used to, after he had refused the crown; but was out of countenance, and chagrin, as if he were conscious of not having been true to himself; and much more apprehensive of danger to his person than he had used to be. Insomuch as he was not easy of access, nor so much seen abroad; and seemed to be in some disorder when his eyes found any stranger in the room; upon whom they were still fixed. When he intended to go to Hampton Court, which was his principal delight and diversion, it was never known, till he was in the coach, which way he would go; and he was still hemmed in by his guards both before and behind; and the coach in which he went was always thronged as full as it could be, with his servants; who were armed; and he seldom returned the same way he went; and rarely lodged two nights together in one chamber, but had many furnished and prepared, to which his own key conveyed him and those he would have with him, when he had a mind to go to bed: which made his fears the more taken notice of, and public, because he had never been accustomed to those precautions.

But that which chiefly broke his peace, was the death of his daughter Claypole; who had been always his greatest joy, and who, in her sickness, which was of a nature the physicians knew not how to deal with, had several conferences with him, which exceedingly perplexed him. Though nobody was near enough to hear the particulars, yet her often mentioning, in the pains she endured, the blood her father had spilt, made people conclude that she had presented his worst actions to his consideration. And though he never made the least show of remorse for any of those actions, it is very certain that either what she said or her death affected him wonderfully.

Whatever it was, about the middle of August he was seized on by a common tertian ague, from which, he believed, a little ease and divertisement at Hampton Court would have freed him. But the fits grew stronger, and his spirits much abated: so that he returned again to Whitehall, when his physicians began to think him in danger, though the preachers, who prayed always about him, and told God Almighty what great things he had done for him, and how much more need he had still of his service, declared as from God that he should recover: and he did not think he should die, till even the time that his spirits failed him. Then he declared to them, 'that he did appoint his son to succeed him, his eldest son Richard'; and so expired upon the third day of September, 1658, a day he thought always very propitious to him, and on which he had twice triumphed for several victories; a day very memorable for the greatest storm of wind that had been ever known, for some hours before and after his death, which overthrew trees, houses, and made great wrecks at sea; and [the tempest] was so universal, that the effects of it were terrible both in France and Flanders, where all people trembled at it; for, besides the wrecks all along the sea-coast, many boats were cast away in the very rivers; and within few days after, the circumstance of his death, that accompanied that storm, was known.

He was one of those men, *quos vituperare ne inimici quidem possunt, nisi ut simul laudent;** for he could never have done half that mischief without great parts of courage, industry, and judgment. He must have had a wonderful understanding in the natures and humours of men, and as great a dexterity in applying them; who, from a private and obscure birth, (though of a good family,) without interest or estate, alliance or friendship, could raise himself to such a height, and compound and knead such opposite and contradictory tempers, humours, and interests into a consistence, that contributed to his designs, and to their own destruction; whilst himself grew insensibly powerful enough to cut off those by whom he had climbed, in the instant that they projected to demolish their own building. What Velleius Paterculus said of Cinna may very justly be said of him, *ausum eum, quae nemo auderet bonus; perfecisse, quae a nullo, nisi fortissimo, perfici possent.** Without doubt, no man with more wickedness ever attempted any thing, or brought to pass what he desired more wickedly, more in the face and contempt of religion, and moral honesty; yet wickedness as great as his could never have accomplished those trophies without the assistance of a great spirit, an admirable circumspection and sagacity, and a most magnanimous resolution.

When he appeared first in the parliament, he seemed to have a person in no degree gracious, no ornament of discourse, none of those talents which use to reconcile the affections of the stander by: yet as he grew into place and authority, his parts seemed to be raised, as if he had had concealed faculties, till he had occasion to use them; and when he was to act the part of a great man, he did it without any indecency, notwithstanding the want of custom.

After he was confirmed and invested protector by the *Humble*

Petition and Advice, he consulted with very few upon any action of importance, nor communicated any enterprise he resolved upon with more than those who were to have principal parts in the execution of it; nor with them sooner than was absolutely necessary. What he once resolved, in which he was not rash, he would not be dissuaded from, nor endure any contradiction of his power and authority; but extorted obedience from them who were not willing to yield it.

When he had laid some very extraordinary tax upon the city, one Cony, an eminent fanatic, and one who had heretofore served him very notably, positively refused to pay his part; and loudly dissuaded others from submitting to it, 'as an imposition notoriously against the law, and the property of the subject, which all honest men were bound to defend'. Cromwell sent for him, and cajoled him with the memory of 'the old kindness, and friendship, that had been between them; and that of all men he did not expect this opposition from him, in a matter that was so necessary for the good of the commonwealth'. But it was always his fortune to meet with the most rude and obstinate behaviour from those who had formerly been governed by him; and they commonly put him in mind of some expressions and sayings of his own, in cases of the like nature: so this man remembered him, how great an enemy he had expressed himself to such grievances, and had declared, 'that all who submitted to them, and paid illegal taxes, were more to blame, and greater enemies to their country, than they who had imposed them; and that the tyranny of princes could never be grievous, but by the tameness and stupidity of the people'. When Cromwell saw that he could not convert him, he told him, 'that he had a will as stubborn as his, and he would try which of them two should be master'. Thereupon, with some terms of reproach and contempt, he committed the man to prison; whose courage was nothing abated by it; but as soon as the term came, he brought his habeas corpus in the king's bench, which they then called the upper bench. Maynard, who was of council with the prisoner, demanded his liberty with great confidence, both upon the illegality of the commitment, and the illegality of the imposition, as being laid without any lawful authority. The judges could not maintain or defend either, and enough declared what their sentence would be; and therefore the protector's attorney required a farther day, to answer what had been urged. Before that day, Maynard was committed to the Tower, for presuming to question or make doubt of his authority; and the judges were sent for, and severely reprehended for suffering that license; when they, with all humility, mentioned the law and Magna Carta, Cromwell told them, 'their magna f—— should not control his actions; which he knew were for the safety of the commonwealth'. He asked them, 'who made them judges? whether they had any authority to sit there, but what he gave them? and if his authority were at an end, they knew well enough what would become of themselves; and therefore advised them to be more tender of that which could only preserve them'; and so dismissed them with caution, 'that they should not suffer the lawyers to prate what it would not become them to hear'.

Thus he subdued a spirit that had been often troublesome to the most sovereign power, and made Westminster-hall as obedient, and subservient to his commands, as any of the rest of his quarters. In all other matters, which did not concern the life of his jurisdiction, he seemed to have great reverence for the law, rarely interposing between party and party. As he proceeded with this kind of indignation and haughtiness with those who were refractory, and dared to contend with his greatness, so towards all who complied with his good pleasure, and courted his protection, he used a wonderful civility, generosity and bounty.

To reduce three nations, which perfectly hated him, to an entire obedience to all his dictates; to awe and govern those nations by an army that was indevoted to him, and wished his ruin, was an instance of a very prodigious address. But his greatness at home was but a shadow of the glory he had abroad. It was hard to discover which feared him most, France, Spain, or the Low Countries, where his friendship was current at the value he put upon it. As they did all sacrifice their honour and their interest to his pleasure, so there is nothing he could have demanded, that either of them would have denied him.

He was not a man of blood, and totally declined Machiavel's method;* which prescribes, upon any alteration of government, as a thing absolutely necessary, to cut off all the heads of those, and extirpate their families, who are friends to the old one. It was confidently reported that in the council of officers it was more than once proposed 'that there might be a general massacre of all the royal party, as the only expedient to secure the government', but that

Cromwell would never consent to it; it may be, out of too much contempt of his enemies. In a word, as he had all the wickedness against which damnation is denounced, and for which hell-fire is prepared, so he had some virtues which have caused the memory of some men in all ages to be celebrated; and he will be looked upon by posterity as a brave bad man.

3   [*The Return of Charles II*] from the *Diary*

SAMUEL PEPYS

In May 1660 Pepys sailed to Holland as Admiral's secretary to Edward Mountagu (referred to in the *Diary* as 'My Lord'; later Earl of Sandwich) as part of the fleet which was to bring back Charles II (1630–85) from his exile. On board ship Pepys shared quarters with Thomas Clarke ('the Doctor'), later a royal physician. As the entry for 25 May implies, the King, who was over six feet tall, caught his head against a beam in the captain's state room; the mark was subsequently gilded.

23 [May 1660]. The Doctor and I waked very merry, only my eye was very red and ill in the morning from yesterday's hurt.

In the morning came infinite of people on board from the King, to go along with him.

My Lord, Mr Crew, and others go on shore to meet the King as he comes off from shore.

Where (Sir R. Stayner bringing His Majesty into the boat) I hear that His Majesty did with a great deal of affection kiss my Lord upon his first meeting.

The King, with the two Dukes, the Queen of Bohemia, Princess Royal, and Prince of Orange, came on board; where I in their coming in kissed the King's, Queen and Princess's hands, having done the other before. Infinite shooting off of the guns, and that in a disorder on purpose, which was better than if it had been otherwise.

All day nothing but Lords and persons of honour on board, that we were exceeding full.

Dined in a great deal of state, the royal company by themselves in the coach, which was a blessed sight to see.

I dined with Dr Clarke, Dr Quarterman, and Mr Darcy in my cabin.

This morning Mr Lucy came on board, to whom and his company of the King's guard in another ship my Lord did give three dozen of bottles of wine. He made friends between Mr Pierce and I.

After dinner, the King and Duke upon the [quarter-deck table] altered the name of some of the ships, *viz.* the *Naseby* into *Charles*—the *Richard, James*; the *Speaker, Mary*—the *Dunbar* (which was not in company with us) the *Henry*—*Winsby, Happy Return*—*Wakefield, Richmond*—*Lamport*, the *Henrietta*—*Cheriton*, the *Speedwell*—*Bradford*, the *Success*.

That done, the Queen, Princess Royal, and Prince of Orange took leave of the King, and the Duke of York went on board the *London*, and the Duke of Gloucester the *Swiftsure*—which done, we weighed anchor, and with a fresh gale and most happy weather we set sail for England—all the afternoon the King walking here and there, up and down (quite contrary to what I thought him to have been), very active and stirring.

Upon the quarter-deck he fell in discourse of his escape from Worcester. Where it made me ready to weep to hear the stories that he told of his difficulties that he had passed through. As his travelling four days and three nights on foot, every step up to the knees in dirt, with nothing but a green coat and a pair of country breeches on, and a pair of country shoes that made him so sore all over his feet that he could scarce stir.

Yet he was forced to run away from a miller and other company that took them for rogues.

His sitting at table at one place, where the master of the house, that had not seen him in eight years, did know him but kept it private; when at the same table there was one that had been of his own regiment at Worcester, could not know him but made him drink the King's health, and said that the King was at least four fingers higher than he.

Another place, he was by some servants of the house made to drink, that they might know him not to be a Roundhead, which they swore he was.

In another place, at his inn, the master of the house, as the King was standing with his hands upon the back of a chair by the fire-side, he kneeled down and kissed his hand privately, saying that he would not ask him who he was, but bid God bless him whither that he was going. Then the difficulty of getting a boat to get into France, where he was fain to plot with the master thereof to keep his design from the four men and a boy (which was all his ship's company), and so got to Feckam in France.

At Roane he looked so poorly that the people went into the rooms before he went away, to see whether he had not stole something or other. In the evening I went up to my Lord to write letters for England—which we sent away, with word of our coming, by Mr Edw. Pickering. The King supped alone in the coach. After that I got a dish, and we four supped in my cabin as at noon.

About bed-time my Lord Bartlet (who I had offered my service to before) sent for me to get him a bed, who with much ado I did get to bed to my Lord Middlesex in the great cabin below; but I was cruelly troubled before I could dispose of him and quit myself of him.

So to my cabin again, where the company still was and were telling more of the King's difficulties. As, how he was fain to eat a piece of bread and cheese out of a poor boy's pocket.

How at a Catholic house, he was fain to lie in the priest's hole a good while in the house for his privacy.

After that our company broke up, and the Doctor and I to bed. We have all the Lords Commissioners on board us, and many others. Under sail all night and most glorious weather.

24. Up, and made myself as fine as I could with the linen stockings and wide canons that I bought the other day at Hague. Extraordinary press of noble company and great mirth all the day. There dined with me in my cabin (that is, the carpenter's) Dr Earle and Mr Hollis, the King's Chaplains. Dr Scarborough, Dr Quarterman, and Dr Clarke, physicians; Mr Darcy and Mr Fox (both very fine gentlemen), the King's servants. Where we had brave discourse.

Walking upon the decks, where persons of honour all the afternoon—among others, Thom. Killigrew (a merry droll, but a gentleman of great esteem with the King): among many merry stories, he told one how he writ a letter three or four days ago to the Princess Royal about a Queen Dowager of Judæa and Palestine that was in The Hague incognita, that made love to the King, &c.; which was Mr Cary (a courtier's) wife that had been a nun, who are all married to Jesus.

At supper the three doctors of physic again at my cabin—where I put Dr Scarborough in mind of what I heard him say about the use of the eyes. Which he owned, that children do in every day's experience look several ways with both their eyes, till custom teaches them otherwise. And that we do now see but with one eye—our eyes looking in parallel lines.

After this discourse I was called to write a pass for my Lord Mandeville to take up horses to London. Which I wrote in the King's name and carried it to him to sign, which was the first and only one that ever he signed in the ship *Charles*. To bed—coming in sight of land a little before night.

25. By the morning we were come close to the land and everybody made ready to get on shore.

The King and the two dukes did eat their breakfast before they went, and there being set some ship's diet before them, only to show them the manner of the ship's diet, they eat of nothing else but pease and pork and boiled beef.

I had Mr Darcy at my cabin and Dr Clarke, who eat with me and told me how the King had given £50 to Mr Sheply for my Lord's servants, and £500 among the officers and common men of the ship. I spoke with the Duke of York about business, who called me Pepys by name, and upon my desire did promise me his future favour.

Great expectation of the King's making some knights, but there was none. About noon (though the brigantine that Beale made was there ready to carry him), yet he would go in my Lord's barge with the two dukes; our captain steered, and my Lord went along bare with him. I went, and Mr Mansell and one of the King's footmen, with a dog that the King loved (which shit in the boat, which made us laugh and me think that a King and all that belong to him are but just as others are) went in a boat by ourselves; and so got on shore when the King did, who was received by General Monck with all imaginable love and respect at his entrance upon the land at Dover. Infinite the crowd of people and the gallantry of the horsemen, citizens, and noblemen of all sorts.

The Mayor of the town came and gave him his white staff, the badge of his place, which the King did give him again. The Mayor also presented him from the town a very rich Bible, which he took and said it was the thing that he loved above all things in the world.

A canopy was provided for him to stand under, which he did; and talked awhile with General Monck and others; and so into a stately coach there set for him; and so away straight through the town toward Canterbury without making any stay at Dover.

The shouting and joy expressed by all is past imagination. I seeing that my Lord did not stir out of his barge, I got into a boat and so into his barge, whither Mr John Crew stepped and spoke a word or two to my Lord; and so returned. We back to the ship; and going, did see a man almost drowned, that fell out of his boat into the sea but with much ado was got out.

My Lord almost transported with joy that he hath done all this without any the least blur and obstruction in the world that would give an offence to any, and with the great honour that he thought it would be to him.

Being overtook by the brigantine, my Lord and we went out of our barge into it; and so went on board with Sir W. Batten and the Vice- and Rear-Admirals.

At night my Lord supped, and Mr Tho. Crew, with Captain Stoakes. I supped with the Captain, who told me what the King had given us. My Lord returned late and at his coming did give me order to cause the mark to be gilded, and a crown and *C. R.* to be made at the head of the coach table, where the King today with his own hand did mark his height—which accordingly I caused the painter to do; and is now done, as is to be seen.

4   [*The Return of Charles II*] from the *Diary*

JOHN EVELYN

29 [May]. This day came in his majesty Charles the Second to London after a sad and long exile, and calamitous suffering both of the king and church, being seventeen years. This was also his birthday, and with a triumph of above 20,000 horse and foot, brandishing their swords and shouting with unexpressible joy: the ways strewed with flowers, the bells ringing, the streets hung with tapestry, fountains running with wine; the mayor, aldermen, all the companies in their liveries, chains of gold, banners; lords and nobles, cloth of silver, gold, and velvet everybody clad in, the windows and balconies all set with ladies, trumpets, music, and myriads of people flocking the streets and was as far as Rochester, so as they were seven hours in

passing the city, even from two in the afternoon till nine at night. I stood in the Strand and beheld it, and blessed God. And all this without one drop of blood, and by that very army which rebelled against him: but it was the Lord's doing, *et mirabile in oculis nostris*:* for such a restoration was never seen in the mention of any history, ancient or modern, since the return of the Babylonian captivity, nor so joyful a day, and so bright, ever seen in this nation: this happening when to expect or effect it was past all human policy.

5 *Astraea Redux: A Poem on the Happy Restoration and Return of His Sacred Majesty Charles the Second*

JOHN DRYDEN

First published June 1660. The Latin title means 'Justice brought back', referring to the Roman goddess of justice who left the world in disgust at the wickedness of human beings. Her return inaugurates a second Saturnian golden age, and the return of Charles II is imagined as inaugurating a second Augustan age: the Roman Emperor Augustus (63 BCE–CE 14) brought peace, stability, and a literary golden age (with luminaries such as Horace, Ovid, and Virgil) after a protracted period of civil war following the murder of Julius Caesar. The association of Charles with Augustus was commonplace in the poems greeting his return, but the term 'Augustan' was not explicitly applied to the period's literary achievement until 1690, when Francis Atterbury wondered 'whether in Charles II's reign English did not come to its full perfection; and whether it has not had its Augustan age as well as the Latin' (Preface to Edmund Waller's *Poems* (1690)).

Iam redit et virgo, redeunt Saturnia regna.

VIRGIL

Now with a general peace the world was blessed,
While ours, a world divided from the rest,
A dreadful quiet felt, and worser far
Than arms, a sullen interval of war:
Thus when black clouds draw down the labouring skies,
Ere yet abroad the wingèd thunder flies,
An horrid stillness first invades the ear,
And in that silence we the tempest fear.

Th' ambitious Swede like restless billows tossed,*
On this hand gaining what on that he lost,   10
Though in his life he blood and ruin breathed,
To his now guideless kingdom peace bequeathed;
And heaven that seemed regardless of our fate,
For France and Spain did miracles create,*
Such mortal quarrels to compose in peace
As nature bred and interest did increase.
We sighed to hear the fair Iberian bride
Must grow a lily to the lily's side,
While our cross stars denied us Charles his bed
Whom our first flames and virgin love did wed.   20
For his long absence church and state did groan,
Madness the pulpit, faction seized the throne;
Experienced age in deep despair was lost
To see the rebel thrive, the loyal crossed;
Youth that with joys had unacquainted been
Envied grey hairs that once good days had seen:
We thought our sires, not with their own content,
Had ere we came to age our portion spent.
Nor could our nobles hope their bold attempt
Who ruined crowns would coronets exempt: 30
For when by their designing leaders taught
To strike at power which for themselves they sought,
The vulgar, gulled into rebellion, armed;
Their blood to action by the prize was warmed.
The sacred purple then and scarlet gown*
Like sanguine dye to elephants was shown.*
Thus when the bold Typhoeus scaled the sky,*
And forced great Jove from his own heaven to fly,
(What king, what crown from treason's reach is free,
If Jove and heaven can violated be?)   40
The lesser gods that shared his prosperous state
All suffered in the exiled Thunderer's fate.
The rabble now such freedom did enjoy
As winds at sea that use it to destroy:
Blind as the Cyclops, and as wild as he,*
They owned a lawless savage liberty,
Like that our painted ancestors so prized

Ere empire's arts their breasts had civilized.
How great were then our Charles his woes, who thus
Was forced to suffer for himself and us!   50
He, tossed by Fate, and hurried up and down,
Heir to his father's sorrows with his crown,
Could taste no sweets of youth's desirèd age,
But found his life too true a pilgrimage.
Unconquered yet in that forlorn estate,
His manly courage overcame his fate.
His wounds he took like Romans on his breast,
Which by his virtue were with laurels dressed.
As souls reach heaven while yet in bodies pent,
So did he live above his banishment.   60
That sun which we beheld with cozened eyes
Within the water, moved along the skies.
How easy 'tis when Destiny proves kind
With full-spread sails to run before the wind;
But those that 'gainst stiff gales laveering go
Must be at once resolved and skilful too.
He would not like soft Otho hope prevent*
But stayed and suffered Fortune to repent:
These virtues Galba in a stranger sought,
And Piso to adopted empire brought.   70
How shall I then my doubtful thoughts express
That must his sufferings both regret and bless!
For when his early valour heaven had crossed,
And all at Worcester but the honour lost,*
Forced into exile from his rightful throne
He made all countries where he came his own;
And viewing monarchs' secret arts of sway
A royal factor for their kingdoms lay.
Thus banished David spent abroad his time,*
When to be God's anointed was his crime,   80
And when restored made his proud neighbours rue
Those choice remarks he from his travels drew.
Nor is he only by afflictions shown
To conquer others' realms, but rule his own:
Recov'ring hardly what he lost before,
His right endears it much, his purchase more.

Inured to suffer ere he came to reign,
No rash procedure will his actions stain;
To business ripened by digestive thought,
His future rule is into method brought: 90
As they who first proportion understand
With easy practice reach a master's hand.
Well might the ancient poets then confer
On night the honoured name of counsellor,
Since struck with rays of prosperous fortune blind,
We light alone in dark afflictions find.
In such adversities to sceptres trained,
The name of Great his famous grandsire gained;*
Who yet a king alone in name and right,
With hunger, cold and angry Jove did fight;   100
Shocked by a covenanting league's vast powers,
As holy and as catholic as ours,
Till Fortune's fruitless spite had made it known
Her blows not shook but riveted his throne.

　　Some lazy ages, lost in sleep and ease,
No action leave to busy chronicles;*
Such whose supine felicity but makes
In story chasms, in epoches mistakes;
O'er whom Time gently shakes his wings of down
Till with his silent sickle they are mown: 110
Such is not Charles his too, too active age,
Which governed by the wild distempered rage
Of some black star infecting all the skies,
Made him at his own cost like Adam wise.
Tremble ye nations who, secure before,
Laughed at those arms that 'gainst ourselves we bore;
Roused by the lash of his own stubborn tail
Our lion now will foreign foes assail.
With alga who the sacred altar strows?
To all the sea-gods Charles an offering owes: 120
A bull to thee, Portunus, shall be slain,*
A lamb to you, the tempests of the main:
For those loud storms that did against him roar
Have cast his shipwracked vessel on the shore.
Yet as wise artists mix their colours so

That by degrees they from each other go,
Black steals unheeded from the neighbouring white
Without offending the well-cozened sight:
So on us stole our blessèd change, while we
Th' effect did feel, but scarce the manner see.   130
Frosts that constrain the ground, and birth deny
To flowers, that in its womb expecting lie,
Do seldom their usurping power withdraw,
But raging floods pursue their hasty thaw:
Our thaw was mild, the cold not chased away,
But lost in kindly heat of lengthened day.
Heaven would no bargain for its blessings drive,
But what we could not pay for, freely give.
The Prince of Peace would, like himself, confer*
A gift unhoped without the price of war: 140
Yet as he knew his blessing's worth, took care
That we should know it by repeated prayer,
Which stormed the skies and ravished Charles from thence,
As heaven itself is took by violence.
Booth's forward valour only served to show*
He durst that duty pay we all did owe:
Th' attempt was fair, but heaven's prefixèd hour
Not come; so like the watchful traveller
That by the moon's mistaken light did rise,
Lay down again, and closed his weary eyes.   150
'Twas Monck whom Providence designed to loose*
Those real bonds false freedom did impose.
The blessèd saints that watched this turning scene
Did from their stars with joyful wonder lean
To see small clues draw vastest weights along,
Not in their bulk but in their order strong.
Thus pencils can by one slight touch restore
Smiles to that changèd face that wept before.
With ease such fond chimeras we pursue
As fancy frames for fancy to subdue,   160
But when ourselves to action we betake
It shuns the mint like gold that chemists make.
How hard was then his task, at once to be
What in the body natural we see

Man's architect distinctly did ordain
The charge of muscles, nerves and of the brain;
Through viewless conduits spirits to dispense,
The springs of motion from the seat of sense.
'Twas not the hasty product of a day,
But the well-ripened fruit of wise delay.　　　170
He like a patient angler, ere he strook
Would let them play a while upon the hook.
Our healthful food the stomach labours thus,
At first embracing what it straight doth crush.
Wise leeches will not vain receipts obtrude,
While growing pains pronounce the humours crude;
Deaf to complaints, they wait upon the ill
Till some safe crisis authorize their skill.
Nor could his acts too close a vizard wear
To scape their eyes whom guilt had taught to fear,　　　180
And guard with caution that polluted nest
Whence Legion twice before was dispossessed;*
Once sacred house which when they entered in
They thought the place could sanctify a sin,
Like those that vainly hoped kind heaven would wink
While to excess on martyrs' tombs they drink:
And as devouter Turks first warn their souls
To part, before they taste forbidden bowls,
So these when their black crimes they went about
First timely charmed their useless conscience out.　　　190
Religion's name against itself was made;
The shadow served the substance to invade:
Like zealous missions they did care pretend
Of souls in show, but made the gold their end.
Th' incensèd powers beheld with scorn from high
An heaven so far distant from the sky,
Which durst with horses' hoofs that beat the ground
And martial brass belie the thunder's sound.
'Twas hence at length just Vengeance thought it fit
To speed their ruin by their impious wit.　　　200
Thus Sforza, cursed with a too fertile brain,*
Lost by his wiles the power his wit did gain.
Henceforth their fogue must spend at lesser rate

Than in its flames to wrap a nation's fate.
Suffered to live, they are like helots set*
A virtuous shame within us to beget:
For by example most we sinned before,
And glass-like, clearness mixed with frailty bore.
But since reformed by what we did amiss,
We by our sufferings learn to prize our bliss: 210
Like early lovers whose unpractised hearts
Were long the May-game of malicious arts,
When once they find their jealousies were vain
With double heat renew their fires again.
'Twas this produced the joy that hurried o'er
Such swarms of English to the neighbouring shore,
To fetch that prize by which Batavia made*
So rich amends for our impoverished trade.
O had you seen from Scheveline's barren shore*
(Crowded with troops, and barren now no more)   220
Afflicted Holland to his farewell bring
True sorrow, Holland to regret a king;
While waiting him his royal fleet did ride,
And willing winds to their low'red sails denied,
The wavering streamers, flags and standard out,
The merry seamen's rude but cheerful shout,
And last the cannons' voice that shook the skies⎫
And, as it fares in sudden ecstasies,   ⎬
At once bereft us both of ears and eyes.   ⎭
The *Naseby* now no longer England's shame,*   230
But better to be lost in Charles his name
(Like some unequal bride in nobler sheets)
Receives her lord: the joyful *London* meets
The princely York, himself alone a freight;
The *Swiftsure* groans beneath great Gloucester's weight.
Secure as when the halcyon breeds, with these*
He that was born to drown might cross the seas.
Heaven could not own a providence and take
The wealth three nations ventured at a stake.
The same indulgence Charles his voyage blessed   240
Which in his right had miracles confessed.
The winds that never moderation knew,

Afraid to blow too much, too faintly blew;
Or out of breath with joy could not enlarge
Their straitened lungs, or conscious of their charge.
The British Amphitrite smooth and clear*
In richer azure never did appear;
Proud her returning Prince to entertain
With the submitted fasces of the main.*

And welcome now, great monarch, to your own;   250
Behold th' approaching cliffs of Albion;
It is no longer motion cheats your view,
As you meet it, the land approacheth you.
The land returns, and in the white it wears
The marks of penitence and sorrow bears.
But you, whose goodness your descent doth show,
Your heavenly parentage, and earthly too;
By that same mildness which your father's crown
Before did ravish, shall secure your own.
Not tied to rules of policy, you find   260
Revenge less sweet than a forgiving mind.
Thus when th' Almighty would to Moses give*
A sight of all he could behold and live,
A voice before his entry did proclaim
Long-suffering, goodness, mercy in his name.
Your power to justice doth submit your cause,
Your goodness only is above the laws,
Whose rigid letter while pronounced by you
Is softer made. So winds that tempests brew
When through Arabian groves they take their flight,   270
Made wanton with rich odours, lose their spite.
And as those lees that trouble it, refine
The agitated soul of generous wine,
So tears of joy for your returning spilt,
Work out and expiate our former guilt.
Methinks I see those crowds on Dover's strand,
Who in their haste to welcome you to land
Choked up the beach with their still growing store,
And made a wilder torrent on the shore;
While spurred with eager thoughts of past delight,   280

Those who had seen you court a second sight,
Preventing still your steps, and making haste
To meet you often wheresoe'er you passed.
How shall I speak of that triumphant day
When you renewed th' expiring pomp of May?
(A month that owns an interest in your name:
You and the flowers are its peculiar claim.)
That star that at your birth shone out so bright
It stained the duller sun's meridian light,
Did once again its potent fires renew,   290
Guiding our eyes to find and worship you.
   And now time's whiter series is begun,
Which in soft centuries shall smoothly run;
Those clouds that overcast your morn shall fly
Dispelled to farthest corners of the sky.
Our nation with united interest blessed,
Not now content to poise, shall sway the rest:
Abroad your empire shall no limits know,
But like the sea in boundless circles flow.
Your much-loved fleet shall with a wide command   300
Besiege the petty monarchs of the land:
And as old Time his offspring swallowed down,
Our ocean in its depths all seas shall drown.
Their wealthy trade from pirates' rapine free,
Our merchants shall no more adventurers be:
Nor in the farthest east those dangers fear
Which humble Holland must dissemble here.
Spain to your gift alone her Indies owes,
For what the powerful takes not, he bestows;
And France that did an exile's presence fear   310
May justly apprehend you still too near.
At home the hateful names of parties cease
And factious souls are wearied into peace.
The discontented now are only they
Whose crimes before did your just cause betray:
Of those your edicts some reclaim from sins,
But most your life and blessed example wins.
O happy prince, whom heaven hath taught the way
By paying vows, to have more vows to pay!

O happy age! O times like those alone   320
By Fate reserved for great Augustus' throne!
When the joint growth of arms and arts foreshow
The world a monarch, and that monarch *you*.

6   From *Last Instructions to a Painter*

ANDREW MARVELL

Written 1667 (dated 4 September 1667 in Bodleian Library MS Eng. Poet.
d. 49); circulated in manuscript. The attribution to Marvell is probable,
but not certain. The genre had started in England with Edmund Waller's
'Instructions to a Painter' (1666), which presented an encomiastic portrait
of the Duke of York, who as Lord High Admiral was responsible for the
English navy. But as the war against the Dutch went badly, parodic rejoin-
ders to Waller's poem proliferated (see *Yale POAS*, vol. i), presenting
satirical characters of the inefficient and corrupt courtiers who were seen
by opposition writers as responsible for the poor state of the nation's
defences. *Last Instructions* presents a gallery of such portraits, before
turning to the humiliating destruction of the English fleet in the River
Medway by the Dutch admiral De Ruyter in June 1667. Coming less than
a year after the Fire of London, this disaster added to disenchantment
with Charles and his government. The extract printed here also provides a
heroic (and homoerotic) portrait of the young soldier Archibald Douglas,
who died on one of the ships burnt by the Dutch.

Ruyter the while, that had our ocean curbed,
Sailed now among our rivers undisturbed,
Surveyed their crystal streams and banks so green
And beauties ere this never naked seen.
Through the vain sedge, the bashful nymphs he eyed:
Bosoms, and all which from themselves they hide.
The sun much brighter, and the skies more clear,
He finds the air and all things sweeter here.   530
The sudden change, and such a tempting sight
Swells his old veins with fresh blood, fresh delight.
Like am'rous victors he begins to shave,
And his new face looks in the English wave.
His sporting navy all about him swim
And witness their complaisance in their trim.

Their streaming silks play through the weather fair
And with inveigling colours court the air,
While the red flags breathe on their topmasts high
Terror and war, but want an enemy.   540
Among the shrouds the seamen sit and sing,
And wanton boys on every rope do cling.
Old Neptune springs the tides and water lent
(The gods themselves do help the provident),
And where the deep keel on the shallow cleaves,
With trident's lever, and great shoulder heaves,
Aeolus their sails inspires with eastern wind,*
Puffs them along, and breathes upon them kind.
With pearly shell the Tritons all the while
Sound the sea-march and guide to Sheppey Isle.   550
    So have I seen in April's bud arise
A fleet of clouds, sailing along the skies;
The liquid region with their squadrons filled,
Their airy sterns the sun behind does gild;
And gentle gales them steer, and heaven drives,
When, all on sudden, their calm bosom rives
With thunder and lightning from each armèd cloud;
Shepherds themselves in vain in bushes shroud.
Such up the stream the Belgic navy glides
And at Sheerness unloads its stormy sides.   560
    Spragge there, though practised in the sea command,*
With panting heart lay like a fish on land,
And quickly judged the fort was not tenáble
(Which, if a house, yet were not tenantáble)
No man can sit there safe: the cannon pours
Thorough the walls untight and bullet showers,
The neighbourhood ill, and an unwholesome seat,
So at the first salute resolves retreat,
And swore that he would never more dwell there
Until the city put it in repair.   570
So he in front, his garrison in rear,
March straight to Chatham to increase the fear.*
    There our sick ships unrigged in summer lay
Like moulting fowl, a weak and easy prey,
For whose strong bulk earth scarce could timber find,

The ocean water, or the heavens wind:
Those oaken giants of the ancient race,
That ruled all seas and did our Channel grace.
The conscious stag so, once the forest's dread,
Flies to the wood and hides his armless head.   580
Ruyter forthwith a squadron does untack;
They sail securely through the river's track.
An English pilot too (O shame, O sin!)
Cheated of pay, was he that showed them in.
Our wretched ships within their fate attend,
And all our hopes now on frail chain depend:*
(Engine so slight to guard us from the sea,
It fitter seemed to captivate a flea).
A skipper rude shocks it without respect,
Filling his sails more force to re-collect.   590
Th' English from shore the iron deaf invoke
For its last aid: 'Hold chain, or we are broke.'
But with her sailing weight, the Holland keel,
Snapping the brittle links, does thorough reel,
And to the rest the opened passage show;
Monck from the bank the dismal sight does view.*
Our feathered gallants, which came down that day
To be spectators safe of the new play,
Leave him alone when first they hear the gun
(Cornbury the fleetest) and to London run.*   600
Our seamen, whom no danger's shape could fright,
Unpaid, refuse to mount our ships for spite,
Or to their fellows swim on board the Dutch,
Which show the tempting metal in their clutch.
Oft had he sent of Duncombe and of Legge*
Cannon and powder, but in vain, to beg;
And Upnor Castle's ill-deserted wall,
Now needful, does for ammunition call.
He finds, wheresoe'er he succour might expect,
Confusion, folly, treachery, fear, neglect.   610
But when the *Royal Charles* (what rage, what grief)*
He saw seized, and could give her no relief;
That sacred keel which had, as he, restored
His exiled sovereign on its happy board,

And thence the British admiral became,
Crowned, for that merit, with their master's name;
That pleasure-boat of war, in whose dear side
Secure so oft he had this foe defied,
Now a cheap spoil, and the mean victor's slave,
Taught the Dutch colours from its top to wave;   620
Of former glories the reproachful thought,
With present shame compared, his mind distraught.
Such from Euphrates' bank, a tigress fell
After the robber for her whelps doth yell;
But sees enraged the river flow between,
Frustrate revenge and love, by loss more keen,
At her own breast her useless claws does arm:
She tears herself, since him she cannot harm.
    The guards, placed for the chain's and fleet's defence,
Long since were fled on many a feigned pretence.   630
Daniel had there adventured, man of might,*
Sweet painter, draw his picture while I write.
Paint him of person tall, and big of bone,
Large limbs like ox, not to be killed but shown.
Scarce can burnt ivory feign an hair so black,
Or face so red, thine ochre and thy lac.
Mix a vain terror in his martial look,
And all those lines by which men are mistook;
But when, by shame constrained to go on board,
He heard how the wild cannon nearer roared,   640
And saw himself confined like sheep in pen,
Daniel then thought he was in lion's den.
And when the frightful fireships he saw,
Pregnant with sulphur, to him nearer draw,
Captain, lieutenant, ensign, all make haste
Ere in the fiery furnace they be cast—
Three children tall, unsinged, away they row,
Like Shadrack, Meschack, and Abednego.*
    Not so brave Douglas, on whose lovely chin
The early down but newly did begin,   650
And modest beauty yet his sex did veil,
While envious virgins hope he is a male.
His yellow locks curl back themselves to seek,

Nor other courtship knew but to his cheek.
Oft, as he in chill Esk or Seine by night
Hardened and cooled his limbs, so soft, so white,
Among the reeds, to be espied by him,
The nymphs would rustle; he would forward swim.
They sighed and said, 'Fond boy, why so untame
That fliest love's fires, reserved for other flame?'   660
Fixed on his ship, he faced that horrid day
And wondered much at those that run away.
Nor other fear himself could comprehend
Than lest heaven fall ere thither he ascend,
But entertains the while his time too short
With birding at the Dutch, as if in sport,
Or waves his sword, and could he them conjùre
Within its circle, knows himself secure.
The fatal bark him boards with grappling fire,
And safely through its port the Dutch retire.   670
That precious life he yet disdains to save
Or with known art to try the gentle wave.
Much him the honours of his ancient race
Inspire, nor would he his own deeds deface,
And secret joy in his calm soul does rise
That Monck looks on to see how Douglas dies.
Like a glad lover, the fierce flames he meets,
And tries his first embraces in their sheets.
His shape exact, which the bright flames enfold,
Like the sun's statue stands of burnished gold.   680
Round the transparent fire about him glows,
As the clear amber on the bee does close,
And as on angels' heads their glories shine,
His burning locks adorn his face divine.
But when in his immortal mind he felt
His altering form and soldered limbs to melt,
Down on the deck he laid himself and died,
With his dear sword reposing by his side;
And on the flaming plank so rests his head
As one that's warmed himself and gone to bed.   690
His ship burns down, and with his relics sinks,
And the sad stream beneath his ashes drinks.

Fortunate boy, if either pencil's fame,
Or if my verse can propagate thy name,
When Oeta and Alcides are forgot,*
Our English youth shall sing the valiant Scot.
　　Each doleful day still with fresh loss returns:
The *Loyal London* now a third time burns,
And the true *Royal Oak* and *Royal James*,
Allied in fate, increase, with theirs, her flames.　　　　　　　700
Of all our navy none should now survive,
But that the ships themselves were taught to dive,
And the kind river in its creek them hides,
Fraughting their piercèd keels with oozy tides.
　　Up to the bridge contagious terror struck:
The Tower itself with the near danger shook,
And were not Ruyter's maw with ravage cloyed,
E'en London's ashes had been then destroyed.
Officious fear, however, to prevent
Our loss, does so much more our loss augment:　　　　　　　710
The Dutch had robbed those jewels of the crown;
Our merchantmen, lest they be burned, we drown.
So when the fire did not enough devour,
The houses were demolished near the Tower.
Those ships that yearly from their teeming hole
Unloaded here the birth of either pole—
Furs from the north and silver from the west,
Wines from the south, and spices from the east;
From Gambo gold, and from the Ganges gems—*
Take a short voyage underneath the Thames,　　　　　　　720
Once a deep river, now with timber floored,
And shrunk, least navigable, to a ford.
　　Now (nothing more at Chatham left to burn),
The Holland squadron leisurely return,
And spite of Ruperts and of Albemarles,*
To Ruyter's triumph lead the captive *Charles*.
The pleasing sight he often does prolong:
Her masts erect, tough cordage, timbers strong,
Her moving shapes, all these he does survey,
And all admires, but most his easy prey.　　　　　　　730
The seamen search her all within, without:

Viewing her strength, they yet their conquest doubt;
Then with rude shouts, secure, the air they vex,
With gamesome joy insulting on her decks.
Such the feared Hebrew, captive, blinded, shorn,*
Was led about in sport, the public scorn.
   Black day accursed! On thee let no man hale
Out of the port, or dare to hoist a sail,
Nor row a boat in thy unlucky hour.
Thee, the year's monster, let thy dam devour,   740
And constant time, to keep his course yet right,
Fill up thy space with a redoubled night.
When agèd Thames was bound with fetters base,
And Medway chaste ravished before his face,
And their dear offspring murdered in their sight,
Thou and thy fellows held'st the odious light.
Sad change since first that happy pair was wed,
When all the rivers graced their nuptial bed,
And Father Neptune promised to resign
His empire old to their immortal line!   750
Now with vain grief their vainer hopes they rue,
Themselves dishonoured, and the gods untrue,
And to each other, helpless couple, moan,
As the sad tortoise for the sea does groan.
But most they for their darling *Charles* complain,
And were it burnt, yet less would be their pain.
To see that fatal pledge of sea command
Now in the ravisher De Ruyter's hand,
The Thames roared, swooning Medway turned her tide,
And were they mortal, both for grief had died.   760

7   *[A Satire on Charles II]*

JOHN WILMOT, EARL OF ROCHESTER

Written 1673, and circulated in manuscript. Rochester is said to have
handed the King a copy of this satire by mistake. Many poems in the
1670s satirized Charles II for his sexual affairs; this one refers to two of his
mistresses, Louise de Keroualle, Duchess of Portsmouth ('Carwell'), and
Nell Gwyn the actress. But discontent with Charles also arose from his

Francophile policies and crypto-Catholic tendencies, hence the allusion to Louis XIV's vigorous military campaigns which were seen by many to threaten Protestant states.

In th' isle of Britain, long since famous grown
For breeding the best cunts in Christendom,
There reigns (and oh, long may he reign and thrive)
The easiest king and best-bred man alive.
Him no ambition moves to get renown,
Like the French fool who wanders up and down,
Starving his people, hazarding his crown.
Peace is his aim, his gentleness is such,
And love he loves, for he loves fucking much.
Nor are his high desires above his strength,   10
His sceptre and his prick are of a length,
And she may sway the one who plays with th' other,
And make him little wiser than his brother.
Restless he rolls about from whore to whore,
A merry monarch, scandalous and poor.
Poor prince, thy prick, like thy buffoons at court,
Will govern thee because it makes thee sport.
'Tis sure the sauciest that did ever swive,
The proudest peremptory prick alive.
Though safety, law, religion, life lay on 't,   20
'Twould break through all to make its way to cunt.
To Carwell, the most dear of all his dears,
The best relief of his declining years,
Oft he bewails his fortune and her fate,
Which made her love so well, and yet too late.
For though in her he settles well his tarse,
Yet his dull graceless ballocks hang an arse.
This you'd believe had I but time to tell ye
The pains it costs the poor laborious Nelly,
Whilst she employs hands, fingers, mouth and thighs   30
Ere she can raise the member she enjoys.
I hate all monarchs, and the thrones they sit on,
From the hector of France to the cully of Britain.

8   *Absalom and Achitophel*

JOHN DRYDEN

Published November 1681. The poem was designed to influence public
opinion at the time of the trial of the Earl of Shaftesbury for treason.
Shaftesbury, formerly Lord Chancellor, was now the leader of the opposition Whig party, which sought to have Charles's Catholic brother
James, Duke of York, excluded from the succession; the Whigs argued
instead for a regency, or the succession of the king's illegitimate son
James, Duke of Monmouth, in order to preserve Protestant liberties.
Several Exclusion Bills were introduced in Parliament, but none passed
into law. Dryden's poem, written in defence of the King and the settled
constitution and against the Whig appeal to a turbulent democracy, is a
biblical allegory which casts contemporary politicians as Old Testament
figures, drawing principally on 2 Samuel 13–18. The protagonists are
the sexually promiscuous but divinely anointed King David (Charles II),
his beloved but potentially rebellious son Absalom (James Scott, Duke
of Monmouth (1649–85)), and the devious counsellor Achitophel
(Anthony Ashley Cooper, Earl of Shaftesbury (1621–83)). Dryden stops
the narrative before it reaches the tragic conclusion related in the Bible.
Alongside these major players are the supporting figures on either side,
many of whom are given memorably epigrammatic character sketches:
these are identified in the Explanatory Notes. A *Second Part* followed in
1682, written largely by Nahum Tate, but including some character
sketches by Dryden (see 42).

> In pious times, ere priestcraft did begin,
> Before polygamy was made a sin,
> When man on many multiplied his kind,
> Ere one to one was cursedly confined;
> When nature prompted, and no law denied
> Promiscuous use of concubine and bride;
> Then Israel's monarch, after heaven's own heart,*
> His vigorous warmth did variously impart
> To wives and slaves: and wide as his command
> Scattered his maker's image through the land.   10
> Michal, of royal blood, the crown did wear,*
> A soil ungrateful to the tiller's care:
> Not so the rest, for several mothers bore
> To godlike David several sons before;

But since like slaves his bed they did ascend
No true succession could their seed attend.
Of all this numerous progeny was none
So beautiful, so brave as Absolon:
Whether, inspired by some diviner lust,
His father got him with a greater gust,   20
Or that his conscious destiny made way
By manly beauty to imperial sway.
Early in foreign fields he won renown,
With kings and states allied to Israel's crown:
In peace the thoughts of war he could remove,
And seemed as he were only born for love.
Whate'er he did was done with so much ease,
In him alone 'twas natural to please:
His motions all accompanied with grace,
And paradise was opened in his face.   30
With secret joy indulgent David viewed
His youthful image in his son renewed;
To all his wishes nothing he denied,
And made the charming Annabel his bride.*
What faults he had (for who from faults is free?)
His father could not, or he would not see.
Some warm excesses which the law forbore
Were construed youth that purged by boiling o'er;
And Amnon's murder by a specious name*
Was called a just revenge for injured fame.   40
Thus praised and loved the noble youth remained,
While David undisturbed in Sion reigned.
But life can never be sincerely blessed:
Heaven punishes the bad, and proves the best.
The Jews, a headstrong, moody, murmuring race
As ever tried th' extent and stretch of grace,
God's pampered people, whom, debauched with ease,
No king could govern, nor no god could please
(Gods they had tried of every shape and size
That god-smiths could produce, or priests devise);   50
These Adam-wits, too fortunately free
Began to dream they wanted liberty,
And when no rule, no precedent was found

Of men, by laws less circumscribed and bound
They led their wild desires to woods and caves,
And thought that all but savages were slaves.
They who when Saul was dead, without a blow,
Made foolish Ishbosheth the crown forgo,*
Who banished David did from Hebron bring
And with a general shout proclaimed him King: 60
Those very Jews, who, at their very best
Their humour more than loyalty expressed,
Now wondered why so long they had obeyed
An idol monarch which their hands had made;
Thought they might ruin him they could create,
Or melt him to that golden calf, a state.
But these were random bolts: no formed design
Nor interest made the factious crowd to join;
The sober part of Israel, free from stain,
Well knew the value of a peaceful reign,   70
And looking backward with a wise affright
Saw seams of wounds dishonest to the sight;
In contemplation of whose ugly scars
They cursed the memory of civil wars.
The moderate sort of men, thus qualified,
Inclined the balance to the better side,
And David's mildness managed it so well
The bad found no occasion to rebel.
But when to sin our biased nature leans,
The careful devil is still at hand with means,   80
And providently pimps for ill desires:
The Good Old Cause revived a plot requires;*
Plots, true or false, are necessary things
To raise up commonwealths and ruin kings.
    Th' inhabitants of old Jerusalem
Were Jebusites, the town so called from them,*
And theirs the native right—
But when the chosen people grew more strong,
The rightful cause at length became the wrong,
And every loss the men of Jebus bore   90
They still were thought God's enemies the more.
Thus worn and weakened, well or ill content,

Submit they must to David's government:
Impoverished, and deprived of all command,
Their taxes doubled as they lost their land,
And, what was harder yet to flesh and blood,
Their gods disgraced, and burned like common wood.
This set the heathen priesthood in a flame,
For priests of all religions are the same:
Of whatsoe'er descent their godhead be,   100
Stock, stone or other homely pedigree,
In his defence his servants are as bold
As if he had been born of beaten gold.
The Jewish rabbins, though their enemies,*
In this conclude them honest men and wise;
For 'twas their duty, all the learnèd think,
T' espouse his cause by whom they eat and drink.
From hence began that plot, the nation's curse,*
Bad in itself, but represented worse;
Raised in extremes, and in extremes decried,   110
With oaths affirmed, with dying vows denied;
Not weighed or winnowed by the multitude,
But swallowed in the mass, unchewed and crude.
Some truth there was, but dashed and brewed with lies,
To please the fools and puzzle all the wise.
Succeeding times did equal folly call
Believing nothing, or believing all.
Th' Egyptian rites the Jebusites embraced,*
Where gods were recommended by their taste:
Such savoury deities must needs be good   120
As served at once for worship and for food.
By force they could not introduce these gods,
For ten to one in former days was odds,
So fraud was used (the sacrificer's trade):
Fools are more hard to conquer than persuade.
Their busy teachers mingled with the Jews,
And raked for converts ev'n the court and stews;
Which Hebrew priests the more unkindly took
Because the fleece accompanies the flock.
Some thought they God's anointed meant to slay   130
By guns, invented since full many a day:

Our author swears it not, but who can know
How far the devil and Jebusites may go?
This plot, which failed for want of common sense,
Had yet a deep and dangerous consequence:
For, as when raging fevers boil the blood
The standing lake soon floats into a flood,
And every hostile humour which before
Slept quiet in its channels, bubbles o'er;
So several factions from this first fermènt   140
Work up to foam, and threat the government.
Some by their friends, more by themselves thought wise,
Opposed the power to which they could not rise.
Some had in courts been great, and thrown from thence
Like fiends, were hardened in impenitence.
Some by their monarch's fatal mercy grown
From pardoned rebels, kinsmen to the throne,
Were raised in power and public office high—
Strong bands, if bands ungrateful men could tie.

    Of these the false Achitophel was first: 150
A name to all succeeding ages cursed.
For close designs and crooked counsels fit,
Sagacious, bold, and turbulent of wit;
Restless, unfixed in principles and place,
In power unpleased, impatient of disgrace.
A fiery soul, which working out its way
Fretted the pigmy body to decay,
And o'erinformed the tenement of clay.
A daring pilot in extremity:
Pleased with the danger, when the waves went high   160
He sought the storms; but for a calm unfit
Would steer too nigh the sands to boast his wit.
Great wits are sure to madness near allied,
And thin partitions do their bounds divide:
Else why should he, with wealth and honour blessed,
Refuse his age the needful hours of rest?
Punish a body which he could not please,
Bankrupt of life, yet prodigal of ease?
And all to leave what with his toil he won
To that unfeathered, two-legged thing, a son: 170

Got while his soul did huddled notions try,
And born a shapeless lump, like anarchy.
In friendship false, implacable in hate,
Resolved to ruin or to rule the state;
To compass this the triple bond he broke,*
The pillars of the public safety shook,
And fitted Israel for a foreign yoke.
Then, seized with fear, yet still affecting fame,
Usurped a patriot's all-atoning name.*
[So easy still it proves in factious times   180
With public zeal to cancel private crimes:
How safe is treason, and how sacred ill,
Where none can sin against the people's will;
Where crowds can wink, and no offence be known,
Since in another's guilt they find their own.
Yet fame deserved no enemy can grudge:
The statesman we abhor, but praise the judge.
In Israel's courts ne'er sat an abbethdin
With more discerning eyes, or hands more clean:
Unbribed, unsought, the wretched to redress,   190
Swift of despatch, and easy of access.]
O, had he been content to serve the crown
With virtues only proper to the gown,
Or had the rankness of the soil been freed
From cockle that oppressed the noble seed,
David for him his tuneful harp had strung,
And heaven had wanted one immortal song.
But wild ambition loves to slide, not stand,
And fortune's ice prefers to virtue's land.
Achitophel, grown weary to possess   200
A lawful fame and lazy happiness,
Disdained the golden fruit to gather free,
And lent the crowd his arm to shake the tree.
Now, manifest of crimes contrived long since
He stood at bold defiance with his prince;
Held up the buckler of the people's cause
Against the crown, and skulked behind the laws.
The wished occasion of the plot he takes,
Some circumstances finds, but more he makes.

By buzzing emissaries fills the ears   210
Of listening crowds with jealousies and fears
Of arbitrary counsels brought to light,
And proves the King himself a Jebusite.
Weak arguments! which yet he knew full well
Were strong with people easy to rebel:
For, governed by the moon, the giddy Jews
Tread the same track when she the prime renews;
And once in twenty years, their scribes record,
By natural instinct they change their lord.
Achitophel still wants a chief, and none   220
Was found so fit as warlike Absolon:
Not that he wished his greatness to create
(For politicians neither love nor hate),
But for he knew his title not allowed
Would keep him still depending on the crowd,
That kingly power, thus ebbing out, might be
Drawn to the dregs of a democracy.
Him he attempts with studied arts to please,
And sheds his venom in such words as these:

    'Auspicious Prince! at whose nativity   230
Some royal planet ruled the southern sky;
Thy longing country's darling and desire,
Their cloudy pillar and their guardian fire;*
Their second Moses, whose extended wand
Divides the seas, and shows the promised land;
Whose dawning day in every distant age
Has exercised the sacred prophets' rage;
The people's prayer, the glad diviner's theme,
The young men's vision, and the old men's dream!
Thee, saviour, thee, the nation's vows confess,   240
And never satisfied with seeing, bless.
Swift, unbespoken pomps thy steps proclaim,
And stammering babes are taught to lisp thy name.
How long wilt thou the general joy detain,
Starve and defraud the people of thy reign;
Content ingloriously to pass thy days
Like one of virtue's fools that feeds on praise,
Till thy fresh glories which now shine so bright

Grow stale and tarnish with our daily sight?
Believe me, royal youth, thy fruit must be   250
Or gathered ripe, or rot upon the tree.
Heaven has to all allotted, soon or late,
Some lucky revolution of their fate;
Whose motions, if we watch and guide with skill
(For human good depends on human will),
Our Fortune rolls, as from a smooth descent,
And from the first impression takes the bent:
But if unseized, she glides away like wind,
And leaves repenting folly far behind.
Now, now she meets you with a glorious prize,   260
And spreads her locks before her as she flies.
Had thus old David, from whose loins you spring,
Not dared, when Fortune called him, to be King,
At Gath an exile he might still remain,
And heaven's anointing oil had been in vain.
Let his successful youth your hopes engage,
But shun th' example of declining age:
Behold him setting in his western skies,
The shadows length'ning as the vapours rise.
He is not now, as when on Jordan's sand   270
The joyful people thronged to see him land,
Cov'ring the beach, and black'ning all the strand:
But like the Prince of Angels from his height
Comes tumbling downward with diminished light;
Betrayed by one poor plot to public scorn
(Our only blessing since his cursed return):
Those heaps of people which one sheaf did bind
Blown off and scattered by a puff of wind.
What strength can he to your designs oppose,
Naked of friends, and round beset with foes?   280
If Pharaoh's doubtful succour he should use,*
A foreign aid would more incense the Jews:
Proud Egypt would dissembled friendship bring,
Foment the war, but not support the King;
Nor would the royal party e'er unite
With Pharaoh's arms t' assist the Jebusite;
Or if they should, their interest soon would break,

And with such odious aid make David weak.
All sorts of men by my successful arts
Abhorring kings, estrange their altered hearts   290
From David's rule; and 'tis the general cry
"Religion, Commonwealth and Liberty".
If you as champion of the public good
Add to their arms a chief of royal blood,
What may not Israel hope, and what applause
Might such a general gain by such a cause?
Not barren praise alone, that gaudy flower
Fair only to the sight, but solid power:
And nobler is a limited command
Given by the love of all your native land,   300
Than a successive title, long and dark,
Drawn from the mouldy rolls of Noah's ark.'
    What cannot praise effect in mighty minds,
When flattery soothes, and when ambition blinds!
Desire of power, on earth a vicious weed,
Yet, sprung from high, is of celestial seed:
In God 'tis glory; and when men aspire
'Tis but a spark too much of heavenly fire.
Th' ambitious youth, too covetous of fame,
Too full of angel's metal in his frame,   310
Unwarily was led from virtue's ways,
Made drunk with honour, and debauched with praise.
Half loath, and half consenting to the ill
(For loyal blood within him struggled still),
He thus replied: 'And what pretence have I
To take up arms for public liberty?
My father governs with unquestioned right,
The faith's defender, and mankind's delight:
Good, gracious, just, observant of the laws,
And heaven by wonders has espoused his cause.   320
Whom has he wronged in all his peaceful reign?
Who sues for justice to his throne in vain?
What millions has he pardoned of his foes,
Whom just revenge did to his wrath expose?
Mild, easy, humble, studious of our good,
Inclined to mercy, and averse from blood.

If mildness ill with stubborn Israel suit,
His crime is God's belovèd attribute.
What could he gain, his people to betray,
Or change his right for arbitrary sway?* 330
Let haughty Pharaoh curse with such a reign
His fruitful Nile, and yoke a servile train.
If David's rule Jerusalem displease,
The dog-star heats their brains to this disease.
Why then should I, encouraging the bad,
Turn rebel, and run popularly mad?
Were he a tyrant who by lawless might
Oppressed the Jews and raised the Jebusite,
Well might I mourn; but nature's holy bands
Would curb my spirits and restrain my hands: 340
The people might assert their liberty,
But what was right in them were crime in me.
His favour leaves me nothing to require,
Prevents my wishes, and outruns desire.
What more can I expect while David lives?
All but his kingly diadem he gives,
And that—' But there he paused, then sighing said,
'Is justly destined for a worthier head.
For when my father from his toils shall rest,
And late augment the number of the blessed, 350
His lawful issue shall the throne ascend,
Or the collateral line where that shall end.
His brother, though oppressed with vulgar spite,
Yet dauntless and secure of native right,
Of every royal virtue stands possessed,
Still dear to all the bravest, and the best.
His courage foes, his friends his truth proclaim,
His loyalty the King, the world his fame.
His mercy ev'n th' offending crowd will find,
For sure he comes of a forgiving kind. 360
Why should I then repine at heaven's decree,
Which gives me no pretence to royalty?
Yet O that Fate, propitiously inclined,
Had raised my birth, or had debased my mind;
To my large soul not all her treasure lent,

And then betrayed it to a mean descent.
I find, I find my mounting spirits bold,
And David's part disdains my mother's mould.
Why am I scanted by a niggard birth?
My soul disclaims the kindred of her earth,   370
And made for empire whispers me within,
"Desire of greatness is a godlike sin."'

   Him staggering so when hell's dire agent found,
While fainting virtue scarce maintained her ground,
He pours fresh forces in, and thus replies:

   'Th' eternal God, supremely good and wise,
Imparts not these prodigious gifts in vain;
What wonders are reserved to bless your reign!
Against your will your arguments have shown
Such virtue's only given to guide a throne.   380
Not that your father's mildness I condemn,
But manly force becomes the diadem,
'Tis true, he grants the people all they crave,
And more perhaps than subjects ought to have:
For lavish grants suppose a monarch tame,
And more his goodness than his wit proclaim.
But when should people strive their bonds to break,
If not when kings are negligent or weak?
Let him give on till he can give no more,
The thrifty Sanhedrin shall keep him poor:*   390
And every shekel which he can receive
Shall cost a limb of his prerogative.
To ply him with new plots shall be my care,
Or plunge him deep in some expensive war;
Which when his treasure can no more supply
He must with the remains of kingship buy.
His faithful friends our jealousies and fears
Call Jebusites, and Pharaoh's pensioners;
Whom when our fury from his aid has torn
He shall be naked left to public scorn.   400
The next successor, whom I fear and hate,
My arts have made obnoxious to the state,
Turned all his virtues to his overthrow,
And gained our elders to pronounce a foe.

His right for sums of necessary gold
Shall first be pawned, and afterwards be sold;
Till time shall ever-wanting David draw
To pass your doubtful title into law:
If not, the people have a right supreme
To make their kings, for kings are made for them. 410
All empire is no more than power in trust,
Which when resumed can be no longer just.*
Succession, for the general good designed,
In its own wrong a nation cannot bind:
If altering that the people can relieve,
Better one suffer than a nation grieve.
The Jews well know their power: ere Saul they chose
God was their King, and God they durst depose.
Urge now your piety, your filial name,
A father's right, and fear of future fame; 420
The public good, that universal call
To which ev'n heaven submitted, answers all.
Nor let his love enchant your generous mind:
'Tis nature's trick to propagate her kind.
Our fond begetters, who would never die,
Love but themselves in their posterity.
Or let his kindness by th' effects be tried,
Or let him lay his vain pretence aside.
God said he loved your father: could he bring
A better proof than to anoint him King? 430
It surely showed he loved the shepherd well
Who gave so fair a flock as Israel.
Would David have you thought his darling son?
What means he then to alienate the crown?
The name of godly he may blush to bear:
'Tis after God's own heart to cheat his heir.
He to his brother gives supreme command:
To you, a legacy of barren land;
Perhaps th' old harp on which he thrums his lays,
Or some dull Hebrew ballad in your praise. 440
Then the next heir, a prince severe and wise,
Already looks on you with jealous eyes;
Sees through the thin disguises of your arts,

And marks your progress in the people's hearts.
Though now his mighty soul its grief contains,
He meditates revenge who least complains;
And like a lion slumbering in the way,
Or sleep dissembling while he waits his prey,
His fearless foes within his distance draws,
Constrains his roaring and contracts his paws;   450
Till at the last, his time for fury found,
He shoots with sudden vengeance from the ground,
The prostrate vulgar passes o'er and spares,
But with a lordly rage his hunters tears.
Your case no tame expedients will afford:
Resolve on death, or conquest by the sword,
Which for no less a stake than life you draw;
And self-defence is nature's eldest law.
Leave the warm people no considering time,
For then rebellion may be thought a crime: 460
Prevail yourself of what occasion gives,
But try your title while your father lives;
And that your arms may have a fair pretence,
Proclaim you take them in the King's defence,
Whose sacred life each minute would expose
To plots from seeming friends and secret foes.
And who can sound the depth of David's soul?
Perhaps his fear his kindness may control.*
He fears his brother though he loves his son
For plighted vows too late to be undone.   470
If so, by force he wishes to be gained,
Like women's lechery, to seem constrained.
Doubt not, but when he most affects the frown
Commit a pleasing rape upon the crown;
Secure his person to secure your cause:
They who possess the prince possess the laws.'
    He said; and this advice above the rest
With Absalom's mild nature suited best:
Unblamed of life (ambition set aside),
Not stained with cruelty, nor puffed with pride;   480
How happy had he been if destiny
Had higher placed his birth, or not so high!

His kingly virtues might have claimed a throne,
And blessed all other countries but his own;
But charming greatness since so few refuse
'Tis juster to lament him than accuse.
Strong were his hopes a rival to remove,
With blandishments to gain the public love;
To head the faction while their zeal was hot,
And popularly prosecute the plot.   490
To farther this, Achitophel unites
The malcontents of all the Israelites,
Whose differing parties he could wisely join
For several ends, to serve the same design.
The best, and of the princes some were such,
Who thought the power of monarchy too much,
Mistaken men, and patriots in their hearts,
Not wicked, but seduced by impious arts:
By these the springs of property were bent,
And wound so high they cracked the government.   500
The next for interest sought t' embroil the state,
To sell their duty at a dearer rate;
And make their Jewish markets of the throne,
Pretending public good, to serve their own.
Others thought kings an useless, heavy load,
Who cost too much, and did too little good:
These were for laying honest David by
On principles of pure good husbandry.
With them joined all th' haranguers of the throng
That thought to get preferment by the tongue.   510
Who follow next a double danger bring,
Not only hating David, but the King—
The Solymæan rout, well versed of old*
In godly faction, and in treason bold;
Cowering and quaking at a conqueror's sword,
But lofty to a lawful prince restored,
Saw with disdain an ethnic plot begun,
And scorned by Jebusites to be outdone.
Hot Levites headed these, who pulled before*
From th' ark, which in the Judges' days they bore,   520
Resumed their cant, and with a zealous cry

Pursued their old beloved theocracy,
Where Sanhedrin and priest enslaved the nation
And justified their spoils by inspiration;
For who so fit for reign as Aaron's race
If once dominion they could found in grace?*
These led the pack, though not of surest scent
Yet deepest-mouthed against the government.
A numerous host of dreaming saints succeed,
Of the true old enthusiastic breed;   530
'Gainst form and order they their power employ,
Nothing to build, and all things to destroy.
But far more numerous was the herd of such
Who think too little, and who talk too much.
These, out of mere instinct, they knew not why,
Adored their fathers' god, and property;
And by the same blind benefit of fate
The devil and the Jebusite did hate:
Born to be saved, ev'n in their own despite,
Because they could not help believing right.   540
Such were the tools, but a whole hydra more
Remains, of sprouting heads too long to score.
    Some of their chiefs were princes of the land:
In the first rank of these did Zimri stand;*
A man so various that he seemed to be
Not one, but all mankind's epitome.
Stiff in opinions, always in the wrong,
Was everything by starts, and nothing long;
But in the course of one revolving moon
Was chemist, fiddler, statesman, and buffoon: 550
Then all for women, painting, rhyming, drinking,
Besides ten thousand freaks that died in thinking.
Blessed madman, who could every hour employ
With something new to wish, or to enjoy!
Railing and praising were his usual themes,
And both, to show his judgement, in extremes:
So over-violent, or over-civil,
That every man with him was god or devil.
In squandering wealth was his peculiar art:
Nothing went unrewarded but desert.   560

Beggared by fools, whom still he found too late,
He had his jest, and they had his estate.
He laughed himself from court, then sought relief
By forming parties, but could ne'er be chief;
For, spite of him, the weight of business fell
On Absalom and wise Achitophel.
Thus wicked but in will, of means bereft,
He left not faction, but of that was left.

    Titles and names 'twere tedious to rehearse
Of lords below the dignity of verse.   570
Wits, warriors, Commonwealthsmen were the best,
Kind husbands and mere nobles all the rest.
And therefore in the name of dullness be
The well-hung Balaam and cold Caleb free;*
And canting Nadab let oblivion damn,*
Who made new porridge for the paschal lamb.
Let friendship's holy band some names assure;
Some their own worth, and some let scorn secure.
Nor shall the rascal rabble here have place,
Whom kings no titles gave, and God no grace: 580
Not bull-faced Jonas, who could statutes draw*
To mean rebellion, and make treason law.
But he, though bad, is followed by a worse,
The wretch who heaven's anointed dared to curse:
Shimei, whose youth did early promise bring*
Of zeal to God, and hatred to his King,
Did wisely from expensive sins refrain,
And never broke the sabbath but for gain:
Nor ever was he known an oath to vent,
Or curse, unless against the government.   590
Thus heaping wealth by the most ready way
Among the Jews, which was to cheat and pray;
The city to reward his pious hate
Against his master, chose him magistrate:
His hand a vare of justice did uphold,
His neck was loaded with a chain of gold.
During his office treason was no crime,
The sons of Belial had a glorious time:*
For Shimei, though not prodigal of pelf,

Yet loved his wicked neighbour as himself.   600
When two or three were gathered to declaim⎫
Against the monarch of Jerusalem,   ⎬
Shimei was always in the midst of them;   ⎭
And if they cursed the King when he was by,
Would rather curse than break good company.
If any durst his factious friends accuse,
He packed a jury of dissenting Jews,
Whose fellow-feeling in the godly cause
Would free the suffering saint from human laws;
For laws are only made to punish those   610
Who serve the King, and to protect his foes.
If any leisure time he had from power
(Because 'tis sin to misemploy an hour)
His business was, by writing, to persuade
That kings were useless, and a clog to trade:
And that his noble style he might refine,
No Rechabite more shunned the fumes of wine.*
Chaste were his cellars, and his shrieval board
The grossness of a city feast abhorred:
His cooks with long disuse their trade forgot;   620
Cool was his kitchen, though his brains were hot.
Such frugal virtue malice may accuse,
But sure 'twas necessary to the Jews,
For towns once burnt such magistrates require
As dare not tempt God's providence by fire.
With spiritual food he fed his servants well,
But free from flesh that made the Jews rebel;
And Moses' laws he held in more account
For forty days of fasting in the mount.

To speak the rest, who better are forgot,   630
Would tire a well-breathed witness of the plot.
Yet Corah, thou shalt from oblivion pass:*
Erect thyself, thou monumental brass,
High as the serpent of thy metal made,
While nations stand secure beneath thy shade.
What though his birth were base, yet comets rise
From earthy vapours ere they shine in skies:
Prodigious actions may as well be done

By weaver's issue as by prince's son.
This arch-attestor for the public good   640
By that one deed ennobles all his blood.
Who ever asked the witnesses' high race
Whose oath with martyrdom did Stephen grace?
Ours was a Levite, and as times went then
His tribe were God Almighty's gentlemen.
Sunk were his eyes, his voice was harsh and loud,
Sure signs he neither choleric was, nor proud:
His long chin proved his wit, his saintlike grace
A church vermilion and a Moses face.
His memory, miraculously great,   650
Could plots exceeding man's belief repeat;
Which therefore cannot be accounted lies,
For human wit could never such devise.
Some future truths are mingled in his book,
But where the witness failed, the prophet spoke.
Some things like visionary flights appear:
The Spirit caught him up, the Lord knows where,
And gave him his rabbinical degree
Unknown to foreign university.
His judgement yet his memory did excel,   660
Which pieced his wondrous evidence so well,
And suited to the temper of the times
Then groaning under Jebusitic crimes.
Let Israel's foes suspect his heavenly call,
And rashly judge his writ apocryphal;
Our laws for such affronts have forfeits made:
He takes his life who takes away his trade.
Were I myself in witness Corah's place
The wretch who did me such a dire disgrace
Should whet my memory, though once forgot,   670
To make him an appendix of my plot.
His zeal to heaven made him his prince despise,
And load his person with indignities:
But zeal peculiar privilege affords,
Indulging latitude to deeds and words;
And Corah might for Agag's murder call*
In terms as coarse as Samuel used to Saul.

What others in his evidence did join
(The best that could be had for love or coin)
In Corah's own predicament will fall,   680
For witness is a common name to all.
    Surrounded thus with friends of every sort,
Deluded Absalom forsakes the court;
Impatient of high hopes, urged with renown,
And fired with near possession of a crown;
Th' admiring crowd are dazzled with surprise,
And on his goodly person feed their eyes.
His joy concealed, he sets himself to show,
On each side bowing popularly low;
His looks, his gestures and his words he frames,   690
And with familiar ease repeats their names.
Thus, formed by nature, furnished out with arts,
He glides unfelt into their secret hearts;
Then with a kind compassionating look,
And sighs bespeaking pity ere he spoke,
Few words he said, but easy those and fit,
More slow than Hybla drops, and far more sweet:*
    'I mourn, my countrymen, your lost estate,
Though far unable to prevent your fate;
Behold a banished man, for your dear cause   700
Exposed a prey to arbitrary laws!
Yet O that I alone could be undone,
Cut off from empire, and no more a son!
Now all your liberties a spoil are made, ⎫
Egypt and Tyrus intercept your trade,* ⎬
And Jebusites your sacred rites invade. ⎭
My father, whom with reverence yet I name,
Charmed into ease, is careless of his fame;
And bribed with petty sums of foreign gold
Is grown in Bathsheba's embraces old;*   710
Exalts his enemies, his friends destroys,
And all his power against himself employs.
He gives, and let him give, my right away.
But why should he his own, and yours, betray?
He only, he can make the nation bleed,
And he alone from my revenge is freed.

Take then my tears' (with that he wiped his eyes),
''Tis all the aid my present power supplies.
No court informer can these arms accuse,
These arms may sons against their fathers use;   720
And 'tis my wish the next successor's reign
May make no other Israelite complain.'
    Youth, beauty, graceful action seldom fail,
But common interest always will prevail:
And pity never ceases to be shown
To him who makes the people's wrongs his own.
The crowd (that still believe their kings oppress)
With lifted hands their young Messiah bless,
Who now begins his progress to ordain
With chariots, horsemen and a numerous train.   730
From east to west his glories he displays,*
And like the sun the promised land surveys.
Fame runs before him as the morning star,
And shouts of joy salute him from afar;
Each house receives him as a guardian god,
And consecrates the place of his abode:
But hospitable treats did most commend
Wise Issachar, his wealthy western friend.
This moving court that caught the people's eyes,
And seemed but pomp, did other ends disguise: 740
Achitophel had formed it with intent
To sound the depths, and fathom, where it went,
The people's hearts, distinguish friends from foes,
And try their strength before they came to blows.
Yet all was coloured with a smooth pretence
Of specious love, and duty to their prince;
Religion, and redress of grievances,
Two names that always cheat and always please,
Are often urged; and good King David's life
Endangered by a brother and a wife.   750
Thus in a pageant show a plot is made,
And peace itself is war in masquerade.
O foolish Israel! never warned by ill,
Still the same bait, and circumvented still!
Did ever men forsake their present ease,

In midst of health imagine a disease,
Take pains contingent mischiefs to foresee,
Make heirs for monarchs, and for God decree?
What shall we think? Can people give away*
Both for themselves and sons, their native sway?   760
Then they are left defenceless to the sword
Of each unbounded arbitrary lord:
And laws are vain by which we right enjoy,
If kings unquestioned can those laws destroy.
Yet if the crowd be judge of fit and just,
And kings are only officers in trust,
Then this resuming cov'nant was declared
When kings were made, or is for ever barred:
If those who gave the sceptre could not tie
By their own deed their own posterity,   770
How then could Adam bind his future race?
How could his forfeit on mankind take place?
Or how could heavenly justice damn us all,
Who ne'er consented to our father's fall?
Then kings are slaves to those whom they command,
And tenants to their people's pleasure stand.
Add that the power for property allowed
Is mischievously seated in the crowd:
For who can be secure of private right
If sovereign sway may be dissolved by might?   780
Nor is the people's judgement always true:
The most may err as grossly as the few,
And faultless kings run down by common cry
For vice, oppression and for tyranny.
What standard is there in a fickle rout,
Which flowing to the mark runs faster out?*
Nor only crowds, but Sanhedrins may be
Infected with this public lunacy,
And share the madness of rebellious times
To murder monarchs for imagined crimes.   790
If they may give and take whene'er they please,
Not kings alone (the Godhead's images)
But government itself at length must fall
To nature's state, where all have right to all.

Yet grant our lords the people kings can make,
What prudent men a settled throne would shake?
For whatsoe'er their sufferings were before,
That change they covet makes them suffer more.
All other errors but disturb a state,
But innovation is the blow of fate.   800
If ancient fabrics nod, and threat to fall,
To patch the flaws and buttress up the wall
Thus far 'tis duty; but here fix the mark,
For all beyond it is to touch our ark.*
To change foundations, cast the frame anew,
Is work for rebels who base ends pursue,
At once divine and human laws control,
And mend the parts by ruin of the whole.
The tampering world is subject to this curse,
To physic their disease into a worse.   810

    Now what relief can righteous David bring?
How fatal 'tis to be too good a King!
Friends he has few, so high the madness grows;
Who dare be such must be the people's foes.
Yet some there were, ev'n in the worst of days,
Some let me name, and naming is to praise.

    In this short file Barzillai first appears:*
Barzillai crowned with honour and with years.
Long since the rising rebels he withstood
In regions waste beyond the Jordan's flood,   820
Unfortunately brave to buoy the state,
But sinking underneath his master's fate.
In exile with his godlike prince he mourned,
For him he suffered, and with him returned.
The court he practised, not the courtier's art;
Large was his wealth, but larger was his heart,
Which well the noblest objects knew to choose,
The fighting warrior and recording Muse.
His bed could once a fruitful issue boast,
Now more than half a father's name is lost.   830
His eldest hope, with every grace adorned,
By me (so heaven will have it) always mourned,
And always honoured, snatched in manhood's prime

By' unequal Fates, and providence's crime.
Yet not before the goal of honour won,   ⎫
All parts fulfilled of subject and of son;   ⎬
Swift was the race, but short the time to run. ⎭
O narrow circle, but of power divine,
Scanted in space, but perfect in thy line!
By sea, by land, thy matchless worth was known,   840
Arms thy delight, and war was all thy own:
Thy force infused the fainting Tyrians propped,
And haughty Pharaoh found his fortune stopped.
O ancient honour, O unconquered hand,
Whom foes unpunished never could withstand!
But Israel was unworthy of thy name:
Short is the date of all immoderate fame.
It looks as heaven our ruin had designed,
And durst not trust thy fortune and thy mind.
Now free from earth, thy disencumbered soul   850
Mounts up and leaves behind the clouds and starry pole.
From thence thy kindred legions mayest thou bring
To aid the guardian angel of thy King.
Here stop my Muse, here cease thy painful flight,
No pinions can pursue immortal height:
Tell good Barzillai thou canst sing no more,
And tell thy soul she should have fled before:
Or fled she with his life, and left this verse
To hang on her departed patron's hearse?
Now take thy steepy flight from heaven, and see   860
If thou canst find on earth another he;
Another he would be too hard to find,
See then whom thou canst see not far behind.
Zadok the priest, whom, shunning power and place,*
His lowly mind advanced to David's grace;
With him the Sagan of Jerusalem,*
Of hospitable soul and noble stem;
Him of the western dome, whose weighty sense
Flows in fit words and heavenly eloquence:
The prophets' sons by such example led,   870
To learning and to loyalty were bred,
For colleges on bounteous kings depend,

And never rebel was to arts a friend.
To these succeed the pillars of the laws,
Who best could plead, and best can judge a cause.
Next them a train of loyal peers ascend:
Sharp-judging Adriel the Muses' friend,*
Himself a Muse; in Sanhedrin's debate
True to his prince, but not a slave of state;
Whom David's love with honours did adorn   880
That from his disobedient son were torn.
Jotham, of piercing wit and pregnant thought,*
Endued by nature, and by learning taught
To move assemblies, who but only tried
The worse awhile, then chose the better side;
Nor chose alone, but turned the balance too—
So much the weight of one brave man can do.
Hushai, the friend of David in distress,*
In public storms of manly steadfastness;
By foreign treaties he informed his youth,   890
And joined experience to his native truth.
His frugal care supplied the wanting throne,
Frugal for that, but bounteous of his own;
'Tis easy conduct when exchequers flow,
But hard the task to manage well the low,
For sovereign power is too depressed or high
When kings are forced to sell, or crowds to buy.
Indulge one labour more, my weary Muse,
For Amiel, who can Amiel's praise refuse?*
Of ancient race by birth, but nobler yet   900
In his own worth, and without title great:
The Sanhedrin long time as chief he ruled,
Their reason guided and their passion cooled;
So dexterous was he in the crown's defence,
So formed to speak a loyal nation's sense,
That as their band was Israel's tribes in small
So fit was he to represent them all.
Now rasher charioteers the seat ascend,
Whose loose careers his steady skill commend:
They like th' unequal ruler of the day*   910
Misguide the seasons and mistake the way,

While he withdrawn at their mad labour smiles,
And safe enjoys the sabbath of his toils.
　　These were the chief, a small but faithful band⎫
Of worthies, in the breach who dared to stand,　⎬
And tempt th' united fury of the land.　　　　　⎭
With grief they viewed such powerful engines bent
To batter down the lawful government,
A numerous faction with pretended frights
In Sanhedrins to plume the regal rights,　　　　　　　　　920
The true successor from the court removed,
The plot by hireling witnesses improved.
These ills they saw, and as their duty bound
They showed the King the danger of the wound:
That no concessions from the throne would please,
But lenitives fomented the disease;
That Absalom, ambitious of the crown,
Was made the lure to draw the people down;
That false Achitophel's pernicious hate
Had turned the plot to ruin church and state;　　　　　　930
The council violent, the rabble worse,
That Shimei taught Jerusalem to curse.
　　With all these loads of injuries oppressed,
And long revolving in his careful breast
Th' event of things, at last his patience tired,
Thus from his royal throne by heaven inspired
The godlike David spoke: with awful fear
His train their maker in their master hear:
　　'Thus long have I, by native mercy swayed,
My wrongs dissembled, my revenge delayed;　　　　　　940
So willing to forgive th' offending age,
So much the father did the King assuage.
But now so far my clemency they slight,
Th' offenders question my forgiving right.
That one was made for many they contend,
But 'tis to rule, for that's a monarch's end.
They call my tenderness of blood my fear,
Though manly tempers can the longest bear.
Yet since they will divert my native course,
'Tis time to show I am not good by force.　　　　　　　950

Those heaped affronts that haughty subjects bring
Are burdens for a camel, not a King:
Kings are the public pillars of the state,
Born to sustain and prop the nation's weight;
If my young Samson will pretend a call*
To shake the column, let him share the fall.
[But O that yet he would repent and live,
How easy 'tis for parents to forgive!
With how few tears a pardon might be won
From nature, pleading for a darling son!]   960
Poor pitied youth, by my paternal care
Raised up to all the height his frame could bear:
Had God ordained his fate for empire born,
He would have given his soul another turn;
Gulled with a patriot's name, whose modern sense
Is one that would by law supplant his prince;
The people's brave, the politician's tool,
Never was patriot yet, but was a fool.
Whence comes it that religion and the laws
Should more be Absalom's than David's cause?   970
His old instructor, ere he lost his place,
Was never thought endued with so much grace.
Good heavens, how faction can a patriot paint!
My rebel ever proves my people's saint.
Would they impose an heir upon the throne?
Let Sanhedrins be taught to give their own.
A King's at least a part of government,
And mine as requisite as their consent;
Without my leave a future King to choose
Infers a right the present to depose: 980
True, they petition me t' approve their choice,
But Esau's hands suit ill with Jacob's voice.*
My pious subjects for my safety pray,
Which to secure they take my power away.
From plots and treasons heaven preserve my years,
But save me most from my petitioners.
Unsatiate as the barren womb or grave,
God cannot grant so much as they can crave.
What then is left, but with a jealous eye

To guard the small remains of royalty?   990
The law shall still direct my peaceful sway,
And the same law teach rebels to obey.
Votes shall no more established power control,
Such votes as make a part exceed the whole:
No groundless clamours shall my friends remove,
Nor crowds have power to punish ere they prove.
For gods and godlike kings their care express,
Still to defend their servants in distress.
O that my power to saving were confined;
Why am I forced, like heaven, against my mind   1000
To make examples of another kind?
Must I at length the sword of justice draw?
O cursed effects of necessary law!
How ill my fear they by my mercy scan;
Beware the fury of a patient man.
Law they require; let law then show her face:
They could not be content to look on grace
Her hinder parts, but with a daring eye
To tempt the terror of her front, and die.*
By their own arts 'tis righteously decreed   1010
Those dire artificers of death shall bleed.
Against themselves their witnesses will swear,
Till viper-like their mother plot they tear,*
And suck for nutriment that bloody gore
Which was their principle of life before.
Their Belial with their Belzebub will fight,
Thus on my foes my foes shall do me right.
Nor doubt th' event, for factious crowds engage
In their first onset all their brutal rage;
Then let 'em take an unresisted course,   1020
Retire and traverse, and delude their force:
But when they stand all breathless, urge the fight,
And rise upon 'em with redoubled might;
For lawful power is still superior found,
When long driven back, at length it stands the ground.'

    He said. Th' Almighty, nodding, gave consent,
And peals of thunder shook the firmament.
Henceforth a series of new time began,

The mighty years in long procession ran;
Once more the godlike David was restored,   1030
And willing nations knew their lawful lord.

9   [*Two Attacks on Titus Oates*]

ANONYMOUS

Titus Oates (1649–1705) was the principal figure in the Popish Plot
(1678–9). He alleged that there was a Catholic conspiracy to take over
the government, and as a result of the mendacious testimony which he
and others provided, some 35 people were executed, including Edward
Coleman, former secretary to the Duke of York, and Richard Langhorne
(see 74). His allegations at one point implicated the Queen. Oates was
educated briefly at the Catholic college at St Omers, and claimed to have a
doctorate from Salamanca. Both pamphlets exploit Oates's homosexuality.

(a) *A Hue and Cry after Dr T. O.*

Printed in 1681 as a single sheet suitable for pasting up on a wall, it takes
the form of a notice for the apprehension of a runaway criminal. Oates's
grotesque appearance is alluded to in Dryden's *Absalom and Achitophel*
(8), ll. 646–9. Cf. 44i.

O yes! O yes! O yes!
If there be any man, woman, or child, in city, town, or country,
that can tell tale or tidings of a Salamanca doctor, stolen, strayed,
banished, or kidnapped out of Whitehall on Tuesday last. His marks
are as followeth: the off-leg behind something shorter than the other,
and cloven foot on the nether side; his face rainbow colour, and the
rest of his body black; two slouching ears, ready to be cropped* next
spring, if they do not drop off before; his mouth is in the middle of
his face, exactly between the upper part of his forehead and the lower
part of his chin; he hath a short neck, which makes him defy the
pillory; a thin chin, and somewhat sharp, bending up almost to his
nose; he hath few or no teeth on the upper jaw, but bites with
his tongue;* his voice something resembles that of the guinea-pig's;
his habit is covered with a black gown, which was made at Salamanca
and Oxford both at once, because he took his degrees at both places

at one time; his eyes are very small, and sunk, and is supposed to be either thick-eyed or moon-blind, by reason he did not know C[oleman] by candle-light, though he had before sworn treason against him; he has a natural bob-tail, because he never was docked nor gelded; he seldom frequents the company of women, but keeps private communication with four bums, to make good the old proverb, 'Lying together makes swine to love'; his food is the entrails and blood of loyalists; his drink the tears of widows and orphans; he is one that hath endeavoured to make the king great by taking away the lives of his friends by perjury, which by consequence must expose his sacred majesty to the fury of the mobile; he is one that brought forty commissions from St Omers, and distributed them all for old hats and old shoes to the papists, though no body ever saw one of them but himself; he hath 40,000 black bills under his gown, which he hath concealed these three years, and no body ever saw them but himself; his usual haunts are Dick's coffee house, Aldersgate Street, B——'s conventicle, and St Lobb's convent in Swallow Street; he is one that preached b——y* before the weavers, in respect to his father being one of the same trade and tribe; he is one that swears quite through B——l's* conscience, or the thick basis of the Monument; he is one whose ingratitude to his benefactors calls them rogues and rascals, and endeavours to swear their lives and estates away by perjury; he is one that brought nothing but rags and lice into Whitehall, but carried away cart-loads of goods, whereof part was his famous library,* viz: that famous *History of Tom Thumb, Guzman, The Spanish Rogue, The French Rogue, Don Thomazo Dangerfieldo, English Rogue, All the Famous Histories of Robin Hood and Little John, The History of Wat Tyler and Jack Straw*, all the infamous works of Smith, Janeway, Curtis and Care, as also the great works of that unreverend divine R. B[axte]r, and another brave book, much admired by the doctor, called Hobbes's *Leviathan*; also two brace of bums, with a masculine chambermaid which he keeps to scour his yard; all which, and a great deal more, he hath purchased by the price of blood and damnation, since he creeped into Whitehall and created himself 'Saviour of the Nation'; he is one that has sworn it to be his duty to the devil to make the k[ing] to prosecute the qu[een], and to disinherit his royal brother, and to make the son rebel against the father. 'Tis supposed he herds somewhere in the c——.*

These are some part of the marks of the beast:* whoever can give any account of him, let them repair to Dick's coffee house, Lying Curtis, Elephant Smith, or Mrs Richard, and they shall have the doctor's wheel of fortune for their pains, and perhaps be called as many rascals to boot as the doctor used to call the king's lifeguards.

(b) *Strange and Wonderful News from Southwark,*
Declaring how a sham doctor got two aldermen students of the same university with child, how they longed for venison, and what ensued upon it

Published as a pamphlet in 1684. In the early 1680s, local elections in London and Southwark had often returned Whig aldermen and mayors who used their positions to oppose the king, sometimes by packing juries with Whig supporters.

I know there have been so many Gargantua stories of this Panta-gruel* doctor, and himself found in so many lies, that if I writ gospel I should not be believed; and that these two aldermen were got with child, and by the same Salamanca doctor, I do not question but to make as clear or clearer to you than ever he did Don John or the Popish Plot. If the doctor has brought such infamy on his name as not to be credited when he speaks truth, it's no fault of mine. I'll tell you the truth, and shame the devil: the doctor I cannot put out of countenance.

In the forest of New Troy,* there [are] several famous colleges for correction of vice and instruction of good manners and discipline, as St Bridewell, St Newgate, and that beyond the river, which for its eminency before the rest is called King's College.* Thither two foul-mouthed aldermen that had defamed the government were sent to learn better language and the civility of the schools, where after they had spent some months, as other blockheads of the university do, without the least improvement, in comes a profligate vagabond that had passed his degrees before in the Counter and Newgate, sent hither in like manner after a great many unparalleled villainous actions, murders, perjuries, blasphemies, and bitter revilings, to learn to govern that unruly member.

The joy of the aldermen was unspeakable, to find a doctor so well qualified in those principles, and whom they had themselves nursed up in those principles, to be joined to them in the same class. This quack doctor, this priest *party per pale*,* this friar in Jack Presbyter's jump, is entertained their chaplain, and soon made free of their board and bed—which he liked as well as the other, being as great a sodomite as an epicure, and women were scarce in that university. But it's all one, the good aldermen supplied that defect, which he exercised by turns as the spirit moved him. This piece of Italian gallantry was managed with such art and secrecy that though they were mutual rivals to each other, yet neither of the aldermen suspected, or was jealous of the other. Each of them thought he was alone blessed in the doctor's favour. The doctor, blessed in both, thought himself happier than either. But as the devil would have it, mischief will out; this loving intrigue is discovered, and the amour that was carried on to everyone's thought in secret, is now come to light. Few months had passed when they began to conceive the monstrous effects of this unhuman conjunction: the aldermen look big upon't, their bellies and mouths began to meet, and were in as close copulation as the doctor's nose and chin. In fine (for there's no more concealing the roguery) the aldermen were both with child, and the doctor the father. The doctor denied it point blank, saying it was between themselves, that they had got one another with child, and let them look to it, he would father none of their brats. The aldermen complain to the overseers; they upon better proof than the doctor's bind him over to save the parish harmless;* the poor doctor was never so hard put to it lest his spurious issue should be lost or he bound to maintain it himself. His only hopes were he might palm it upon the court, but having laid a bastard there before, and being catched in it, made him suspect the same sham would not pass twice; and for the country, from the rank seed he sprung he could expect no entertainment but amongst the horses. 'The loyal city has crushed the cockatrice head that was thrown out of court; what wolf shall I find to cherish my orsons?' The aldermen, taking the doctor into their arms, bid him not be concerned: they and the brethren would take care for the babes. And now, as it is the custom with people that are breeding, the squeamish aldermen began to long for every toy that came into their head; nor did the doctor like a kind breeding father want his longings. The aldermen longed for change of government, the doctor for change of bedfellows; the aldermen for change of air, the doctor for change of diet and lodging; the aldermen long for a new hash of anarchy, the doctor for a fricassee of democracy; the aldermen for a commonwealth, the doctor for a parliament; the aldermen for a chest of burgundy, the doctor for a venison pasty. The burgundy is sent for, the venison bespoke, and now piping hot entering the enchanted gates, when lo! a crew of Hungarian* sharpers, fellow-students of the same university, as claiming a property, seized upon the premises, which with all their hopes vanished in an instant. Such is the fate of transitory things. *Multa cadunt:** the bottles were off, ere a glass could touch the longing lips, and the pasty devoured before the doctor could come within smell of the plot; so far were these cannibals from considering the condition of the hungry doctor or his brace of prostitutes, that they left him neither corpse nor coffin, nor half an ounce of crust, though the doctor offered a guinea to save their longings. On this miscarriage of the pasty they are all like to miscarry. To see himself thus shamefully baulked struck the doctor into a convulsion, and the aldermen into fits of the mother, with the excess of which they fell immediately into labour. In much pain and many pangs they lay complaining, but all to little purpose, for the Observator* had informed Latona* what a monstrous production it would prove, begot in conjunction of Capricorn on a Gemini of cits. The goddess denied her assistance, and, which was worse, the witch Cellier* sat cross-legged, by which spell it was impossible for them to be delivered till Sir Thomas* instead of the chamberlain came to assist the doctor; the groaning-board doctor all the while praying by, by which means they were delivered of the monster, which like Gargantua stalked through the father's mouth, or Minerva with scratches and thumps out of the dull brain of Jupiter.* Thus the brats through the maggots of a hot, unruly brain, having like the viper eat their way into the world, they were sent into the city to be nursed, till the next kind keeping assembly provide better for 'em, or the law for the father in the mean time.

10   [*The Character of Charles II*] from the *Diary*

JOHN EVELYN

The entry is for the day of Charles's death.

[6 February 1685] A prince of many virtues, not bloody or cruel; his countenance fierce, his voice great, proper of person, every motion became him; a lover of the sea and skilful in shipping; not affecting other studies, yet he had a laboratory and knew of many empirical medicines, and the easier mechanical mathematics; loved planting, building, and brought in a politer way of living, which passed to luxury and intolerable expense. He had a particular talent in telling stories and facetious passages, of which he had innumerable, which made some buffoons and vicious wretches too presumptuous and familiar, not worthy the favours they abused. He took delight to have a number of little spaniels follow him, and lie in his bedchamber, where often times he suffered the bitches to puppy and give suck, which rendered it very offensive, and indeed made the whole court nasty and stinking. An excellent prince, doubtless, had he been less addicted to women, which made him uneasy and always in want to supply their unmeasurable profusion, and to the detriment of many indigent persons who had signally served both him and his father. Easily and frequently he changed favourites to his great prejudice etc. As to other public transactions and unhappy miscarriages, 'tis not here I intend to number them; but certainly never had king more glorious opportunities to have made himself, his people, and all Europe happy, and prevented innumerable mischiefs, had not his too easy nature resigned him to be managed by crafty men, and some abandoned and profane wretches, who corrupted his otherwise sufficient parts, disciplined as he had been by many afflictions during his banishment: which gave him much experience and knowledge of men and things; but those wicked creatures took him off from all application becoming so great a king. The history of his reign will certainly be the most wonderful for the variety of matter and accidents above any extant of many former ages: the sad, tragical death of his father, his banishment and hardships, his miraculous restoration, conjurations against him, parliaments, wars, plagues, fires, comets, revolutions abroad happening in his time, with a thousand other particulars. He was ever kind to me, and very gracious upon all occasions, and therefore I cannot without ingratitude but deplore his loss, which for many respects (as well as duty) I do with all my soul.

. . .

I am never to forget the unexpressable luxury and profaneness, gaming, and all dissolution, and as it were total forgetfulness of God (it being Sunday evening) which this day sennight I was witness of: the king sitting and toying with his concubines Portsmouth, Cleveland, and Mazarin,* etc; a French boy singing love songs in that glorious gallery, whilst about twenty of the great courtiers and other dissolute persons were at basset round a large table, a bank of at least 2000 in gold before them, upon which two gent[lemen] that were with me made reflections with astonishment, it being a scene of utmost vanity; and surely, as they thought, would never have an end. Six days after, was all in the dust.

11   *Tarquin and Tullia*

ARTHUR MAINWARING

Written 1689, and circulated in manuscript. This Jacobite satire uses a Roman story allegorically: the Roman king Tullius (James II) is deposed by Tarquin (William III) with the connivance of his daughter Tullia (Mary, James's daughter and William's wife). Much of the rhetoric is indebted to *Absalom and Achitophel* (8).

> In times when princes cancelled nature's law
> And declarations (which themselves did draw),
> When children used their parents to dethrone
> And gnawed their way like vipers to a crown,*
> Tarquin, a savage, proud, ambitious prince,
> Prompt to expel, yet thoughtless of defence,
> The envied sceptre did from Tullius snatch,
> The Roman King, and father by the match.
>   To form his party (histories report)
> A sanctuary was opened in his court,   10

Where glad offenders safely might resort.
Great was the crowd, and wondrous the success
(For those were fruitful times of wickedness),
And all that lived obnoxious to the laws
Flocked to Prince Tarquin, and embraced his cause.
   'Mongst these, a pagan priest for refuge fled,*
A prophet deep in godly faction read,
A sycophant that knew the modish way
To cant and plot, to flatter and betray,
To whine and sin, to scribble and recant,   20
A shameless author, and a lustful saint.
To serve all times, he could distinctions coin,
And with great ease flat contradictions join.
A traitor now, once loyal in extreme,
(And then obedience was his only theme)
He sang in temples the most passive lays*
And wearied monarchs with repeated praise,
But managed awkwardly that lawful part,
For to vent lies and treason was his art,
And pointed libels at crowned heads to dart.   30
This priest, and others learnèd to defame,
First murdered injured Tullius in his name,
With blackest calumnies their sovereign load:
A poisoned brother, and dark league abroad,*
A son unjustly topped upon the throne,*
Which yet was proved undoubtedly his own,
Though as the law was there, 'twas his behoof
Who dispossessed the heir, to bring the proof.
This hellish charge they backed with dismal frights—
The loss of property, and sacred rights,   40
And freedom—words which all false patriots use,
The surest names the Romans to abuse,
Jealous of kings, and always malcontent,
Forward to change, yet certain to repent.
   Whilst thus the plotters needful fears create,
Tarquin with open force invades the state.
Lewd nobles join him with their feeble might,
And atheist fools for dear religion fight;
The priests their boasted principles disown,

And level their harangues against the throne. 50
Vain promises the people's minds allure;
Slight were their ills, but desperate the cure.
'Tis hard for kings to steer an equal course,
And they who banish one, oft get a worse;
Those heavenly bodies we admire above,
Do every day irregularly move.
Yet Tullius, 'tis decreed, must lose his crown
For faults that were his counsel's, not his own.
He now in vain commands ev'n those he paid:
By darling troops deserted, and betrayed 60
By creatures which his genial warmth had made.

    Of these a captain of the guards was worst,*
Whose memory to this day stands accursed.
This rogue, advanced to military trust
By his own whoredom and his sister's lust,
Forsook his master after dreadful vows,
And plotted to betray him to his foes.
The kindest master to the vilest slave,
As free to give, as he was sure to crave.

    His haughty female, who (as books declare) 70
Did always toss wide nostrils in the air,
Was to the younger Tullia governess
And did attend her, when, in borrowed dress,
She fled by night from Tullius in distress.
This wretch by letters did invite his foes
And used all arts her father to depose:
A father always generously bent,
So kind that he her wishes did prevent.

    'Twas now high time for Tullius to retreat
When even his daughter hastened his defeat, 80
When faith and duty vanished, and no more
The name of father, nor of king, he bore:
A king whose right his foes could ne'er dispute,
So mild, that mercy was his attribute.
Affable, kind, and easy of access,
Swift to relieve, unwilling to oppress,
Rich without taxes, yet in payment just,
So honest, that he hardly could distrust.

His active soul did ne'er from labours cease,
Valiant in war, and sedulous in peace,   90
Studious with traffic to enrich the land,
Strong to protect, and skilful to command,
Liberal and splendid, not without excess,
Loth to revenge, and willing to caress.
In sum, how godlike must his nature be,
Whose only fault was too much piety.

    This king removed, th' assembled states thought fit
That Tarquin in the vacant throne should sit,
Voted him regent in their senate house,
And with an empty name endowed his spouse—   100
The elder Tullia, who (some authors feign)
Drove o'er her father's corpse a trembling wain.
But she, more guilty, numerous wains did drive
To crush her father, and her king, alive;
In glad remembrance of his hastened fall
Resolved to institute a weekly ball;
She, jolly glutton, grew in bulk and chin,
Feasted on rapine and enjoyed her sin;
With luxury she did weak reason force,
Debauched good nature, and crammed down remorse.   110
Yet when she drunk cool tea in liberal sups
The sobbing dame was maudlin in her cups.

    But brutal Tarquin never did relent,
Too hard to melt, too wicked to repent,
Cruel in deeds, more merciless in will,
And blest with natural delight in ill.
From a wise guardian he received his doom,
To walk the 'change, and not to govern Rome;
He swore his native honours to disown,
And did by perjury ascend the throne.   120
Oh! had that oath his swelling pride repressed,
Rome then had been with peace and plenty blessed;
But Tarquin, guided by destructive fate,
Wasted the country, and embroiled the state,
Transported to their foes the Roman pelf,
And by their ruin hoped to save himself.
Innumerable woes oppressed the land

When it submitted to his cursed command;
So just was Heaven that 'twas hard to tell
Whether its guilt or losses did excel.   130
Men who renounced their God for dearer trade
Were then the guardians of religion made;
Rebels were sainted, foreigners did reign,
Outlaws returned, preferments to obtain,
With frogs and toads and all their croaking train.
No native knew their features nor their birth;
They seemed the greasy offspring of the earth.
The trade was sunk, the fleet and army spent,
Devouring taxes swallowed lesser rent,
(Taxes imposed by no authority: 140
Each lewd collection was a robbery).
Bold self-creating men did statutes draw,
Skilled to establish villainy by law,
Fanatic drivers, whose unjust careers
Produced new ills exceeding former fears.
   Yet authors, here, except that faithful band
Which the prevailing faction did withstand,
And some who bravely stood in the defence
Of baffled justice and their injured prince.
These shine to aftertimes; each sacred name   150
Stands still recorded in the books of fame.

12   From *The Works of Virgil*

JOHN DRYDEN

Published 1697 in Dryden's complete translation of *The Works of Virgil*. Dryden's translation of Virgil is not an allegory of contemporary politics, but its account of the fall of Troy and the wanderings of Aeneas is inflected with a sense of the loss of empire and homeland, and the pain of exile—in part an expression of Dryden's own position as a Jacobite and Roman Catholic after the Revolution of 1688–9.

(a) [*The Death of Priam*]

From Book II of the *Aeneis*, in which Aeneas tells Dido the story of the capture of Troy by the Greeks, and the death of King Priam.

Perhaps you may of Priam's fate inquire.
He, when he saw his regal town on fire,
His ruined palace, and his entering foes,
On every side, inevitable woes:
In arms disused invests his limbs, decayed
Like them with age: a late and useless aid.
His feeble shoulders scarce the weight sustain: ⎫
Loaded, not armed, he creeps along with pain, ⎬
Despairing of success, ambitious to be slain. ⎭
Uncovered but by heaven, there stood in view   700
An altar: near the hearth a laurel grew,
Doddered with age, whose boughs encompass round
The household gods, and shade the holy ground.
Here Hecuba, with all her helpless train
Of dames, for shelter sought, but sought in vain.
Driven like a flock of doves along the sky,
Their images they hug, and to their altars fly.
The queen, when she beheld her trembling lord,
And hanging by his side a heavy sword,
'What rage' she cried 'has seized my husband's mind?   710
What arms are these, and to what use designed?
These times want other aids! Were Hector here,
E'en Hector now in vain, like Priam, would appear.
With us, one common shelter thou shalt find,
Or in one common fate with us be joined.'
She said, and with a last salute embraced
The poor old man, and by the laurel placed.
Behold Polites, one of Priam's sons,
Pursued by Pyrrhus, there for safety runs.
Through swords and foes, amazed and hurt, he flies   720
Through empty courts, and open galleries.
Him Pyrrhus, urging with his lance, pursues,
And often reaches, and his thrusts renews.
The youth, transfixed, with lamentable cries

Expires before his wretched parents' eyes:
Whom gasping at his feet when Priam saw,
The fear of death gave place to nature's law;
And, shaking more with anger than with age,
'The gods' said he 'requite thy brutal rage!
(As sure they will, barbarian, sure they must,   730
If there be gods in heaven, and gods be just)
Who tak'st in wrongs an insolent delight,
With a son's death t' infect a father's sight.
Not he, whom thou and lying fame conspire
To call thee his—not he, thy vaunted sire*
Thus used my wretched age: the gods he feared,
The laws of nature and of nations heard.
He cheered my sorrows, and, for sums of gold,
The bloodless carcass of my Hector sold;
Pitied the woes a parent underwent,   740
And sent me back in safety from his tent.'

    This said, his feeble hand a javelin threw,
Which, fluttering, seemed to loiter as it flew:
Just, and but barely, to the mark it held,
And faintly tinkled on the brazen shield.

    Then Pyrrhus thus: 'Go thou from me to fate,
And to my father my foul deeds relate.
Now die!' With that he dragged the trembling sire,
Sliddering through clottered blood and holy mire
(The mingled paste his murdered son had made),   750
Hauled from beneath the violated shade,
And on the sacred pile the royal victim laid.
His right hand held his bloody falchion bare;
His left he twisted in his hoary hair;
Then, with a speeding thrust his heart he found:
The lukewarm blood came rushing through the wound,
And sanguine streams distained the sacred ground.
Thus Priam fell, and shared one common fate
With Troy in ashes, and his ruined state:
He, who the sceptre of all Asia swayed,   760
Whom monarchs like domestic slaves obeyed;
On the bleak shore now lies th' abandoned king,
A headless carcass, and a nameless thing.

(b) [*A Vision of the Future of Rome*]

From Book VI of the *Aeneis*, in which Aeneas, visiting the underworld, is
shown by his father Anchises a vision of the future of Rome. Anchises
speaks.

'Let others better mould the running mass ⎫
Of metals, and inform the breathing brass, ⎬
And soften into flesh a marble face; ⎭   1170
Plead better at the bar; describe the skies,
And when the stars descend, and when they rise.
But, Rome, 'tis thine alone, with awful sway, ⎫
To rule mankind, and make the world obey: ⎬
Disposing peace and war thy own majestic way. ⎭
To tame the proud, the fettered slave to free,
These are imperial arts, and worthy thee.'
   He paused—and, while with wondering eyes
      they viewed
The passing spirits, thus his speech renewed:
'See great Marcellus! how, untired in toils,*   1180
He moves with manly grace, how rich with
      regal spoils!
He, when his country (threatened with alarms)
Requires his courage and his conquering arms,
Shall more than once the Punic bands affright,
Shall kill the Gaulish king in single fight;
Then to the Capitol in triumph move,
And the third spoils shall grace Feretrian Jove.'
   Æneas here beheld, of form divine,
A godlike youth in glittering armour shine,
With great Marcellus keeping equal pace;   1190
But gloomy were his eyes, dejected was his face.
He saw, and, wondering, asked his airy guide,
'What, and of whence, was he who pressed the
      hero's side?
His son, or one of his illustrious name?
How like the former, and almost the same!
Observe the crowds that compass him around:
All gaze and all admire, and raise a shouting sound;

But hovering mists around his brows are spread,
And night, with sable shades, involves his head.'
'Seek not to know' the ghost replied with tears   1200
'The sorrows of thy sons in future years.
This youth, the blissful vision of a day,
Shall just be shown on earth, and snatched away.
The gods too high had raised the Roman state,
Were but their gifts as permanent as great!
What groans of men shall fill the Martian field,
How fierce a blaze his flaming pile shall yield!
What funeral pomp shall floating Tiber see,
When, rising from his bed, he views the sad solemnity!
No youth shall equal hopes of glory give,   1210
No youth afford so great a cause to grieve.
The Trojan honour, and the Roman boast,
Admired when living, and adored when lost!
Mirror of ancient faith in early youth,
Undaunted worth, inviolable truth!
No foe, unpunished, in the fighting field
Shall dare thee, foot to foot, with sword and shield;
Much less in arms oppose thy matchless force,
When thy sharp spurs shall urge thy foaming horse.
Ah! couldst thou break through Fate's severe decree,   1220
A new Marcellus shall arise in thee!
Full canisters of fragrant lilies bring,
Mixed with the purple roses of the spring:
Let me with funeral flowers his body strow; ⎫
This gift which parents to their children owe, ⎬
This unavailing gift, at least, I may bestow!' ⎭

TOWN AND COUNTRY

From *Paradise Lost*, Book IX

JOHN MILTON

Satan, in the garden of Eden in the guise of a serpent, is spying on Eve.

Beyond his hope, Eve separate he spies,
Veiled in a cloud of fragrance, where she stood,
Half spied, so thick the roses bushing round
About her glowed, oft stooping to support
Each flower of slender stalk, whose head though gay
Carnation, purple, azure, or specked with gold,
Hung drooping unsustained; them she upstays   430
Gently with myrtle band, mindless the while
Herself, though fairest unsupported flower,
From her best prop so far, and storm so nigh.
Nearer he drew, and many a walk traversed
Of stateliest covert, cedar, pine, or palm,
Then voluble and bold, now hid, now seen
Among thick-woven arborets and flowers
Embordered on each bank, the hand of Eve:
Spot more delicious than those gardens feigned
Or of revived Adonis, or renowned   440
Alcinous, host of old Laertes' son,
Or that, not mystic, where the sapient king
Held dalliance with his fair Egyptian spouse.*
Much he the place admired, the person more.
As one who long in populous city pent,
Where houses thick and sewers annoy the air,
Forth issuing on a summer's morn to breathe

Among the pleasant villages and farms
Adjoined, from each thing met conceives delight,
The smell of grain, or tedded grass, or kine,   450
Or dairy, each rural sight, each rural sound;
If chance with nymph-like step fair virgin pass,
What pleasing seemed, for her now pleases more,
She most, and in her look sums all delight.
Such pleasure took the serpent to behold
This flowery plat, the sweet recess of Eve
Thus early, thus alone.

14   From *The Country Wife*

              WILLIAM WYCHERLEY

First performed and printed 1675. Extract from the beginning of Act II.
Mr Pinchwife has brought his wife Margery up from the country to
London; but he is jealous, and anxious to keep her away from any place
where she might meet attractive young men. Her sister-in-law Alethea
('Truth') is an habituée of London, and immediately tells her of the most
fashionable areas for promenading: the Mulberry Garden (on the site of
the present Buckingham Palace), St James's Park, and the New Exchange,
a shopping complex in the Strand.

[*Pinchwife's lodging in London*]

[*Enter*] *Mrs Margery Pinchwife and Alethea; Mr Pinchwife
peeping behind at the door*

Mrs Pinchwife. Pray, sister, where are the best fields and woods to
walk in, in London?

Alethea. A pretty question! Why, sister, Mulberry Garden, and St
James's Park; and for close walks, the New Exchange.

Mrs P. Pray, sister, tell me why my husband looks so grum here in
town? And keeps me up so close, and will not let me go a-walking,
nor let me wear my best gown yesterday?

Aleth. Oh, he's jealous, sister.

Mrs P. Jealous? What's that?

Aleth. He's afraid you should love another man.

Mrs P. How should he be afraid of my loving another man, when he will not let me see any but himself.

Aleth. Did he not carry you yesterday to a play?

Mrs P. Ay, but we sat amongst ugly people; he would not let me come near the gentry, who sat under us, so that I could not see 'em. He told me, none but naughty women sat there, whom they toused and moused—but I would have ventured, for all that.

Aleth. But how did you like the play?

Mrs P. Indeed I was aweary of the play—but I liked hugeously the actors; they are the goodliest, proper'st men, sister.

Aleth. Oh, but you must not like the actors, sister!

Mrs P. Ay, how should I help it, sister? Pray, sister, when my husband comes in, will you ask leave for me to go a-walking?

Aleth. (*aside*). A-walking, ha ha! Lord, a country gentlewoman's leisure is the drudgery of a foot-post, and she requires as much airing as her husband's horses.

Enter Mr Pinchwife to them

But here comes your husband; I'll ask, though I'm sure he'll not grant it.

Mrs P. He says he won't let me go abroad, for fear of catching the pox.

Aleth. Fie! 'The smallpox' you should say.

Mrs P. Oh my dear, dear bud, welcome home. Why dost thou look so froppish? Who has nangered thee?

Pinch. You're a fool.

Mrs Pinchwife goes aside, and cries

Aleth. Faith, so she is, for crying for no fault—poor, tender creature!

Pinch. What, you would have her as impudent as yourself, as arrant a gill-flirt, a gadder, a magpie, and—to say all—a mere notorious town-woman?

Aleth. Brother, you are my only censurer; and the honour of your family shall sooner suffer in your wife there, than in me, though I take the innocent liberty of the town.

Pinch. Hark you, mistress, do not talk so before my wife. The innocent liberty of the town!

Aleth. Why, pray, who boasts of any intrigue with me? What lampoon has made my name notorious? What ill women frequent my lodgings? I keep no company with any women of scandalous reputations.

Pinch. No, you keep the men of scandalous reputations company.

Aleth. Where? Would you not have me civil? Answer 'em in a box at the plays? In the drawing-room at Whitehall? In St James's Park, Mulberry Garden, or—

Pinch. Hold, hold; do not teach my wife where the men are to be found. I believe she's the worse for your town documents already. I bid you keep her in ignorance, as I do.

Mrs P. Indeed, be not angry with her, bud; she will tell me nothing of the town, though I ask her a thousand times a day.

Pinch. Then you are very inquisitive to know, I find?

Mrs P. Not I indeed, dear; I hate London. Our place-house in the country is worth a thousand of 't; would I were there again.

Pinch. So you shall, I warrant. But were you not talking of plays, and players, when I came in? [*To Alethea*] You are her encourager in such discourses.

Mrs P. No indeed, dear; she chid me just now for liking the player-men.

Pinch. (*aside*). Nay, if she be so innocent as to own to me her liking them, there is no hurt in't.—Come, my poor rogue; but thou lik'st none better than me?

Mrs P. Yes, indeed, but I do; the player men are finer folks.

Pinch. But you love none better than me?

Mrs P. You are mine own dear bud, and I know you; I hate a stranger.

Pinch. Ay, my dear, you must love me only, and not be like the naughty town-women, who only hate their husbands, and love every man else—love plays, visits, fine coaches, fine clothes, fiddles, balls, treats, and so lead a wicked town-life.

Mrs P. Nay, if to enjoy all these things be a town-life, London is not so bad a place, dear.

Pinch. How! If you love me, you must hate London.

Aleth. (*aside*). The fool has forbid me discovering to her the pleasures of the town, and he is now setting her agog upon them himself.

Mrs P. But, husband, do the town-women love the player-men too?

Pinch. Yes, I warrant you.

Mrs P. Ay, I warrant you.

Pinch. Why, you do not, I hope?

Mrs P. No, no, bud. But why have we no player-men in the country?

Pinch. Ha! Mistress Minx, ask me no more to go to a play.

Mrs P. Nay, why, love? I did not care for going; but when you forbid me, you make me (as 'twere) desire it.

Aleth. (*aside*). So 'twill be in other things, I warrant.

Mrs P. Pray, let me go to a play, dear.

Pinch. Hold your peace; I won't.

Mrs P. Why, love?

Pinch. Why? I'll tell you.

Aleth. (*aside*). Nay, if he tell her, she'll give him more cause to forbid her that place.

Mrs P. Pray, why, dear?

Pinch. First, you like the actors, and the gallants may like you.

Mrs P. What, a homely country girl? No, bud, nobody will like me.

Pinch. I tell you, yes, they may.

Mrs P. No, no, you jest—I won't believe you; I will go.

Pinch. I tell you then, that one of the lewdest fellows in town, who saw you there, told me he was in love with you.

Mrs P. Indeed! Who, who, pray who was't?

Pinch. (*aside*). I've gone too far, and slipped before I was aware. How overjoyed she is!

Mrs P. Was it any Hampshire gallant, any of our neighbours? I promise you, I am beholding to him.

Pinch. I promise you, you lie—for he would but ruin you, as he has done hundreds. He has no other love for women but that; such as he, look upon women like basilisks, but to destroy 'em.

Mrs P. Ay, but if he loves me, why should he ruin me? Answer me to that. Methinks he should not; I would do him no harm.

Aleth. Ha ha ha!

Pinch. 'Tis very well—but I'll keep him from doing you any harm, or me either.

> *Enter Sparkish and Harcourt*

But here comes company; get you in, get you in.

Mrs P. But pray, husband, is he a pretty gentleman that loves me?

Pinch. In, baggage, in.

> *Thrusts her in; shuts the door*

15   *A Satire in Imitation of the Third of Juvenal*

JOHN OLDHAM

Written May 1682, published in his *Poems, and Translations* (1683). Oldham's imitation of Juvenal's *Satire III* transfers the scene from Rome to London, following the example of Boileau, who had imitated the same poem in his *Satires I* and *VI*, applying Juvenal's criticisms to Paris. The intemperate rhetoric imitates Juvenal's manner, and the roughness of metre and rhyme (while characteristic of Oldham) were considered appropriate for satire.

The poet brings in a friend of his, giving him an account why he removes from London to live in the country

> Though much concerned to leave my dear old friend,
> I must however his design commend
> Of fixing in the country: for were I
> As free to choose my residence as he,
> The Peak, the Fens, the Hundreds, or Land's End,*
> I would prefer to Fleet Street, or the Strand.
> What place so desert, and so wild is there, ⎫
> Whose inconveniencies one would not bear, ⎬
> Rather than the alarms of midnight fire, ⎭

The falls of houses, knavery of cits, 10
The plots of factions, and the noise of wits,
And thousand other plagues, which up and down
Each day and hour infest the cursèd town?
    As fate would have it, on the appointed day
Of parting hence, I met him on the way,
Hard by Mile End, the place so famed of late*
In prose and verse, for the great faction's treat;
Here we stood still, and after compliments
Of course, and wishing his good journey hence,
I asked what sudden causes made him fly 20
The once loved town, and his dear company:
When, on the hated prospect looking back,
Thus with just rage the good old Timon spake:*
    'Since virtue here in no repute is had,
Since worth is scorned, learning and sense unpaid,
And knavery the only thriving trade;
Finding my slender fortune every day
Dwindle and waste insensibly away,
I, like a losing gamester, thus retreat,
To manage wiselier my last stake of fate; 30
While I have strength, and want no staff to prop
My tott'ring limbs, ere age has made me stoop
Beneath its weight, ere all my thread be spun,
And life has yet in store some sands to run,
'Tis my resolve to quit the nauseous town.
    'Let thriving Morecraft choose his dwelling there,*
Rich with the spoils of some young spendthrift heir:
Let the plot-mongers stay behind, whose art
Can truth to sham, and sham to truth convert:
Whoever has an house to build or set, 40
His wife, his conscience, or his oath to let:
Whoever has, or hopes for offices,
A navy, guard, or custom-house's place:
Let sharping courtiers stay, who there are great
By putting the false dice on king and state:
Where they, who once were grooms and footboys known,
Are now to fair estates and honours grown;
Nor need we envy them, or wonder much

At their fantastic greatness, since they're such
Whom Fortune oft in her capricious freaks   50
Is pleased to raise from kennels and the jakes
To wealth and dignity above the rest,
When she is frolic, and disposed to jest.
   'I live in London? What should I do there?
I cannot lie, nor flatter, nor forswear:
I can't commend a book, or piece of wit
(Though a lord were the author) dully writ:
I'm no Sir Sidrophel to read the stars,*
And cast nativities for longing heirs,
When fathers shall drop off: no Gadbury*   60
To tell the minute when the King shall die,
And you know what—come in: nor can I steer,⎫
And tack about my conscience, whensoe'er   ⎬
To a new point I see religion veer.   ⎭
Let others pimp to courtier's lechery,
I'll draw no city cuckold's curse on me:
Nor would I do it, though to be made great,
And raised to the chief Minister of State.
Therefore I think it fit to rid the town
Of one that is an useless member grown.   70
   'Besides, who has pretence to favour now,   ⎫
But he who hidden villainy does know,   ⎬
Whose breast does with some burning secret glow?⎭
By none thou shalt preferred or valued be
That trusts thee with an honest secrecy:
He only may to great men's friendship reach,
Who great men, when he pleases, can impeach.
Let others thus aspire to dignity;
For me, I'd not their envied grandeur buy
For all th' Exchange is worth, that Paul's will cost,   80
Or was of late in the Scotch voyage lost.*
What would it boot, if I, to gain my end,   ⎫
Forego my quiet, and my ease of mind,   ⎬
Still feared, at last betrayed, by my great friend?⎭
   'Another cause, which I must boldly own,
And not the least, for which I quit the town,
Is to behold it made the common shore

Where France does all her filth and ordure pour:
What spark of true old English rage can bear
Those who were slaves at home, to lord it here?   90
We've all our fashions, language, compliments,
Our music, dances, curing, cooking thence;
And we shall have their poisoning too ere long,
If still in the improvement we go on.
   'What wouldst thou say, great Harry, shouldst thou view*
Thy gaudy, fluttering race of English now,
Their tawdry clothes, pulvilios, essences,
Their Chedreux perruques, and those vanities*
Which thou, and they of old did so despise?
What wouldst thou say to see th' infected town   100
With the foul spawn of foreigners o'errun?
Hither from Paris, and all parts they come,
The spew and vomit of their jails at home:
To court they flock, and to St James his Square,
And wriggle into great men's service there:
Footboys at first, till they, from wiping shoes,
Grow by degrees the masters of the house:
Ready of wit, hardened of impudence,
Able with ease to put down either Haynes,*
Both the King's player, and King's evidence;   110
Flippant of talk, and voluble of tongue,
With words at will, no lawyer better hung:
Softer than flattering court parasite,
Or city trader when he means to cheat;
No calling or profession comes amiss:
A needy monsieur can be what he please,
Groom, page, valet, quack, operator, fencer,
Perfumer, pimp, jack-pudding, juggler, dancer:
Give but the word, the cur will fetch and bring,
Come over to the Emperor, or King: 120
Or, if you please, fly o'er the pyramid,
Which Aston and the rest in vain have tried.*
   'Can I have patience, and endure to see
The paltry foreign wretch take place of me,
Whom the same wind and vessel brought ashore,
That brought prohibited goods, and dildoes o'er?

Then, pray, what mighty privilege is there
For me, that at my birth drew English air?
And where's the benefit to have my veins
Run British blood, if there's no difference   130
'Twixt me and him the statute freedom gave,*
And made a subject of a true-born slave?

   'But nothing shocks, and is more loathed by me,
Than the vile rascal's fulsome flattery:
By help of this false magnifying glass,
A louse or flea shall for a camel pass:
Produce an hideous wight, more ugly far ⎫
Than those ill shapes which in old hangings are, ⎬
He'll make him straight a *beau garçon* appear: ⎭
Commend his voice and singing, though he bray   140
Worse than Sir Martin Mar-all in the play:*
And, if he rhyme, shall praise for standard wit
More scurvy sense than Prynne and Vicars writ.*

   'And here's the mischief, though we say the same,
He is believed, and we are thought to sham:
Do you but smile, immediately the beast
Laughs out aloud, though he ne'er heard the jest:
Pretend you're sad, he's presently in tears,
Yet grieves no more than marble, when it wears
Sorrow in metaphor: but speak of heat,   150
"O God! how sultry 'tis!" he'll cry, and sweat
In depth of winter: straight, if you complain
Of cold, the weather-glass is sunk again:
Then he'll call for his frieze campaign, and swear
'Tis beyond eighty, he's in Greenland here.*
Thus he shifts scenes, and oft'ner in a day
Can change his face, than actors at a play:
There's nought so mean can 'scape the flatt'ring sot,
Not his Lord's snuff-box, nor his powder-spot:
If he but spit, or pick his teeth, he'll cry, ⎫
"How everything becomes you! Let me die, ⎬   160
Your lordship does it most judiciously!" ⎭
And swear 'tis fashionable if he sneeze,
Extremely taking, and it needs must please.

   'Besides, there's nothing sacred, nothing free

From the hot satyr's rampant lechery:
Nor wife, nor virgin-daughter can escape,
Scarce thou thyself or son avoid a rape:
All must go padlocked: if nought else there be,
Suspect thy very stables' chastity.   170
By this the vermin into secrets creep,
Thus families in awe they strive to keep.
What living for an Englishman is there,   ⎫
Where such as these get head, and domineer, ⎬
Whose use and custom 'tis, never to share   ⎭
A friend, but love to reign without dispute,
Without a rival, full and absolute?
Soon as the insect gets his Honour's ear,
And flyblows some of 's pois'nous malice there,
Straight I'm turned off, kicked out of doors, discarded,   180
And all my former service disregarded.

   'But leaving these messieurs, for fear that I
Be thought of the silk-weavers' mutiny,*
From the loathed subject let us hasten on,
To mention other grievances in town:
And further, what respect at all is had
Of poor men here? and how's their service paid,
Though they be ne'er so diligent to wait,
To sneak, and dance attendance on the great?
No mark of favour is to be obtained   190
By one that sues, and brings an empty hand;
And all his merit is but made a sport,
Unless he glut some cormorant at court.

   ''Tis now a common thing, and usual here,
To see the son of some rich usurer
Take place of nobles, keep his first-rate whore,
And for a vaulting bout or two give more
Than a guard-captain's pay: meanwhile the breed
Of peers, reduced to poverty and need,
Are fain to trudge to the Bankside, and there   200
Take up with porters' leavings, suburb ware;
There spend that blood, which their great ancestor ⎫
So nobly shed at Cressy heretofore,   ⎬
At brothel-fights in some foul common shore.   ⎭

'Produce an evidence, though just he be
As righteous Job, or Abraham, or he
Whom Heaven, when whole nature shipwrecked was,
Thought worth the saving, of all human race;
Or t' other, who the flaming deluge 'scaped,*
When Sodom's lechers angels would have raped;   210
How rich he is, must the first question be,
Next for his manners and integrity:
They'll ask what equipage he keeps, and what
He's reckoned worth in money and estate;
For shrieve how oft he has been known to fine,
And with how many dishes he does dine.
For look what cash a person has in store,
Just so much credit has he, and no more:
Should I upon a thousand Bibles swear, ⎫
And call each saint throughout the calendar ⎬   220
To vouch my oath, it won't be taken here: ⎭
The poor slight Heav'n and thunderbolts, they think,
And Heav'n itself does at such trifles wink.

'Besides, what store of gibing scoffs are thrown
On one that's poor, and meanly clad in town;
If his apparel seem but overworn,
His stockings out at heel, or breeches torn:
One takes occasion his ripped shoe to flout,
And swears 't has been at prison-grates hung out;*
Another shrewdly jeers his coarse cravat,   230
Because himself wears point; a third his hat,
And most unmercifully shows his wit
If it be old, or does not cock aright.
Nothing in poverty so ill is borne,
As its exposing men to grinning scorn,
To be by tawdry coxcombs pissed upon,
And made the jesting stock of each buffoon.
"Turn out there, friend!" cries one at church, "the pew
Is not for such mean scoundrel curs as you:
'Tis for your betters kept:" belike some sot   240
That knew no father, was on bulks begot,
But now is raised to an estate and pride,
By having the kind proverb on his side:*

Let Gripe and Cheatwell take their places there,
And Dash, the scrivener's gaudy sparkish heir,
That wears three ruined orphans on his back.
Meanwhile, you in the alley stand and sneak,
And you therewith must rest contented, since
Almighty wealth does put such difference.
What citizen a son-in-law will take,   250
Bred ne'er so well, that can't a jointure make?
What man of sense, that's poor, e'er summoned is
Amongst the Common Council to advise?
At vestry-consults when does he appear,   ⎫
For choosing of some parish officer,   ⎬
Or making leather buckets for the choir?*   ⎭
   ''Tis hard for any man to rise, that feels
His virtue clogged with poverty at heels;
But harder 'tis by much in London, where
A sorry lodging, coarse and slender fare,   260
Fire, water, breathing, everything is dear:
Yet such as these an earthen dish disdain,
With which their ancestors, in Edgar's reign,
Were served, and thought it no disgrace to dine,
Though they were rich, had store of leather coin.
Low as their fortune is, yet they despise
A man that walks the streets in homely frieze:
To speak the truth, great part of England now
In their own cloth will scarce vouchsafe to go:
Only, the statute's penalty to save,   270
Some few perhaps wear woollen in the grave.*
Here all go gaily dressed, although it be
Above their means, their rank, and quality:
The most in borrowed gallantry are clad,
For which the tradesmen's books are still unpaid:
This fault is common in the meaner sort,   ⎫
That they must needs affect to bear the port ⎬
Of gentlemen, though they want income for't. ⎭
   'Sir, to be short, in this expensive town
There's nothing without money to be done: 280
What will you give to be admitted there,
And brought to speech of some court minister?

What will you give to have the quarter-face,
The squint and nodding go-by of his Grace?
His porter, groom, and steward must have fees,
And you may see the tombs and Tower for less:*
Hard fate of suitors! who must pay, and pray
To livery-slaves, yet oft go scorned away.

   'Whoe'er at Barnet or St Albans fears
To have his lodging drop about his ears,   290
Unless a sudden hurricane befall,
Or such a wind as blew old Noll to hell?*
Here we build slight, what scarce outlasts the lease,
Without the help of props and buttresses:
And houses nowadays as much require
To be insured from falling, as from fire.
There buildings are substantial, though less neat,
And kept with care both wind- and water-tight:
There you in safe security are blessed,
And nought but conscience to disturb your rest.   300

   'I am for living where no fires affright,
No bells rung backward break my sleep at night:*
I scarce lie down, and draw my curtains here,
But straight I'm roused by the next house on fire:
Pale, and half dead with fear, myself I raise,
And find my room all over in a blaze;
By this 't has seized on the third stairs, and I
Can now discern no other remedy,
But leaping out at window to get free:
For if the mischief from the cellar came,   310
Be sure the garret is the last takes flame.

   'The moveables of Pordage were a bed*
For him and's wife, a piss-pot by its side,
A looking-glass upon the cupboard's head,
A comb-case, candlestick, and pewter spoon
For want of plate, with desk to write upon:
A box without a lid served to contain
Few authors, which made up his Vatican:*
And there his own immortal works were laid,
On which the barbarous mice for hunger preyed.   320
Pordage had nothing, all the world does know,

And yet should he have lost this nothing too,
No one the wretched bard would have supplied
With lodging, house-room, or a crust of bread.
  'But if the fire burn down some great man's house,
All straight are interested in the loss:
The court is straight in mourning sure enough,
The Act, Commencement, and the term put off:*
Then we mischances of the town lament,
And fasts are kept, like judgments to prevent.   330
Out comes a brief immediately, with speed
To gather charity as far as Tweed.
Nay, while 'tis burning, some will send him in
Timber and stone to build his house again;
Others choice furniture: here some rare piece
Of Rubens or Van Dyck presented is,
There a rich suit of Mortlake tapestry,*
A bed of damask or embroidery:
One gives a fine scrutoire, or cabinet,
Another a huge massy dish of plate,   340
Or bag of gold: thus he at length gets more
By kind misfortune than he had before:
And all suspect it for a laid design,
As if he did himself the fire begin.
Could you but be advised to leave the town,
And from dear plays, and drinking friends be drawn,
An handsome dwelling might be had in Kent,
Surrey, or Essex, at a cheaper rent
Than what you're forced to give for one half year
To lie, like lumber, in a garret here: 350
A garden there, and well that needs no rope,
Engine, or pains to crane its waters up:
Water is there through nature's pipes conveyed,
For which no custom or excise is paid.
Had I the smallest spot of ground, which scarce
Would summer half a dozen grasshoppers,
Not larger than my grave, though hence remote ⎫
Far as St Michael's Mount, I would go to't, ⎬
Dwell there content, and thank the Fates to boot. ⎭
  'Here want of rest a-nights more people kills   360

Than all the College, and the weekly bills:*
Where none have privilege to sleep, but those
Whose purses can compound for their repose:
In vain I go to bed, or close my eyes;
Methinks the place the middle region is,
Where I lie down in storms, in thunder rise:
The restless bells such din in steeples keep,
That scarce the dead can in their churchyards sleep:
Huzzas of drunkards, bellmen's midnight rhymes,
The noise of shops, with hawkers' early screams,   370
Besides the brawls of coachmen, when they meet
And stop in turnings of a narrow street,
Such a loud medley of confusion make,
As drowsy Archer on the bench would wake.*

   'If you walk out in business ne'er so great,
Ten thousand stops you must expect to meet:
Thick crowds in every place you must charge through,
And storm your passage wheresoe'er you go;
While tides of followers behind you throng,
And, pressing on your heels, shove you along: 380
One with a board or rafter hits your head,
Another with his elbow bores your side;
Some tread upon your corns, perhaps in sport,
Meanwhile your legs are cased all o'er with dirt.
Here you the march of a slow funeral wait,
Advancing to the church with solemn state:
There a sedan and lackeys stop your way,
That bears some punk of honour to the play:
Now you some mighty piece of timber meet,
Which tott'ring threatens ruin to the street: 390
Next a huge Portland stone, for building Paul's,
Itself almost a rock, on carriage rolls;
Which, if it fall, would cause a massacre,
And serve at once to murder and inter.

   'If what I've said can't from the town affright,
Consider other dangers of the night:
When brickbats are from upper storeys thrown,
And emptied chamber-pots come pouring down
From garret windows: you have cause to bless

The gentle stars, if you come off with piss: 400
So many fates attend, a man had need
Ne'er walk without a surgeon by his side,
And he can hardly now discreet be thought,
That does not make his will ere he go out.
   'If this you 'scape, twenty to one you meet
Some of the drunken scourers of the street,
Flushed with success of warlike deeds performed,
Of constables subdued, and brothels stormed:
These, if a quarrel or a fray be missed,
Are ill at ease a–nights, and want their rest: 410
For mischief is a lechery to some,
And serves to make them sleep like laudanum.
Yet heated, as they are, with youth and wine,
If they discern a train of flambeaux shine,
If a great man with his gilt coach appear, }
And a strong guard of footboys in the rear,
The rascals sneak, and shrink their heads for fear.
Poor me, who use no light to walk about,
Save what the parish or the skies hang out,
They value not: 'tis worth your while to hear } 420
The scuffle, if that be a scuffle where
Another gives the blows, I only bear:
He bids me stand: of force I must give way,
For 'twere a senseless thing to disobey,
And struggle here, where I'd as good oppose
Myself to Preston and his mastiffs loose.*
"Who's there?" he cries, and takes you by the throat;
"Dog! are you dumb? Speak quickly, else my foot
Shall march about your buttocks: whence d'ye come?
From what bulk-ridden strumpet reeking home? 430
Saving your reverend pimpship, where d'ye ply?
How may one have a job of lechery?"
If you say anything, or hold your peace
And silently go off, 'tis all a case:
Still he lays on: nay well, if you 'scape so:
Perhaps he'll clap an action on you too
Of battery, nor need he fear to meet
A jury to his turn, shall do him right,

And bring him in large damage for a shoe
Worn out, besides the pains, in kicking you.   440
A poor man must expect nought of redress
But patience: his best in such a case
Is to be thankful for the drubs, and beg
That they would mercifully spare one leg
Or arm unbroke, and let him go away
With teeth enough to eat his meat next day.
  'Nor is this all which you have cause to fear:
Oft we encounter midnight padders here,
When the exchanges and the shops are close, ⎫
And the rich tradesman in his counting-house⎬   450
To view the profits of the day withdraws. ⎭
Hither in flocks from Shooter's Hill they come,
To seek their prize and booty nearer home:
"Your purse!" they cry; 'tis madness to resist,
Or strive, with a cocked pistol at your breast:
And these each day so strong and numerous grow,
The town can scarce afford them jail-room now.
Happy the times of the old Heptarchy,*
Ere London knew so much of villainy:
Then fatal carts through Holborn seldom went,   460
And Tyburn with few pilgrims was content:*
A less, and single prison then would do,
And served the city and the county too.
  'These are the reasons, sir, which drive me hence,
To which I might add more, would time dispense
To hold you longer; but the sun draws low,
The coach is hard at hand, and I must go:
Therefore, dear sir, farewell; and when the town
From better company can spare you down,
To make the country with your presence blessed,   470
Then visit your old friend amongst the rest:
There I'll find leisure to unlade my mind
Of what remarks I now must leave behind:
The fruits of dear experience, which, with these
Improved, will serve for hints and notices;
And when you write again, may be of use
To furnish satire for your daring muse.'

16　　*A Letter from Artemisa in the Town to Chloe in the Country*

JOHN WILMOT, EARL OF ROCHESTER

Probably written in 1669; circulated in manuscript; first printed in two separate editions 1679.

Chloe, in verse by your command I write;
Shortly you'll bid me ride astride, and fight:
These talents better with our sex agree
Than lofty flights of dangerous poetry.
Amongst the men, I mean the men of wit
(At least they passed for such before they writ)
How many bold advent'rers for the bays,
Proudly designing large returns of praise,
Who durst that stormy, pathless world explore,
Were soon dashed back, and wrecked on the dull shore, }　10
Broke of that little stock they had before!
How would a woman's tott'ring bark be tossed,
Where stoutest ships, the men of wit, are lost?
When I reflect on this, I straight grow wise,
And my own self thus gravely I advise.
Dear Artemisa, poetry's a snare:
Bedlam has many mansions: have a care.*
Your muse diverts you, makes the reader sad;
You fancy you're inspired, he thinks you're mad.
Consider too, 'twill be discreetly done　　　　　　20
To make yourself the fiddle of the town,
To find th' ill-humoured pleasure at their need,
Cursed if you fail, and scorned though you succeed.
Thus, like an arrant woman, as I am, }
No sooner well convinced writing's a shame, }
That whore is scarce a more reproachful name }
Than poetess—
As men that marry, or as maids that woo,
Because it is the worst thing they can do,
Pleased with the contradiction and the sin,　　　　30
Methinks I stand on thorns till I begin.*

Y' expect at least to hear what loves have passed
In this lewd town, since you and I met last.
What change has happened of intrigues, and whether
The old ones last, and who and who's together.
But how, my dearest Chloe, shall I set
My pen to write what I would fain forget,
Or name that lost thing, love, without a tear,
Since so debauched by ill-bred customs here?
Love, the most generous passion of the mind,   40
The softest refuge innocence can find,
The safe director of unguided youth,
Fraught with kind wishes, and secured by truth;
That cordial drop heaven in our cup has thrown,
To make the nauseous draught of life go down,
On which one only blessing God might raise
In lands of atheists, subsidies of praise:
For none did e'er so dull and stupid prove,
But felt a God, and blessed his power in love:
This only joy for which poor we were made,   50
Is grown like play to be an arrant trade;
The rooks creep in, and it has got of late
As many little cheats and tricks as that.
But what yet more a woman's heart would vex,
'Tis chiefly carried on by our own sex;
Our silly sex, who born like monarchs free;
Turn gypsies for a meaner liberty,
And hate restraint, though but from infamy.*
They call whatever is not common, 'nice',
And deaf to nature's rule, or love's advice,   60
Forsake the pleasure to pursue the vice.
To an exact perfection they have wrought
The action love; the passion is forgot.
'Tis below wit, they tell you, to admire,
And e'en without approving they desire.
Their private wish obeys the public voice,
'Twixt good and bad, whimsy decides, not choice.
Fashions grow up for taste, at forms they strike;*
They know what they would have, not what
     they like.

Bovey's a beauty, if some few agree*   70
To call him so; the rest to that degree
Affected are, that with their ears they see.

   Where I was visiting the other night,
Comes a fine lady with her humble knight,
Who had prevailed on her, through her own skill,
At his request, though much against her will,
To come to London.
As the coach stopped, we heard her voice more loud
Than a great-bellyed woman's in a crowd,
Telling the knight that her affairs require   80
He for some hours obsequiously retire.
I think she was ashamed to have him seen—
Hard fate of husbands! The gallànt had been,
Though a diseased ill-favoured fool, brought in.
'Dispatch', says she, 'that business you pretend,
Your beastly visit to your drunken friend;
A bottle ever makes you look so fine!
Methinks I long to smell you stink of wine.
Your country drinking breath's enough to kill—
Sour ale corrected with a lemon peel.   90
Prithee farewell—we'll meet again anon'.
The necessary thing bows, and is gone.
She flies upstairs, and all the haste does show
That fifty antic postures will allow,
And then bursts out: 'Dear Madam, am not I
The altered'st creature breathing? Let me die,
I find myself ridiculously grown
Embarrassée with being out of town,*
Rude and untaught, like any Indian Queen;*
My country nakedness is strangely seen.   100
How is love governed? Love, that rules the state—
And pray, who are the men most worn of late?
When I was married, fools were *à la mode*;
The men of wit were then held *incommode*,
Slow of belief, and fickle in desire,
Who ere they'll be persuaded, must enquire,
As if they came to spy, not to admire.
With searching wisdom fatal to their ease,

They still find out why what may, should not please;
Nay, take themselves for injured, when we dare   110
Make 'em think better of us than we are:
And if we hide our frailties from their sights,
Call us deceitful jilts, and hypocrites.
They little guess, who at our arts are grieved,
The perfect joy of being well deceived;
Inquisitive as jealous cuckolds grow,   ⎫
Rather than not be knowing, they will know   ⎬
What, being known, creates their certain woe.   ⎭
Women should these of all mankind avoid;
For wonder by clear knowledge is destroyed.   120
Woman, who is an arrant bird of night,
Bold in the dusk before a fool's dull sight,
Should fly when reason brings the glaring light.
But the kind, easy fool, apt to admire   ⎫
Himself, trusts us; his follies all conspire   ⎬
To flatter his, and favour our desire.   ⎭
Vain of his proper merit, he with ease
Believes we love him best, who best can please.
On him our gross, dull, common flatteries pass,
Ever most joyful, when most made an ass.   130
Heavy to apprehend, though all mankind
Perceives us false, the fop concerned is blind,
Who doting on himself,
Thinks everyone that sees him of his mind.
These are true women's men.'—Here forced
     to cease
Through want of breath, not will to hold her peace,
She to the window runs, where she had spied
Her much esteemed dear friend the monkey tied.
With forty smiles, as many antic bows,
As if 't had been the lady of the house,   140
The dirty, chattering monster she embraced,
And made it this fine tender speech at last:
'Kiss me, thou curious miniature of man;
How odd thou art! how pretty! how Japan!*
Oh, I could live and die with thee!'—then on
For half an hour in compliment she run.

I took this time to think what Nature meant
When this mixed thing into the world she sent,
So very wise, yet so impertinent.
One who knew everything; who God thought fit   150
Should be an ass through choice, not want of wit:
Whose foppery, without the help of sense,
Could ne'er have rose to such an excellence.
Nature's as lame in making a true fop
As a philosopher; the very top
And dignity of folly we attain
By studious search and labour of the brain,
By observation, counsel, and deep thought:
God never made a coxcomb worth a groat.
We owe that name to industry, and arts: 160
An eminent fool must be a fool of parts.
And such a one was she, who had turned o'er
As many books as men; loved much, read more,
Had a discerning wit; to her was known
Everyone's fault and merit but her own.
All the good qualities that ever blessed
A woman so distinguished from the rest,
Except discretion only, she possessed.
But now, '*Mon cher*, dear pug,' she cries, '*adieu*',
And the discòurse broke off does thus renew: 170
'You smile to see me, whom the world perchance
Mistakes to have some wit, so far advance
The interest of fools, that I approve
Their merit more than men's of wit in love.
But in our sex too many proofs there are
Of such whom wits undo, and fools repair.
This in my time was so observed a rule,
Hardly a wench in town but had her fool.
The meanest common slut, who long was grown
The jest and scorn of every pit buffoon,   180
Had yet left charms enough to have subdued
Some fop or other, fond to be thought lewd.*
Foster could make an Irish lord a Nokes,*
And Betty Morris had her city cokes.*
A woman's ne'er so ruined but she can

Be still revenged on her undoer man.
How lost so e'er, she'll find some lover more
A lewd abandoned fool, than she a whore.
That wretched thing Corinna, who had run
Through all the several ways of being undone,   190
Cozened at first by love, and living then
By turning the too dear-bought trick on men:
Gay were the hours, and winged with joys
    they flew,
When first the town her early beauties knew;
Courted, admired, and loved, with presents fed,
Youth in her looks, and pleasure in her bed,
Till Fate, or her ill angel, thought it fit
To make her dote upon a man of wit,
Who found 'twas dull to love above a day,
Made his ill-natured jest, and went away.   200
Now scorned by all, forsaken, and oppressed,
She's a *memento mori* to the rest.
Diseased, decayed, to take up half a crown
Must mortgage her long scarf, and Mantua gown.*
Poor creature! Who, unheard of as a fly,
In some dark hole must all the winter lie,
And want and dirt endure a whole half year,
That for one month she tawdry may appear.
In Easter Term she gets her a new gown,
When my young master's worship comes to town,   210
From pedagogue and mother just set free,
The heir and hopes of a great family,
Which with strong ale and beef the country rules,
And ever since the conquest have been fools:
And now with careful prospect to maintain
This character, lest crossing of the strain
Should mend the booby breed, his friends
    provide
A cousin of his own to be his bride;
And thus set out—
With an estate, no wit, and a young wife   220
(The solid comforts of a coxcomb's life),
Dunghill and pease forsook, he comes to town,

Turns spark, learns to be lewd, and is undone.
Nothing suits worse with vice than want of sense:
Fools are still wicked at their own expense.
This o'ergrown schoolboy lost Corinna wins,
And at first dash to make an ass begins:
Pretends to like a man who has not known
The vanities nor vices of the town;
Fresh in his youth, and faithful in his love,   230
Eager of joys which he does seldom prove,
Healthful and strong, he does no pains endure,
But what the fair one he adores can cure;
Grateful for favours does the sex esteem,
And libels none for being kind to him;*
Then of the lewdness of the times complains,
Rails at the wits and atheists, and maintains
'Tis better than good sense, than power, or wealth,
To have a love untainted, youth, and health.*
The unbred puppy, who had never seen   240
A creature look so gay, or talk so fine,
Believes, then falls in love, and then in debt,
Mortgages all, e'en to the ancient seat,
To buy this mistress a new house for life;
To give her plate and jewels robs his wife,
And when to th' height of fondness he is grown,
'Tis time to poison him, and all's her own.
Thus meeting in her common arms his fate,
He leaves her bastard heir to his estate;
And as the race of such an owl deserves,   250
His own dull lawful progeny he starves.
Nature, who never made a thing in vain,
But does each insect to some end ordain,
Wisely provides kind keeping fools, no doubt,
To patch up vices men of wit wear out.'
Thus she ran on two hours, some grains of sense
Still mixed with volleys of impertinence.
But now 'tis time I should some pity show ⎫
To Chloe, since I cannot choose but know ⎬
Readers must reap the dullness writers sow.⎭   260
By the next post such stories I will tell

As joined with these shall to a volume swell,
As true as heaven, more infamous than hell;
But you are tired, and so am I.—Farewell.

17   *To the Postboy*

JOHN WILMOT, EARL OF ROCHESTER

Written after 17 June 1676. While spoken in the persona of Rochester, it
may not have been written by him (see *Works*, ed. Love, p. 367).

Son of a whore, God damn you, can you tell
A peerless peer the readiest way to hell?
I've out-swilled Bacchus, sworn of my own make*
Oaths would fright Furies, and make Pluto quake;
I've swived more whores more ways than Sodom's walls
E'er knew, or the College of Rome's Cardinals:
Witness heroic scars, look here, ne'er go,
Cerecloths and ulcers from the top to toe;
Frighted at my own mischiefs I have fled,
And bravely left my life's defender dead;*   10
Broke houses to break chastity, and dyed
That floor with murder which my lust denied:
Pox on it—why do I speak of these poor things;
I have blasphemed my God and libelled kings:
The readiest way to hell—come, quick, ne'er stir—
Boy. The readiest way, my Lord, 's by Rochester.

18   *Régime de vivre**

ANONYMOUS

Written *c.*1673. It satirizes the rakish lifestyle exemplified by the Earl of
Rochester, and often appears in manuscripts along with poems by him.

I rise at eleven, I dine about two,
I get drunk before seven, and the next thing I do

I send for my whore, when for fear of a clap
I spend in her hand, and I spew in her lap.
There we quarrel and scold, till I fall asleep,
When the bitch, growing bold, to my pocket does creep.
Then slyly she leaves me, and to revenge the affront
At once she bereaves me of money and cunt.
If by chance then I wake, hot-headed and drunk,
What a coil do I make for the loss of my punk!   10
I storm, and I roar, and I fall in a rage,
And missing my whore, I bugger my page.
Then crop-sick all morning, I rail at my men,
And in bed I lie yawning till eleven again.

19   *A Satirical Flash*

SIR PHILIP WODEHOUSE

Written 1670. Wodehouse (b. 1608) seems to distance himself from
Restoration fashion by both his subject and style: the compact, angular
rhetoric and verse-movement of this poem are reminiscent of Tudor and
early Stuart satire (by poets such as Donne, Jonson, Marston, or Hall).

Facit indignatio versum*
O tempora! O mores!*

The modes-man's catechism. Does he eat well?
Drink reason off, till fancy boom and swell?
Keeps he a *mademoiselle*, a dame of pleasure,
'Pon whom he pours his purse, his love, his leisure?
Is he French dressed? Wears he a bush or wig
That's worth his herd, and as his glory big?
Keeps he gay equipage, an uncouth pride,
A brace of footboys, not to run but ride,
Mounting the coach's prow and poop, wherein
He hurries into debt and deadly sin?   10
(Which two, to pray against he does defy,
As superstitions in his litany.)
Can he with ladies complimentally

Toy, and decoy, with lip-adultery?
If baffled in his foul address, can he
Make a false bravo of his victory?
For if his miss won't jostle, then he may
Swear she's not chaste, but loathly to say nay.
Scorns he all scholarship as pedantry?
All wise old men as doting gravity?   20
Only well-read in the philosophy
Of the modern bard of Malmesbury?*
Yet huffs and hectors it, sits judge of wit,
Whilst he betrays his own in doing it?
And sets as *censor morum* too, in chair
Of scorn, wherein h' has neither ear nor air.
Can he transvest into bold drollery
Grave *Galateus*' rules of modesty?*
And make a comment 'pon the *point Venise*,
Read ladies' laces, which to which agrees?   30
Has he been travelled? And come home, contemns
His country? Modes as old and base condemns?
Yet nothing brings but congees and a hug
From France or Spain? From Italy their shrug?
Can he despise all wiser than himself?
All frugaller as huggers of their pelf?
Can he wear townships trimly on his back,
And soak his timber in large butts of sack?
Has he an ássurance or confidence
Which fools cajoles to think he has some sense?   40
Can he live counter as antipodes,
Act sin all night, all day but sleep and dress?
Can he affront his own damnation?
Stave off its thought till doomsday? Hopes there's none?
Then may he well commence an *A-la-mode*,
And ride to Rhadamanth the Hyde Park road.*
     Lo, a new sect of virtuosos! Who
Outbrave old virtue, would her truth undo!
But 't will not be: for she's eternal, and she
Against the powers of man and dev'l stands free.   50

20   [*Vanity Fair*] from *The Pilgrim's Progress*

JOHN BUNYAN

Written during Bunyan's imprisonment, and published 1678. Christian has been warned to leave the City of Destruction, where he was born, and is making a journey towards the Celestial City in the company of Faithful, when they come to a town called Vanity, where the inhabitants hold a year-long fair.

Then I saw in my dream, that when they were got out of the wilderness, they presently saw a town before them, and the name of that town is Vanity, and at the town there is a fair kept, called Vanity Fair: it is kept all the year long; it beareth the name of Vanity Fair, because the town where tis kept is lighter than vanity; and also because all that is there sold, or that cometh thither, is vanity. As is the saying of the wise, 'all that cometh is vanity'.

This fair is no new-erected business, but a thing of ancient standing; I will show you the original of it.

Almost five thousand years agone, there were pilgrims walking to the Celestial City, as these two honest persons are: and Beelzebub, Apollyon, and Legion,* with their companions, perceiving by the path that the pilgrims made, that their way to the city lay through this town of Vanity, they contrived here to set up a fair; a fair wherein should be sold of all sorts of vanity, and that it should last all the year long. Therefore at this fair are all such merchandise sold, as houses, lands, trades, places, honours, preferments, titles, countries, kingdoms, lusts, pleasures, and delights of all sorts, as whores, bawds, wives, husbands, children, masters, servants, lives, blood, bodies, souls, silver, gold, pearls, precious stones, and what not.

And, moreover, at this fair there is at all times to be seen jugglings, cheats, games, plays, fools, apes, knaves, and rogues, and that of all sorts.

Here are to be seen, too, and that for nothing, thefts, murders, adulteries, false swearers, and that of a blood-red colour.

And, as in other fairs of less moment, there are the several rows and streets, under their proper names, where such and such wares are vended; so here likewise you have the proper places, rows, streets (viz., countries and kingdoms) where the wares of this fair are soonest to be found. Here is the Britain Row, the French Row, the Italian Row, the Spanish Row, the German Row, where several sorts of vanities are to be sold. But, as in other fairs, some one commodity is as the chief of all the fair, so the ware of Rome and her merchandise is greatly promoted in this fair; only our English nation, with some others, have taken a dislike thereat.

Now, as I said, the way to the Celestial City lies just through this town where this lusty fair is kept; and he that will go to the city, and yet not go through this town, must needs go out of the world. The Prince of princes himself, when here, went through this town to his own country, and that upon a fair-day too; yea, and as I think, it was Beelzebub, the chief lord of this fair, that invited him to buy of his vanities; yea, would have made him lord of the fair, would he but have done him reverence as he went through the town.* Yea, because he was such a person of honour, Beelzebub had him from street to street, and showed him all the kingdoms of the world in a little time, that he might, if possible, allure that Blessed One to cheapen and buy some of his vanities; but he had no mind to the merchandise, and therefore left the town without laying out so much as one farthing upon these vanities. This fair, therefore, is an ancient thing, of long standing, and a very great fair.

Now these pilgrims, as I said, must needs go through this fair. Well, so they did: but, behold, even as they entered into the fair, all the people in the fair were moved, and the town itself as it were in a hubbub about them; and that for several reasons: for—

First, The pilgrims were clothed with such kind of raiment as was diverse from the raiment of any that traded in that fair. The people, therefore, of the fair made a great gazing upon them: some said they were fools, some they were bedlams, and some they were outlandish men.

Secondly, And as they wondered at their apparel, so they did likewise at their speech; for few could understand what they said; they naturally spoke the language of Canaan,* but they that kept the fair were the men of this world, so that from one end of the fair to the other, they seemed barbarians each to the other.

Thirdly, But that which did not a little amuse the merchandisers was, that these pilgrims set very light by all their wares; they cared not so much as to look upon them; and if they called upon them to buy, they would put their fingers in their ears, and cry, 'Turn away mine eyes from beholding vanity',* and look upwards, signifying that their trade and traffic was in heaven.

One chanced mockingly, beholding the carriages of the men, to say unto them, 'What will ye buy?' But they, looking gravely upon him, said, 'We buy the truth'. At that there was an occasion taken to despise the men the more, some mocking, some taunting, some speaking reproachfully, and some calling upon others to smite them. At last things came to an hubbub and great stir in the fair, insomuch that all order was confounded. Now was word presently brought to the great one of the fair, who quickly came down, and deputed some of his most trusty friends to take these men into examination, about whom the fair was almost overturned. So the men were brought to examination; and they that sat upon them, asked them whence they came, whither they went, and what they did there in such an unusual garb? The men told them that they were pilgrims and strangers in the world, and that they were going to their own country, which was the heavenly Jerusalem, and that they had given none occasion to the men of the town, nor yet to the merchandisers, thus to abuse them, and to let them in their journey, except it was for that, when one asked them what they would buy, they said they would buy the truth. But they that were appointed to examine them did not believe them to be any other than bedlams and mad, or else such as came to put all things into a confusion in the fair. Therefore they took them and beat them, and besmeared them with dirt, and then put them into the cage, that they might be made a spectacle to all the men of the fair. There, therefore, they lay for some time, and were made the objects of any man's sport, or malice, or revenge, the great one of the fair laughing still at all that befell them. But the men being patient, and not rendering railing for railing, but contrariwise blessing, and giving good words for bad, and kindness for injuries done, some men in the fair that were more observing, and less prejudiced than the rest, began to check and blame the baser sort for their continual abuses done by them to the men; they, therefore, in angry manner, let fly at them again, counting them as bad as the men in the cage, and telling them that they seemed confederates, and should be made partakers of their misfortunes. The other replied that, for aught they could see, the men were quiet, and sober, and intended nobody any harm; and that there were many that traded in their fair that were more worthy to be put into the cage, yea, and pillory too, than were the men that they had abused. Thus, after divers words had passed on both sides (the men behaving themselves all the while very wisely and soberly before them) they fell to some blows among themselves, and did harm one to another. Then were these two poor men brought before their examiners again, and there charged as being guilty of the late hubbub that had been in the fair. So they beat them pitifully, and hanged irons upon them, and led them in chains up and down the fair, for an example and a terror to others, lest any should further speak in their behalf, or join themselves unto them. But Christian and Faithful behaved themselves yet more wisely, and received the ignominy and shame that was cast upon them with so much meekness and patience, that it won to their side, though but few in comparison of the rest, several of the men in the fair. This put the other party yet into a greater rage, insomuch that they concluded the death of these two men. Wherefore they threatened that neither the cage nor irons should serve their turn, but that they should die, for the abuse they had done, and for deluding the men of the fair.

Then were they remanded to the cage again, until further order should be taken with them. So they put them in, and made their feet fast in the stocks.

Here also they called again to mind what they had heard from their faithful friend Evangelist, and was the more confirmed in their way and sufferings by what he told them would happen to them. They also now comforted each other, that whose lot it was to suffer, even he should have the best on't; therefore each man secretly wished that he might have that preferment: but committing themselves to the all-wise dispose of him that ruleth all things, with much content they abode in the condition in which they were, until they should be otherwise disposed of.

Then a convenient time being appointed, they brought them forth to their trial, in order to their condemnation. When the time was come, they were brought before their enemies and arraigned. The judge's name was Lord Hategood. Their indictment was one and the same in substance, though somewhat varying in form, the contents whereof was this:

'That they were enemies to and disturbers of their trade; that they had made commotions and divisions in the town, and had won a party to their own most dangerous opinions, in contempt of the law of their prince.'

Then Faithful began to answer, that he had only set himself against that which had set itself against him that is higher than the highest. 'And', said he, 'as for disturbance, I make none, being myself a man of peace; the party that were won to us, were won by beholding our truth and innocence, and they are only turned from the worse to the better. And as to the king you talk of, since he is Beelzebub, the enemy of our Lord, I defy him and all his angels.'

Then proclamation was made, that they that had aught to say for their lord the king against the prisoner at the bar, should forthwith appear and give in their evidence. So there came in three witnesses, to wit, Envy, Superstition, and Pickthank. They was then asked if they knew the prisoner at the bar; and what they had to say for their lord the king against him.

Then stood forth Envy, and said to this effect: 'My Lord, I have known this man a long time, and will attest upon my oath before this honourable bench that he is—'

JUDGE: 'Hold! Give him his oath.' So they sware him. Then he said:

[ENVY]: 'My Lord, this man, notwithstanding his plausible name, is one of the vilest men in our country. He neither regardeth prince nor people, law nor custom, but doth all that he can to possess all men with certain of his disloyal notions, which he in the general calls principles of faith and holiness. And, in particular, I heard him once myself affirm that Christianity and the customs of our town of Vanity were diametrically opposite, and could not be reconciled. By which saying, my Lord, he doth at once not only condemn all our laudable doings, but us in the doing of them.'

JUDGE: Then did the Judge say to him, 'Hast thou any more to say?'

ENVY: 'My Lord, I could say much more, only I would not be tedious to the court. Yet, if need be, when the other gentlemen have given in their evidence, rather than anything shall be wanting that will despatch him, I will enlarge my testimony against him.' So he was bid stand by. Then they called Superstition, and bid him look upon the prisoner. They also asked what he could say for their lord the king against him. Then they sware him; so he began.

SUPERSTITION: 'My Lord, I have no great acquaintance with this man, nor do I desire to have further knowledge of him; however, this

I know, that he is a very pestilent fellow, from some discourse that the other day I had with him in this town; for then talking with him, I heard him say that our religion was nought; and such by which a man could by no means please God. Which sayings of his, my Lord, your Lordship very well knows what necessarily thence will follow, to wit, that we still do worship in vain, are yet in our sins, and finally shall be damned; and this is that which I have to say.'

Then was Pickthank sworn, and bid say what he knew in behalf of their lord the king against the prisoner at the bar.

PICKTHANK: 'My Lord, and you gentlemen all, this fellow I have known of a long time, and have heard him speak things that ought not to be spoke; for he hath railed on our noble prince Beelzebub, and hath spoke contemptibly of his honourable friends, whose names are the Lord Old Man, the Lord Carnal Delight, the Lord Luxurious, the Lord Desire of Vain Glory, my old Lord Lechery, Sir Having Greedy, with all the rest of our nobility: and he hath said, moreover, that if all men were of his mind, if possible, there is not one of these noblemen should have any longer a being in this town. Besides, he hath not been afraid to rail on you, my Lord, who are now appointed to be his judge, calling you an ungodly villain, with many other suchlike vilifying terms, with which he hath bespattered most of the gentry of our town.' When this Pickthank had told his tale, the Judge directed his speech to the prisoner at the bar, saying, 'Thou runagate, heretic, and traitor, hast thou heard what these honest gentlemen have witnessed against thee?'

FAITHFUL: 'May I speak a few words in my own defence?'

JUDGE: 'Sirrah, sirrah, thou deservest to live no longer, but to be slain immediately upon the place; yet, that all men may see our gentleness towards thee, let us hear what thou hast to say.'

FAITHFUL: '1. I say, then, in answer to what Mr Envy hath spoken, I never said aught but this, that what rule, or laws, or custom, or people, were flat against the word of God, are diametrically opposite to Christianity. If I have said amiss in this, convince me of my error, and I am ready here before you to make my recantation.

'2. As to the second, to wit, Mr Superstition, and his charge against me, I said only this, that in the worship of God there is required a divine faith; but there can be no divine faith without a divine revelation of the will of God. Therefore, whatever is thrust into the worship of God that is not agreeable to divine revelation, cannot be done but by an human faith, which faith will not profit to eternal life.

'3. As to what Mr Pickthank hath said, I say (avoiding terms, as that I am said to rail, and the like) that the prince of this town, with all the rabblement his attendants, by this gentleman named, are more fit for a being in hell, than in this town and country: and so the Lord have mercy upon me.'

Then the Judge called to the jury (who all this while stood by, to hear and observe): 'Gentlemen of the jury, you see this man about whom so great an uproar hath been made in this town. You have also heard what these worthy gentlemen have witnessed against him. Also you have heard his reply and confession. It lieth now in your breasts to hang him or save his life; but yet I think meet to instruct you into our law.

'There was an Act made in the days of Pharaoh the Great, servant to our prince, that lest those of a contrary religion should multiply and grow too strong for him, their males should be thrown into the river. There was also an Act made in the days of Nebuchadnezzar the Great, another of his servants, that whoever would not fall down and worship his golden image, should be thrown into a fiery furnace. There was also an Act made in the days of Darius, that whoso, for some time, called upon any god but his, should be cast into the lions' den.* Now the substance of these laws this rebel has broken, not only in thought (which is not to be borne), but also in word and deed, which must therefore needs be intolerable.

'For that of Pharaoh, his law was made upon a supposition, to prevent mischief, no crime being yet apparent; but here is a crime apparent. For the second and third, you see he disputeth against our religion; and for the treason he hath confessed, he deserveth to die the death.'

Then went the jury out, whose names were Mr Blind-man, Mr No-good, Mr Malice, Mr Love-lust, Mr Live-loose, Mr Heady, Mr High-mind, Mr Enmity, Mr Liar, Mr Cruelty, Mr Hate-light, and Mr Implacable; who every one gave in his private verdict against him among themselves, and afterwards unanimously concluded to bring him in guilty before the Judge. And first, Mr Blind-man, the fore-man, said, 'I see clearly that this man is an heretic.' Then said Mr

No-good, 'Away with such a fellow from the earth.' 'Ay,' said Mr Malice, 'for I hate the very looks of him.' Then said Mr Love-lust, 'I could never endure him.' 'Nor I,' said Mr Live-loose, 'for he would always be condemning my way.' 'Hang him, hang him,' said Mr Heady. 'A sorry scrub', said Mr High-mind. 'My heart riseth against him', said Mr Enmity. 'He is a rogue', said Mr Liar. 'Hanging is too good for him', said Mr Cruelty. 'Let's despatch him out of the way', said Mr Hate-light. Then said Mr Implacable, 'Might I have all the world given me, I could not be reconciled to him; therefore, let us forthwith bring him in guilty of death.' And so they did; therefore he was presently condemned to be had from the place where he was, to the place from whence he came, and there to be put to the most cruel death that could be invented.

They therefore brought him out, to do with him according to their law, and first they scourged him, then they buffeted him, then they lanced his flesh with knives; after that they stoned him with stones, then pricked him with their swords; and last of all they burned him to ashes at the stake. Thus came Faithful to his end. Now, I saw that there stood behind the multitude a chariot and a couple of horses, waiting for Faithful, who (so soon as his adversaries had despatched him) was taken up into it, and straightway was carried up through the clouds, with sound of trumpet, the nearest way to the Celestial Gate. But as for Christian, he had some respite, and was remanded back to prison. So he there remained for a space; but he that over-rules all things, having the power of their rage in his own hand, so wrought it about that Christian for that time escaped them, and went his way.

And as he went, he sang:

> Well, Faithful, thou hast faithfully profest
> Unto thy Lord; with him thou shalt be blest,
> When faithless ones, with all their vain delights,
> Are crying out under their hellish plights:
> Sing, Faithful, sing, and let thy name survive;
> For, though they killed thee, thou art yet alive!

21   [*The Fire of London*] from the *Diary*

SAMUEL PEPYS

The fire began early in the morning of 2 September 1666, in the King's baker's shop in Pudding Lane. It burnt for four days, covered 436 acres, destroyed 89 churches and about 13,200 houses, and gutted St Paul's Cathedral, the Guildhall, and the Royal Exchange.

1 [September]. Up and at the office all the morning, and then dined at home. Got my new closet made mighty clean against tomorrow. Sir W. Penn and my wife and Mercer and I to *Polichenelly*, but were there horribly frighted to see young Killigrew come in with a great many more young sparks; but we hid ourselves, so as we think they did not see us. By and by they went away, and then we were at rest again; and so the play being done, we to Islington and there eat and drank and mighty merry—and so home, singing; and after a letter or two at the office, to bed.

2. *Lord's day*. Some of our maids sitting up late last night to get things ready against our feast today, Jane called us up, about 3 in the morning, to tell us of a great fire they saw in the City. So I rose, and slipped on my nightgown and went to her window, and thought it to be on the back side of Mark Lane at the furthest; but being unused to such fires as followed, I thought it far enough off, and so went to bed again and to sleep. About 7 rose again to dress myself, and there looked out at the window and saw the fire not so much as it was, and further off. So to my closet to set things to rights after yesterday's cleaning. By and by Jane comes and tells me that she hears that above 300 houses have been burned down tonight by the fire we saw, and that it was now burning down all Fish Street by London Bridge. So I made myself ready presently, and walked to the Tower and there got up upon one of the high places, Sir J. Robinson's little son going up with me; and there I did see the houses at that end of the bridge all on fire, and an infinite great fire on this and the other side the end of the bridge—which, among other people, did trouble me for poor little Mitchell* and our Sarah on the bridge. So down, with my heart full of trouble, to the Lieutenant of the Tower, who tells me that it begun this morning in the King's baker's house in Pudding Lane, and that it hath burned down St Magnus Church and most part of

Fish Street already. So I down to the waterside and there got a boat and through bridge, and there saw a lamentable fire. Poor Mitchell's house, as far as the Old Swan, already burned that way and the fire running further, that in a very little time it got as far as the Steelyard while I was there. Everybody endeavouring to remove their goods, and flinging into the river or bringing them into lighters that lay off. Poor people staying in their houses as long as till the very fire touched them, and then running into boats or clambering from one pair of stair by the waterside to another. And among other things, the poor pigeons I perceive were loath to leave their houses, but hovered about the windows and balconies till they were some of them burned, their wings, and fell down.

Having stayed, and in an hour's time seen the fire rage every way, and nobody to my sight endeavouring to quench it, but to remove their goods and leave all to the fire; and having seen it get as far as the Steelyard, and the wind mighty high and driving it into the city, and everything, after so long a drought, proving combustible, even the very stones of churches, and among other things, the poor steeple by which pretty Mrs [Horsley] lives, and whereof my old school-fellow Elborough is parson, taken fire in the very top and there burned till it fall down—I to Whitehall with a gentleman with me who desired to go off from the Tower to see the fire in my boat—to Whitehall, and there up to the King's closet in the chapel, where people came about me and I did give them an account dismayed them all; and word was carried in to the King, so I was called for and did tell the King and Duke of York what I saw, and that unless his Majesty did command houses to be pulled down, nothing could stop the fire. They seemed much troubled, and the King commanded me to go to my Lord Mayor from him and command him to spare no houses but to pull down before the fire every way. The Duke of York bid me tell him that if he would have any more soldiers, he shall; and so did my Lord Arlington afterward, as a great secret. Here meeting with Captain Cocke, I in his coach, which he lent me, and Creed with me, to Paul's; and there walked along Watling Street as well as I could, every creature coming away loaden with goods to save—and here and there sick people carried away in beds. Extraordinary good goods carried in carts and on backs. At last met my Lord Mayor in Canning Street, like a man spent, with a handkerchief about his neck. To the King's message, he cried like a fainting woman, 'Lord, what can I do? I am spent! People will not obey me. I have been pull[ing] down houses. But the fire overtakes us faster than we can do it.' That he needed no more soldiers; and that for himself, he must go and refresh himself, having been up all night. So he left me, and I him, and walked home—seeing people all almost distracted and no manner of means used to quench the fire. The houses too, so very thick thereabouts, and full of matter for burning, as pitch and tar, in Thames Street—and warehouses of oil and wines and brandy and other things. Here I saw Mr Isaac Houblon, that handsome man—prettily dressed and dirty at his door at Dowgate, receiving some of his brothers' things whose houses were on fire; and as he says, have been removed twice already, and he doubts (as it soon proved) that they must be in a little time removed from his house also—which was a sad consideration. And to see the churches all filling with goods, by people who themselves should have been quietly there at this time.

By this time it was about 12 o'clock, and so home and there find my guests, which was Mr Wood and his wife, Barbary Shelden, and also Mr Moone—she mighty fine, and her husband, for aught I see, a likely man. But Mr Moone's design and mine, which was to look over my closet and please him with the sight thereof, which he hath long desired, was wholly disappointed, for we were in great trouble and disturbance at this fire, not knowing what to think of it. However, we had an extraordinary good dinner, and as merry as at this time we could be.

While at dinner, Mrs Batelier came to enquire after Mr Woolfe and Stanes (who it seems are related to them), whose houses in Fish Street are all burned, and they in a sad condition. She would not stay in the fright.

As soon as dined, I and Moone away and walked through the City, the streets full of nothing but people and horses and carts loaden with goods, ready to run over one another, and removing goods from one burned house to another—they now removing out of Canning Street (which received goods in the morning) into Lombard Street and further; and among others, I now saw my little goldsmith Stokes receiving some friend's goods, whose house itself was burned the day after. We parted at Paul's, he home and I to Paul's Wharf, where I had appointed a boat to attend me; and took in Mr Carcasse and his brother, whom I met in the street, and carried them below and above bridge, to and again, to see the fire, which was now got further, both below and above, and no likelihood of stopping it. Met with the King and Duke of York in their barge, and with them to Queenhithe and there called Sir Rd. Browne to them. Their order was only to pull down houses apace, and so below bridge at the waterside; but little was or could be done, the fire coming upon them so fast. Good hopes there was of stopping it at the Three Cranes above, and at Bottolph's Wharf below bridge, if care be used; but the wind carries it into the City, so as we know not by the waterside what it doth there. River full of lighter[s] and boats taking in goods, and good goods swimming in the water; and only, I observed that hardly one lighter or boat in three that had the goods of a house in, but there was a pair of virginals in it. Having seen as much as I could now, I away to Whitehall by appointment, and there walked to St James's Park, and there met my wife and Creed and Wood and his wife and walked to my boat, and there upon the water again, and to the fire up and down, it still increasing and the wind great. So near the fire as we could for smoke; and all over the Thames, with one's face in the wind you were almost burned with a shower of firedrops—this is very true—so as houses were burned by these drops and flakes of fire, three or four, nay five or six houses, one from another. When we could endure no more upon the water, we to a little alehouse on the Bankside over against the Three Cranes, and there stayed till it was dark almost and saw the fire grow; and as it grow darker, appeared more and more, and in corners and upon steeples and between churches and houses, as far as we could see up the hill of the City, in a most horrid malicious bloody flame, not like the fine flame of an ordinary fire. Barbary and her husband away before us. We stayed till, it being darkish, we saw the fire as only one entire arch of fire from this to the other side the bridge, and in a bow up the hill, for an arch of above a mile long. It made me weep to see it. The churches, houses, and all on fire and flaming at once, and a horrid noise the flames made, and the cracking of houses at their ruin. So home with a sad heart, and there find everybody discoursing and lamenting the fire; and poor Tom Hater came with some few of his goods saved out of his house, which is burned upon Fish Street hill. I invited him to lie at my house, and did receive his goods: but was deceived in his lying there, the noise coming every moment of the growth of the fire, so as we were forced to begin to pack up our own goods and prepare for their removal. And did by moonshine (it being brave, dry, and moonshine and warm weather) carry much of my goods into the garden, and Mr Hater and I did remove my money and iron chests into my cellar—as thinking that the safest place. And got my bags of gold into my office ready to carry away, and my chief papers of accounts also there, and my tallies into a box by themselves. So great was our fear, as Sir W. Batten had carts come out of the country to fetch away his goods this night. We did put Mr Hater, poor man, to bed a little; but he got but very little rest, so much noise being in my house, taking down of goods.

3. About 4 o'clock in the morning, my Lady Batten sent me a cart to carry away all my money and plate and best things to Sir W. Rider's at Bethnall Green; which I did, riding myself in my night-gown in the cart; and Lord, to see how the streets and the highways are crowded with people, running and riding and getting of carts at any rate to fetch away thing[s]. I find Sir W. Rider tired with being called up all night and receiving things from several friends. His house full of goods—and much of Sir W. Batten and Sir W. Penn's. I am eased at my heart to have my treasure so well secured. Then home with much ado to find a way. Nor any sleep all this night to me nor my poor wife. But then, and all this day, she and I and all my people labouring to get away the rest of our things, and did get Mr Tooker to get me a lighter to take them in, and we did carry them (myself some) over Tower Hill, which was by this time full of people's goods, bringing their goods thither. And down to the lighter, which lay at the next quay above the Towerdock. And here was my neighbour's wife, Mrs [Buckworth], with her pretty child and some few of her things, which I did willingly give way to be saved with mine. But there was no passing with anything through the postern, the crowd was so great.

The Duke of York came this day by the office and spoke to us, and did ride with his guard up and down the City to keep all quiet (he being now General, and having the care of all).

This day, Mercer* being not at home, but against her mistress' order gone to her mother's, and my wife going thither to speak with W. Hewer, met her there and was angry; and her mother saying that she was not a prentice girl, to ask leave every time she goes abroad, my wife with good reason was angry, and when she came home, bid her be gone again. And so she went away, which troubled me; but yet less than it would, because of the condition we are in fear of coming into in a little time, of being less able to keep one in her quality. At night, lay down a little upon a quilt of W. Hewer in the office (all my own things being packed up or gone); and after me, my poor wife did the like—we having fed upon the remains of yesterday's dinner, having no fire nor dishes, nor any opportunity of dressing anything.

4. Up by break of day to get away the remainder of my things, which I did by a lighter at the Irongate; and my hands so few, that it was the afternoon before we could get them all away.

Sir W. Penn and I to Tower Street, and there met the fire burning three or four doors beyond Mr Howell's; whose goods, poor man (his trays and dishes, shovels etc., were flung all along Tower Street in the kennels, and people working therewith from one end to the other), the fire coming on in that narrow street, on both sides, with infinite fury. Sir W. Batten, not knowing how to remove his wine, did dig a pit in the garden and laid it in there; and I took the opportunity of laying all the papers of my office that I could not otherwise dispose of. And in the evening Sir W. Penn and I did dig another and put our wine in it, and I my parmesan cheese as well as my wine and some other things.

The Duke of York was at the office this day at Sir W. Penn's, but I happened not to be within. This afternoon, sitting melancholy with Sir W. Penn in our garden and thinking of the certain burning of this office without extraordinary means, I did propose for the sending up of all our workmen from Woolwich and Deptford yards (none whereof yet appeared), and to write to Sir W. Coventry to have the Duke of York's permission to pull down houses rather than lose this office, which would much hinder the King's business. So Sir W. Penn he went down this night, in order to the sending them up tomorrow morning; and I wrote to Sir W. Coventry about the business, but received no answer.

This night Mrs Turner (who, poor woman, was removing her goods all this day—good goods, into the garden, and knew not how to dispose of them)—and her husband supped with my wife and I at night in the office, upon a shoulder of mutton from the cook's, without any napkin or anything, in a sad manner but were merry. Only, now and then walking into the garden and saw how horridly the sky looks, all on a fire in the night, was enough to put us out of our wits; and indeed it was extremely dreadfull—for it looks just as if it was at us, and the whole heaven on fire. I after supper walked in the dark down to Tower Street, and there saw it all on fire at the Trinity house on that side and the Dolphin tavern on this side, which was very near us—and the fire with extraordinary vehemence. Now begins the practice of blowing up of houses in Tower Street, those next the Tower, which at first did frighten people more than anything; but it stop[ped] the fire where it was done—it bringing down the houses to the ground in the same places they stood, and then it was easy to quench what little fire was in it, though it kindled nothing almost. W. Hewer this day went to see how his mother did, and comes late home, but telling us how he hath been forced to remove her to Islington, her house in Pie Corner being burned. So that it is got so far that way and all the Old Bailey, and was running down to Fleet Street. And Paul's is burned, and all Cheapside. I wrote to my father this night; but the post-house being burned, the letter could not go.

5. I lay down in the office again upon W. Hewer's quilt, being mighty weary and sore in my feet with going till I was hardly able to stand. About 2 in the morning my wife calls me up and tells of new cries of 'Fire!'—it being come to Barking Church, which is the bottom of our lane. I up; and finding it so, resolved presently to take her away; and did, and took my gold (which was about £2350), W. Hewer, and Jane down by Poundy's boat to Woolwich. But Lord, what a sad sight it was by moonlight to see the whole City almost on fire—that you might see it plain at Woolwich, as if you were by it. There when I came, I find the gates* shut, but no guard kept at all; which troubled me, because of discourses now begun that there is plot in it and that the French had done it. I got the gates open, and to Mr Shelden's, where I locked up my gold and charged my wife and W. Hewer never to leave the room without one of them in it night nor day. So back again, by the way seeing my goods well in the lighters at Deptford and watched well by people. Home, and whereas I expected to have seen our house on fire, it being now about 7 o'clock, it was not. But to the fire, and there find greater hopes than I expected; for my confidence of finding our office on fire was such, that I durst not ask anybody how it was with us, till I came and saw it not burned. But going to the fire, I find, by the blowing up of houses and the great help given by the workmen out of the King's yards, sent up by Sir W. Penn, there is a good stop given to it, as well at

Mark Lane end as ours—it having only burned the dial of Barking Church, and part of the porch, and was there quenched. I up to the top of Barking steeple, and there saw the saddest sight of desolation that I ever saw. Everywhere great fires. Oil-cellars and brimstone and other things burning. I became afeared to stay there long; and therefore down again as fast as I could, the fire being spread as far as I could see it, and to Sir W. Penn's and there eat a piece of cold meat, having eaten nothing since Sunday but the remains of Sunday's dinner.

Here I met with Mr Young and Whistler; and having removed all my things, and received good hopes that the fire at our end is stopped, they and I walked into the town and find Fenchurch Street, Gracious Street, and Lombard Street all in dust. The Exchange a sad sight, nothing standing there of all the statues or pillars but Sir Tho. Gresham's picture in the corner. Walked into Moorfields (our feet ready to burn, walking through the town among the hot coals) and find that full of people, and poor wretches carrying their goods there, and everybody keeping his goods together by themselves (and a great blessing it is to them that it is fair weather for them to keep abroad night and day); drank there, and paid twopence for a plain penny loaf.

Thence homeward, having passed through Cheapside and Newgate market, all burned—and seen Anthony Joyce's house in fire. And took up (which I keep by me) a piece of glass of Mercer's chapel in the street, where much more was, so melted and buckled with the heat of the fire, like parchment. I also did see a poor cat taken out of a hole in the chimney joining to the wall of the Exchange, with the hair all burned off the body and yet alive. So home at night, and find there good hopes of saving our office—but great endeavours of watching all night and having men ready; and so we lodged them in the office, and had drink and bread and cheese for them. And I lay down and slept a good night about midnight— though when I rose, I hear that there had been a great alarm of French and Dutch being risen—which proved nothing. But it is a strange thing to see how long this time did look since Sunday, having been alway full of variety of actions, and little sleep, that it looked like a week or more. And I had forgot almost the day of the week.

6. Up about 5 o'clock, and there met Mr Gawden at the gate of the office (I intending to go out, as I used every now and then to do,

to see how the fire is) to call our men to Bishopsgate, where no fire had yet been near, and there is now one broke out—which did give great grounds to people, and to me too, to think that there is some kind of plot in this (on which many by this time have been taken, and it hath been dangerous for any stranger to walk in the streets); but I went with the men and we did put it out in a little time, so that that was well again. It was pretty to see how hard the women did work in the kennells sweeping of water; but then they would scold for drink and be as drunk as devils. I saw good butts of sugar broke open in the street, and people go and take handfuls out and put into beer and drink it. And now all being pretty well, I took boat and over to Southwark, and took boat on the other side the bridge and so to Westminster, thinking to shift myself, being all in dirt from top to bottom. But could not there find any place to buy a shirt or pair of gloves, Westminster Hall being full of people's goods—those in Westminster having removed all their goods, and the Exchequer money put into vessels to carry to Nonsuch. But to the Swan, and there was trimmed. And then to Whitehall, but saw nobody, and so home. A sad sight to see how the river looks—no houses nor church near it to the Temple—where it stopped. At home did go with Sir W. Batten and our neighbour Knightly (who, with one more, was the only man of any fashion left in all the neighbourhood hereabouts, they all removing their goods and leaving their houses to the mercy of the fire) to Sir R. Ford's, and there dined, in an earthen platter a fried breast of mutton, a great many of us. But very merry; and indeed as good a meal, though as ugly a one, as ever I had in my life. Thence down to Deptford, and there with great satisfaction landed all my goods at Sir G. Carteret's, safe, and nothing missed I could see, or hurt. This being done to my great content, I home; and to Sir W. Batten's, and there with Sir R. Ford, Mr Knightly, and one Withers, a professed lying rogue, supped well; and mighty merry and our fears over. From them to the office and there slept, with the office full of labourers, who talked and slept and walked all night long there. But strange it was to see Clothworkers Hall on fire these three days and nights in one body of flame—it being the cellar, full of oil.

7. Up by 5 o'clock and, blessed be God, find all well, and by water to Paul's wharf. Walked thence and saw all the town burned, and a miserable sight of Paul's church, with all the roofs fallen and the body of the choir fallen into St Faith's—Paul's school also—

Ludgate—Fleet Street—my father's house, and the church, and a good part of the Temple the like. So to Creed's lodging near the New Exchange, and there find him laid down upon a bed—the house all unfurnished, there being fears of the fire's coming to them. There borrowed a shirt of him—and washed. To Sir W. Coventry at St James's, who lay without curtains, having removed all his goods—as the King at Whitehall and everybody had done and was doing. He hopes we shall have no public distractions upon this fire, which is what everybody fears—because of the talk of the French having a hand in it. And it is a proper time for discontents—but all men's minds are full of care to protect themselves and save their goods. The Militia is in arms everywhere. Our fleets, he tells me, have been in sight one of another, and most unhappily by foul weather were parted, to our great loss, as in reason they do conclude—the Dutch being come out only to make a show and please their people; but in very bad condition as to stores, victuals, and men. They are at Bullen, and our fleet come to St Ellen's.* We have got nothing, but have lost one ship, but he knows not what.

Thence to the Swan and there drank; and so home and find all well. My Lord Brouncker at Sir W. Batten's, and tells us the General* is sent for up to come to advise with the King about business at this juncture, and to keep all quiet—which is great honour to him, but I am sure is but a piece of dissimulation. So home and did give order for my house to be made clean; and then down to Woolwich and there find all well. Dined, and Mrs Markeham came to see my wife. So I up again, and calling at Deptford for some things of W. Hewer, he being with me; and then home and spent the evening with Sir R. Ford, Mr Knightly, and Sir W. Penn at Sir W. Batten's. This day our merchants first met at Gresham College, which by proclamation is to be their Exchange. Strange to hear what is bid for houses all up and down here—a friend of Sir W. Rider's having £150 for what he used to let for £40 per annum. Much dispute where the Custom House shall be; thereby the growth of the City again to be foreseen. My Lord Treasurer, they say, and others, would have it at the other end of the town. I home late to Sir W. Penn, who did give me a bed – but without curtains or hangings, all being down. So here I went the first time* into a naked bed, only my drawers on—and did sleep pretty well; but still, both sleeping and waking, had a fear of fire in my heart, that I took little rest. People do all the world over cry out of the simplicity of my Lord Mayor* in general, and more particularly in this business of the fire, laying it all upon him. A proclamation is come out for markets to be kept at Leadenhall and Mile End Green and several other places about the town, and Tower Hill, and all churches to be set open to receive poor people.

22   [*The Fire of London*] from *Annus Mirabilis*

JOHN DRYDEN

Published 1667. *Annus Mirabilis, The Year of Wonders, 1666* describes the two major events of that year, the naval war against the Dutch, and the Fire of London. The title means 'wonderful year'.

209

Transitum to the Fire of London.

But ah! how unsincere are all our joys!
  Which sent from heaven, like lightning make no stay:
Their palling taste the journey's length destroys,
  Or grief sent post o'ertakes them on the way.

210

Swelled with our late successes on the foe,
  Which France and Holland wanted power to cross,
We urge an unseen Fate to lay us low,
  And feed their envious eyes with English loss.   840

211

Each element his dread command obeys,
  Who makes or ruins with a smile or frown;
Who as by one he did our nation raise,
  So now he with another pulls us down.*

212

Yet, London, Empress of the northern clime,
  By an high fate thou greatly didst expire:
ᶻGreat as the world's, which at the death of time
  Must fall, and rise a nobler frame by fire.

(z) Cum mare cum tellus correptaque regia coeli ardeat, etc. OVID.*

213

As when some dire usurper heaven provides
    To scourge his country with a lawless sway;   850
His birth perhaps some petty village hides,
    And sets his cradle out of Fortune's way:

214

Till fully ripe his swelling fate breaks out,
    And hurries him to mighty mischiefs on;
His prince surprised at first no ill could doubt,
    And wants the power to meet it when 'tis known.

215

Such was the rise of this prodigious fire,
    Which in mean buildings first obscurely bred,
From thence did soon to open streets aspire,
    And straight to palaces and temples spread.   860

216

The diligence of trades, and noiseful gain,
    And luxury, more late, asleep were laid:
All was the night's, and in her silent reign
    No sound the rest of nature did invade.

217

In this deep quiet, from what source unknown,
    Those seeds of fire their fatal birth disclose;
And first, few scattering sparks about were blown,
    Big with the flames that to our ruin rose.

218

Then in some close-pent room it crept along,
    And smouldering as it went, in silence fed;   870
Till th' infant monster, with devouring strong,
    Walked boldly upright with exalted head.

219

Now like some rich or mighty murderer
    Too great for prison, which he breaks with gold,
Who fresher for new mischiefs does appear,
    And dares the world to tax him with the old:

220

So scapes th' insulting fire his narrow jail,
　　And makes small outlets into open air;
There the fierce winds his tender force assail,
　　And beat him downward to his first repair.　　880

221

ᵃThe winds like crafty courtesans withheld
　　His flames from burning but to blow them more,
And every fresh attempt he is repelled,
　　With faint denials, weaker than before.

(a) Like crafty etc.: Haec arte tractabat cupidum virum, ut illius animum inopia accenderet.*

222

And now no longer letted of his prey
　　He leaps up at it with enraged desire,
O'erlooks the neighbours with a wide survey
　　And nods at every house his threatening fire.

223

The ghosts of traitors from the bridge descend*
　　With bold fanatic spectres to rejoice;*　　890
About the fire into a dance they bend,
　　And sing their sabbath notes with feeble voice.*

224

Our guardian angel saw them where he sate
　　Above the palace of our slumbering King;
He sighed, abandoning his charge to Fate,
　　And drooping, oft looked back upon the wing.

225

At length the crackling noise and dreadful blaze
　　Called up some waking lover to the sight,
And long it was ere he the rest could raise,
　　Whose heavy eyelids yet were full of night.　　900

226

The next to danger, hot pursued by Fate,
  Half–clothed, half–naked, hastily retire,
And frighted mothers strike their breasts too late
  For helpless infants left amidst the fire.

227

Their cries soon waken all the dwellers near:
  Now murmuring noises rise in every street;
The more remote run stumbling with their fear,
  And in the dark men jostle as they meet.

228

So weary bees in little cells repose,
  But if night–robbers lift the well–stored hive   910
An humming through their waxen city grows,
  And out upon each other's wings they drive.

229

Now streets grow thronged and busy as by day:
  Some run for buckets to the hallowed choir,
Some cut the pipes, and some the engines play,
  And some more bold mount ladders to the fire.

230

In vain: for from the east a Belgian wind
  His hostile breath through the dry rafters sent;
The flames impelled soon left their foes behind
  And forward with a wanton fury went.   920

231

A quay of fire ran all along the shore
  [b]And lightened all the river with the blaze;
The wakened tides began again to roar,
  And wondering fish in shining waters gaze.

(b) Sigaea igni freta lata relucent. VIRG*.

232

Old father Thames raised up his reverend head,
  But feared the fate of Simois would return;*
Deep in his ooze he sought his sedgy bed,
  And shrunk his waters back into his urn.

233

The fire, meantime, walks in a broader gross,
  To either hand his wings he opens wide:
He wades the streets, and straight he reaches 'cross
  And plays his longing flames on th' other side.

234

At first they warm, then scorch, and then they take;
  Now with long necks from side to side they feed:
At length grown strong their mother fire forsake,
  And a new colony of flames succeed.

235

To every nobler portion of the town
  The curling billows roll their restless tide;
In parties now they straggle up and down
  As armies unopposed for prey divide.

236

One mighty squadron, with a side wind sped,
  Through narrow lanes his cumbered fire does haste,
By powerful charms of gold and silver led
  The Lombard bankers and the Change to waste.

237

Another backward to the Tower would go,
  And slowly eats his way against the wind;
But the main body of the marching foe
  Against th' imperial palace is designed.

238

Now day appears, and with the day the King,
  Whose early care had robbed him of his rest;
Far off the cracks of falling houses ring,
  And shrieks of subjects pierce his tender breast.

930

940

950

239

Near as he draws, thick harbingers of smoke
　　With gloomy pillars cover all the place;
Whose little intervals of night are broke
　　By sparks that drive against his sacred face.

240

More than his guards his sorrows made him known,
　　And pious tears which down his cheeks did shower;
The wretched in his grief forgot their own,
　　So much the pity of a king has power.　　　　　960

241

He wept the flames of what he loved so well,
　　And what so well had merited his love:
For never prince in grace did more excel,
　　Or royal city more in duty strove.

242

Nor with an idle care did he behold:
　　Subjects may grieve, but monarchs must redress.
He cheers the fearful and commends the bold,
　　And makes despairers hope for good success.

243

Himself directs what first is to be done,
　　And orders all the succours which they bring:　　　970
The helpful and the good about him run
　　And form an army worthy such a King.

244

He sees the dire contagion spread so fast
　　That where it seizes all relief is vain;
And therefore must unwillingly lay waste
　　That country which would else the foe maintain.

245

The powder blows up all before the fire:
　　Th' amazèd flames stand gathered on a heap,
And from the precipice's brink retire,
　　Afraid to venture on so large a leap.　　　　　980

246

Thus fighting fires awhile themselves consume,
　　But straight, like Turks, forced on to win or die,
They first lay tender bridges of their fume
　　And o'er the breach in unctuous vapours fly.

247

Part stays for passage till a gust of wind
　　Ships o'er their forces in a shining sheet;
Part creeping under ground their journey blind,
　　And climbing from below their fellows meet.

248

Thus to some desert plain or old wood side
　　Dire night-hags come from far to dance their round,　990
And o'er broad rivers on their fiends they ride,
　　Or sweep in clouds above the blasted ground.

249

No help avails: for hydra-like the fire
　　Lifts up his hundred heads to aim his way;
And scarce the wealthy can one half retire
　　Before he rushes in to share the prey.

250

The rich grow suppliant, and the poor grow proud;
　　Those offer mighty gain, and these ask more:
So void of pity is th' ignoble crowd
　　When others' ruin may increase their store.　1000

251

As those who live by shores with joy behold
　　Some wealthy vessel split or stranded nigh,
And from the rocks leap down for shipwrecked gold,
　　And seek the tempest which the others fly:

252

So these but wait the owners' last despair,
　　And what's permitted to the flames invade;
Ev'n from their jaws they hungry morsels tear,
　　And on their backs the spoils of Vulcan lade.

253

The days were all in this lost labour spent,
 And when the weary King gave place to night   1010
His beams he to his royal brother lent,
 And so shone still in his reflective light.

254

Night came, but without darkness or repose,
 A dismal picture of the general doom,
Where souls distracted when the trumpet blows
 And half unready with their bodies come.

255

Those who have homes, when home they do repair
 To a last lodging call their wandering friends;
Their short, uneasy sleeps are broke with care,
 To look how near their own destruction tends.   1020

256

Those who have none sit round where once it was,
 And with full eyes each wonted room require,
Haunting the yet warm ashes of the place,
 As murdered men walk where they did expire.

257

Some stir up coals and watch the Vestal fire,*
 Others in vain from sight of ruin run,
And while through burning labyrinths they retire
 With loathing eyes repeat what they would shun.

258

The most in fields like herded beasts lie down,
 To dews obnoxious on the grassy floor;   1030
And while their babes in sleep their sorrows drown,
 Sad parents watch the remnants of their store.

259

While by the motion of the flames they guess
 What streets are burning now, and what are near;
An infant, waking, to the paps would press,
 And meets, instead of milk, a falling tear.

260

No thought can ease them but their sovereign's care,
    Whose praise th' afflicted as their comfort sing:
Even those whom want might drive to just despair
    Think life a blessing under such a King.   1040

261

Meantime he sadly suffers in their grief,
    Out-weeps an hermit, and out-prays a saint:
All the long night he studies their relief,
    How they may be supplied, and he may want.

262

King's Prayer.

'O God', said he, 'thou patron of my days,
    Guide of my youth in exile and distress!
Who me unfriended brought'st by wondrous ways
    The kingdom of my fathers to possess;

263

Be thou my judge, with what unwearied care
    I since have laboured for my people's good,   1050
To bind the bruises of a civil war
    And stop the issues of their wasting blood.

264

Thou who hast taught me to forgive the ill,
    And recompense as friends the good misled,
If mercy be a precept of thy will,
    Return that mercy on thy servant's head.

265

Or if my heedless youth has stepped astray,
    Too soon forgetful of thy gracious hand;
On me alone thy just displeasure lay,
    But take thy judgements from this mourning land.   1060

266

We all have sinned, and thou hast laid us low
  As humble earth from whence at first we came;
Like flying shades before the clouds we show,
  And shrink like parchment in consuming flame.

267

O let it be enough what thou hast done,
  When spotted deaths ran armed through every street*
With poisoned darts which not the good could shun,
  The speedy could out-fly, or valiant meet.

268

The living few, and frequent funerals then,
  Proclaimed thy wrath on this forsaken place;   1070
And now those few who are returned again
  Thy searching judgements to their dwellings trace.

269

O pass not, Lord, an absolute decree,
  Or bind thy sentence unconditional;
But in thy sentence our remorse foresee,
  And in that foresight this thy doom recall.

270

Thy threatenings, Lord, as thine, thou mayest revoke;
  But if immutable and fixed they stand,
Continue still thyself to give the stroke,
  And let not foreign foes oppress thy land.'   1080

271

Th' Eternal heard, and from the heavenly choir
  Chose out the cherub with the flaming sword;
And bad him swiftly drive th' approaching fire
  From where our naval magazines were stored.

272

The blessèd minister his wings displayed,
  And like a shooting star he cleft the night;
He charged the flames, and those that disobeyed
  He lashed to duty with his sword of light.

273

The fugitive flames, chastised, went forth to prey
    On pious structures by our fathers reared,   1090
By which to heaven they did affect the way
    Ere faith in churchmen without works was heard.

274

The wanting orphans saw with watery eyes
    Their founder's charity in dust laid low,
And sent to God their ever-answered cries,
    For he protects the poor who made them so.

275

Nor could thy fabric, Paul's, defend thee long,
    Though thou wert sacred to thy maker's praise;
Though made immortal by a poet's song,
    And poets' songs the Theban walls could raise.*   1100

276

The daring flames peeped in, and saw from far
    The awful beauties of the sacred choir;
But since it was profaned by civil war
    Heaven thought it fit to have it purged by fire.

277

Now down the narrow streets it swiftly came,
    And widely opening did on both sides prey:
This benefit we sadly owe the flame,
    If only ruin must enlarge our way.

278

And now four days the sun had seen our woes,
    Four nights the moon beheld th' incessant fire;   1110
It seemed as if the stars more sickly rose,
    And farther from the feverish north retire.

279

In th' empyrean heaven (the blessed abode)
    The thrones and the dominions prostrate lie,*
Not daring to behold their angry God,
    And an hushed silence damps the tuneful sky.

280

At length th' Almighty cast a pitying eye,
  And mercy softly touched his melting breast;
He saw the town's one half in rubbish lie,
  And eager flames give on to storm the rest.   1120

281

An hollow crystal pyramid he takes,
  In firmamental waters dipped above;
Of it a broad extinguisher he makes,
  And hoods the flames that to their quarry strove.

282

The vanquished fires withdraw from every place,
  Or full with feeding sink into a sleep;
Each household genius shows again his face,
  And from the hearths the little Lares creep.

283

Our King this more-than-natural change beholds;
  With sober joy his heart and eyes abound: 1130
To the All-good his lifted hands he folds,
  And thanks him low on his redeemèd ground.

284

As when sharp frosts had long constrained the earth
  A kindly thaw unlocks it with mild rain;
And first the tender blade peeps up to birth,
  And straight the green fields laugh with promised grain:*

285

By such degrees the spreading gladness grew
  In every heart which fear had froze before;
The standing streets with so much joy they view
  That with less grief the perished they deplore.   1140

286

The father of the people opened wide
  His stores, and all the poor with plenty fed:
Thus God's Anointed God's own place supplied,
  And filled the empty with his daily bread.

287

This royal bounty brought its own reward,
  And in their minds so deep did print the sense,
That if their ruins sadly they regard,
  'Tis but with fear the sight might drive him thence.

288

City's request to the King not to leave them.

But so may he live long that town to sway
  Which by his auspice they will nobler make,
As he will hatch their ashes by his stay,
  And not their humble ruins now forsake.

1150

289

They have not lost their loyalty by fire,
  Nor is their courage or their wealth so low
That from his wars they poorly would retire,
  Or beg the pity of a vanquished foe.

290

Not with more constancy the Jews of old
  By Cyrus from rewarded exile sent,
Their royal city did in dust behold
  Or with more vigour to rebuild it went.*

1160

291

The utmost malice of their stars is past,
  And two dire comets which have scourged the town
In their own plague and fire have breathed their last,
  Or dimly in their sinking sockets frown.

292

Now frequent trines the happier lights among,
  And high-raised Jove from his dark prison freed*
(Those weights took off that on his planet hung)
  Will gloriously the new-laid work succeed.

293

Methinks already from this chymic flame
  I see a city of more precious mould: 1170
Rich as the town which gives the ᶜIndies name,
  With silver paved, and all divine with gold.

(c) *Mexico.*

294

Already, labouring with a mighty fate,
  She shakes the rubbish from her mounting brow,
And seems to have renewed her charter's date
  Which heaven will to the death of time allow.

295

More great than human, now, and more ᵈAugust,
  New deified she from her fires does rise:
Her widening streets on new foundations trust,
  And opening, into larger parts she flies.   1180

(d) *Augusta, the old name of London.*

296

Before, she like some shepherdess did show
  Who sate to bathe her by a river's side;
Not answering to her fame, but rude and low,
  Nor taught the beauteous arts of modern pride.

297

Now like a maiden queen she will behold
  From her high turrets hourly suitors come:
The east with incense and the west with gold
  Will stand like suppliants to receive her doom.

298

The silver Thames, her own domestic flood,
  Shall bear her vessels like a sweeping train,   1190
And often wind (as of his mistress proud)
  With longing eyes to meet her face again.

299

The wealthy Tagus and the wealthier Rhine
   The glory of their towns no more shall boast;
And Seine, that would with Belgian rivers join,
   Shall find her lustre stained and traffic lost.

300

The venturous merchant who designed more far,
   And touches on our hospitable shore,
Charmed with the splendour of this northern star
   Shall here unlade him and depart no more.   1200

301

Our powerful navy shall no longer meet
   The wealth of France or Holland to invade:
The beauty of this town, without a fleet,
   From all the world shall vindicate her trade.

302

And while this famed emporium we prepare,
   The British ocean shall such triumphs boast
That those who now disdain our trade to share
   Shall rob like pirates on our wealthy coast.

303

Already we have conquered half the war,
   And the less dangerous part is left behind: 1210
Our trouble now is but to make them dare,
   And not so great to vanquish as to find.

304

Thus to the eastern wealth through storms we go,
   But now, the Cape once doubled, fear no more:
A constant trade-wind will securely blow,
   And gently lay us on the spicy shore.

23 *A Country Life*

KATHERINE PHILIPS

Probably written 1650, published 1664. Philips had recently married, and left London for west Wales.

How sacred, and how innocent
　　A country life appears,
How free from tumult, discontent,
　　From flattery and fears.
That was the first and happiest life,
　　When man enjoyed himself;
Till pride exchangèd peace for strife,
　　And happiness for pelf.
'Twas here the poets were inspired,
　　And sang their mysteries,　　　　　　　　　10
And while the listening world admired,
　　Men's minds did civilize.
That golden age did entertain
　　No passion but of love;
The thoughts of ruling or of gain
　　Did ne'er their fancies move.
None then did envy neighbour's wealth,
　　Nor plot to wrong his bed;
Happy in friendship and in health,
　　On roots, not beasts, they fed.　　　　　　　20
They knew no law nor physic then,
　　Nature was all their wit;
And if there yet remain to man
　　Content, sure this is it.
What blessing doth this world afford,
　　To tempt or bribe desire?
Her courtship is all fire and sword:
　　Who would not then retire?
Then welcome, dearest solitude,
　　My great felicity;　　　　　　　　　　　　30
Though some are pleased to call thee rude,
　　Thou art not so, but we.

Such as do covet only rest,
    A cottage will suffice:
It is not brave to be possessed
    Of earth, but to despise.
Opinion is the rate of things,
    From hence our peace doth flow;
I have a better fate than kings
    Because I think it so.   40
When all the stormy world doth roar,
    How unconcerned am I!
I cannot fear to tumble lower
    That never would be high.
Secure in these unenvied walls,
    I think not on the state,
And pity no man's case that falls
    From his ambition's height.
Silence and innocence are safe:
    A heart that's nobly true   50
At all these little arts can laugh
    That do the world subdue.
While others revel it in state,
    Here I'll contented sit.
And think I have as good a fate
    As wealth or pomp admit.
Let some in courtship take delight,
    And to th' Exchange resort;*
There revel out a winter's night,
    Not making love, but sport.   60
These never knew a noble flame,
    'Tis lust, scorn, or design:
While vanity plays all their game,
    Let peace and honour mine.
When the inviting spring appears,
    To Hyde Park let them go,
And hasting thence be full of fears
    To lose Spring Garden show.*
Let others (nobler) seek to gain
    In knowledge happy fate,   70
And others busy them in vain

To study ways of state.
But I, resolvèd from within,
    Confirmèd from without,
In privacy intend to spin
    My future minutes out.
I from this hermitage of mine
    Do banish all wild toys,
And nothing that is not divine
    Shall dare to tempt my joys.   80
There are below but two things good:
    Friendship and honesty,
And only these of all I would
    Ask for felicity.
In this retired integrity,
    Free from both war and noise,
I live not by necessity,
    But wholly by my choice.

24   *From Horace, 'Epode II'*

JOHN DRYDEN

Published 1685 in the Dryden–Tonson miscellany *Sylvae*. Horace's *Epode II* was one of the most popular poems in praise of country life, and had been translated by Ben Jonson (1640) and Abraham Cowley (in his *Essays*, 1668).

How happy in his low degree,
How rich in humble poverty is he
    Who leads a quiet country life!
    Discharged of business, void of strife,
And from the griping scrivener free.
(Thus ere the seeds of vice were sown,
    Lived men in better ages born,
Who ploughed with oxen of their own
    Their small paternal field of corn.)
Nor trumpets summon him to war,   10
    Nor drums disturb his morning sleep,

Nor knows he merchants' gainful care,
  Nor fears the dangers of the deep.
The clamours of contentious law,
  And court and state he wisely shuns,
Nor bribed with hopes nor dared with awe
  To servile salutations runs:
But either to the clasping vine
  Does the supporting poplar wed,
Or with his pruning hook disjoin   20
  Unbearing branches from their head,
  And grafts more happy in their stead;
Or climbing to a hilly steep
  He views his herds in vales afar,
Or shears his overburdened sheep;
  Or mead for cooling drink prepares
  Of virgin honey in the jars.*
Or in the now declining year,
  When bounteous Autumn rears his head,
He joys to pull the ripened pear,   30
  And clustering grapes with purple spread.
The fairest of his fruit he serves,
  Priapus, thy rewards;*
Sylvanus too his part deserves,*
  Whose care the fences guards.
Sometimes beneath an ancient oak,
  Or on the matted grass he lies;
No god of sleep he need invoke,
  The stream that o'er the pebbles flies
  With gentle slumber crowns his eyes.   40
The wind that whistles through the sprays
  Maintains the consort of the song,
And hidden birds with native lays
  The golden sleep prolong.
But when the blast of winter blows,
  And hoary frost inverts the year,
Into the naked woods he goes,
  And seeks the tusky boar to rear
  With well-mouthed hounds and pointed spear;
Or spreads his subtle nets from sight,   50

With twinkling glasses to betray
The larks that in the meshes light,
  Or makes the fearful hare his prey.
Amidst his harmless easy joys
  No anxious care invades his health,
Nor love his peace of mind destroys,
  Nor wicked avarice of wealth.
But if a chaste and pleasing wife,
To ease the business of his life,
  Divides with him his household care,   60
  Such as the Sabine matrons were,
Such as the swift Apulian's bride,*
  Sunburnt and swarthy though she be,
Will fire for winter nights provide,
  And without noise will oversee
  His children and his family,
And order all things till he come
Sweaty and overlaboured home;
If she in pens his flocks will fold,
  And then produce her dairy store,   70
With wine to drive away the cold,
  And unbought dainties of the poor;
Not oysters of the Lucrine lake*
  My sober appetite would wish,
  Nor turbot, or the foreign fish
That rolling tempests overtake,
  And hither waft the costly dish;
Not heathpout, or the rarer bird
  Which Phasis or Ionia yields,*
More pleasing morsels would afford   80
  Than the fat olives of my fields,
Than shards or mallows for the pot,
  That keep the loosened body sound;
Or than the lamb that falls by lot
  To the just guardian of my ground.*
Amidst these feasts of happy swains,
  The jolly shepherd smiles to see
His flock returning from the plains;
  The farmer is as pleased as he

To view his oxen, sweating smoke,   90
Bear on their necks the loosened yoke;
To look upon his menial crew
    That sit around his cheerful hearth,
And bodies spent in toil renew
    With wholesome food and country mirth.
This Morecraft said within himself,*
    Resolved to leave the wicked town
    And live retired upon his own;
        He called his money in:
But the prevailing love of pelf   100
Soon split him on the former shelf,
        And put it out again.

25   *The Country Mouse*

                    ABRAHAM COWLEY

First printed in Cowley's *Verses Written upon Several Occasions* (1663),
then incorporated in his essay 'Of Agriculture' in his posthumous *Works*
(1668), followed here, which also includes translations from Virgil's
Georgic II, and Horace's *Epode II* (cf. **28** and **24**). It imitates part of
Horace's *Serm.* II. vi.

At the large foot of a fair hollow tree,
Close to ploughed ground, seated commodiously,
His ancient and hereditary house,
There dwelt a good, substantial country mouse;
Frugal and grave, and careful of the main,
Yet one who once did nobly entertain
A city mouse, well-coated, sleek and gay,
A mouse of high degree, which lost his way,
Wantonly walking forth to take the air,
And arrived early, and belighted, there   10
For a day's lodging. The good hearty host
(The ancient plenty of his hall to boast)
Did all the stores produce that might excite,
With various tastes, the courtier's appetite:

Fitches and beans, peason, and oats and wheat,
And a large chestnut, the delicious meat
Which Jove himself, were he a mouse, would eat.
And for a *hautgoût* there was mixed with these
The sward of bacon and the coat of cheese:
The precious relics, which at harvest he   20
Had gathered from the reapers' luxury.
'Freely,' said he, 'fall on, and never spare!
The bounteous gods will for tomorrow care!'
And thus at ease on beds of straw they lay,
And to their genius sacrificed the day.

    Yet the nice guest's epicurean mind
(Though breeding made him civil seem, and kind)
Despised this country feast, and still his thought
Upon the cakes and pies of London wrought.
'Your bounty and civility,' said he,   30
'Which I'm surprised in these rude parts to see,
Shows that the gods have given you a mind
Too noble for the fate which here you find.
Why should a soul so virtuous and so great
Lose itself thus in an obscure retreat?
Let savage beasts lodge in a country den;
You should see towns, and manners know, and men,
And taste the gen'rous luxury of the court,
Where all the mice of quality resort;
Where thousand beauteous shes about you move,   40
And by high fare are pliant made to love.
We all ere long must render up our breath;
No cave or hole can shelter us from death.
Since life is so uncertain, and so short,
Let's spend it all in feasting and in sport.
Come, worthy sir, come with me, and partake
All the great things that mortals happy make!'
    Alas, what virtue hath sufficient arms
T' oppose bright honour and soft pleasure's charms?
What wisdom can their magic force repel?   50
It draws the rev'rend hermit from his cell.
It was the time when witty poets tell
'That Phoebus into Thetis' bosom fell;*

She blushed at first, and then put out the light,
And drew the modest curtains of the night.'
Plainly the truth to tell, the sun was set,
When to the town our wearied travellers get.
To a lord's house, as lordly as can be,
Made for the use of pride and luxury,
They come; the gentle courtier at the door   60
Stops, and will hardly enter in before:
'But 'tis, sir, your command, and, being so,
I'm sworn t' obedience'; and so in they go.

    Behind a hanging in a spacious room
(The richest work of Mortlake's noble loom)*
They wait a while, their wearied limbs to rest,
Till silence should invite them to their feast;
'About the hour that Cynthia's silver light*
Had touched the pale meridies of the night.'

    At last, the various supper being done,   70
It happened that the company was gone
Into a room remote, servants and all,
To please their nobles' fancies with a ball.
Our host leads forth his stranger, and does find
All fitted to the bounties of his mind.
Still on the table half-filled dishes stood,
And with delicious bits the floor was strewed.
The courteous mouse presents him with the best,
And both with fat varieties are blessed.
Th' industrious peasant everywhere does range,   80
And thanks the gods for his life's happy change.

    Lo, in the midst of a well-freighted pie
They both at last glutted and wanton lie!
When see the sad reverse of prosp'rous fate,
And what fierce storms on mortal glories wait!
With hideous noise down the rude servants come;
Six dogs before run barking into th' room:
The wretched gluttons fly with wild affright,
And hate the fullness which retards their flight.
Our trembling peasant wishes now in vain   90
That rocks and mountains covered him again.
Oh, how the change of his poor life he cursed:

'This, of all lives,' said he, 'is sure the worst!
Give me again, ye gods, my cave and wood;
With peace, let tares and acorns be my food!'

26　　　　　　　　*The Garden*

ANDREW MARVELL

Probably written *c*.1668; published 1681 in his posthumous *Miscellaneous Poems*.

I

How vainly men themselves amaze
To win the palm, the oak, or bays;*
And their uncessant labours see
Crowned from some single herb or tree,
Whose short and narrow vergèd shade
Does prudently their toils upbraid,
While all flowers and all trees do close
To weave the garlands of repose.

2

Fair Quiet, have I found thee here,
And Innocence, thy sister dear:　　　　　　10
Mistaken long, I sought you then
In busy companies of men.
Your sacred plants, if here below,*
Only among the plants will grow.
Society is all but rude,
To this delicious solitude.*

3

No white nor red was ever seen
So am'rous as this lovely green.
Fond lovers, cruel as their flame,
Cut in these trees their mistress' name.　　　　　20
Little, alas, they know or heed
How far these beauties hers exceed!
Fair trees, wheres'e'er your barks I wound,
No name shall but your own be found.

4

When we have run our passion's heat,
Love hither makes his best retreat.
The gods that mortal beauty chase
Still in a tree did end their race:
Apollo hunted Daphne so,
Only that she might laurel grow;   30
And Pan did after Syrinx speed,
Not as a nymph, but for a reed.*

5

What wondrous life in this I lead!*
Ripe apples drop about my head;
The luscious clusters of the vine
Upon my mouth do crush their wine;
The nectarene and curious peach
Into my hands themselves do reach;
Stumbling on melons as I pass,
Ensnared with flowers, I fall on grass.   40

6

Meanwhile the mind from pleasure less*
Withdraws into its happiness:
The mind, that ocean where each kind
Does straight its own resemblance find;*
Yet it creates, transcending these,
Far other worlds and other seas,
Annihilating all that's made
To a green thought in a green shade.

7

Here at the fountain's sliding foot,
Or at some fruit-tree's mossy root,   50
Casting the body's vest aside,
My soul into the boughs does glide:*
There like a bird it sits and sings,
Then whets and combs its silver wings;
And till prepared for longer flight,
Waves in its plumes the various light.

8

Such was that happy garden-state
While man there walked without a mate:
After a place so pure and sweet,
What other help could yet be meet?   60
But 'twas beyond a mortal's share
To wander solitary there:
Two paradises 'twere in one
To live in paradise alone.

9

How well the skilful gardener drew
Of flowers and herbs this dial new,
Where from above the milder sun
Does through a fragrant zodiac run;
And as it works, th' industrious bee
Computes its time as well as we.   70
How could such sweet and wholesome hours
Be reckoned, but with herbs and flowers?

27   *In Imitation of Horace, Ode IX, Lib. I*

WILLIAM CONGREVE

Published 1693 in the Dryden–Tonson miscellany *Examen Poeticum*.
Dryden had also published an imitation of this ode in *Sylvae* (1685).

Vides ut alta, etc.

1

Bless me, 'tis cold! How chill the air!
How naked does the world appear!
But see, big with the offspring of the north,
    The teeming clouds bring forth:
A shower of soft and fleecy rain
Falls to new-clothe the earth again.
Behold the mountain tops around,
As if with fur of ermines crowned:
    And lo! how by degrees

The universal mantle hides the trees 10
   In hoary flakes, which downward fly
As if it were the autumn of the sky.
Trembling, the groves sustain the weight, and bow
   Like agèd limbs, which feebly go
Beneath a venerable head of snow.

II

Diffusive cold does the whole earth invade,
Like a disease, through all its veins 'tis spread,
And each late living stream is numbed and dead.
Let's melt the frozen hours, make warm the air;
Let cheerful fires Sol's feeble beams repair; 20
   Fill the large bowl with sparkling wine;
   Let's drink till our own faces shine,
     Till we like suns appear,
    To light and warm the hemisphere.
Wine can dispense to all both light and heat,
   They are with wine incorporate:
That powerful juice with which no cold dares mix,
Which still is fluid, and no frost can fix;
   Let that but in abundance flow,
And let it storm and thunder, hail and snow: 30
   'Tis heaven's concern; and let it be
   The care of heaven still, for me:
These winds, which rend the oaks and plough the seas,
    Great Jove can, if he please,
   With one commanding nod appease.

III

   Seek not to know tomorrow's doom:
   That is not ours, which is to come.
   The present moment's all our store,
    The next, should heaven allow,*
    Than this will be no more: 40
So all our life is but one instant now.
    Look on each day you've passed
   To be a mighty treasure won;
   And lay each moment out in haste:
    We're sure to live too fast,

And cannot live too soon.
Youth does a thousand pleasures bring,
Which from decrepit age will fly;
    Sweets that wanton i' th' bosom of the spring*
    In winter's cold embraces die.   50

IV

Now Love, that everlasting boy, invites*
To revel while you may in soft delights:
    Now the kind nymph yields all her charms,
    Nor yields in vain to youthful arms.
Slowly she promises at night to meet,
But eagerly prevents the hour with swifter feet.
    To gloomy groves and òbscure shades she flies,
    There veils the bright confession of her eyes.
        Unwillingly she stays,
        Would more unwillingly depart,   60
          And in soft sighs conveys
          The whispers of her heart.
    Still she invites and still denies,
    And vows she'll leave you if y' are rude;
    Then from her ravisher she flies,
        But flies to be pursued.
If from his sight she does herself convey,
With a feigned laugh she will herself betray,
And cunningly instruct him in the way.

28   From *The Georgics*, Book II

JOHN DRYDEN

Published 1697 in Dryden's complete translation of *The Works of Virgil*.

O happy, if he knew his happy state,
The swain, who, free from business and debate,   640
Receives his easy food from nature's hand,
And just returns of cultivated land!
No palace with a lofty gate he wants,

T' admit the tides of early visitants,
With eager eyes devouring as they pass
The breathing figures of Corinthian brass.
No statues threaten from high pedestals;
No Persian arras hides his homely walls
With antique vests, which through their shady fold
Betray the streaks of ill-dissembled gold: 650
He boasts no wool, whose native white is dyed
With purple poison of Assyrian pride;
No costly drugs of Araby defile
With foreign scents the sweetness of his oil:
But easy quiet, a secure retreat,
A harmless life that knows not how to cheat,
With home-bred plenty the rich owner bless,
And rural pleasures crown his happiness.
Unvexed with quarrels, undisturbed with noise,
The country king his peaceful realm enjoys—   660
Cool grots, and living lakes, the flowery pride
Of meads, and streams that through the valley glide,
And shady groves that easy sleep invite,
And after toilsome days, a soft repose at night.
Wild beasts of nature in his woods abound;
And youth, of labour patient, plough the ground,
Inured to hardship, and to homely fare.
Nor venerable age is wanting there,
In great examples to the youthful train;
Nor are the gods adored with rites profane.   670
From hence Astræa took her flight, and here*
The prints of her departing steps appear.

  Ye sacred Muses! with whose beauty fired,
My soul is ravished, and my brain inspired;
Whose priest I am, whose holy fillets wear,
Would you your poet's first petition hear:
Give me the ways of wandering stars to know,
The depths of heaven above, and earth below;
Teach me the various labours of the moon,
And whence proceed th' eclipses of the sun;   680
Why flowing tides prevail upon the main,
And in what dark recess they shrink again;

What shakes the solid earth; what cause delays
The summer nights, and shortens winter days.
But if my heavy blood restrain the flight⎫
Of my free soul, aspiring to the height   ⎬
Of nature, and unclouded fields of light,⎭
My next desire is, void of care and strife,
To lead a soft, secure, inglorious life:
A country cottage near a crystal flood,   690
A winding valley, and a lofty wood.
Some god conduct me to the sacred shades,
Where Bacchanals are sung by Spartan maids,
Or lift me high to Hemus' hilly crown,
Or in the plains of Tempe lay me down,
Or lead me to some solitary place,
And cover my retreat from human race.

   Happy the man, who, studying nature's laws,
Through known effects can trace the secret cause;
His mind possessing in a quiet state,   700
Fearless of Fortune, and resigned to Fate.
And happy too is he who decks the bowers
Of sylvans, and adores the rural powers;
Whose mind, unmoved, the bribes of courts can see,
Their glittering baits, and purple slavery;
Nor hopes the people's praise, nor fears their frown,⎫
Nor, when contending kindred tear the crown,*   ⎬
Will set up one, or pull another down.⎭

   Without concern he hears, but hears from far,
Of tumults, and descents, and distant war;   710
Nor with a superstitious fear is awed,
For what befalls at home, or what abroad.
Nor envies he the rich their heapy store,
Nor his own peace disturbs with pity for the poor.
He feeds on fruits which of their own accord
The willing ground and laden trees afford.
From his loved home no lucre him can draw;⎫
The senate's mad decrees he never saw;   ⎬
Nor heard, at bawling bars, corrupted law.⎭
Some to the seas, and some to camps resort,   720
And some with impudence invade the court:

In foreign countries others seek renown;
With wars and taxes others waste their own,
And houses burn, and household gods deface,
To drink in bowls which glittering gems enchase,
To loll on couches, rich with citron steads,
And lay their guilty limbs in Tyrian beds.
This wretch in earth entombs his golden ore,
Hovering and brooding on his buried store.
Some patriot fools to pop'lar praise aspire   730
By public speeches, which worse fools admire;
While from both benches, with redoubled sounds,
Th' applause of lords and commoners abounds.
Some through ambition, or through thirst of gold,
Have slain their brothers, or their country sold;
And, leaving their sweet homes, in exile run
To lands that lie beneath another sun.

   The peasant, innocent of all these ills, ⎫
With crookèd ploughs the fertile fallows tills, ⎬
And the round year with daily labour fills. ⎭
                          740
From hence the country markets are supplied:
Enough remains for household charge beside,
His wife and tender children to sustain,
And gratefully to feed his dumb deserving train.
Nor cease his labours till the yellow field
A full return of bearded harvest yield:
A crop so plenteous as the land to load,
O'ercome the crowded barns, and lodge on ricks abroad.
Thus every several season is employed,
Some spent in toil, and some in ease enjoyed.   750
The yeaning ewes prevent the springing year;
The laded boughs their fruits in autumn bear:
'Tis then the vine her liquid harvest yields,
Baked in the sunshine of ascending fields.
The winter comes; and then the falling mast
For greedy swine provides a full repast:
Then olives, ground in mills, their fatness boast,
And winter fruits are mellowed by the frost.
His cares are eased with intervals of bliss;
His little children, climbing for a kiss,   760

Welcome their father's late return at night;
His faithful bed is crowned with chaste delight.
His kine with swelling udders ready stand,
And, lowing for the pail, invite the milker's hand.
His wanton kids, with budding horns prepared,
Fight harmless battles in his homely yard:
Himself in rustic pomp on holidays ⎤
To rural powers a just oblation pays, ⎬
And on the green his careless limbs displays. ⎦
The hearth is in the midst; the herdsmen round   770
The cheerful fire provoke his health in goblets crowned.
He calls on Bacchus, and propounds the prize; ⎤
The groom his fellow-groom at butts defies, ⎬
And bends his bow, and levels with his eyes; ⎦
Or stripped for wrestling, smears his limbs with oil,
And watches with a trip his foe to foil.
Such was the life the frugal Sabines led;
So Remus and his brother-god were bred,
From whom th' austere Etrurian virtue rose;*
And this rude life our homely fathers chose.   780
Old Rome from such a race derived her birth
(The seat of empire and the conquered earth),
Which now on seven high hills triumphant reigns,
And in that compass all the world contains,
Ere Saturn's rebel son usurped the skies,*
When beasts were only slain for sacrifice,*
While peaceful Crete enjoyed her ancient lord,
Ere sounding hammers forged th' inhuman sword,
Ere hollow drums were beat, before the breath
Of brazen trumpets rung the peals of death,   790
The good old god his hunger did assuage
With roots and herbs, and gave the golden age.
But over-laboured with so long a course,
'Tis time to set at ease the smoking horse.

29 *To My Honoured Kinsman John Driden of Chesterton*

JOHN DRYDEN

Published in *Fables Ancient and Modern* (1700). John Driden (1635–1708) was the poet's cousin, a country gentleman and MP for Huntingdon. Dryden said that 'In the description which I have made of a Parliament Man, I think I have not onely drawn the features of my worthy Kinsman, but have also given my Own opinion, of what an Englishman in Parliament oughto [*sic*] be; & deliver it as a Memorial of my own Principles to all Posterity' (*Letters*, p. 120).

How blest is he, who leads a country life,
Unvexed with anxious cares, and void of strife!
Who studying peace, and shunning civil rage,
Enjoyed his youth, and now enjoys his age:
All who deserve his love, he makes his own,
And to be loved himself, needs only to be known.
   Just, good, and wise, contending neighbours come ⎫
From your award to wait their final doom;   ⎬
And, foes before, return in friendship home.   ⎭
Without their cost, you terminate the cause,   10
And save th' expense of long litigious laws,
Where suits are traversed, and so little won,
That he who conquers is but last undone.
Such are not your decrees; but so designed,   ⎫
The sanction leaves a lasting peace behind,   ⎬
Like your own soul, serene; a pattern of your mind. ⎭
   Promoting concord, and composing strife,
Lord of yourself, uncumbered with a wife;
Where, for a year, a month, perhaps a night,
Long penitence succeeds a short delight: 20
Minds are so hardly matched, that e'en the first,
Though paired by heaven, in paradise were cursed.
For man and woman, though in one they grow,
Yet, first or last, return again to two.
He to God's image, she to his was made;
So, farther from the fount, the stream at random strayed.
   How could he stand, when put to double pain,

He must a weaker than himself sustain!
Each might have stood, perhaps, but each alone;
Two wrestlers help to pull each other down.   30

   Not that my verse would blemish all the fair; ⎫
But yet, if some be bad, 'tis wisdom to beware; ⎬
And better shun the bait, than struggle in the snare. ⎭
Thus have you shunned, and shun the married state,
Trusting as little as you can to fate.

   No porter guards the passage of your door
T' admit the wealthy, and exclude the poor:
For God, who gave the riches, gave the heart
To sanctify the whole, by giving part:
Heaven, who foresaw the will, the means has wrought,   40
And to the second son a blessing brought:
The first-begotten had his father's share;
But you, like Jacob, are Rebecca's heir.*

   So may your stores and fruitful fields increase;
And ever be you blest, who live to bless.
As Ceres sowed, where'er her chariot flew;*
As heaven in deserts rained the bread of dew,
So free to many, to relations most,
You feed with manna your own Israel host.*

   With crowds attended of your ancient race,   50
You seek the champian sports, or sylvan chase:
With well-breathed beagles you surround the wood,
E'en then industrious of the common good:
And often have you brought the wily fox
To suffer for the firstlings of the flocks;
Chased e'en amid the folds, and made to bleed,
Like felons, where they did the murderous deed.
This fiery game your active youth maintained,
Not yet by years extinguished, though restrained;
You season still with sports your serious hours,   60
For age but tastes of pleasures, youth devours.
The hare in pastures or in plains is found,
Emblem of human life, who runs the round,
And after all his wandering ways are done, ⎫
His circle fills, and ends where he begun, ⎬
Just as the setting meets the rising sun. ⎭

Thus princes ease their cares; but happier he
Who seeks not pleasure through necessity,
Than such as once on slippery thrones were placed,
And, chasing, sigh to think themselves are chased.   70

So lived our sires, ere doctors learned to kill,
And multiplied with theirs the weekly bill:
The first physicians by debauch were made:
Excess began, and sloth sustains the trade
Pity the generous kind their cares bestow
To search forbidden truths (a sin to know)*
To which, if human science could attain,
The doom of death, pronounced by God, were vain.
In vain the leech would interpose delay,
Fate fastens first, and vindicates the prey.   80
What help from art's endeavours can we have?
Gibbons but guesses, nor is sure to save:
But Maurus sweeps whole parishes, and peoples every grave.
And no more mercy to mankind will use,
Than when he robbed and murdered Maro's Muse.
Wouldst thou be soon dispatched, and perish whole?
Trust Maurus with thy life, and Milbourne with thy soul.*

By chase our long-lived fathers earned their food;
Toil strung the nerves, and purified the blood:
But we, their sons, a pampered race of men,   90
Are dwindled down to threescore years and ten.
Better to hunt in fields, for health unbought,
Than fee the doctor for a nauseous draught.
The wise for cure on exercise depend;
God never made his work for man to mend.

The tree of knowledge, once in Eden placed,
Was easy found, but was forbid the taste;
O, had our grandsire walked without his wife,
He first had sought the better plant of life!
Now both are lost: yet wandering in the dark,   100
Physicians for the tree have found the bark.
They, labouring for relief of human kind,
With sharpened sight some remedies may find;
Th' apothecary-train is wholly blind.
From files a random recipe they take,

And many deaths of one prescription make.
Garth, generous as his Muse, prescribes and gives;*
The shopman sells, and by destruction lives:
Ungrateful tribe! who, like the viper's brood,
From medicine issuing, suck their mother's blood!   110
Let these obey; and let the learn'd prescribe,
That men may die without a double bribe;
Let them but under their superiors kill,
When doctors first have signed the bloody bill:
He scapes the best who, nature to repair,
Draws physic from the fields, in draughts of vital air.

    You hoard not health for your own private use,
But on the public spend the rich prodùce;
When, often urged, unwilling to be great,
Your country calls you from your loved retreat,   120
And sends to senates, charged with common care,
Which none more shuns, and none can better bear.
Where could they find another formed so fit
To poise with solid sense a sprightly wit?
Were these both wanting (as they both abound)
Where could so firm integrity be found?

    Well-born and wealthy, wanting no support,
You steer betwixt the country and the court;
Nor gratify whate'er the great desire,
Nor grudging give what public needs require.   130
Part must be left, a fund when foes invade,
And part employed to roll the watery trade;
E'en Canaan's happy land, when worn with toil,
Required a sabbath-year to mend the meagre soil.

    Good senators (and such are you) so give
That kings may be supplied, the people thrive.
And he, when want requires, is truly wise
Who slights not foreign aids, nor over-buys,
But on our native strength in time of need relies.
Münster was bought, we boast not the success,*   140
Who fights for gain for greater makes his peace.

    Our foes, compelled by need, have peace embraced;*
The peace both parties want is like to last;
Which if secure, securely we may trade;

Or not secure, should never have been made.
Safe in ourselves, while on ourselves we stand,
The sea is ours, and that defends the land.
Be then the naval stores the nation's care,
New ships to build, and battered to repair.

Observe the war, in every annual course; 150
What has been done, was done with British force:
Namur subdued is England's palm alone,*
The rest besieged, but we constrained the town:
We saw th' event that followed our success:
France, though pretending arms, pursued the peace,
Obliged by one sole treaty to restore
What twenty years of war had won before.
Enough for Europe has our Albion fought:
Let us enjoy the peace our blood has bought.
When once the Persian king was put to flight, 160
The weary Macedons refused to fight:
Themselves their own mortality confessed,
And left the son of Jove to quarrel for the rest.*

Ev'n victors are by victories undone;
Thus Hannibal, with foreign laurels won,
To Carthage was recalled, too late to keep his own.*
While sore of battle, while our wounds are green,
Why should we tempt the doubtful die again?
In wars renewed uncertain of success,
Sure of a share as umpires of the peace. 170

A patriot both the king and country serves,
Prerogative, and privilege preserves:
Of each our laws the certain limit show;
One must not ebb, nor t'other overflow:
Betwixt the prince and parliament we stand,
The barriers of the state on either hand:
May neither overflow, for then they drown the land.
When both are full, they feed our blest abode,
Like those that watered once the paradise of God.

Some overpoise of sway by turns they share; 180
In peace the people, and the prince in war:
Consuls of moderate power in calms were made;
When the Gauls came, one sole dictator swayed.

Patriots in peace assert the people's right,
With noble stubbornness resisting might;
No lawless mandates from the court receive,
Nor lend by force, but in a body give.
Such was your generous grandsire; free to grant*
In parliaments that weighed their prince's want:
But so tenacious of the common cause,　　　　　　190
As not to lend the king against his laws;
And in a loathsome dungeon doomed to lie, ⎤
In bonds retained his birthright liberty, ⎬
And shamed oppression, till it set him free. ⎦

O true descendant of a patriot line,
Who, while thou shar'st their lustre, lend'st them thine,
Vouchsafe this picture of thy soul to see;
'Tis so far good as it resembles thee:
The beauties to th' original I owe,
Which when I miss, my own defects I show.　　　　200
Nor think the kindred Muses thy disgrace;
A poet is not born in every race.
Two of a house few ages can afford,
One to perform, another to record.
Praiseworthy actions are by thee embraced,
And 'tis my praise to make thy praises last.
For ev'n when death dissolves our human frame, ⎤
The soul returns to heaven, from whence it came, ⎬
Earth keeps the body, verse preserves the fame. ⎦

LITERATURE AND THEATRE

30   From *Paradise Lost*, Book III

JOHN MILTON

In this passage, the blind Milton prays that heavenly light will illuminate
him and inspire his poetry, as he turns from describing the fallen angels in
Books I–II to giving an account of God and heaven in Book III. Milton
imagines heavenly light in two ways, (i) as the first of God's creations
('offspring of heaven first-born', l. 1); (ii) as an aspect of God himself, and
so, like him, uncreated and 'eternal' (ll. 2–3).

> Hail, holy Light, offspring of heaven first-born,
> Or of the eternal co-eternal beam
> May I express thee unblamed? Since God is light,*
> And never but in unapproachèd light
> Dwelt from eternity, dwelt then in thee,
> Bright effluence of bright essence increate.*
> Or hear'st thou rather pure ethereal stream,
> Whose fountain who shall tell? Before the sun,
> Before the heavens thou wert, and at the voice
> Of God, as with a mantle didst invest   10
> The rising world of waters dark and deep,
> Won from the void and formless infinite.
> Thee I revisit now with bolder wing,
> Escaped the Stygian pool, though long detained
> In that obscure sojòurn, while in my flight
> Through utter and through middle darkness borne
> With other notes than to the Orphean lyre*
> I sung of chaos and eternal night,
> Taught by the heavenly Muse to venture down

The dark descent, and up to reascend,   20
Though hard and rare: thee I revisit safe,
And feel thy sovereign vital lamp; but thou
Revisit'st not these eyes, that roll in vain
To find thy piercing ray, and find no dawn;
So thick a drop serene hath quenched their orbs,*
Or dim suffusion veiled. Yet not the more
Cease I to wander where the Muses haunt
Clear spring, or shady grove, or sunny hill,
Smit with the love of sacred song; but chief
Thee Sion and the flowery brooks beneath   30
That wash thy hallowed feet, and warbling flow,
Nightly I visit: nor sometimes forget
Those other two equalled with me in fate,
So were I equalled with them in renown,
Blind Thamyris, and blind Maeonides,
And Tiresias and Phineus prophets old.*
Then feed on thoughts, that voluntary move
Harmonious numbers; as the wakeful bird*
Sings darkling, and in shadiest covert hid
Tunes her nocturnal note. Thus with the year   40
Seasons return, but not to me returns
Day, or the sweet approach of even or morn,
Or sight of vernal bloom, or summer's rose,
Or flocks, or herds, or human face divine;
But cloud instead, and ever-during dark
Surrounds me, from the cheerful ways of men
Cut off, and for the book of knowledge fair
Presented with a universal blank
Of nature's works to me expunged and razed,
And wisdom at one entrance quite shut out.   50
So much the rather thou celestial Light
Shine inward, and the mind through all her powers
Irradiate, there plant eyes, all mist from thence
Purge and disperse, that I may see and tell
Of things invisible to mortal sight.

31   *On Mr Milton's 'Paradise Lost'*

ANDREW MARVELL

Printed in the second edition of *Paradise Lost* (1674). The fourth issue of
the first edition (1668) had added Milton's defence of his decision to write
the poem in blank verse rather than rhyming couplets, which were the
fashionable form; Marvell alludes to this in ll. 45–54.

When I beheld the poet blind, yet bold,
In slender book his vast design unfold,
Messiah crowned, God's reconciled decree,*
Rebelling angels, the forbidden tree,
Heaven, hell, earth, chaos, all; the argument
Held me a while, misdoubting his intent,
That he would ruin (for I saw him strong)
The sacred truths to fable and old song:
So Samson groped the temple's posts in spite,
The world o'erwhelming to revenge his sight.*   10

   Yet as I read, soon growing less severe,
I liked his project, the success did fear;
Through that wide field how he his way should find
O'er which lame faith leads understanding blind;
Lest he perplexed the things he would explain,
And what was easy he should render vain.

   Or if a work so infinite he spanned,
Jealous I was that some less skillful hand
(Such as disquiet always what is well,
And by ill imitating would excel)   20
Might hence presume the whole creation's day
To change in scenes, and show it in a play.*

   Pardon me, mighty poet, nor despise
My causeless, yet not impious, surmise.
But I am now convinced, and none will dare
Within thy labours to pretend a share.
Thou hast not missed one thought that could be fit,
And all that was improper dost omit:
So that no room is here for writers left,
But to detect their ignorance or theft.   30

That majesty which through thy work doth reign
Draws the devout, deterring the profane;
And things divine thou treat'st of in such state
As them preserves, and thee, inviolate:
At once delight and horror on us seize,
Thou sing'st with so much gravity and ease;
And above human flight dost soar aloft,
With plume so strong, so equal, and so soft.
The bird named from that paradise you sing
So never flags, but always keeps on wing.　　　　40

　　Where couldst thou words of such a compass find?
Whence furnish such a vast expense of mind?
Just heaven thee, like Tiresias, to requite,
Rewards with prophecy thy loss of sight.

　　Well mightst thou scorn thy readers to allure
With tinkling rhyme, of thy own sense secure;
While the Town Bays writes all the while and spells,*
And like a pack-horse tires without his bells.
Their fancies like our bushy points appear:
The poets tag them, we for fashion wear.　　　　50
I too, transported by the mode, offend,
And while I meant to praise thee, must commend.
Thy verse created like thy theme sublime
In number, weight, and measure, needs not rhyme.

32　　*A Letter from the Country to a Friend in*
Town, Giving an Account of the Author's
Inclinations to Poetry

JOHN OLDHAM

Written July 1678, published in Oldham's *Some New Pieces* (1681). It was prompted by a verse letter from Oldham's barrister friend John Spenser (printed in *Poems*, ed. Brooks and Selden, pp. 534–41).

　　As to that poet (if so great a one as he,*
　　May suffer in comparison with me)
　　When heretofore in Scythian exile pent,

To which he by ungrateful Rome was sent:
If a kind paper from his country came,
And wore subscribed some known and faithful name,
That, like a powerful cordial, did infuse
New life into his speechless gasping Muse;
And straight his genius, which before did seem
Bound up in ice, and frozen as the clime,   10
By its warm force and friendly influence thawed,
Dissolved apace, and in soft numbers flowed:
Such welcome here, dear sir, your letter had
With me, shut up in close constraint as bad:
Not eager lovers, held in long suspense,
With warmer joy, and a more tender sense,
Meet those kind lines which all their wishes bless,
And sign and seal delivered happiness.
My grateful thoughts so throng to get abroad,
They overrun each other in the crowd: 20
To you with hasty flight they take their way,
And hardly for the dress of words will stay.

    Yet pardon, if this only fault I find,
That while you praise too much, you are less kind:
Consider, sir, 'tis ill and dang'rous thus
To overlay a young and tender Muse:
Praise, the fine diet which we're apt to love,
If given to excess does hurtful prove:
Where it does weak, distempered stomachs meet,
That surfeits, which should nourishment create.   30
Your rich perfumes such fragrancy dispense,
Their sweetness overcomes and palls my sense;
On my weak head you heap so many bays,
I sink beneath 'em, quite oppressed with praise,
And a resembling fate with him receive   ⎫
Who in too kind a triumph found his grave,   ⎬
Smothered with garlands which applauders gave. ⎭

    To you these praises justlier all belong,
By alienating which, yourself you wrong:
Whom better can such commendations fit   40
Than you, who so well teach and practise wit?
Verse, the great boast of drudging fools, from some,

Nay most of scribblers, with much straining come:
They void 'em dribbling, and in pain they write,
As if they had a strangury of wit:
Your pen uncalled they readily obey,
And scorn your ink should flow so fast as they:
Each strain of yours so easy does appear, ⎫
Each such a graceful negligence does wear, ⎬
As shows you have none, and yet want no care: ⎭   50
None of your serious pains or time they cost,
But what thrown by, you can afford for lost.
If such the fruits of your loose leisure be,
Your careless minutes yield such poetry,
We guess what proofs your genius would impart,
Did it employ you, as it does divert:
But happy you, more prudent and more wise,
With better aims have fixed your noble choice;
While silly I all thriving arts refuse, ⎫
And all my hopes, and all my vigour lose ⎬   60
In service on that worst of jilts, a Muse, ⎭
For gainful business court ignoble ease,
And in gay trifles waste my ill-spent days.

   Little I thought, my dearest friend, that you
Would thus contribute to my ruin too:
O'errun with filthy poetry and rhyme,
The present reigning evil of the time,
I lacked, and (well I did myself assure)
From your kind hand I should receive a cure:
When, lo! instead of healing remedies,   70
You cherish and encourage the disease:
Inhuman, you help the distemper on,
Which was before but too inveterate grown:
As a kind looker on, who int'rest shares,
Though not in's stake, yet in his hopes and fears,
Would to his friend a pushing gamester do,
Recall his elbow when he hastes to throw;
Such a wise course you should have took with me,
A rash and vent'ring fool in poetry.
Poets are cullies, whom rook fame draws in,   80
And wheedles with deluding hopes to win:

But when they hit, and most successful are,
They scarce come off with a bare saving share.

   Oft, I remember, did wise friends dissuade,
And bid me quit the trifling barren trade:
Oft have I tried (Heaven knows) to mortify
This vile and wicked lust of poetry;
But still unconquered it remains within,
Fixed as an habit, or some darling sin.
In vain I better studies there would sow,   90
Often I've tried, but none will thrive or grow:
All my best thoughts, when I'd most serious be,
Are never from its foul infection free:
Nay (God forgive me) when I say my prayers,
I scarce can help polluting them with verse:
That fabulous wretch of old reversed I seem,*
Who turn whate'er I touch to dross and rhyme.

   Oft to divert the wild caprice, I try ⎫
If sovereign wisdom and philosophy   ⎬
Rightly applied, will give a remedy: ⎭   100
Straight the great Stagyrite I take in hand,*
Seek nature and my self to understand:
Much I reflect on his vast worth and fame,
And much my low and grovelling aims condemn,
And quarrel, that my ill-packed fate should be
This vain, this worthless thing called poetry:
But when I find this unregarded toy
Could his important thoughts and pains employ,
By reading there, I am but more undone,
And meet that danger which I went to shun.   110
Oft when ill humour, chagrin, discontent, ⎫
Give leisure my wild follies to resent,   ⎬
I thus against myself my passion vent: ⎭
'Enough, mad rhyming sot, enough for shame,
Give o'er, and all thy quills to tooth-picks damn;
Didst ever thou the altar rob, or worse, ⎫
Kill the priest there, and maids receiving force? ⎬
What else could merit this so heavy curse? ⎭
The greatest curse I can, I wish on him,
(If there be any greater than to rhyme)   120

Who first did of the lewd invention think,
First made two lines with sounds resembling clink,
And, swerving from the easy paths of prose,
Fetters and chains did on free sense impose:
Cursed too be all the fools, who since have went
Misled in steps of that ill precedent:
Want be entailed their lot:'——and on I go,
Wreaking my spite on all the jingling crew:
Scarce the belovèd Cowley 'scapes, though I
Might sooner my own curses fear, than he: 130
And thus resolved against the scribbling vein,
I deeply swear never to write again.

   But when bad company and wine conspire
To kindle and renew the foolish fire,
Straightways relapsed, I feel the raving fit
Return, and straight I all my oaths forget:
The spirit, which I thought cast out before, ⎫
Enters again with stronger force and power, ⎬
Worse than at first, and tyrannizes more. ⎭
No sober good advice will then prevail,   140
Nor from the raging frenzy me recall:
Cool reason's dictates me no more can move
Than men in drink, in Bedlam, or in love:
Deaf to all means which might most proper seem
Towards my cure, I run stark mad in rhyme:
A sad, poor, haunted wretch, whom nothing less
Than prayers of the church can dispossess.

   Sometimes, after a tedious day half spent,
When fancy long has hunted on cold scent,
Tired in the dull and fruitless chase of thought,   150
Despairing I grow weary, and give out:
As a dry lecher pumped of all my store,
I loathe the thing, 'cause I can do't no more:
But when I once begin to find again
Recruits of matter in my pregnant brain,
Again more eager I the hunt pursue,
And with fresh vigour the loved sport renew:
Tickled with some strange pleasure which I find,
And think a secrecy to all mankind,

I please myself with the vain, false delight, 160
And count none happy but the fops that write.

 'Tis endless, sir, to tell the many ways
Wherein my poor deluded self I please:
How, when the fancy lab'ring for a birth,
With unfelt throes brings its rude issue forth:
How after, when imperfect shapeless thought
Is by the judgement into fashion wrought.
When at first search I traverse o'er my mind,
Nought but a dark and empty void I find:
Some little hints at length, like sparks, break thence, 170
And glimm'ring thoughts just dawning into sense:
Confused a while the mixed ideas lie,
With nought of mark to be discovered by,
Like colours undistinguished in the night,
Till the dusk images, moved to the light,
Teach the discerning faculty to choose
Which it had best adopt, and which refuse.
Here rougher strokes, touched with a careless dash,
Resemble the first sitting of a face:
There finished draughts in form more full appear, 180
And to their justness ask no further care.
Meanwhile with inward joy I proud am grown
To see the work successfully go on;
And prize myself in a creating power
That could make something, what was nought before.
 Sometimes a stiff, unwieldy thought I meet,
Which to my laws will scarce be made submit:
But when, after expense of pains and time,
'Tis managed well, and taught to yoke in rhyme,
I triumph more than joyful warriors would, 190
Had they some stout and hardy foe subdued,
And idly think, less goes to their command,
That makes armed troops in well-placed order stand,
Than to the conduct of my words, when they
March in due ranks, are set in just array.
 Sometimes on wings of thought I seem on high, ⎫
As men in sleep, though motionless they lie, ⎬
Fledged by a dream, believe they mount and fly: ⎭

So witches some enchanted wand bestride,
And think they through the airy regions ride, } 200
Where fancy is both traveller, way, and guide:
Then straight I grow a strange exalted thing,
And equal in conceit at least a king:
As the poor drunkard, when wine stums his brains,
Anointed with that liquor, thinks he reigns.
Bewitched by these delusions 'tis I write,
(The tricks some pleasant devil plays in spite)
And when I'm in the freakish trance, which I,
Fond silly wretch, mistake for ecstasy,
I find all former resolutions vain, 210
And thus recant them, and make new again:
    'What was't I rashly vowed? Shall ever I
Quit my beloved mistress, poetry?
Thou sweet beguiler of my lonely hours,
Which thus glide unperceived with silent course;
Thou gentle spell, which undisturbed dost keep
My breast, and charm intruding care asleep:
They say, thou'rt poor and unendowed; what though?
For thee I this vain, worthless world forgo:
Let wealth and honour be for Fortune's slaves, 220
The alms of fools, and prize of crafty knaves:
To me thou art whate'er th' ambitious crave,
And all that greedy misers want, or have:
In youth or age, in travel or at home,
Here or in town, at London or at Rome,
Rich or a beggar, free or in the Fleet,
Whate'er my fate is, 'tis my fate to write.'
    Thus I have made my shrifted Muse confess
Her secret feebles and her weaknesses:
All her hid faults she sets exposed to view, 230
And hopes a gentle cònfessor in you:
She hopes an easy pardon for her sin, }
Since 'tis but what she is not wilful in, }
Nor yet has scandalous nor open been. }
Try if your ghostly counsel can reclaim
The heedless wanton from her guilt and shame:
At least be not ungenerous to reproach

That wretched frailty which you've helped debauch.
   'Tis now high time to end, for fear I grow
More tedious than old doters when they woo,   240
Than travelled fops, when far-fetched lies they prate,
Or flattering poets, when they dedicate.
No dull forgiveness I presume to crave,
Nor vainly for my tiresome length ask leave:
Lest I, as often formal coxcombs use,
Prolong that very fault I would excuse:
May this the same kind welcome find with you,
As yours did here, and ever shall; adieu.

33   *To the Memory of Mr Oldham*

JOHN DRYDEN

Published along with memorial poems by several other writers in Oldham's posthumous collection, *The Remains of Mr John Oldham in Verse and Prose* (1684). For Oldham see the biographical note, and **15** and **32**.

Farewell, too little and too lately known,
Whom I began to think and call my own;
For sure our souls were near allied, and thine
Cast in the same poetic mould with mine.
One common note on either lyre did strike,
And knaves and fools we both abhorred alike:
To the same goal did both our studies drive,
The last set out the soonest did arrive.
Thus Nisus fell upon the slippery place,
While his young friend performed and won the race.*   10
O early ripe! to thy abundant store
What could advancing age have added more?
It might (what Nature never gives the young)
Have taught the numbers of thy native tongue;
But satire needs not those, and wit will shine
Through the harsh cadence of a rugged line:
A noble error, and but seldom made,
When poets are by too much force betrayed.

Thy generous fruits, though gathered ere their prime ⎫
Still showed a quickness; and maturing time   ⎬ 20
But mellows what we write to the dull sweets of rhyme. ⎭
Once more, hail and farewell; farewell thou young,
But ah too short, Marcellus of our tongue;*
Thy brows with ivy, and with laurels bound;*
But fate and gloomy night encompass thee around.

34   *An Allusion to Horace*

JOHN WILMOT, EARL OF ROCHESTER

Written in the winter of 1675–6; circulated in manuscript; first printed in
the 1680 edition. The poem imitates Horace's *Serm.* I. x, in
which Horace criticizes a number of Latin writers; however, all his butts
were already dead, whereas Rochester satirizes contemporaries, notably
Dryden.

The 10th Satire of the 1st Book
Nempe incomposito dixi pede etc.

Well Sir, 'tis granted, I said Dryden's rhymes
Were stol'n, unequal, nay dull many times:
What foolish patron is there found of his,*
So blindly partial to deny me this?
But that his plays, embroidered up and down
With wit and learning, justly pleased the town,
In the same paper I as freely own.
Yet having this allowed, the heavy mass
That stuffs up his loose volumes must not pass:
For by that rule, I might as well admit   10
Crowne's tedious scenes for poetry, and wit.*
'Tis therefore not enough, when your false sense
Hits the false judgement of an audience
Of clapping fools, assembling a vast crowd,
Till the thronged playhouse crack with the dull load;
Though ev'n that talent merits in some sort
That can divert the rabble and the court:
Which blundering Settle never could attain,*
And puzzling Otway labours at in vain.*

But within due proportions circumscribe 20
Whate'er you write; that with a flowing tide
The style may rise, yet in its rise forbear
With useless words t' oppress the wearied ear.
Here be your language lofty, there more light,
Your rhetoric with your poetry unite:
For elegance sake, sometimes allay the force
Of epithets, 'twill soften the discòurse;
A jest in scorn points out and hits the thing
More home than the morosest satyr's sting.
Shakespeare and Jonson did herein excel, 30
And might in this be imitated well;
Whom refined Etherege copies not at all,*
But is himself a sheer original.
Nor that slow drudge, in swift pindaric strains,
Flatman, who Cowley imitates with pains,*
And rides a jaded Muse, whipped with loose reins.
When Lee makes temp'rate Scipio fret and rave,*
And Hannibal a whining amorous slave,
I laugh, and wish the hot-brained fustian fool
In Busby's hands, to be well lashed at school.* 40
Of all our modern wits, none seems to me
Once to have touched upon true comedy,
But hasty Shadwell, and slow Wycherley.*
Shadwell's unfinished works do yet impart
Great proofs of force of nature, none of art:
With just, bold strokes he dashes here and there,
Showing great mastery with little care;
And scorns to varnish his good touches o'er,
To make the fools, and women, praise 'em more.
But Wycherley earns hard whate'er he gains, 50
He wants no judgement, nor he spares no pains;
He frequently excels, and at the least
Makes fewer faults than any of the best.
Waller, by nature for the bays designed,*
With force, and fire, and fancy unconfined,
In panegyrics does excel mankind:
He best can turn, enforce, and soften things,
To praise great conquerors, or to flatter kings.

For pointed satires, I would Buckhurst choose,*
The best good man, with the worst-natured Muse.   60
For songs and verses mannerly obscene,
That can stir nature up by spring unseen,
And without forcing blushes warm the Queen—
Sedley has that prevailing, gentle art,*
That can with a resistless charm impart
The loosest wishes to the chastest heart;
Raise such a conflict, kindle such a fire,
Betwixt declining virtue and desire,
Till the poor vanquished maid dissolves away
In dreams all night, in sighs and tears all day.   70
　　Dryden in vain tried this nice way of wit,
For he to be a tearing blade thought fit;
But when he would be sharp, he still was blunt,
To frisk his frolic fancy, he'd cry, 'Cunt!'
Would give the ladies a dry bawdy bob,
And thus he got the name of Poet Squab.
But to be just, 'twill to his praise be found,
His excellencies more than faults abound.
Nor dare I from his sacred temples tear
That laurel which he best deserves to wear.   80
But does not Dryden find e'en Jonson dull?
Fletcher and Beaumont uncorrect, and full
Of lewd lines, as he calls 'em? Shakespeare's style
Stiff and affected; to his own the while*
Allowing all the justness that his pride
So arrogantly had to these denied?
And may not I have leave impartially
To search and censure Dryden's works, and try
If those gross faults his choice pen does commit
Proceed from want of judgement, or of wit?   90
Or if his lumpish fancy does refuse
Spirit and grace to his loose slattern Muse?
Five hundred verses ev'ry morning writ
Proves you no more a poet, than a wit:
Such scribbling authors have been seen before:
Mustapha, The English Princess, forty more,*
Were things perhaps composed in half an hour.

To write what may securely stand the test
Of being well read over thrice at least,
Compare each phrase, examine every line,   100
Weigh every word, and every thought refine;
Scorn all applause the vile rout can bestow,
And be content to please those few who know.
Canst thou be such a vain, mistaken thing,
To wish thy works might make a playhouse ring
With the unthinking laughter and poor praise
Of fops and ladies, factious for thy plays?
Then send a cunning friend to learn thy doom
From the shrewd judges of the drawing room.
I've no ambition on that idle score,   110
But say with Betty Morris heretofore,*
When a court lady called her Bulkeley's whore,*
'I please one man of wit, am proud on't too,
Let all the coxcombs dance to bed to you.'
Should I be troubled when the purblind knight,*
Who squints more in his judgement than his sight,
Picks silly faults, and censures what I write?
Or when the poor-fed poets of the town
For scraps and coach-room cry my verses down?
I loathe the rabble; 'tis enough for me   120
If Sedley, Shadwell, Shepherd, Wycherley,*
Godolphin, Butler, Buckhurst, Buckingham,*
And some few more, whom I omit to name,
Approve my sense: I count their censure fame.

35   *An Elegy on the Earl of Rochester*

                    ANNE WHARTON

Written 1680; published in a shortened version in 1685 (omitting ll. 18–27
and 44–80), and much admired.

Deep waters silent roll: so grief like mine
Tears never can relieve, nor words define.
Stop, then, stop your vain source, weak springs of grief;

Let tears flow from their eyes whom tears relieve.
They from their heads show the light trouble there:
Could my heart weep, its sorrows 'twould declare.
Weep drops of blood, my heart, thou'st lost thy pride,
The cause of all thy hopes and fears, thy guide:
He would have led thee right in wisdom's way,
And 'twas thy fault whene'er thou went'st astray;   10
And since thou stray'dst when guided and led on,
Thou wilt be surely lost when left alone.
It is thy elegy I write, not his:
He lives immortal, and in highest bliss.
But thou art dead, alas! my heart, thou'rt dead;
He lives, that lovely soul, for ever fled,
And thou 'mongst crowds on earth art burièd.
He led thee up the steep and high ascent
To poetry, the sacred way he went;
He taught thy infant Muse the art betime,   20
Though then the way was difficult to climb,
Since Daphne prostituted has her tree,*
We well may scorn the gift of poetry.
Then she was his alone, constant and fair,
And taught us all desire, and all despair:
But now, like other beauties oft enjoyed,
Her charms are gone, and all her lovers cloyed.
Great was thy loss, which thou canst ne'er express,
Nor was th' insensible dull nation's less.
He civilized the rude, and taught the young;   30
Made fools grow wise; such artful magic hung
Upon his useful, kind, instructing tongue.
His lively wit was of himself a part,
Not, as in other men, the work of art:
For though his learning, like his wit, was great,
Yet sure all learning came below his wit;
As God's immediate gifts are better far
Than those we borrow from his likeness here.*
He was—but I want words, and ne'er can tell;
But this I know, he did mankind excel.   40
He was what no man ever was before,
Nor can indulgent Nature give us more,

For to make him sh' exhausted all her store.
His childhood flamed with that poetic rage
With which he since informed and blessed the age;
Then, when his limbs were weak, his wit was strong,
Good sense before plain words adorned his tongue.
No wonder that he left the world so soon:
The little time he had was all his own;
No part of it in childhood stole away, 50
And yet this matchless pattern went astray.
When such as he can err, and angels fall,
What hopes have we ever to climb at all?
God saw his drooping star, and cast him down
That he might raise his soul to be his own.
God saw, and loved him; saw this chiefest part
Of his creation from his precepts start;
Blessed him with dying pains, and gave him more
In that last, mournful gift than all before;
Gave him a penitence so fixed, so true 60
A greater penitence no saint e'er knew;
Which done, the merciful Creator said:
'This creature of my own is perfect made;
No longer fit to dwell with men below,
He'll be a wonder amongst angels now.
I'll straight to those exalted spirits show
What stupid men cannot enough admire.'
He stopped, and his best finished work expired,
And the triumphant soul to heaven aspired:
To heaven, where everlasting glories shine, 70
To heaven, where cherubims with angels join
To welcome him whom we'll no more deplore,
Since so well landed on that happy shore.
He who could here below such wonders sing,
What will he now to heaven's eternal king!
And since our joys in him were here so great,
What will they be when we immortal meet!
With ecstasy these thoughts inflame my mind:
Methinks I leave this case of flesh behind,
And to him, winged with joy, out-fly the wind. 80

36   *The Miseries of Visits*

ANONYMOUS

Probably written 1680. The poem illustrates how manuscript poems were
circulated, and refers to Captain Robert Julian, called the 'Secretary to the
Muses', whose scriptorium was responsible for producing many manuscript copies of satirical and erotic poems which could not be printed.

> Pox on the rhyming fops that plague the town,
> With libelling the court, and railing at the gown!
> A man can make no visits now, but his caress
> Is a lewd satire shown, with 'Pray, sir, guess
> Whose style it is!' 'Good faith, sir, I don't care,
> For truly I read none that treas'nous are.'
> Then he replies, 'Lord, 'tis the wittiest thing,
> 'Tis smart on Nelly, Portsmouth, and the King.'*
> Just as he speaks, comes Julian passing by,
> His pockets stuffed with scurrilous poetry.   10
> My friend cries, 'Hem!', and adds to that a bow.
> 'Thou slave to th' Muses, what's the newest now?'
> 'S'blood, sir,' says he, 'You're sick o' th' old disease;
> You want new papers: damn me, where's my fees?'
> A guinea's tossed, with 'Julian, you're a rogue.'
> We're straight presented with what's now in vogue:
> There was obscene Rochester's chief stories
> Of matrix, glances, dildo, and clitoris,
> With Dorset's tawdry nonsense dressed for sale,
> This motto on 't: 'Brave Buckhurst ne'er did fail.'   20
> 'God's blood and wounds', cries Julian, 'that's grown stale,
> I scarce can put it off for Nantes and ale.'
> The next was smoothly writ by squinting Car*
> On Pembroke's drunken tricks, his bull and bear.*
> Behen was there, with bawdry in a veil,*
> But swearing bloodily, as in a jail.
> Mulgrave appeared with his base borrowed wit,*
> And Dryden at his heels a-owning it.
> There was lewd Buckingham's lank poetry,
> But stuffed so full of horrid blasphemy   30

Made Julian doubt there was no deity.
Fierce Dryden's satire we desired to view,
For we had heard he mourned in black and blue;
He searched for it, but ['t] was not to be found:
'Twas put i' the gazette for a hundred pound.
The tavern was the next resort, where I,
Quite weary of their tippling company,
Went home, a-cursing of this wretched age
That couples each old lady with her page,
And whores the chastest virgin with her dog,   40
Calling the best of kings a senseless log.*

37   [*A Critique of Shakespeare*]

MARGARET CAVENDISH, DUCHESS OF NEWCASTLE

Published in *CCXI Sociable Letters* (1664), 224–8. Cavendish's explan-
ation of Shakespeare's qualities counters a common contemporary view
that his work was coarse, and emphasizes his capacity to enter into the
experience of many different characters.

Madam,

I wonder how that person you mention in your letter could either
have the conscience or confidence to dispraise Shakespeare's plays,
as to say they were made up only with clowns, fools, watchmen, and
the like. But to answer that person (though Shakespeare's wit will
answer for himself) I say that it seems by his judging, or censuring,
he understands not plays or wit: for to express properly, rightly,
usually, and naturally a clown's or fool's humour, expressions,
phrases, garbs, manners, actions, words, and course of life, is as
witty, wise, judicious, ingenious, and observing as to write and
express the expressions, phrases, garbs, manners, actions, words, and
course of life of kings and princes; and to express naturally, to the
life, a mean country wench as a great lady, a courtesan as a chaste
woman, a mad man as a man in his right reason and senses, a drunkard as a sober man, a knave as an honest man, and so a clown as a
well-bred man, and a fool as a wise man: nay, it expresses and declares
a greater wit to express and deliver to posterity the extravagancies of

madness, the subtlety of knaves, the ignorance of clowns, and the simplicity of naturals or the craft of feigned fools, than to express regularities, plain honesty, courtly garbs, or sensible discourses; for 'tis harder to express nonsense than sense, and ordinary conversations than that which is unusual; and 'tis harder, and requires more wit, to express a jester than a grave statesman. Yet Shakespeare did not want wit to express to the life all sorts of persons, of what quality, profession, degree, breeding, or birth soever: nor did he want wit to express the divers and different humours or natures, or several passions, in mankind; and so well he hath expressed in his plays all sorts of persons, as one would think he had been transformed into every one of those persons he hath described; and as sometimes one would think he was really himself the clown or jester he feigns, so one would think he was also the King and Privy Counsellor; also, as one would think he were really the coward he feigns, so one would think he were the most valiant and experienced soldier. Who would not think he had been such a man as his Sir John Falstaff? And who would not think he had been Harry the Fifth? And certainly Julius Caesar, Augustus Caesar, and Antonius did never really act their parts better, if so well, as he hath described them; and I believe that Antonius and Brutus did not speak better to the people than he hath feigned them. Nay, one would think that he had been metamorphosed from a man to a woman, for who could describe Cleopatra better than he hath done, and many other females of his own creating, as Nan Page, Mrs Page, Mrs Ford, the doctor's maid, Beatrice, Mrs Quickly, Doll Tearsheet, and others too many to relate? And in his tragic vein he presents passions so naturally, and misfortunes so probably, as he pierces the souls of his readers with such a true sense and feeling thereof that it forces tears through their eyes, and almost persuades them they are really actors (or at least present) at those tragedies. Who would not swear he had been a noble lover, that could woo so well? And there is not any person he hath described in his book, but his readers might think they were well acquainted with them. Indeed, Shakespeare had a clear judgement, a quick wit, a spreading fancy, a subtle observation, a deep apprehension, and a most eloquent elocution; truly, he was a natural orator as well as a natural poet, and he was not an orator to speak well only on some subjects, as lawyers, who can make eloquent orations at the bar, and plead subtly and wittily in law cases, or divines, that can preach eloquent sermons or dispute subtly and wittily in theology, but take them from that, and put them to other subjects, and they will be to seek; but Shakespeare's wit and eloquence was general, for and upon all subjects; he rather wanted subjects for his wit and eloquence to work on, for which he was forced to take some of his plots out of history, where he only took the bare designs, the wit and language being all his own; and so much he had above others, that those who writ after him were forced to borrow of him, or rather, to steal from him. I could mention divers places that others of our famous poets have borrowed, or stolen; but lest I should discover the persons, I will not mention the places or parts, but leave it to those that read his plays and others' to find them out. I should not have needed to write this to you, for his works would have declared the same truth: but I believe those that dispraised his plays dispraised them more out of envy than simplicity or ignorance; for those that could read his plays could not be so foolish to condemn them, only the excellency of them caused an envy to them. By this we may perceive envy doth not leave a man in the grave, it follows him after death, unless a man be buried in oblivion; but if he leave anything to be remembered, envy and malice will be still throwing aspersion upon it, or striving to pull it down by detraction. But leaving Shakespeare's works to their own defence, and his detractors to their envy, and you to your better employments than reading my letter, I rest,

Madam,

Your faithful friend
and humble servant.

38 [*A Critique of Shakespeare and his Contemporaries*]

RICHARD FLECKNOE

From 'A Short Discourse of the English Stage', prefixed to his play *Love's Kingdom* (1664). Flecknoe compares Shakespeare with his Jacobean contemporaries Ben Jonson (?1573–1637), who was famous chiefly for his comedies, and the partnership of Francis Beaumont (1584–1616) and John Fletcher (1579–1625), who specialized in tragicomedy, and whose plays were popular on the early Restoration stage. Flecknoe also compares English with French drama; the French tended to prefer 'regular' plays which obeyed the neo-classical unities of time, place, and action, and avoided intricate plots and extended time-schemes.

For plays, Shakespeare was one of the first who inverted the dramatic style from dull history to quick comedy, upon whom Jonson refined; as Beaumont and Fletcher first writ in the heroic way, upon whom Suckling* and others endeavoured to refine again; one saying wittily of his *Aglaura*, that 'twas full of fine flowers, but they seemed rather stuck than growing there; as another, of Shakespeare's writings, that 'twas a fine garden, but it wanted weeding.

There are few of our English plays (excepting only some few of Jonson's) without some faults or other; and if the French have fewer than our English, 'tis because they confine themselves to narrower limits, and consequently have less liberty to err.

The chief faults of ours are our huddling too much matter together, and making them too long and intricate; we imagining we never have intrigue enough till we lose ourselves and auditors, who should be led in a maze but not a mist, and through turning and winding ways, but so still as they may find their way at last.

A good play should be like a good stuff, closely and evenly wrought, without any breaks, thrums, or loose ends in 'um, or like a good picture, well painted and designed: the plot or contrivement, the design; the writing, the colours; and counterplot, the shadowings, with other embellishments; or finally, it should be like a well contrived garden, cast into its walks and counterwalks, betwixt an alley and a wilderness, neither too plain nor too confused. Of all arts, that of the dramatic poet is the most difficult and most subject to censure; for in all others they write only of some particular subject, as the mathematician of mathematics, or philosopher of philosophy; but in that the poet must write of everything, and everyone undertakes to judge of it.

. . .

To compare our English dramatic poets together (without taxing them) Shakespeare excelled in a natural vein, Fletcher in wit, and Jonson in gravity and ponderousness of style; whose only fault was he was too elaborate; and had he mixed less erudition with his plays they had been more pleasant and delightful than they are. Comparing him with Shakespeare, you shall see the difference betwixt nature and art; and with Fletcher, the difference betwixt wit and judgement: wit being an exuberant thing, like Nilus, never more commendable than when it overflows; but judgement a staid and reposed thing, always containing itself within its bounds and limits.

39   [*A Critique of Shakespeare and Jonson*]

JOHN DRYDEN

(a) From *Of Dramatic Poesy: An Essay*

Published 1668. The essay is written as a dialogue between four friends, who are thinly disguised representations of contemporaries: Eugenius ('the well-born') is Charles Sackville, later Earl of Dorset (see notes to p. 180); Crites ('the critical') is Sir Robert Howard (1626–98), poet and dramatist, and Dryden's brother-in-law; Lisideus is Sir Charles Sedley (see notes to p. 180); and Neander ('the new man') is Dryden himself. The discussion ranges over the relative merits of the ancients and the moderns; of English and French drama; of blank verse and rhyme; and of the major Jacobean playwrights, Shakespeare, Jonson, and Beaumont and Fletcher. The present extract is spoken by Neander.

To begin, then, with Shakespeare: he was the man who of all modern, and perhaps ancient poets, had the largest and most comprehensive soul. All the images of nature were still present to him, and he drew them not laboriously, but luckily; when he describes anything, you more than see it, you feel it too. Those who accuse him to have wanted learning* give him the greater commendation: he was naturally learned; he needed not the spectacles of books to read nature; he looked inwards, and found her there. I cannot say he is everywhere alike; were he so, I should do him injury to compare him with the greatest of mankind. He is many times flat, insipid; his comic wit degenerating into clenches, his serious swelling into bombast. But he is always great when some great occasion is presented to him; no man can say he ever had a fit subject for his wit, and did not then raise himself as high above the rest of poets,

quantum lenta solent inter viburna cupressi.*

The consideration of this made Mr Hales of Eton* say that there was no subject of which any poet ever writ, but he would produce it much better treated of in Shakespeare; and however others are now generally preferred before him, yet the age wherein he lived, which had contemporaries with him Fletcher and Jonson, never equalled them to him in their esteem. And in the last King's court, when Ben's reputation was at highest, Sir John Suckling,* and with him the greater part of the courtiers, set our Shakespeare far above him.

Beaumont and Fletcher, of whom I am next to speak, had, with the advantage of Shakespeare's wit, which was their precedent, great natural gifts improved by study; Beaumont especially being so accurate a judge of plays that Ben Jonson, while he lived, submitted all his writings to his censure, and, 'tis thought, used his judgement in correcting, if not contriving, all his plots. What value he had for him, appears by the verses he writ to him;* and therefore I need speak no farther of it. The first play which brought Fletcher and him in esteem was their *Philaster*: for before that, they had written two or three very unsuccessfully, as the like is reported of Ben Jonson before he writ *Every Man in his Humour*. Their plots were generally more regular than Shakespeare's, especially those which were made before Beaumont's death; and they understood and imitated the conversation of gentlemen much better; whose wild debaucheries, and quickness of wit in repartees, no poet can ever paint as they have done. This humour of which Ben Jonson derived from particular persons, they made it not their business to describe: they represented all the passions very lively, but above all love. I am apt to believe the English language in them arrived to its highest perfection: what words have since been taken in, are rather superfluous than necessary. Their plays are now the most pleasant and frequent entertainments of the stage; two of theirs being acted through the year for one of Shakespeare's or Jonson's: the reason is because there is a certain gaiety in their comedies, and pathos in their more serious plays, which suits generally with all men's humours. Shakespeare's language is likewise a little obsolete, and Ben Jonson's wit comes short of theirs.

As for Jonson, to whose character I am now arrived, if we look upon him while he was himself (for his last plays were but his dotages), I think him the most learned and judicious writer which any theatre ever had. He was a most severe judge of himself as well as others. One cannot say he wanted wit, but rather that he was frugal of it. In his works you find little to retrench or alter. Wit and language, and humour also in some measure, we had before him; but something of art was wanting to the drama till he came. He managed his strength to more advantage than any who preceded him. You seldom find him making love in any of his scenes, or endeavouring to move the passions; his genius was too sullen and saturnine to do it gracefully, especially when he knew he came after those who had performed both to such an height. Humour was his proper sphere, and in that he delighted most to represent mechanic people. He was deeply conversant in the ancients, both Greek and Latin, and he borrowed boldly from them: there is scarce a poet or historian among the Roman authors of those times whom he has not translated in *Sejanus* and *Catiline*. But he has done his robberies so openly that one may see he fears not to be taxed by any law. He invades authors like a monarch, and what would be theft in other poets is only victory in him. With the spoils of these writers he so represents old Rome to us in its rites, ceremonies, and customs, that if one of their poets had written either of his tragedies, we had seen less of it than in him. If there was any fault in his language, 'twas that he weaved it too closely and laboriously in his serious plays: perhaps, too, he did a little too much Romanize our tongue, leaving the words which he translated almost as much Latin as he found them: wherein, though he learnedly followed the idiom of their language, he did not enough comply with ours. If I would compare him with Shakespeare, I must acknowledge him the more correct poet, but Shakespeare the greater wit. Shakespeare was the Homer, or father of our dramatic poets, Jonson was the Virgil, the pattern of elaborate writing; I admire him, but I love Shakespeare. To conclude of him, as he has given us the most correct plays, so in the precepts which he has laid down in his *Discoveries** we have as many and profitable rules for perfecting the stage as any wherewith the French can furnish us.

(b) *Epilogue to 'The Second Part of The Conquest of Granada'*

Performed 1671, published 1672. The remarks on Jonson in this epilogue were much criticized by contemporaries, and when he published the play Dryden added a 'Defence of the Epilogue' in which he argued that language and manners had become more refined since the days of Jonson (*Works*, xi. 203–18).

They who have best succeeded on the stage
Have still conformed their genius to their age.
Thus Jonson did mechanic humour show,
When men were dull, and conversation low.
Then comedy was faultless, but 'twas coarse:
Cob's tankard was a jest, and Otter's horse.*
And as their comedy, their love was mean:
Except, by chance, in some one laboured scene
Which must atone for an ill-written play.
They rose, but at their height could seldom stay.   10
Fame then was cheap, and the first comer sped;
And they have kept it since, by being dead.
But were they now to write when critics weigh
Each line, and every word, throughout a play,
None of 'em, no not Jonson in his height,
Could pass, without allowing grains for weight.
Think it not envy that these truths are told:
Our poet's not malicious, though he's bold.
'Tis not to brand 'em that their faults are shown,
But, by their errors, to excuse his own.   20
If love and honour now are higher raised,
'Tis not the poet, but the age is praised.
Wit's now arrived to a more high degree,
Our native language more refined and free.
Our ladies and our men now speak more wit
In conversation, than those poets writ.
Then one of these is, consequently, true:
That what this poet writes comes short of you,
And imitates you ill (which most he fears),
Or else his writing is not worse than theirs.   30
Yet, though you judge (as sure the critics will)
That some before him writ with greater skill,
In this one praise he has their fame surpassed,
To please an age more gallant than the last.

(c) From *The Grounds of Criticism in Tragedy*

Published 1679 as part of the prefatory material to Dryden's adaptation of
Shakespeare's *Troilus and Cressida*.

If Shakespeare be allowed, as I think he must, to have made his characters distinct, it will easily be inferred that he understood the nature of the passions, because it has been proved already that confused passions make undistinguishable characters: yet I cannot deny that he has his failings; but they are not so much in the passions themselves as in his manner of expression: he often obscures his meaning by his words, and sometimes makes it unintelligible. I will not say of so great a poet that he distinguished not the blown, puffy style from true sublimity; but I may venture to maintain that the fury of his fancy often transported him beyond the bounds of judgement, either in coining of new words and phrases, or racking words which were in use into the violence of a catachresis. 'Tis not that I would explode the use of metaphors from passions, for Longinus* thinks 'em necessary to raise it: but to use 'em at every word, to say nothing without a metaphor, a simile, an image, or description, is I doubt to smell a little too strongly of the buskin. I must be forced to give an example of expressing passion figuratively; but that I may do it with respect to Shakespeare, it shall not be taken from anything of his: 'tis an exclamation against Fortune, quoted in his *Hamlet* but written by some other poet:

> Out, out, thou strumpet Fortune! all you gods,
> In general synod, take away her power;
> Break all the spokes and felleys from her wheel,
> And bowl the round nave down the hill of heav'n,
> As low as to the fiends.

And immediately after, speaking of Hecuba, when Priam was killed before her eyes:

> The mobbled queen ran up and down,
> Threatening the flame with bisson rheum; a clout about
>   that head
> Where late the diadem stood; and for a robe,
> About her lank and all o'er-teemèd loins,
> A blanket in th' alarm of fear caught up.
> Who this had seen, with tongue in venom steep'd
> 'Gainst Fortune's state would treason have pronounced;
> But if the gods themselves did see her then,
> When she saw Pyrrhus make malicious sport

> In mincing with his sword her husband's limbs,
> The instant burst of clamour that she made
> (Unless things mortal move them not at all)*
> Would have made milch the burning eyes of heav'n,
> And passion in the gods.*

What a pudder is here kept in raising the expression of trifling thoughts! Would not a man have thought that the poet had been bound prentice to a wheelwright for his first rant? and had followed a ragman for the clout and blanket in the second? Fortune is painted on a wheel, and therefore the writer, in a rage, will have poetical justice done upon every member of that engine: after this execution, he bowls the nave downhill, from heaven to the fiends (an unreasonable long mark, a man would think); 'tis well there are no solid orbs to stop it in the way, or no element of fire to consume it: but when it came to the earth, it must be monstrous heavy to break ground as low as to the centre. His making milch the burning eyes of heaven was a pretty tolerable flight too, and I think no man ever drew milk out of eyes before him: yet, to make the wonder greater, these eyes were burning. Such a sight indeed were enough to have raised passion in the gods; but to excuse the effects of it, he tells you perhaps they did not see it. Wise men would be glad to find a little sense couched under all these pompous words; for bombast is commonly the delight of that audience which loves poetry, but understands it not: and as commonly has been the practice of those writers who, not being able to infuse a natural passion into the mind, have made it their business to ply the ears and to stun their judges by the noise. But Shakespeare does not often thus; for the passions in his scene between Brutus and Cassius* are extremely natural, the thoughts are such as arise from the matter, the expression of 'em not viciously figurative. I cannot leave this subject before I do justice to that divine poet by giving you one of his passionate descriptions: 'tis of Richard the Second when he was deposed, and led in triumph through the streets of London by Henry of Bullingbrook: the painting of it is so lively, and the words so moving, that I have scarce read anything comparable to it in any other language. Suppose you have seen already the fortunate usurper passing through the crowd, and followed by the shouts and acclamations of the people; and now behold King Richard entering upon the scene: consider the wretchedness of his condition, and his carriage in it; and refrain from pity if you can:

> As in a theatre, the eyes of men,
> After a well-graced actor leaves the stage,
> Are idly bent on him that enters next,
> Thinking his prattle to be tedious:
> Even so, or with much more contempt, men's eyes
> Did scowl on Richard: no man cried, 'God save him':
> No joyful tongue gave him his welcome home,
> But dust was thrown upon his sacred head,
> Which with such gentle sorrow he shook off,
> His face still combating with tears and smiles
> (The badges of his grief and patience),
> That had not God (for some strong purpose) steeled
> The hearts of men, they must perforce have melted,
> And barbarism itself have pitied him.*

To speak justly of this whole matter: 'tis neither height of thought that is discommended, nor pathetic vehemence, nor any nobleness of expression in its proper place; but 'tis a false measure of all these, something which is like 'em, and is not them; 'tis the Bristol-stone, which appears like a diamond; 'tis an extravagant thought, instead of a sublime one; 'tis roaring madness, instead of vehemence; and a sound of words, instead of sense. If Shakespeare were stripped of all the bombast in his passions, and dressed in the most vulgar words, we should find the beauties of his thoughts remaining; if his embroideries were burnt down, there would still be silver at the bottom of the melting-pot: but I fear (at least let me fear it for myself) that we who ape his sounding words have nothing of his thought, but are all outside; there is not so much as a dwarf within our giant's clothes. Therefore, let not Shakespeare suffer for our sakes; 'tis our fault, who succeed him in an age which is more refined, if we imitate him so ill that we copy his failings only, and make a virtue of that in our writings which in his was an imperfection.

For what remains, the excellency of that poet was, as I have said, in the more manly passions, Fletcher's in the softer: Shakespeare writ better betwixt man and man, Fletcher, betwixt man and woman: consequently, the one described friendship better, the other love: yet

Shakespeare taught Fletcher to write love, and Juliet and Desde-mona are originals. 'Tis true, the scholar had the softer soul, but the master had the kinder. Friendship is both a virtue and a passion essentially; love is a passion only in its nature, and is not a virtue but by accident: good nature makes friendship, but effeminacy love. Shakespeare had an universal mind, which comprehended all char-acters and passions; Fletcher a more confined and limited: for though he treated love in perfection, yet honour, ambition, revenge, and generally all the stronger passions, he either touched not, or not masterly. To conclude all, he was a limb of Shakespeare.

40   *Preface to 'The Sullen Lovers'*

THOMAS SHADWELL

Printed 1668. This was one of a series of prefaces, prologues, and epi-logues in which Dryden and Shadwell debated various topics: the merits of Ben Jonson (whom Shadwell professed to emulate, and Dryden admired with reservations: see **39**); whether comedy should entertain (as Dryden thought) or instruct (as Shadwell claimed); the relative merits of the comedy of repartee (practised by Dryden) and Jonsonian humours (espoused by Shadwell); and the right of authors to borrow from ancient and modern writers. The quarrel would come to a head in *Mac Flecknoe* (**41**), where Dryden ridiculed Shadwell's pretensions to Jonsonian and classical principles.

Reader,

The success of this play, as it was much more than it deserved, so was much more than I expected; especially in this very critical age, when every man pretends to be a judge, and some, that never read three plays in their lives, and never understood one, are as positive in their judgement of plays as if they were all Jonsons. But had I been used with all the severity imaginable, I should patiently have submit-ted to my fate; not like the rejected authors of our time, who when their plays are damned, will strut, and huff it out, and laugh at the ignorance of the age: or like some other of our modern fops, that declare they are resolved to justify their plays with their swords (though perhaps their courage is as little as their wit), such as peep through their loop-holes in the theatre to see who looks grum upon their plays: and if they spy a gentle squire making faces, he, poor soul, must be hectored till he likes 'em, while the more stubborn bully-rock damns, and is safe; such is their discretion in the choice of their men. Such gentlemen as these, I must confess, had need pretend they cannot err. These will huff and look big upon the success of an ill play stuffed full of songs and dances (which have that constraint upon 'em too, that they seldom seem to come in willingly); when in such plays the composer and the dancing-master are the best poets, and yet the unmerciful scribbler would rob them of all the honour.

I am so far from valuing myself (as the phrase is) upon this play, that perhaps no man is a severer judge of it than myself; yet if anything could have made me proud of it, it would have been the great favour and countenance it received from His Majesty and their Royal Highnesses.

But I could not persuade myself that they were so favourable to the play for the merit of it, but out of a princely generosity to encourage a young beginner that did what he could to please them, and that otherwise might have been balked for ever: 'tis to this I owe the success of the play, and am as far from presumption of my own merits in it, as one ought to be who receives an alms.

The first hint I received was from the report of a play of Molière's* of three Acts, called *Les Fâcheux*, upon which I wrote a great part of this before I read that; and after it came to my hands, I found so little for my use (having before upon that hint designed the fittest characters I could for my purpose), that I have made use of but two short scenes, viz., the first scene in the Second Act between Stanford and Roger, and Molière's story of piquet, which I have translated into backgammon, both of them so varied you would not know them. But I freely confess my theft, and am ashamed on't, though I have the example of some that never yet wrote play without stealing most of it; and (like men that lie so long, till they believe themselves) at length by continual thieving reckon their stolen goods their own too; which is so ignoble a thing, that I cannot but believe that he that makes a common practice of stealing other men's wit, would, if he could with the same safety, steal anything else.

I have in this play, as near as I could, observed the three unities of time, place, and action; the time of the drama does not exceed six hours, the place is in a very narrow compass, and the main action of the play, upon which all the rest depend, is the sullen love betwixt

Stanford and Emilia, which kind of love is only proper to their characters. I have here, as often as I could naturally, kept the scenes unbroken,* which (though it be not so much practised, or so well understood, by the English) yet among the French poets is accounted a great beauty. But after these frivolous excuses, the want of design in the play has been objected against me; which fault (though I may endeavour a little to extenuate) I dare not absolutely deny. I conceive, with all submission to better judgements, that no man ought to expect such intrigues in the little actions of comedy, as are required in plays of a higher nature. But in plays of humour, where there are so many characters as there are in this, there is yet less design to be expected: for if, after I had formed three or four forward prating fops in the play, I had made it full of plot and business; at the latter end, where the turns ought to be many, and suddenly following one another, I must have let fall the humour, which I thought would be pleasanter than intrigues could have been without it; and it would have been easier to me to have made a plot than to hold up the humour.

Another objection that has been made by some, is that there is the same thing over and over: which I do not apprehend, unless they blame the unity of the action; yet Horace, *De Arte Poetica*, says:

> *sit quod vis, simplex dumtaxat et unum.*

Or whether it be the carrying on of the humours to the last, which the same author directs me to do

> *si quid inexpertum scenæ committis et audes*
> *personam formare novam, servetur ad imum,*
> *qualis ab incepto processerit, et sibi constet.*

I have endeavoured to represent variety of humours (most of the persons of the play differing in their characters from one another), which was the practice of Ben Jonson, whom I think all dramatic poets ought to imitate, though none are like to come near; he being the only person that appears to me to have made perfect representations of human life. Most other authors that I ever read, either have wild romantic tales, wherein they strain love and honour to that ridiculous height that it becomes burlesque; or in their lower comedies content themselves with one or two humours at most, and those not near so perfect characters as the admirable Jonson always made, who never wrote comedy without seven or eight considerable humours. I never saw one, except that of Falstaff, that was in my judgement comparable to any of Jonson's considerable humours. You will pardon this digression when I tell you he is the man, of all the world, I most passionately admire for his excellency in dramatic poetry.

Though I have known some of late so insolent to say that Ben Jonson wrote his best plays without wit; imagining that all the wit in plays consisted in bringing two persons upon the stage to break jests and to bob one another, which they call repartee; not considering that there is more wit and invention required in the finding out good humour, and matter proper for it, than in all their smart repartees. For in the writing of a humour, a man is confined not to swerve from the character, and obliged to say nothing but what is proper to it; but in the plays which have been wrote of late, there is no such thing as perfect character, but the two chief persons are most commonly a swearing, drinking, whoring ruffian for a lover, and an impudent, ill-bred tomrig for a mistress, and these are the fine people of the play; and there is that latitude in this, that almost anything is proper for them to say; but their chief subject is bawdy and profaneness, which they call 'brisk writing', when the most dissolute of men, that relish those things well enough in private, are shocked at 'em in public. And methinks, if there were nothing but the ill manners of it, it should make poets avoid that indecent way of writing.

But perhaps you may think me as impertinent as any one I represent; that, having so many faults of my own, should take the liberty to judge of others, to impeach my fellow-criminals. I must confess, it is very ungenerous to accuse those that modestly confess their own errors; but positive men, that justify all their faults, are common enemies that no man ought to spare, prejudicial to all societies they live in, destructive to all communication, always endeavouring magisterially to impose upon our understandings, against the freedom of mankind. These ought no more to be suffered amongst us than wild beasts: for no corrections that can be laid upon 'em are of power to reform 'em; and certainly it was a positive fool that Solomon spoke of, when he said, 'Bray him in a mortar, and yet he will retain his folly.'*

But I have troubled you too long with this discourse, and am to ask your pardon for it, and the many faults you will find in the play; and

beg you will believe that whatever I have said of it, was intended not
in justification, but excuse of it. Look upon it, as it really was, wrote
in haste, by a young writer, and you will easily pardon it; especially
when you know that the best of our dramatic writers have wrote very
ill plays at first; nay some of 'em have wrote several before they could
get one to be acted, and their best plays were made with great
expense of labour and time. Nor can you expect a very correct play
under a year's pains at the least, from the wittiest man of the nation;
it is so difficult a thing to write well in this kind. Men of quality, that
write for their pleasure, will not trouble themselves with exactness in
their plays; and those that write for profit would find too little
encouragement for so much pains as a correct play would require.

                                                                  Vale.

41   *Mac Flecknoe*

JOHN DRYDEN

Written 1676 and circulated anonymously in manuscript; first authorized
(though still anonymous) printing 1684 in the Dryden–Tonson *Miscellany
Poems*. The poem draws upon issues debated between Dryden and Shadwell over the previous eight years (see **40**), and casts Shadwell as son and
heir not of Ben Jonson (his preferred role) but of Richard Flecknoe (see **38**
and biographical note), a byword for a bad poet.

> All human things are subject to decay,
> And, when Fate summons, monarchs must obey:
> This Flecknoe found, who like Augustus young*
> Was called to empire, and had governed long;
> In prose and verse was owned without dispute
> Through all the realms of nonsense absolute.
> This agèd prince, now flourishing in peace,
> And blessed with issue of a large incrèase,
> Worn out with business, did at length debate
> To settle the succession of the state;   10
> And pondering which of all his sons was fit
> To reign, and wage immortal war with wit,
> Cried, ''Tis resolved; for Nature pleads that he
> Should only rule who most resembles me:

Shadwell alone my perfect image bears,
Mature in dullness from his tender years;
Shadwell alone, of all my sons, is he
Who stands confirmed in full stupidity.
The rest to some faint meaning make pretence,
But Shadwell never deviates into sense.   20
Some beams of wit on other souls may fall,
Strike through and make a lucid interval,
But Shadwell's genuine night admits no ray,
His rising fogs prevail upon the day.
Besides, his goodly fabric fills the eye,
And seems designed for thoughtless majesty:
Thoughtless as monarch oaks that shade the plain,
And, spread in solemn state, supinely reign.
Heywood and Shirley were but types of thee,*
Thou last great prophet of tautology:*   30
Ev'n I, a dunce of more renown than they,
Was sent before but to prepare thy way,*
And coarsely clad in rustic drugget came
To teach the nations in thy greater name.
My warbling lute, the lute I whilom strung
When to King John of Portugal I sung,*
Was but the prelude to that glorious day
When thou on silver Thames didst cut thy way
With well-timed oars before the royal barge,*
Swelled with the pride of thy celestial charge,   40
And big with hymn, commander of an host,
The like was ne'er in Epsom blankets tossed.*
Methinks I see the new Arion sail,*
The lute still trembling underneath thy nail:
At thy well-sharpened thumb from shore to shore
The treble squeaks for fear, the basses roar;
Echoes from Pissing Alley "Shadwell" call,*
And "Shadwell" they resound from Aston Hall.*
About thy boat the little fishes throng,
As at the morning toast that floats along.   50
Sometimes as prince of thy harmonious band
Thou wield'st thy papers in thy threshing hand:
St André's feet ne'er kept more equal time,*

Not ev'n the feet of thy own *Psyche*'s rhyme,
Though they in number as in sense excel:
So just, so like tautology they fell
That pale with envy Singleton forswore*   ⎫
The lute and sword which he in triumph bore, ⎬
And vowed he ne'er would act Villerius more.'* ⎭
Here stopped the good old sire, and wept for joy   60
In silent raptures of the hopeful boy.
All arguments, but most his plays, persuade
That for anointed dullness he was made.

   Close to the walls which fair Augusta bind*
(The fair Augusta, much to fears inclined),
An ancient fabric raised t' inform the sight
There stood of yore, and Barbican it hight:
A watchtower once, but now, so Fate ordains,
Of all the pile an empty name remains.
From its old ruins brothel-houses rise,   70
Scenes of lewd loves, and of polluted joys;
Where their vast courts the mother-strumpets keep,
And undisturbed by watch, in silence sleep.
Near these a nursery erects its head,*
Where queens are formed, and future heroes bred;
Where unfledged actors learn to laugh and cry, ⎫
Where infant punks their tender voices try,   ⎬
And little Maximins the gods defy.*   ⎭
Great Fletcher never treads in buskins here,
Nor greater Jonson dares in socks appear;   80
But gentle Simkin just reception finds*
Amidst this monument of vanished minds.
Pure clinches the suburbian Muse affords,
And Panton waging harmless war with words.*
Here Flecknoe, as a place to Fame well known,
Ambitiously designed his Shadwell's throne;
For ancient Dekker prophesied long since*   ⎫
That in this pile should reign a mighty prince, ⎬
Born for a scourge of wit, and flail of sense, ⎭
To whom true dullness should some *Psyches* owe,   90
But worlds of *Misers* from his pen should flow;
Humourists and *Hypocrites* it should produce,

Whole Raymond families, and tribes of Bruce.*
   Now Empress Fame had published the renown
Of Shadwell's coronation through the town.
Roused by report of Fame, the nations meet
From near Bunhill and distant Watling Street.*
No Persian carpets spread th' imperial way,
But scattered limbs of mangled poets lay:
From dusty shops neglected authors come,   100
Martyrs of pies, and relics of the bum.*
Much Heywood, Shirley, Ogilby there lay,*
But loads of Shadwell almost choked the way.
Bilked stationers for yeomen stood prepared,
And Herringman was captain of the guard.*
The hoary prince in majesty appeared,
High on a throne of his own labours reared.*
At his right hand our young Ascanius state,
Rome's other hope, and pillar of the state:
His brows thick fogs, instead of glories, grace,   110
And lambent dullness played around his face.*
As Hannibal did to the altars come,
Sworn by his sire a mortal foe to Rome,*
So Shadwell swore, nor should his vow be vain,
That he till death true dullness would maintain,
And in his father's right, and realm's defence,
Ne'er to have peace with wit, nor truce with sense.
The king himself the sacred unction made,
As king by office, and as priest by trade:
In his sinister hand, instead of ball   120
He placed a mighty mug of potent ale;
Love's Kingdom to his right he did convey,*
At once his sceptre and his rule of sway,
Whose righteous lore the prince had practised young,
And from whose loins recorded *Psyche* sprung.
His temples last with poppies were o'erspread,
That nodding seemed to consecrate his head.
Just at that point of time, if Fame not lie,
On his left hand twelve reverend owls did fly:
So Romulus, 'tis sung, by Tiber's brook   130
Presage of sway from twice six vultures took.*

Th' admiring throng loud acclamations make,
And omens of his future empire take.
The sire then shook the honours of his head,
And from his brows damps of oblivion shed
Full on the filial dullness; long he stood   ⎫
Repelling from his breast the raging god;   ⎬
At length burst out in this prophetic mood: ⎭
  'Heavens bless my son: from Ireland let him reign
To far Barbados on the western main;   140
Of his dominion may no end be known,
And greater than his father's be his throne.
Beyond *Love's Kingdom* let him stretch his pen;'
He paused, and all the people cried, 'Amen'.
Then thus continued he, 'My son, advance
Still in new impudence, new ignorance.
Success let others teach; learn thou from me
Pangs without birth, and fruitless industry.
Let *Virtuosos* in five years be writ,
Yet not one thought accuse thy toil of wit.   150
Let gentle George in triumph tread the stage,
Make Dorimant betray, and Loveit rage;
Let Cully, Cockwood, Fopling charm the pit,
And in their folly show the writer's wit;*
Yet still thy fools shall stand in thy defence,
And justify their author's want of sense.
Let 'em be all by thy own model made
Of dullness, and desire no foreign aid,
That they to future ages may be known
Not copies drawn, but issue of thy own.   160
Nay, let thy men of wit too be the same,
All full of thee, and differing but in name.
But let no alien Sedley interpose
To lard with wit thy hungry Epsom prose,*
And when false flowers of rhetoric thou wouldst cull,
Trust nature, do not labour to be dull;
But write thy best, and top, and in each line
Sir Formal's oratory will be thine:
Sir Formal, though unsought, attends thy quill,
And does thy northern dedications fill.*   170

Nor let false friends seduce thy mind to fame
By arrogating Jonson's hostile name:
Let father Flecknoe fire thy mind with praise,
And uncle Ogilby thy envy raise.
Thou art my blood, where Jonson has no part;
What share have we in nature or in art?
Where did his wit on learning fix a brand,
And rail at arts he did not understand?
Where made he love in Prince Nicander's vein,*
Or swept the dust in *Psyche*'s humble strain?   180
Where sold he bargains, "whip-stitch, kiss my arse",*
Promised a play and dwindled to a farce?
When did his Muse from Fletcher scenes purloin,
As thou whole Eth'rege dost transfuse to thine?*
But so transfused as oil on water's flow,
His always floats above, thine sinks below.
This is thy province, this thy wondrous way,
New humours to invent for each new play.
This is that boasted bias of thy mind,
By which one way, to dullness, 'tis inclined,   190
Which makes thy writings lean on one side still,
And in all changes that way bends thy will.
Nor let thy mountain belly make pretence*
Of likeness; thine's a tympany of sense:
A tun of man in thy large bulk is writ,
But sure thou'rt but a kilderkin of wit.
Like mine thy gentle numbers feebly creep,
Thy tragic Muse gives smiles, thy comic sleep.
With whate'er gall thou sett'st thyself to write,
Thy inoffensive satires never bite: 200
In thy felonious heart though venom lies
It does but touch thy Irish pen, and dies.*
Thy genius calls thee not to purchase fame
In keen iambics, but mild anagram.
Leave writing plays, and choose for thy command
Some peaceful province in acrostic land:
There thou mayest wings display and altars raise,*
And torture one poor word ten thousand ways.
Or if thou wouldst thy different talents suit,

Set thy own songs, and sing them to thy lute.'   210
He said; but his last words were scarcely heard, ⎫
For Bruce and Longvil had a trap prepared,   ⎬
And down they sent the yet declaiming bard.* ⎭
Sinking he left his drugget robe behind,
Born upwards by a subterranean wind.
The mantle fell to the young prophet's part
With double portion of his father's art.*

42   [*Doeg and Og*] from *The Second Part of
Absalom and Achitophel*

JOHN DRYDEN

The Second Part of Absalom and Achitophel (1682) was mostly written by
Nahum Tate (1652–1715), but this passage is generally agreed to be
Dryden's work. Doeg is the Whig dramatist and pamphleteer Elkanah
Settle (1648–1724), whose reply to *Absalom and Achitophel* (8), called
Absalom Senior: or, Achitophel Transpros'd, included a malicious personal
attack on Dryden. Og is Shadwell (see 40–1).

Doeg, though without knowing how or why,
Made still a blundering kind of melody;
Spurred boldly on, and dashed through thick and thin,
Through sense and nonsense, never out nor in;
Free from all meaning, whether good or bad,
And in one word, heroically mad.
He was too warm on picking work to dwell, ⎫
But faggotted his notions as they fell,   ⎬
And if they rhymed and rattled all was well. ⎭   420
Spiteful he is not, though he wrote a satire,
For still there goes some thinking to ill nature;
He needs no more than birds and beasts to think,
All his occasions are to eat and drink.
If he call 'rogue' and 'rascal' from a garret
He means you no more mischief than a parrot.
The words for friend and foe alike were made,
To fetter 'em in verse is all his trade.

For almonds he'll cry 'whore' to his own mother,*
And call young Absalom King David's brother. 430
Let him be gallows-free by my consent,
And nothing suffer since he nothing meant.
Hanging supposes human soul and reason;
This animal's below committing treason.
Shall he be hanged who never could rebel?
That's a preferment for Achitophel.
The woman that committed buggery
Was rightly sentenced by the law to die,
But 'twas hard fate that to the gallows led
The dog that never heard the statute read. 440
Railing in other men may be a crime,
But ought to pass for mere instinct in him.
Instinct he follows, and no farther knows,
For to write verse with him is to transprose.
'Twere pity treason at his door to lay,
Who 'makes heaven's gate a lock to its own key'.*
Let him rail on, let his invective Muse
Have four and twenty letters to abuse,*
Which if he jumbles to one line of sense
Indict him of a capital offence. 450
In fireworks give him leave to vent his spite,
Those are the only serpents he can write;
The height of his ambition is we know
But to be master of a puppet show:
On that one stage his works may yet appear,
And a month's harvest keeps him all the year.

   Now stop your noses, readers, all and some,⎫
For here's a tun of midnight-work to come, ⎬
Og from a treason-tavern rolling home. ⎭
Round as a globe, and liquored every chink, 460
Goodly and great he sails behind his link;
With all this bulk there's nothing lost in Og,
For every inch that is not fool is rogue:
A monstrous mass of foul corrupted matter,
As all the devils had spewed to make the batter.
When wine has given him courage to blaspheme
He curses God, but God before cursed him;

And if man could have reason, none has more
That made his paunch so rich, and him so poor.
With wealth he was not trusted, for heaven knew   470
What 'twas of old to pamper up a Jew;
To what would he on quail and pheasant swell,
That ev'n on tripe and carrion could rebel?
But though heaven made him poor (with rev'rence speaking)
He never was a poet of God's making.
The midwife laid her hand on his thick skull
With this prophetic blessing: 'Be thou dull.'
Drink, swear and roar, forbear no lewd delight
Fit for thy bulk, do anything but write.
Thou art of lasting make like thoughtless men,   480
A strong nativity—but for the pen.
Eat opium, mingle arsenic in thy drink,
Still thou may'st live avoiding pen and ink.
I see, I see 'tis counsel given in vain,
For treason botched in rhyme will be thy bane.
Rhyme is the rock on which thou art to wreck,
'Tis fatal to thy fame and to thy neck.
Why should thy metre good King David blast?
A psalm of his will surely be thy last.*
Dar'st thou presume in verse to meet thy foes,   490
Thou whom the penny pamphlet foiled in prose?
Doeg, whom God for mankind's mirth has made,
O'ertops thy talent in thy very trade;
Doeg to thee—thy paintings are so coarse—
A poet is, though he's the poet's horse.
A double noose thou on thy neck dost pull
For writing treason, and for writing dull:
To die for faction is a common evil,
But to be hanged for nonsense is the devil.
Hadst thou the glories of thy King expressed,   500
Thy praises had been satire at the best;
But thou in clumsy verse, unlicked, unpointed,
Hast shamefully defied the Lord's Anointed.
I will not rake the dunghill of thy crimes,
For who would read thy life that reads thy rhymes?
But of King David's foes be this the doom,

> May all be like the young man Absalom;
> And for my foes may this their blessing be,
> To talk like Doeg, and to write like thee.

43   *To My Dear Friend Mr Congreve, on his*
        Comedy called 'The Double-Dealer'

JOHN DRYDEN

Printed 1694 with Congreve's play. The poem reflects on Dryden's position after the Revolution of 1688–9, when he was ousted as Poet Laureate
and Historiographer Royal, and succeeded (ironically) by Shadwell. When
Shadwell died in 1692, Thomas Rymer became Historiographer Royal
(see l. 48) and Nahum Tate Poet Laureate. Dryden sees Congreve as his
true successor.

> Well then, the promised hour is come at last;
> The present age of wit obscures the past.
> Strong were our sires; and as they fought they writ,
> Conquering with force of arms and dint of wit;
> Theirs was the giant race before the flood,*
> And thus, when Charles returned, our empire stood.
> Like Janus he the stubborn soil manured,*
> With rules of husbandry the rankness cured;
> Tamed us to manners, when the stage was rude,
> And boist'rous English wit with art indued.   10
> Our age was cultivated thus at length,
> But what we gained in skill we lost in strength.
> Our builders were with want of genius cursed;
> The second temple was not like the first:
> Till you, the best Vitruvius, come at length,
> Our beauties equal, but excel our strength.
> Firm Doric pillars found your solid base,   ⎫
> The fair Corinthian crowns the higher space;   ⎬
> Thus all below is strength, and all above is grace. ⎭ *
> In easy dialogue is Fletcher's praise: 20
> He moved the mind, but had not power to raise.

Great Jonson did by strength of judgement please,
Yet, doubling Fletcher's force, he wants his ease.
In differing talents both adorned their age,
One for the study, t'other for the stage.*
But both to Congreve justly shall submit,
One matched in judgement, both o'er-matched in wit.
In him all beauties of this age we see:
Etherege his courtship, Southerne's purity,*
The satire, wit, and strength of manly Wycherley.   30
All this in blooming youth you have achieved,
Nor are your foiled contemporaries grieved;
So much the sweetness of your manners move,
We cannot envy you, because we love.
Fabius might joy in Scipio, when he saw*
A beardless consul made against the law,
And join his suffrage to the votes of Rome,
Though he with Hannibal was overcome.
Thus old Romano bowed to Raphael's fame,*
And scholar to the youth he taught, became.   40
    O that your brows my laurel had sustained!
Well had I been deposed, if you had reigned;
The father had descended for the son;
For only you are lineal to the throne.
Thus when the state one Edward did depose,
A greater Edward in his room arose.*
But now not I, but poetry is cursed,
For Tom the Second reigns like Tom the First.
But let 'em not mistake my patron's part,*
Nor call his charity their own desert.   50
Yet this I prophesy: thou shalt be seen
(Though with some short parenthesis between)
High on the throne of wit; and seated there
Not mine (that's little) but thy laurel wear.
Thy first attempt an early promise made;*
That early promise this has more than paid.
So bold, yet so judiciously you dare,
That your least praise is to be regular.
Time, place, and action may with pains be wrought,
But genius must be born, and never can be taught.   60

This is your portion, this your native store; ⎫
Heaven that but once was prodigal before, ⎬
To Shakespeare gave as much; she could not give him more. ⎭
   Maintain your post; that's all the fame you need,
For 'tis impossible you should proceed.
Already I am worn with cares and age,
And just abandoning th' ungrateful stage:
Unprofitably kept at heaven's expense,
I live a rent-charge on his providence:
But you, whom every Muse and Grace adorn,   70
Whom I foresee to better fortune born,
Be kind to my remains; and O defend,
Against your judgement, your departed friend!
Let not th' insulting foe my fame pursue,
But shade those laurels which descend to you;
And take for tribute what these lines express:
You merit more; nor could my love do less.

44   [*Ten Prologues and Epilogues*]

The Restoration playhouse was a comparatively intimate space, many of the actors and actresses were well known to the audience, and a rapport was quickly established between them (both during performances and afterwards). Audiences were often boisterous, critical, and inattentive, and some theatregoers seemed mainly interested in displaying their own wit and fashions (44e). The prologues and epilogues which framed each performance provided an opportunity to defend or excuse the play or the performance, and to flatter or insult the audience: so Aphra Behn defends the role of the female playwright (44g), and most texts comment on the manners and judgement of the audience. The actresses, who at the Restoration replaced the boy actors who had taken women's roles in the prewar theatre (44c), were frequently represented in prologues and epilogues as sexually available, though we see that they used their reputation to tease and satirize the men in the audience (44a and j). As the country passed through the political turbulence of the Popish Plot and Exclusion Crisis, the theatre became politicized, and this is reflected in two anti-Whig pieces (44h and i).

(a) 'Epilogue to *Tyrannic Love*'

JOHN DRYDEN

Performed June 1669; published with the play 1670. It is spoken by Ellen ('Nell') Gwyn (1642/50–1687). She was an orange-seller in the Theatre Royal in 1663, and joined the King's Company as an actress the following year. She was the mistress of its leading actor Charles Hart, then mistress of the Earl of Dorset, and became the King's mistress *c.*1668, bearing him two sons. In *Tyrannic Love* (which depicts the martyrdom of St Catharine) she played Valeria, who stabs herself in the final scene. As she says in l. 16, her forte was for comedy rather than tragedy.

*Spoken by Mrs Ellen, when she was to be
carried off dead by the bearers.*

To the bearer:
   Hold, are you mad? you damned confounded dog,
   I am to rise, and speak the Epilogue.

To the audience:
   I come, kind gentlemen, strange news to tell ye,
   I am the ghost of poor departed Nelly.
   Sweet ladies, be not frighted, I'll be civil,
   I'm what I was, a little harmless devil.
   For after death we sprites have just such natures
   We had for all the world when human creatures;
   And therefore I that was an actress here,
   Play all my tricks in hell, a goblin there.   10
   Gallants, look to't, you say there are no sprites,
   But I'll come dance about your beds at nights.
   And faith, you'll be in a sweet kind of taking
   When I surprise you between sleep and waking.
   To tell you true, I walk because I die
   Out of my calling in a tragedy.
   O poet, damned dull poet, who could prove
   So senseless to make Nelly die for love!
   Nay, what's yet worse, to kill me in the prime
   Of Easter term, in tart and cheese-cake time!   20
   I'll fit the fop, for I'll not one word say
   T' excuse his godly out-of-fashion play:

A play which if you dare but twice sit out,
You'll all be slandered, and be thought devout.
But farewell, gentlemen, make haste to me,
I'm sure ere long to have your company.
As for my epitaph when I am gone,
I'll trust no poet, but will write my own:
Here Nelly lies, who though she lived a slattern,
Yet died a princess, acting in St Cathar'n.   30

(b) 'Prologue to *Marriage A-la-Mode*'

JOHN DRYDEN

Performed November 1671; published with the play 1673. Recruitment
for the Third Dutch War had removed some men from the audience.

> Lord, how reformed and quiet we are grown,
> Since all our braves and all our wits are gone:
> Fop-corner now is free from civil war,
> White wig and vizard mask no longer jar.
> France and the fleet have swept the town so clear
> That we can act in peace, and you can hear.
> 'Twas a sad sight, before they marched from home,⎫
> To see our warriors in red waistcoats come ⎬
> With hair tucked up into our tiring room. ⎭
> But 'twas more sad to hear their last adieu;   10
> The women sobbed, and swore they would be true;
> And so they were, as long as e'er they could: ⎫
> But powerful guinea cannot be withstood, ⎬
> And they were made of playhouse flesh and blood. ⎭
> Fate did their friends for double use ordain,⎫
> In wars abroad they grinning honour gain, ⎬
> And mistresses, for all that stay, maintain. ⎭
> Now they are gone, 'tis dead vacation here,
> For neither friends nor enemies appear.
> Poor pensive punk now peeps ere plays begin,   20
> Sees the bare bench, and dares not venture in,
> But manages her last half-crown with care,
> And trudges to the Mall, on foot, for air.

Our city friends so far will hardly come,
They can take up with pleasures nearer home,
And see gay shows, and gaudy scenes elsewhere:
For we presume they seldom come to hear.
But they have now ta'en up a glorious trade,
And cutting Morecraft struts in masquerade.*
There's all our hope, for we shall show today   30
A masking ball to recommend our play:
Nay, to endear 'em more, and let 'em see
We scorn to come behind in courtesy,
We'll follow the new mode which they begin,
And treat 'em with a room, and couch within:*
For that's one way, howe'er the play fall short,
T' oblige the town, the city and the court.

(c) 'Epilogue to *The Parson's Wedding*'

THOMAS KILLIGREW

Probably performed June 1672; published in *Covent Garden Drolery* (1672). Though the prologue and epilogue were for a revival of Killigrew's play, they may not have been written by him. The play was performed by an all-women cast, perhaps as a way of appealing to audiences after the Theatre Royal had been burnt down in January 1672 (see ll. 25–6).

When boys played women's parts, you'd think the stage
Was innocent, in that untempting age.
No: for your amorous fathers then, like you,
Amongst those boys had playhouse misses too:
They set those bearded beauties on their laps,
Men gave 'em kisses, and the ladies claps.
But they, poor hearts, could not supply our room:
They went but females to the tiring room,
While we, in kindness to ourselves, and you,
Can hold out women to our lodgings too.   10
Now, to oppose the humour of that age,
We have this day expelled our men the stage.
Why cannot we as well perform their parts?
No, t'would not take: the tender ladies' hearts

Would then their former charity give o'er:
The madams in disguise would steal no more
To the young actors' chambers, in masked faces,
To leave love-offerings of point and laces.
Nor can we act their parts: alas, too soon
You'd find the cheat in th' empty pantaloon.   20
Well, though we are not women's men, at least
We hope to have you gallants constant guests:
Which, if you grant, and fill our house each day,
We will return your kindnesses this way:
We'll build up a new theatre to gain you,
And turn this to a house to entertain you.

(d) 'Prologue to *The Double Marriage*'

APHRA BEHN

Used at a revival of Fletcher and Massinger's *The Double Marriage*;
published in *Covent Garden Drolery* (1672). Subsequently re-used as the
Prologue to Behn's *Abdelazer* (1677) and the epilogue to her *The Widow
Ranter* (1690). Behn's authorship is not certain.

Gallants, you have so long been absent hence,
That you have almost cooled your diligence;
For while we study or revive a play,
You, like good husbands, in the country stay;
There frugally wear out your summer suit,⎱
And in frieze jerkin after beagles toot, ⎬
Or in montero caps at fieldfares shoot. ⎰
Nay, some are so obdùrate in their sin
That they swear never to come up again,
But all their charge of clothes and treat retrench   10
To gloves and stockings for some country wench.
Even they who in the summer had mishaps
Send up to town for physic for their claps.
The ladies, too, are as resolved as they, ⎱
And, having debts unknown to them, they stay,⎬
And with the gain of cheese and poultry pay. ⎰
Even in their visits they from banquets fall

To entertain with nuts and bottle-ale;
And in discourse with secrecy report
Stale news that passed a twelvemonth since at court.　　20
These of them who are most refined and gay
Now learn the songs of the last summer's play;
While the young daughter does in private mourn:
Her love's in town, and hopes not to return.
These country grievances too great appear,
But, cruel ladies, we have greater here:
You come not sharp, as you were wont, to plays,
But only on the first and second days.*
This made our poet in his visits look
What new strange courses for your time you took;　　30
And to his great regret he found too soon
Damned beasts and ombre spent the afternoon;
So that we cannot hope to see you here
Before the little net-work purse be clear.
Suppose you should have luck—
Yet sitting up so late, as I am told,
You'll lose in beauty what you win in gold;
And what each lady of another says
Will make you new lampoons, and us new plays.

(e) 'Prologue to *The Ordinary*'

ANONYMOUS

Probably performed 1673; published in *A Collection of Poems* (1673). The occasion was a revival of the play by Sir William Cartwright.

From you grave men of business and of trade,
Who were for industry, not pleasure, made,
We seldom do implore, or hope for aid;
For we but rarely are obliged by you:
You come but when y' ave nothing else to do.
Besides, our wit to you needs no excuse,
For you all wit do like a mistress use—
A thing you seldom see—while some are cloyed
With wit, as with a wife too oft enjoyed.

Nay, you will think that wit which is not so: 10
A quibble or a little pun takes you.
Dullness does men for business prepare,
Whilst wit delights in ease, and hates all care.
But to the young brisk men who think it fit
To spend no afternoon but in the pit,*
Whether we will or no, we must submit.
Some come with lusty burgundy half-drunk,
T' eat China oranges, make love to punk,
And briskly mount a bench when th' Act is done,
And comb their much-loved periwigs to the tune; 20
And can sit out a play of three hours long,
Minding no part of't but the dance or song.
These are our trusty friends; but some there are,
Most bloody judges, who no poets spare.
But I have heard some injured authors say
That these most parlous cens'rers of a play
With little wit, which they so much employ,
Which by reflection only they enjoy,
Would even those from whom they took 't destroy.
So does the famed enlight'ner of the night 30
Eclipse the sun, from whom she sh'ad all her light;
And these mock-critics hiss, and whistle loud,
And with their noise outvie bear-baiting crowd.
But, ladies, you are sweet, and soft, and fair,
And will the poet and the actors spare.
But busy men and sparks are welcome now,
The little misses, and great ladies too:
You altogether make a noble show.
Y'ave paid for't, and whatever poets say,
Think or say what you please of this our play. 40

(f) 'Epilogue to *The Man of Mode*'

JOHN DRYDEN

Performed March 1676 at the première of Sir George Etherege's play;
published with the play in the same year. Dryden highlights Etherege's
portrayal of Sir Fopling Flutter, the 'man of mode', and the absurd
affectations of contemporary fashion.

Most modern wits such monstrous fools have shown,
They seemed not of heaven's making, but their own.
Those nauseous harlequins in farce may pass,
But there goes more to a substantial ass!*
Something of man must be exposed to view,
That, gallants, they may more resemble you.
Sir Fopling is a fool so nicely writ
The ladies would mistake him for a wit,
And when he sings, talks loud, and cocks, would cry,
'I vow, methinks he's pretty company,   10
So brisk, so gay, so travelled, so refined!'
As he took pains to graff upon his kind:*
True fops help nature's work, and go to school
To file and finish God A'mighty's fool.
Yet none Sir Fopling him or him can call:
He's knight o' the shire, and represents ye all.
From each he meets he culls whate'er he can,
Legion's his name, a people in a man.
His bulky folly gathers as it goes,
And, rolling o'er you, like a snowball grows.   20
His various modes from various fathers follow,
One taught the toss, and one the new French wallow.
His sword-knot this, his cravat this designed,
And this, the yard-long snake he twirls behind.
From one the sacred periwig he gained,
Which wind ne'er blew, nor touch of hat profaned.
Another's diving bow he did adore,
Which with a shog casts all the hair before,
Till he with full decorum brings it back,
And rises with a water spaniel shake.   30
As for his songs (the ladies' dear delight),
Those sure he took from most of you who write.
Yet every man is safe from what he feared,
For no one fool is hunted from the herd.

(g) 'Epilogue to *Sir Patient Fancy*'

APHRA BEHN

Performed January 1678, spoken by Anne Quin; published with the play the same year.

I here and there o'erheard a coxcomb cry,   *Looking about*
'Ah, rot it!—'tis a woman's comedy:
One, who because she lately chanced to please us,*
With her damned stuff will never cease to tease us.'
What has poor woman done that she must be
Debarred from sense, and sacred poetry?
Why in this age has heaven allowed you more
And women less of wit, than heretofore?
We once were famed in story, and could write
Equal to men; could govern; nay, could fight.   10
We still have passive valour, and can show,
Would custom give us leave, the active too,
Since we no provocations want from you.
For who but we could your dull fopperies bear,
Your saucy love, and your brisk nonsense hear;
Endure your worse-than-womanish affectation,
Which renders you the nuisance of the nation;
Scorned ev'n by all the misses of the town,
A jest to vizard mask—the pit buffoon;
A glass by which th' admiring country fool   20
May learn to dress himself *en ridicule*:
Both striving who shall most ingenious grow
In lewdness, foppery, nonsense, noise, and show.
And yet to these fine things we must submit
Our reason, arms, our laurels, and our wit,
Because we do not laugh at you when lewd,
And scorn and cudgel ye when you are rude.
That we have nobler souls than you, we prove
By how much more we're sensible of love:
Quickest in finding all the subtlest ways   30
To make your joys—why not to make you plays?
We best can find your feebles, know our own,

And jilts and cuckolds now best please the town.
Your way of writing's out of fashion grown;
Method and rule you only understand:
Pursue that way of fooling, and be damned.
Your learnèd cant of action, time, and place*
Must all give way to the unlaboured farce.
To all the men of wit we will subscribe,
But for you half-wits, you unthinking tribe,   40
We'll let you see, whate'er besides we do,
How artfully we copy some of you;
And if you're drawn to th' life, pray tell me then
Why women should not write as well as men?

(h) 'Prologue to *Fools have Fortune*'

ANONYMOUS

Probably performed February 1680. Spoken at the height of the Exclusion Crisis, this prologue is hostile to the Whigs. According to a note on the manuscript it was spoken by Mrs Butler.

Gentlemen, I am an ambassadress:
I come from two poor nations, I confess—
Poets and players, who were always low,
But never were so humble as they're now.
Long with you critics have the poets fought,
And by the stage's help, wit's empire sought;
But whilst you three weak nations fight and brawl,*
Plotters and politics devour you all.
But now my masters, tired with this contèst,
Would league with you for common interest;   10
Not but if wit's destruction be decreed
We have more trades to trust to for a need:
Poets can fall a-writing those romances
Which they call *Protestant Intelligences*;*
Some of our men can dance, and some can trim;
Nokes has a toy shop, Tony Leigh can limn;*
And I believe 'tis known to most of you
Our female actresses have toy shops too.

Nokes has more choice of knacks, none can deny,
But to the fox, what did the cat reply,   20
When the fox boasted of his many wiles
To save himself? The puss with scornful smiles
Climbing a tree, cried, 'Fox, the hunters bawl;
You've many tricks; I have one worth 'em all.'
'Tis seldom a new play with you prevails,
But a new woman almost never fails.
New, did I say? Nay, though the town before
Had rumpled, read, and thumbed her o'er and o'er,
But on the stage no sooner she appears,
But presently the spark prick up their ears,   30
And all in clusters round the scenes betake,
Like boys about a bush to catch a snake.
The charming silver and the price does win,
And then the snake does quickly cast her skin,
And in embroidery struts, and *point Venee*
Who th' other day was daggled to the knee.
You see two excellent trades we can repair:
Then I demand your answer—peace or war?
Will you wit, women, love, and pleasure choose,
Or pamphlets, prating fops, or lying news?   40
You'll be the losers if you let us fall:
I cannot wish more mischief to you all.
Fops will lose brave conveniencies for sin,
And vapouring huffs to quarrel safely in.

(i) 'Prologue to *The City Heiress*'

THOMAS OTWAY

Probably spoken May 1682; printed the same year as a separate broadside, and also with the play. The Prologue was written by Otway and spoken by Elizabeth Barry; the play was by Aphra Behn, and satirized the Earl of Shaftesbury as Sir Timothy Treat-all. By this date the tide had turned against the Whigs. Lines 15–34 refer to Titus Oates (see 8, ll. 632–77, and 9) who had recently been ejected from his lodgings in Whitehall and moved to the City of London. More people were now regarding his allegations as false (the 'sham plots' of l. 41). Lines 35–42 refer to the Whigs' plans for a defiant feast at Haberdashers' Hall on 21 April 1682, which was banned by the King. Tickets, sold at a guinea each, described the occasion as a 'testimony of thankfulness' to God for the protection of the King and the Protestant religion from the Popish Plot.

> How vain have proved the labours of the stage
> In striving to reclaim a vicious age!
> Poets may write, the mischief to impeach—
> You care as little what the poets teach
> As you regard at church what parsons preach.
> But where such follies and such vices reign,
> What honest pen has patience to refrain?
> At church, in pews ye most devoutly snore,
> And here, got dully drunk, ye come to roar.
> Ye go to church to gloat and ogle there,   10
> And come to meet more lewd convenient here.
> With equal zeal ye honour either place,
> And run so very evenly your race
> Y' improve in wit just as you do in grace.
> It must be so, some demon has possessed
> Our land, and we have never since been blessed.
> Y' have seen it all, or heard of its renown:
> In reverend shape it stalked about the town,
> Six yeomen tall attending on its frown.
> Sometimes with humble note, and zealous lore,   20
> 'Twould play the apostolic function o'er,
> But heaven have mercy on us when it swore.*
> Whene'er it swore, to prove the oaths were true,
> Out of its mouth, at random, halters flew
> Round some unwary neck, by magic thrown,
> Though still the cunning devil saved its own.
> For when th' enchantment could no longer last,
> The subtle pug, most dext'rously uncased,
> Left awful form for one more seeming pious,
> And in a moment varied to defy us—   30
> From silken doctor, home-spun Ananias;*
> Left the lewd court, and did in city fix,
> Where still by its old arts it plays new tricks,
> And fills the heads of fools with politics.

This demon lately drew in many a guest
To part with zealous guinea for—no feast.
Who but the most incorrigible fops,
For ever doomed in dismal cells, called shops,
To cheat and damn themselves to get their livings,
Would lay sweet money out in sham thanksgivings?   40
Sham plots you may have paid for o'er and o'er,
But who e'er paid for a sham treat before?
Had you not better sent your offerings all
Hither to us, than Sequestrators' Hall?
I being your steward, justice had been done ye:
I could have entertained you worth your money.

(j) 'Epilogue to *King Arthur*'

JOHN DRYDEN

Performed May or June 1691; published with the play the same year. It
was spoken by Anne Bracegirdle.

I've had today a dozen billets-doux,
From fops, and wits, and cits, and Bow Street beaux;*
Some from Whitehall, but from the Temple more;*
A Covent Garden porter brought me four.*
I have not yet read all: but, without feigning,
We maids can make shrewd guesses at your meaning.
What if, to show your styles, I read 'em here? ⎫
Methinks I hear one cry, 'O Lord, forbear! ⎬
No, madam, no! By heaven, that's too severe!' ⎭
Well then, be safe——   10
But swear henceforwards to renounce all writing, ⎫
And take this solemn oath of my inditing: ⎬
'As you love ease, and hate campaigns and fighting'. ⎭
Yet, 'faith, 'tis just to make some few examples:
What if I showed you one or two for samples?
Pulls one out. Here's one desires my ladyship to meet
At the kind couch above in Bridges Street.*
O sharping knave, that would have you know what
For a poor sneaking treat of chocolate!

Pulls out another. Now, in the name of luck, I'll break   20
  this open,
Because I dreamt last night I had a token.
The superscription is exceeding pretty:
'To the desire of all the town and city'.*
Now, gallants, you must know this precious fop
Is foreman of a haberdasher's shop:
One who devoutly cheats, demure in carriage,
And courts me to the holy bands of marriage.
But with a civil innuendo too:
My overplus of love shall be for you.*
Reads: 'Madam, I swear your looks are so divine,   30
When I set up, your face shall be my sign:
Though times are hard, to show how I adore you,
Here's my whole heart, and half a guinea for you.
But have a care of beaux, they're false, my honey;
And which is worse, have not one rag of money!'
 See how maliciously the rogue would wrong ye;
But I know better things of some among ye.
My wisest way will be to keep the stage,
And trust to the good nature of the age;
And he that likes the music and the play   40
Shall be my favourite gallant today.

45 From *The History of the Royal Society of London*

THOMAS SPRAT

The History of the Royal-Society of London. For the Improving of Natural Knowledge was first published 1667. The Royal Society was founded in 1662 for the promotion of 'natural philosophy', which we would now call 'experimental science'. Sprat's history defends the Society against the contemporary prejudices that its work was frivolous or even ungodly. The first extract envisages the creation of a companion institution to purify and codify the English language, and to refine English literary style; it would have exercised a similar role to that of the Académie française, which had first met in 1634. No such academy materialized in Restoration England, though an informal academy (including Dryden) met for a while under the auspices of the Earl of Roscommon. Dryden showed an interest in the idea of regularizing and purifying the English language in the

Dedication to *Troilus and Cressida* (1679; *Works*, xiii. 222–4). In the second extract, Sprat explains that the Royal Society encourages a plain and sober style in its meetings and publications, particularly rejecting jargon and extravagant metaphor; here he is marking a break with the stylistic exuberance of much early seventeenth-century prose, and with the obfuscatory vocabulary which characterized much contemporary scholastic philosophy, alchemy, and puritan Nonconformist writing. Sprat's ideal of a lucid and accessible style for scientific writing finds a counterpart in the elegant, conversational manner of the period's literary prose, exemplified in Dryden's critical essays.

A Proposal for Erecting an English Academy

I hope now it will not be thought a vain digression, if I step a little aside to recommend the forming of such an assembly to the gentlemen of our nation. I know indeed that the English genius is not so airy and discoursive as that of some of our neighbours, but that we generally love to have reason set out in plain, undeceiving expressions, as much as they to have it delivered with colour and beauty. And besides this, I understand well enough that they have one great assistance to the growth of oratory which to us is wanting; that is, that their nobility live commonly close together in their cities, and ours for the most part scattered in their country houses. For the same reason why our streets are not so well built as theirs will hold also for their exceeding us in the arts of speech. They prefer the pleasures of the town, we those of the field; whereas it is from the frequent conversations in cities that the humour, and wit, and variety, and elegance of language are chiefly to be fetched. But yet, notwithstanding these discouragements, I shall not stick to say that such a project is now seasonable to be set on foot, and may make a great reformation in the manner of our speaking and writing. First, the thing itself is no way contemptible. For the purity of speech and greatness of empire have in all countries still met together. The Greeks spoke best when they were in their glory of conquest. The Romans made those times the standard of their wit when they subdued and gave laws to the world. And from thence, by degrees, they declined to corruption, as their valour, their prudence, and the honour of their arms did decay; and at last did even meet the northern nations halfway in barbarism, a little before they were overrun by their armies.

But besides, if we observe well the English language, we shall find that it seems at this time more than others to require some such aid to bring it to its last perfection. The truth is, it has been hitherto a little too carelessly handled, and, I think, has had less labour spent about its polishing than it deserves. Till the time of King Henry the Eighth there was scarce any man regarded it but Chaucer, and nothing was written in it which one would be willing to read twice, but some of his poetry. But then it began to raise itself a little, and to sound tolerably well. From that age down to the beginning of our late civil wars, it was still fashioning and beautifying itself. In the wars themselves (which is a time wherein all languages use, if ever, to increase by extraordinary degrees; for in such busy and active times there arise more new thoughts of men which must be signified and varied by new expressions), then, I say, it received many fantastical terms which were introduced by our religious sects, and many outlandish phrases which several writers and translators in that great hurry brought in and made free as they pleased, and withal it was enlarged by many sound and necessary forms and idioms which it before wanted. And now, when men's minds are somewhat settled, their passions allayed, and the peace of our country gives us the opportunity of such diversions, if some sober and judicious men would take the whole mass of our language into their hands as they find it, and would set a mark on the ill words, correct those which are to be retained, admit and establish the good, and make some emendations in the accent and grammar, I dare pronounce that our speech would quickly arrive at as much plenty as it is capable to receive, and at the greatest smoothness which its derivation from the rough German will allow it.

Nor would I have this new English academy confined only to the weighing words and letters, but there may be also greater works found out for it. By many signs we may guess that the wits of our nation are not inferior to any other, and that they have an excellent mixture of the spirit of the French and the Spaniard; and I am confident that we only want a few more standing examples, and a little more familiarity with the ancients, to excel all the moderns. Now the best means that can be devised to bring that about, is to settle a fixed and impartial court of eloquence, according to whose censure all books or authors should either stand or fall. And above all, there might be recommended to them one principal work in which we are yet defective, and that is the compiling of a history of our late civil wars. Of all the labours of men's wit and industry, I scarce know any that can be more useful to the world than civil history, if it were written with that sincerity and majesty as it ought to be, as a faithful idea of human actions. And it is observable that almost in all civilized countries it has been the last thing that has come to perfection. I may now say that the English can already show many industrious and worthy pieces in its kind, but yet I have some prophetical imagination in my thoughts that there is still behind something greater than any we have yet seen, reserved for the glory of this age. One reason of this my strong persuasion, is a comparison that I make between the condition of our state and that of the Romans: they at first writ in this way not much better than our monks, only registering in an undigested manner some few naked breviaries of their wars and leagues, and acts of their city magistrates. And indeed, they advanced forward by very slow degrees; for I remember that Tully somewhere complains in these words: *Historia nondum Latinis literis illustrata.** But it was in the peaceful reign of Augustus, after the conclusion of their long civil wars, that most of their perfect historians appeared. And it seems to me that we may expect the same progress amongst us. There lie now ready in bank the most memorable actions of twenty years: a subject of as great dignity and variety as ever passed under any man's hands: the peace which we now enjoy gives leisure and encouragement enough; the effects of such a work would be wonderfully advantageous to the safety of our country, and to his majesty's interest: for there can be no better means to preserve his subjects in obedience for the future than to give them a full view of the miseries that attended rebellion. There are only therefore wanting, for the finishing of so brave an undertaking, the united endeavours of some public minds, who are conversant both in letters and business; and if it were appointed to be the labour of one or two men to compose it, and of such an assembly to revise and correct it, it might certainly challenge all the writings of past or present times.

. . .

Their Manner of Discourse

Thus they have directed, judged, conjectured upon, and improved experiments. But lastly, in these and all other businesses that have come under their care, there is one thing more, about which the Society has been most solicitous; and that is the manner of their discourse: which, unless they had been very watchful to keep in due temper, the whole spirit and vigour of their design had been soon eaten out by the luxury and redundance of speech. The ill effects of this superfluity of talking have already overwhelmed most other arts and professions, insomuch that when I consider the means of happy living, and the causes of their corruption, I can hardly forbear recanting what I said before, and concluding that eloquence ought to be banished out of all civil societies as a thing fatal to peace and good manners. To this opinion I should wholly incline, if I did not find that it is a weapon which may be as easily procured by bad men as good: and that, if these should only cast it away, and those retain it, the naked innocence of virtue would be upon all occasions exposed to the armed malice of the wicked. This is the chief reason that should now keep up the ornaments of speaking in any request, since they are so much degenerated from their original usefulness. They were at first, no doubt, an admirable instrument in the hands of wise men, when they were only employed to describe goodness, honesty, obedience in larger, fairer, and more moving images: to represent truth clothed with bodies, and to bring knowledge back again to our very senses, from whence it was first derived to our understandings. But now they are generally changed to worse uses: they make the fancy disgust the best things if they come sound and unadorned: they are in open defiance against reason, professing not to hold much correspondence with that, but with its slaves, the passions: they give the mind a motion too changeable and bewitching to consist with right practice. Who can behold without indignation how many mists and uncertainties these specious tropes and figures have brought on our knowledge? How many rewards, which are due to more profitable and difficult arts, have been still snatched away by the easy vanity of fine speaking? For now I am warmed with this just anger, I cannot withhold myself from betraying the shallowness of all these seeming mysteries, upon which we writers and speakers look so big. And, in few words, I dare say that of all the studies of men, nothing may be sooner obtained than this vicious abundance of phrase, this trick of metaphors, this volubility of tongue, which makes so great a noise in the world. But I spend words in vain, for the evil is now so inveterate that it is hard to know whom to blame, or where to begin to reform. We all value one another so much upon this beautiful deceit, and labour so long after it, in the years of our education, that we cannot but ever after think kinder of it than it deserves. And indeed, in most other parts of learning I look on it to be a thing almost utterly desperate in its cure, and I think it may be placed amongst those general mischiefs, such as the dissension of Christian princes, the want of practice in religion, and the like; which have been so long spoken against that men are become insensible about them, every one shifting off the fault from himself to others, and so they are only made bare commonplaces of complaint. It will suffice my present purpose to point out what has been done by the Royal Society towards the correcting of its excesses in natural philosophy, to which it is, of all others, a most professed enemy.*

They have therefore been most rigorous in putting in execution the only remedy that can be found for this extravagance, and that has been a constant resolution to reject all the amplifications, digressions, and swellings of style; to return back to the primitive purity and shortness, when men delivered so many things almost in an equal number of words. They have exacted from all their members a close, naked, natural way of speaking, positive expressions, clear senses, a native easiness, bringing all things as near the mathematical plainness as they can; and preferring the language of artisans, countrymen, and merchants before that of wits or scholars.

And here there is one thing not to be passed by, which will render this established custom of the Society well nigh everlasting: and that is, the general constitution of the minds of the English. I have already often insisted on some of the prerogatives of England, whereby it may justly lay claim to be the head of a philosophical league, above all other countries in Europe; I have urged its situation, its present genius, and the disposition of its merchants; and many more such arguments to encourage us still remain to be used. But of all others, this which I am now alleging is of the most weighty and important consideration. If there can be a true character given of the universal temper of any nation under heaven, then certainly this must be ascribed to our countrymen: that they have commonly an unaffected sincerity; that they love to deliver their minds with a sound simplicity; that they have the middle qualities between the reserved, subtle southern and the rough, unhewn northern people; that they are not extremely prone to speak; that they are more concerned what others will think of the strength than of the fineness of what they say; and that an universal modesty possesses them. These qualities are conspicuous, and proper to our soil, that we often hear them objected to us by some of our neighbour satirists, in more disgraceful expressions. For they are wont to revile the English with a want of familiarity, and with a melancholy dumpishness; with slowness, silence, and with the unrefined sullenness of their behaviour. But these are only the reproaches of partiality or ignorance: for they ought rather to be commended for an honourable integrity, for a neglect of circumstances and flourishes, for regarding things of greater moment more than less, for a scorn to deceive as well as to be deceived; which are all the best endowments that can enter into a philosophical mind. So that even the position of our climate, the air, the influence of the heaven, the constitution of the English blood, as well as the embraces of the ocean, seem to join with the labours of the Royal Society to render our country a land of experimental knowledge. And it is a good sign that nature will reveal more of its secrets to the English than to others, because it has already furnished them with a genius so well proportioned for the receiving and retaining its mysteries.

LOVE AND FRIENDSHIP

From *Paradise Lost*, Book IV

JOHN MILTON

This passage celebrates the wedded love of Adam and Eve before the Fall.

> Thus at their shady lodge arrived, both stood,   720
> Both turned, and under open sky adored
> The God that made both sky, air, earth, and heaven
> Which they beheld, the moon's resplendent globe
> And starry pole: 'Thou also mad'st the night,
> Maker omnipotent, and thou the day,
> Which we in our appointed work employed
> Have finished happy in our mutual help,
> And mutual love, the crown of all our bliss
> Ordained by thee, and this delicious place
> For us too large, where thy abundance wants   730
> Partakers, and uncropped falls to the ground.
> But thou hast promised from us two a race
> To fill the earth, who shall with us extol
> Thy goodness infinite, both when we wake,
> And when we seek, as now, thy gift of sleep.'
>   This said unanimous, and other rites
> Observing none, but adoration pure
> Which God likes best, into their inmost bower
> Handed they went; and eased the putting off
> These troublesome disguises which we wear,   740
> Straight side by side were laid, nor turned I ween
> Adam from his fair spouse, nor Eve the rites
> Mysterious of connubial love refused:*

Whatever hypocrites austerely talk
Of purity and place and innocence,
Defaming as impure what God declares
Pure, and commands to some, leaves free to all.
Our maker bids increase: who bids abstain
But our destroyer, foe to God and man?*
Hail wedded love, mysterious law, true source   750
Of human offspring, sole propriety
In Paradise of all things common else.
By thee adulterous lust was driven from men
Among the bestial herds to range, by thee
Founded in reason, loyal, just, and pure,
Relations dear, and all the charities
Of father, son, and brother first were known.
Far be it, that I should write thee sin or blame,
Or think thee unbefitting holiest place,
Perpetual fountain of domestic sweets,   760
Whose bed is undefiled and chaste pronounced,
Present, or past, as saints and patriarchs used.
Here Love his golden shafts employs, here lights
His constant lamp, and waves his purple wings,
Reigns here and revels; not in the bought smile
Of harlots, loveless, joyless, unendeared,
Casual fruition, nor in court amours,
Mixed dance, or wanton masque, or midnight ball,
Or serenade, which the starved lover sings
To his proud fair, best quitted with disdain.   770
These lulled by nightingales embracing slept,
And on their naked limbs the flowery roof
Showered roses, which the morn repaired. Sleep on,
Blest pair; and O yet happiest if ye seek
No happier state, and know to know no more.

47 *A Virgin Life*

JANE BARKER

Published in her *Poetical Recreations* (1688).

Since, O ye powers, ye have bestowed on me
So great a kindness for virginity,
Suffer me not to fall into the powers
Of men's almost omnipotent amours:
But in this happy life let me remain,
Fearless of twenty-five and all its train;
Of slights or scorns, or being called 'old maid',
Those goblins which so many have betrayed,
Like harmless kids that are pursued by men
For safety run into a lion's den.   10
Ah, lovely state! How strange it is to see
What mad conceptions some have made of thee!
As though thy being was all wretchedness,
Or foul deformity i' th' ugliest dress;
Whereas thy beauty's pure, celestial,
Thy thoughts divine, thy words angelical:
And such ought all thy votaries to be,
Or else they're so but for necessity.
A virgin bears the impress of all good,
In that dread name all virtue's understood;   20
So equal all her looks, her mien, her dress,
That nought but modesty seems in excess.
And when she any treats or visits make
'Tis not for tattle but for friendship's sake.
Her neighb'ring poor she does adopt her heirs,
And less she cares for her own good than theirs;
And by obedience testifies she can
Be 's good a subject as the stoutest man.
She to her church such filial duty pays
That one would think she'd lived i' th' pristine days.*   30
Her closet, where she does much time bestow,
Is both her library and chapel too,
Where she enjoys society alone

I' the great Three-One.
She drives her whole life's business to these ends:
To serve her God, enjoy her books, and friends.

48 *On Rosania's Apostasy and Lucasia's Friendship*

KATHERINE PHILIPS

This and **49–50** were published posthumously in *Poems by the most deservedly admired Mrs Katherine Philips the Matchless Orinda* (1667). Philips gave romantic names to members of her circle: Rosania is Mary Aubrey (b. 1631), whose private marriage in 1652 caused a rift between her and Philips; Lucasia is Anne Owen, who joined Philips's circle in 1651, and became her closest friend.

Great soul of friendship, whither art thou fled?
Where dost thou now choose to repose thy head?
Or art thou nothing but voice, air, and name,
Found out to put souls in pursuit of fame?
Thy flames being thought immortal, we may doubt
Whether they e'er did burn, that see them out.

Go, wearied soul, find out thy wonted rest
In the safe harbour of Orinda's breast;
There all unknown adventures thou hast found
In thy late transmigrations, expound;   10
That so Rosania's darkness may be known
To be her want of lustre, not thy own.

Then to the great Lucasia have recourse,
There gather up new excellence and force,
Till by a free, unbiased, clear commèrce,
Endearments which no tongue can e'er rehearse,
Lucasia and Orinda shall thee give
Eternity, and make ev'n friendship live.

Hail, great Lucasia, thou shalt doubly shine:
What was Rosania's own is now twice thine;   20
Thou saw'st Rosania's chariot and her flight,
And so the double portion is thy right:*

Though 'twas Rosania's spirit, be content,
Since 'twas at first from thy Orinda sent.

49 *Lucasia, Rosania, and Orinda parting at a Fountain.*
July 1663

KATHERINE PHILIPS

1

Here, here are our enjoyments done,
   And since the love and grief we wear
   Forbids us either word or tear,
And art wants here expression,
See nature furnish us with one.

2

The kind and mournful nymph which here
   Inhabits in her humble cells,
   No longer her own sorrow tells,
Nor for it now concerned appears,
But for our parting sheds these tears.   10

3

Unless she may afflicted be,
   Lest we should doubt her innocence;
   Since she hath lost her best pretence
Unto a matchless purity;
Our love being clearer far than she.

4

Cold as the streams which from her flow,
   Or (if her privater recess
   A greater coldness can express)
Then cold as those dark beds of snow
Our hearts are at this parting blow.   20

5

But Time, that has both wings and feet,
 Our suffering minutes being spent,
  Will visit us with new content;
And sure, if kindness be so sweet,
'Tis harder to forget than meet.

6

Then though the sad adieu we say,
 Yet as the wine we hither bring,
  Revives, and then exalts the spring;
So let our hopes to meet allay
The fears and sorrows of this day.   30

50   *Orinda to Lucasia*

KATHERINE PHILIPS

1

Observe the weary birds ere night be done,
How they would fain call up the tardy sun,
 With feathers hung with dew,
 And trembling voices too,
They court their glorious planet to appear,
That they may find recruits of spirits there.
 The drooping flowers hang their heads,
 And languish down into their beds:
While brooks more bold and fierce than they,
 Wanting those beams, from whence   10
 All things drink influence,
Openly murmur, and demand the day.

2

Thou, my Lucasia, art far more to me,
Than he to all the under-world can be;
 From thee I've heat and light,
 Thy absence makes my night.

But ah! my friend, it now grows very long,
The sadness weighty, and the darkness strong:
   My tears (its dew) dwell on my cheeks,
   And still my heart thy dawning seeks,   20
And to thee mournfully it cries,
   That if too long I wait,
   Ev'n thou may'st come too late,
And not restore my life, but close my eyes.

51   [*The Death of Nisus and Euryalus*, from Virgil, *Aeneid* IX]

JOHN DRYDEN

Published in the Dryden–Tonson miscellany *Sylvae* (1685). Nisus and his younger friend Euryalus are two of the band of warriors who have escaped from Troy with Aeneas, and have followed him to Italy, where the Trojan forces are opposed by the local inhabitants led by Turnus. According to some interpretations the men are lovers. In Book V, Virgil relates how the friends take part in a race; Nisus is leading, with Salius second and Euryalus third, when Nisus slips, and in falling contrives to trip Salius, thus giving the victory to Euryalus. In this extract from Book IX, Virgil narrates the story of the friends' attempt to break through the enemy lines at night and reach their commander Aeneas.

The war being now broken out betwixt the Trojans and Latins, and Aeneas being overmatched in numbers by his enemies, who were aided by King Turnus, he fortifies his camp, and leaves in it his young son Ascanius under the direction of his chief councillors and captains, while he goes in person to beg succours from King Evander and the Tuscans. Turnus takes advantage of his absence and assaults his camp; the Trojans in it are reduced to great extremities, which gives the poet the occasion of continuing this admirable episode, wherein he describes the friendship, the generosity, the adventures and the death of Nisus and Euryalus.

The Trojan camp the common danger shared;
By turns they watched the walls, and kept the nightly guard.
To warlike Nisus fell the gate by lot
(Whom Hyrtacus on huntress Ida got,

And sent to sea, Aeneas to attend);
Well could he dart the spear, and shafts unerring send.
Beside him stood Euryalus, his ever-faithful friend.
No youth in all the Trojan host was seen
More beautiful in arms, or of a nobler mien;
Scarce was the down upon his chin begun,   10
One was their friendship, their desire was one;
With minds united in the field they warred,
And now were both by choice upon the guard.
Then Nisus thus:
'Or do the gods this warlike warmth inspire,
Or makes each man a god of his desire?
A noble ardour boils within my breast,
Eager of action, enemy of rest,
That urges me to fight, or undertake
Some deed that may my fame immortal make.   20
Thou seest the foe secure; how faintly shine
Their scattered fires, the most in sleep supine,
Dissolved in ease, and drunk with victory;
The few awake the fuming flagon ply,
All hushed around. Now hear what I revolve
Within my mind, and what my labouring thoughts resolve.
Our absent lord both camp and council mourn;
By message both would hasten his return:
The gifts proposed if they confer on thee
(For fame is recompense enough to me)   30
Methinks beneath yon hill I have espied
A way that safely will my passage guide.'
Euryalus stood listening while he spoke,
With love of praise and noble envy struck;
Then to his ardent friend exposed his mind:
'All this alone, and leaving me behind!
Am I unworthy, Nisus, to be joined?
Think'st thou my share of honour I will yield,
Or send thee unassisted to the field?
Not so my father taught my childhood arms,   40
Born in a siege, and bred amongst alarms:
Nor is my youth unworthy of my friend,
Or of the heaven-born hero I attend.*

The thing called life with ease I can disclaim,
And think it oversold to purchase fame.'
To whom his friend:
'I could not think, alas, thy tender years
Would minister new matter to my fears:
Nor is it just thou shouldst thy wish obtain.
So Jove in triumph bring me back again   50
To those dear eyes, or if a god there be
To pious friends propitious more than he.
But if some one, as many sure there are,
Of adverse accidents in doubtful war,
If one should reach my head, there let it fall
And spare thy life: I would not perish all.
Thy youth is worthy of a longer date.
Do thou remain to mourn thy lover's fate,
To bear my mangled body from the foe,
Or buy it back, and funeral rites bestow;   60
Or if hard Fortune shall my corpse deny,
Those dues with empty marble to supply.
O let not me the widow's tears renew,
Let not a mother's curse my name pursue;
Thy pious mother, who in love to thee
Left the fair coast of fruitful Sicily,
Her age committing to the seas and wind,
When every weary matron stayed behind.'
To this Euryalus: 'Thou plead'st in vain,
And but delay'st the cause thou canst not gain;   70
No more, 'tis loss of time.' With that he wakes
The nodding watch; each to his office takes.
The guard relieved, in company they went
To find the council at the royal tent.
Now every living thing lay void of care,
And sleep, the common gift of nature, share.
Meantime the Trojan peers in council sate, ⎤
And called their chief commanders to debate ⎬
The weighty business of th' endangered state: ⎦
What next was to be done, who to be sent   80
T' inform Aeneas of the foe's intent.
In midst of all the quiet camp they held

Nocturnal council; each sustains a shield
Which his o'erlaboured arm can hardly rear,
And leans upon a long projected spear.
Now Nisus and his friend approach the guard,⎫
And beg admittance, eager to be heard,   ⎬
Th' affair important, not to be deferred.   ⎭
Ascanius bids them be conducted in,*
Then thus, commanded, Nisus does begin: 90
'Ye Trojan fathers, lend attentive ears,
Nor judge our undertaking by our years.
The foes securely drenched in sleep and wine
Their watch neglect; their fires but thinly shine:
And where the smoke in thickening vapours flies,
Covering the plain, and clouding all the skies,
Betwixt the spaces we have marked a way,
Close by the gate, and coasting by the sea;
This passage undisturbed and unespied
Our steps will safely to Aeneas guide;   100
Expect each hour to see him back again,
Loaded with spoils of foes in battle slain.
Snatch we the lucky minute while we may.
Nor can we be mistaken in the way,
For hunting in the vale we oft have seen
The rising turrets with the stream between,
And know its winding course, with every ford.'
He paused, and old Alethes took the word:
'Our country gods in whom our trust we place
Will yet from ruin save the Trojan race,   110
While we behold such springing worth appear
In youth so brave, and breasts so void of fear.'
With this he took the hand of either boy,
Embraced them closely both, and wept for joy.
'Ye brave young men, what equal gifts can we,
What recompense for such desert, decree?
The greatest, sure, and best you can receive
The gods, your virtue and your fame will give:
The rest our grateful general will bestow,
And young Ascanius till his manhood owe.'   120
'And I, whose welfare in my father lies,'

Ascanius adds, 'by all the deities,
By our great country, and our household gods,
By hoary Vesta's rites and dark abodes,*
Adjure you both; on you my fortune stands:
That and my faith I plight into your hands.
Make me but happy in his safe return
(For I no other loss but only his can mourn),
Nisus, your gift shall two large goblets be
Of silver, wrought with curious imagery,   130
And high embossed, which when old Priam reigned
My conquering sire at sacked Arisba gained;
And more, two tripods cast in antique mould,
With two great talents of the finest gold;
Besides a bowl which Tyrian art did grave,
The present that Sidonian Dido gave.*
But if in conquered Italy we reign,
When spoils by lot the victors shall obtain,
Thou saw'st the courser by proud Turnus pressed:
That and his golden arms, and sanguine crest   140
And shield, from lot exempted, thou shalt share;
With these, twelve captive damsels young and fair,
Male slaves as many, well appointed all
With vests and arms, shall to thy portion fall:
And last, a fruitful field to thee shall rest,
The large demesnes the Latian king possessed.
But thou, whose years are more to mine allied,
No fate my vowed affection shall divide
From thee, O wondrous youth: be ever mine,
Take full possession, all my soul is thine;   150
My life's companion, and my bosom friend,
One faith, one fame, one fate shall both attend.
My peace shall be committed to thy care,
And to thy conduct my concerns in war.'
Then thus the bold Euryalus replied:
'Whatever fortune, good or bad, betide,
The same shall be my age, as now my youth;
No time shall find me wanting to my truth.
This only from your bounty let me gain
(And this not granted, all rewards are vain):   160

Of Priam's royal race my mother came,
And sure the best that ever bore the name,
Whom neither Troy nor Sicily could hold
From me departing, but o'erspent and old
My fate she followed; ignorant of this
Whatever danger, neither parting kiss*
Nor pious blessing taken, her I leave,
And in this only act of all my life deceive.
By this your hand and conscious night I swear,
My youth so sad a farewell could not bear.   170
Be you her patron, fill my vacant place
(Permit me to presume so great a grace),
Support her age, forsaken and distressed:
That hope alone will fortify my breast
Against the worst of fortunes and of fears.'
He said; th' assistants shed presaging tears,
But above all, Ascanius, moved to see
That image of paternal piety;*
Then thus replied:
'So great beginnings in so green an age   180
Exact that faith which firmly I engage;
Thy mother all the privilege shall claim
Creusa had, and only want the name.*
Whate'er event thy enterprise shall have,
'Tis merit to have borne a son so brave.
By this my head a sacred oath I swear
(My father used it): what returning here,
Crowned with success, I for thyself prepare,*
Thy parent and thy family shall share.'
He said; and weeping while he spoke the word,   190
From his broad belt he drew a shining sword,
Magnificent with gold: Lycaon made,
And in an ivory scabbard sheathed the blade.
This was his gift, while Mnestheus did provide ⎫
For Nisus' arms a grisly lion's hide,   ⎬
And true Alethes changed with him his helm of temper tried. ⎭
Thus armed they went: the noble Trojans wait
Their going forth, and follow to the gate.
With prayers and vows above the rest appears

Ascanius, manly far above his years, 200
And messages committed to their care,
Which all in winds were lost, and empty air.
The trenches first they passed, then took their way
Where their proud foes in pitched pavilions lay,
To many fatal ere themselves were slain.
The careless host dispersed upon the plain
They found, who drunk with wine supinely snore;
Unharnessed chariots stand upon the shore:
Midst wheels, and reins, and arms, the goblet by,
A medley of debauch and war they lie. 210
Observing, Nisus showed his friend the sight,
Then thus: 'Behold a conquest without fight.
Occasion calls the sword to be prepared:
Our way lies there; stand thou upon the guard,
And look behind, while I securely go
To cut an ample passage through the foe.'
Softly he spoke, then stalking took his way
With his drawn sword where haughty Rhamnes lay,
His head raised high, on tapestry beneath,
And heaving from his breast he puffed his breath: 220
A king and prophet by King Turnus loved,
But fate by prescience cannot be removed.
Three sleeping slaves he soon subdues, then spies
Where Rhemus with his proud retinue lies:
His armour-bearer first, and next he kills
His charioteer, entrenched betwixt the wheels
And his loved horses; last invades their lord:
Full on his neck he aims the fatal sword,
The gasping head flies off, a purple flood
Flows from the trunk that wallows in the blood, 230
Which by the spurning heels dispersed around,
The bed besprinkles, and bedews the ground.
Then Lamyrus with Lamus, and the young
Serranus, who with gaming did prolong
The night: oppressed with wine and slumber lay ⎫
The beauteous youth, and dreamt of lucky play— ⎬
More lucky had it been protracted till the day. ⎭
The famished lion thus with hunger bold

O'erleaps the fences of the nightly fold,
The peaceful flock devours, and tears, and draws;   240
Wrapped up in silent fear they lie, and pant beneath his paws.
Nor with less rage Euryalus employs
The vengeful sword, nor fewer foes destroys;
But on th' ignoble crowd his fury flew,
Which Fadus, Hebesus and Rhaetus slew,
With Abaris. In sleep the rest did fall,
But Rhaetus waking, and observing all,
Behind a mighty jar he slunk for fear:
The sharp-edged iron found and reached him there;
Full as he rose he plunged it in his side,   250
The cruel sword returned in crimson dyed.
The wound a blended stream of wine and blood
Pours out; the purple soul comes floating in the flood.
Now where Messapus quartered they arrive,
The fires were fainting there, and just alive;
The warlike horses tied in order fed.
Nisus the discipline observed, and said:
'Our eagerness of blood may both betray:
Behold the doubtful glimmering of the day,
Foe to these nightly thefts: no more, my friend,   260
Here let our glutted execution end;
A lane through slaughtered bodies we have made.'
The bold Euryalus, though loath, obeyed;
Rich arms and arras which they scattered find,
And plate, a precious load they leave behind.
Yet fond of gaudy spoils, the boy would stay
To make the proud caparisons his prey,
Which decked a neighbouring steed.
Nor did his eyes less longingly behold
The girdle studded o'er with nails of gold   270
Which Rhamnes wore: this present long ago
On Remulus did Caedicus bestow,
And absent joined in hospitable ties.
He dying to his heir bequeathed the prize,
Till by the conquering Rutuli oppressed
He fell, and they the glorious gift possessed.
These gaudy spoils Euryalus now bears,

And vainly on his brawny shoulders wears:
Messapus' helm he found amongst the dead,
Garnished with plumes, and fitted to his head.   280
They leave the camp and take the safest road.
Meantime a squadron of their foes abroad,
Three hundred horse, with bucklers armed, they spied,
Whom Volscens by the King's command did guide:
To Turnus these were from the city sent,
And to perform their message sought his tent.
Approaching near their utmost lines they draw,
When bending t'wards the left their captain saw
The faithful pair, for through the doubtful shade ⎤
His glittering helm Euryalus betrayed,   ⎬   290
On which the moon with full reflection played. ⎦
' 'Tis not for nought' cried Volscens from the crowd,
'These men go there', then raised his voice aloud:
'Stand, stand! why thus in arms? and whither bent?
From whence, to whom, and on what errand sent?'
Silent they make away, and haste their flight
To neighbouring woods, and trust themselves to night.
The speedy horsemen spur their steeds to get
'Twixt them and home, and every path beset,
And all the windings of the well-known wood;   300
Black was the brake, and thick with oak it stood,
With fern all horrid, and perplexing thorn,
Where tracks of bears had scarce a passage worn.
The darkness of the shades, his heavy prey,
And fear, misled the younger from his way;
But Nisus hit the turns with happier haste,
Who now, unknowing, had the danger passed,
And Alban lakes (from Alba's name so called)
Where King Latinus then his oxen stalled;
Till turning at the length he stood his ground,   310
And vainly cast his longing eyes around
For his lost friend.
'Ah wretch!' he cried, 'where have I left behind,
Where shall I hope th' unhappy youth to find?
Or what way take?' Again he ventures back,
And treads the mazes of his former track

Through the wild wood; at last he hears the noise
Of trampling horses, and the riders' voice.
The sound approached, and suddenly he viewed
His foes enclosing, and his friend pursued,   320
Forelaid, and taken, while he strove in vain
The covert of the neighbouring wood to gain:
What should he next attempt, what arms employ
With fruitless force to free the captive boy?
Or tempt unequal numbers with the sword,
And die by him whom living he adored?
Resolved on death, his dreadful spear he shook,
And casting to the moon a mournful look,
'Fair Queen', said he, 'who dost in woods delight,*⎫
Grace of the stars, and goddess of the night,   ⎬   330
Be present, and direct my dart aright.   ⎭
If e'er my pious father for my sake
Did on thy altars grateful offerings make,
Or I increased them with successful toils,
And hung thy sacred roof with savage spoils,
Through the brown shadows guide my flying spear
To reach this troop.' Then poising from his ear
The quivering weapon with full force he threw:
Through the divided shades the deadly javelin flew;
On Sulmo's back it splits, the double dart   340
Drove deeper onward and transfixed his heart.
He staggers round, his eyeballs roll in death,
And with short sobs he gasps away his breath.
All stand amazed; a second javelin flies
From his stretched arm, and hisses through the skies.
The lance through Tagus' temples forced its way,
And in his brain-pan warmly buried lay.
Fierce Volscens foams with rage, and gazing round
Descried no author of the fatal wound,
Nor where to fix revenge. 'But thou' he cries   350
'Shalt pay for both', and at the prisoner flies
With his drawn sword. Then, struck with deep despair,
That fatal sight the lover could not bear,
But from his covert rushed in open view,
And sent his voice before him as he flew:

'Me, me, employ your sword on me alone;
The crime confessed; the fact was all my own.
He neither could nor durst, the guiltless youth,
Ye moon and stars bear witness to the truth;
His only fault, if that be to offend,   360
Was too much loving his unhappy friend.'
Too late, alas, he speaks:
The sword, which unrelenting fury guides,
Driven with full force had pierced his tender sides.
Down fell the beauteous youth, the gaping wound
Gushed out a crimson stream, and stained the ground.
His nodding neck reclines on his white breast,
Like a fair flower in furrowed fields oppressed
By the keen share, or poppy on the plain,
Whose heavy head is overcharged with rain.   370
Disdain, despair, and deadly vengeance vowed
Drove Nisus headlong on the hostile crowd;
Volscens he seeks, at him alone he bends,
Born back and pushed by his surrounding friends,
He still pressed on, and kept him still in sight,
Then whirled aloft his sword with all his might.
Th' unerring weapon flew, and winged with death
Entered his gaping mouth and stopped his breath.*
Dying he slew, and staggering on the plain
Sought for the body of his lover slain;   380
Then quietly on his dear breast he fell,
Content in death to be revenged so well.
O happy pair! For if my verse can give
Eternity, your fame shall ever live:
Fixed as the Capitol's foundation lies,*
And spread where'er the Roman eagle flies.

52   From *Secret Love*

JOHN DRYDEN

From Act V, scene i; published 1668. The extract from the final scene of this tragicomedy begins with the Queen inviting Celadon to ask a favour from her; subsequently Celadon and Florimell agree the terms on which they are prepared to marry.

Queen. Your modesty shall not serve the turn; ask something.

Celadon. Then I beg, Madam, you will command Florimell never to be friends with me.

Florimell. Ask again; I grant that without the Queen. But why are you afraid on't?

Cel. Because I am sure as soon as ever you are, you'll marry me.

Flor. Do you fear it?

Cel. No, 'twill come with a fear.

Flor. If you do, I will not stick with you for an oath.

Cel. I require no oath till we come to church; and then after the priest, I hope; for I find it will be my destiny to marry thee.

Flor. If ever I say word after the black gentleman for thee Celadon——

Cel. Then I hope you'll give me leave to bestow a faithful heart elsewhere.

Flor. Ay, but if you would have one you must bespeak it, for I am sure you have none ready made.

Cel. What say you, shall I marry Flavia?

Flor. No, she'll be too cunning for you.

Cel. What say you to Olinda then? She's tall, and fair, and bonny.

Flor. And foolish, and apish, and fickle.

Cel. But Sabina, there's pretty, and young, and loving, and innocent.

Flor. And dwarfish, and childish, and fond, and flippant: if you marry her sister you will get may-poles, and if you marry her you will get fairies to dance about them.

Cel. Nay then the case is clear, Florimell; if you take 'em all from me, 'tis because you reserve me for yourself.

Flor. But this marriage is such a bugbear to me; much might be if we could invent but any way to make it easy.

Cel. Some foolish people have made it uneasy, by drawing the knot faster than they need; but we that are wiser will loosen it a little.

Flor. 'Tis true indeed, there's some difference betwixt a girdle and an halter.

Cel. As for the first year, according to the laudable custom of new-married people, we shall follow one another up into chambers, and down into gardens, and think we shall never have enough of one another.——So far 'tis pleasant enough, I hope.

Flor. But after that, when we begin to live like husband and wife, and never come near one another——what then, sir?

Cel. Why then our only happiness must be to have one mind, and one will, Florimell.

Flor. One mind if thou wilt, but prithee let us have two wills; for I find one will be little enough for me alone. But how if those wills should meet and clash, Celadon?

Cel. I warrant thee for that: husbands and wives keep their wills far enough asunder for ever meeting: one thing let us be sure to agree on, that is, never to be jealous.

Flor. No; but e'en love one another as long as we can; and confess the truth when we can love no longer.

Cel. When I have been at play, you shall never ask me what money I have lost.

Flor. When I have been abroad you shall never enquire who treated me.

Cel. Item, I will have the liberty to sleep all night, without your interrupting my repose for any evil design whatsoever.

Flor. Item, Then you shall bid me good night before you sleep.

Cel. Provided always, that whatever liberties we take with other people, we continue very honest to one another.

Flor. As far as will consist with a pleasant life.

Cel. Lastly, Whereas the names of husband and wife hold forth nothing but clashing and cloying, and dullness and faintness in their signification, they shall be abolished for ever betwixt us.

Flor. And instead of those, we will be married by the more agreeable names of mistress and gallant.

Cel. None of my privileges to be infringed by thee Florimell, under the penalty of a month of fasting-nights.

Flor. None of my privileges to be infringed by thee Celadon, under the penalty of cuckoldom.

Cel. Well, if it be my fortune to be made a cuckold, I had rather thou shouldst make me one than anyone in Sicily: and for my comfort I shall have thee oftener than any of thy servants.

Flor. La ye now, is not such a marriage as good as wenching, Celadon?

Cel. This is very good, but not so good, Florimell.

53   *The Mistress: A Song*

JOHN WILMOT, EARL OF ROCHESTER

An age in her embraces passed
    Would seem a winter's day;
Where life and light with envious haste
    Are torn and snatched away.

But oh, how slowly minutes roll
    When absent from her eyes,
That feed my love, which is my soul;
    It languishes and dies.

For then no more a soul, but shade,
    It mournfully does move,
And haunts my breast, by absence made   10
    The living tomb of love.

You wiser men, despise me not,
    Whose love-sick fancy raves
On shades of souls, and heav'n knows what;
    Short ages live in graves.

Whene'er those wounding eyes so full
    Of sweetness you did see;

Had you not been profoundly dull,
   You had gone mad like me. 20

Nor censure us, you who perceive
   My best belov'd and me
Sigh and lament, complain and grieve:
   You think we disagree.

Alas! 'tis sacred jealousy,
   Love raised to an extreme;
The only proof 'twixt her and me,
   We love, and do not dream.

Fantastic fancies fondly move,
   And in frail joys believe; 30
Taking false pleasure for true love;
   But pain can ne'er deceive.

Kind jealous doubts, tormenting fears,
   And anxious cares, when past,
Prove our hearts' treasure fixed and dear,
   And make us blessed at last.

54 *Against Constancy*

JOHN WILMOT, EARL OF ROCHESTER

Tell me no more of constancy,
   The frivolous pretence
Of cold age, narrow jealousy,
   Disease, and want of sense.

Let duller fools, on whom kind chance
   Some easy heart has thrown,
Despairing higher to advance
   Be kind to one alone.

Old men and weak, whose idle flame
   Their own defects discovers, 10
Since changing can but spread their shame
   Ought to be constant lovers;

But we, whose hearts do justly swell
   With no vainglorious pride,
Who know how we in love excel
   Long to be often tried.

Then bring my bath, and strew my bed,
   As each kind night returns;
I'll change a mistress till I'm dead,
   And fate change me to worms.   20

55   *Upon his Leaving his Mistress*

JOHN WILMOT, EARL OF ROCHESTER

'Tis not that I am weary grown
Of being yours, and yours alone;
But with what face can I incline
To damn you to be only mine?
You whom some kinder power did fashion,
By merit, and by inclination,
The joy at least of one whole nation.

Let meaner spirits of your sex
With humbler aims their thoughts perplex,
And boast, if by their arts they can   10
Contrive to make one happy man;
Whilst moved by an impartial sense,
Favours like Nature you dispense,
With universal influence.

See the kind seed-receiving earth
To every grain affords a birth;
On her no show'rs unwelcome fall,
Her willing womb retains 'em all;
And shall my Celia be confined?
No, live up to thy mighty mind,   20
And be the mistress of mankind.

56   *Song*

JOHN WILMOT, EARL OF ROCHESTER

Absent from thee I languish still,
    Then ask me not, when I return;
The straying fool 'twill plainly kill
    To wish all day, all night to mourn.

Dear, from thine arms then let me fly,
    That my fantastic mind may prove
The torments it deserves to try,
    That tears my fixed heart from my love.

When wearied with a world of woe,
    To thy safe bosom I retire,   10
Where love and peace and truth does flow,
    May I contented there expire;

Lest once more wand'ring from that heav'n
    I fall on some base heart unblest,
Faithless to thee, false, unforgiv'n,
    And lose my everlasting rest.

57   *Love and Life: A Song*

JOHN WILMOT, EARL OF ROCHESTER

All my past life is mine no more,
    The flying hours are gone;
Like transitory dreams giv'n o'er,
Whose images are kept in store
    By memory alone.

Whatever is to come, is not,
    How can it then be mine?
The present moment's all my lot,
And that as fast as it is got,
    Phyllis, is wholly thine.   10

Then talk not of inconstancy,
   False hearts, and broken vows;
If I by miracle can be
This live-long minute true to thee,
   'Tis all that heav'n allows.

58 *A Song of a Young Lady to her Ancient Lover*

JOHN WILMOT, EARL OF ROCHESTER

Ancient person, for whom I
All the flatt'ring youth defy,
Long be it ere thou grow old,
Aching, shaking, crazy, cold;
But still continue as thou art,
Ancient person of my heart.

On thy withered lips and dry,
Which like barren furrows lie,
Brooding kisses I will pour
Shall thy youthful heat restore.   10
Such kind showers in autumn fall,
And a second spring recall:
Nor from thee will ever part,
Ancient person of my heart.

Thy nobler part, which but to name
In our sex would be counted shame,
By age's frozen grasp possessed,
From his ice shall be released:
And soothed by my reviving hand,
In former warmth and vigour stand.   20
All a lover's wish can reach
For thy joy my love shall teach;
And for thy pleasure shall improve,
All that art can add to love.
Yet still I love thee without art,
Ancient person of my heart.

59   *Song*

JOHN WILMOT, EARL OF ROCHESTER

Love a woman! you're an ass,
'Tis a most insipid passion,
To choose out for your happiness
The idlest part of God's creation.

Let the porter and the groom,
Things designed for dirty slaves,
Drudge in fair Aurelia's womb,
To get supplies for age, and graves.

Farewell woman, I intend
Henceforth every night to sit,   10
With my lewd well-natured friend,
Drinking to engender wit.

Then give me health, wealth, mirth and wine,
And if busy love entrenches,
There's a sweet, soft page of mine
Does the trick worth forty wenches.

60   *The Fall: A Song*

JOHN WILMOT, EARL OF ROCHESTER

How blest was the created state
    Of man and woman, ere they fell,
Compared to our unhappy fate;
    We need not fear another hell.

Naked beneath cool shades they lay,
    Enjoyment waited on desire;
Each member did their wills obey,
    Nor could a wish set pleasure higher.

But we, poor slaves to hope and fear,
    Are never of our joys secure;   10

They lessen still as they draw near,
    And none but dull delights endure.

Then Chloris, while I duly pay
    The nobler tribute of my heart;
Be not you so severe to say,
    You love me for a frailer part.

61   *The Imperfect Enjoyment*

JOHN WILMOT, EARL OF ROCHESTER

The subject of this poem is traditional, dating back to Petronius' *Satyricon* and Ovid's *Amores*, III. vii; Aphra Behn (see **64**) and Sir George Etherege also wrote on this topic.

Naked she lay, clasped in my longing arms,
I filled with love, and she all over charms,
Both equally inspired with eager fire,
Melting through kindness, flaming in desire;
With arms, legs, lips, close clinging to embrace,
She clips me to her breast, and sucks me to her face.
Her nimble tongue (love's lesser lightning) played
Within my mouth, and to my thoughts conveyed
Swift orders, that I should prepare to throw
The all–dissolving thunderbolt below.   10
My fluttering soul, sprung with the pointed kiss,
Hangs hovering o'er her balmy brinks of bliss;
But whilst her busy hand would guide that part
Which should convey my soul up to her heart,
In liquid raptures I dissolve all o'er,
Melt into sperm, and spend at every pore:
A touch from any part of her had done 't,
Her hand, her foot, her very look's a cunt.
Smiling, she chides in a kind murmuring noise,
And from her body wipes the clammy joys;   20
When with a thousand kisses wandering o'er
My panting breast, 'And is there then no more?'
She cries. 'All this to love and rapture's due,

Must we not pay a debt to pleasure too?'
But I, the most forlorn, lost man alive,
To show my wished obedience vainly strive;
I sigh, alas! and kiss, but cannot swive.
Eager desires confound my first intent,
Succeeding shame does more success prevent,
And rage, at last, confirms me impotent.   30
Ev'n her fair hand, which might bid heat return
To frozen age, and make cold hermits burn,
Applied to my dead cinder, warms no more
Than fire to ashes could past flames restore.
Trembling, confused, despairing, limber, dry,
A wishing, weak, unmoving lump I lie.
This dart of love, whose piercing point, oft tried,
With virgin blood ten thousand maids has dyed;
Which nature still directed with such art,
That it through every cunt reached every heart;   40
Stiffly resolved, 'twould carelessly invade
Woman or man, nor aught its fury stayed;*
Where'er it pierced, a cunt it found or made:
Now languid lies, in this unhappy hour,
Shrunk up and sapless, like a withered flower.
Thou treacherous, base deserter of my flame,
False to my passion, fatal to my fame;
By what mistaken magic dost thou prove
So true to lewdness, so untrue to love?
What oyster-, cinder-, beggar-, common-whore   50
Didst thou e'er fail in all thy life before?
When vice, disease and scandal lead the way,
With what officious haste dost thou obey!
Like a rude, roaring hector in the streets
That scuffles, cuffs and ruffles all he meets;
But if his King or country claim his aid,
The rascal villain shrinks, and hides his head:
Ev'n so thy brutal valour is displayed,
Breaks every stews, does each small whore invade.
But if great love the onset does command,   60
Base recreant to thy prince, thou dar'st not stand.
Worst part of me, and henceforth hated most,

Through all the town the common fucking post;
On whom each whore relieves her tingling cunt,
As hogs on gates do rub themselves and grunt.
May'st thou to ravenous chancres be a prey,
Or in consuming weepings waste away.
May stranguries and stone thy days attend,
May'st thou ne'er piss, who didst refuse to spend
When all my joys did on false thee depend.   70
And may ten thousand abler pricks agree
To do the wronged Corinna right for thee.

62   *Song*

JOHN WILMOT, EARL OF ROCHESTER

Fair Chloris in a pigsty lay,
    Her tender herd lay by her;
She slept: in murmuring gruntlings they
Complaining of the scorching day
    Her slumbers thus inspire:

She dreamt whilst she with careful pains
    Her snowy arms employed
In ivory pails to fill out grains,
One of her love-convicted swains
    Thus hasting to her cried: 10

'Fly nymph, oh fly, ere 'tis too late,
    A dear-loved life to save,
Rescue your bosom-pig from fate
Who now expires, hung in the gate
    That leads to Flora's cave.

Myself had tried to set him free,
    Rather than brought the news,
But I am so abhorred by thee
That ev'n thy darling's life from me
    I know thou would'st refuse.'   20

Struck with the news, as quick she flies
    As blushes to her face,

Not the bright lightning from the skies
Nor love shot from her brighter eyes
    Move half so swift a pace.

This plot, it seems, the lustful slave
    Had laid against her honour,
Which not one god took care to save,
For he pursues her to the cave
    And throws himself upon her.   30

Now piercèd is her virgin zone,
    She feels the foe within it,
She hears a broken amorous groan,
The panting lover's fainting moan,
    Just in the happy minute.

Frighted she wakes, and waking frigs;
    Nature thus kindly eased
In dreams raised by her murmuring pigs,
And her own thumb between her legs,
    She's innocent and pleased.   40

63   *To a Lady, in a Letter*

JOHN WILMOT, EARL OF ROCHESTER

    Such perfect bliss, fair Chloris, we
        In our enjoyment prove:
    'Tis pity restless jealousy
        Should mingle with our love.

    Let us, since wit has taught us how,
        Raise pleasure to the top:
    You rival bottle must allow,
        I'll suffer rival fop.

    Think not in this that I design
        A treason 'gainst love's charms,   10
    When following the god of wine
        I leave my Chloris' arms:

Since you have that, for all your haste,
   At which I'll ne'er repine,
Will take its liquor off as fast
   As I can take off mine.

There's not a brisk insipid spark
   That flutters in the town,
But with your wanton eyes you mark
   Him out to be your own.   20

Nor do you think it worth your care
   How empty and how dull
The heads of your admirers are,
   So that their bags be full.

All this you freely may confess,
   Yet we ne'er disagree:
For did you love your pleasure less,
   You were no match for me.

Whilst I, my pleasure to pursue,
   Whole nights am taking in   30
The lusty juice of grapes, take you
   The juice of lusty men.

64   *The Disappointment*

APHRA BEHN

Printed in her *Poems on Several Occasions* (1684). It is a version of a poem
by Benech de Cantenac.

I

One day the amorous Lysander
By an impatient passion swayed,
Surprised fair Cloris, that loved maid,
Who could defend herself no longer.
All things did with his love conspire:
That gilded planet of the day,
In his gay chariot drawn by fire,

Was now descending to the sea,
And left no light to guide the world
But what from Cloris' brighter eyes was hurled.　　10

II

In a lone thicket made for love,
Silent as yielding maid's consent,
She with a charming languishment
Permits his force, yet gently strove;
Her hands his bosom softly meet,
But not to put him back designed,
Rather to draw 'em on inclined;
Whilst he lay trembling at her feet
Resistance 'tis in vain to show;
She wants the power to say, 'Ah! What d'ye do?'　　20

III

Her bright eyes sweet, and yet severe,
Where love and shame confus'dly strive,
Fresh vigour to Lysander give;
And breathing faintly in his ear
She cried, 'Cease, cease your vain desire,
Or I'll call out! What would you do?
My dearer honour ev'n to you
I cannot, must not give: retire,
Or take this life, whose chiefest part
I gave you with the conquest of my heart.'　　30

IV

But he, as much unused to fear
As he was capable of love,
The blessèd minutes to improve
Kisses her mouth, her neck, her hair;
Each touch her new desire alarms,
His burning, trembling hand he pressed
Upon her swelling, snowy breast,
While she lay panting in his arms:
All her unguarded beauties lie
The spoils and trophies of the enemy.　　40

V

And now, without respect or fear,
He seeks the object of his vows,
(His love no modesty allows)
By swift degrees advancing where
His daring hand that altar seized
Where gods of love do sacrifice:
That awful throne, that paradise
Where rage is calmed and anger pleased;
That fountain where delight still flows,
And gives the universal world repose.   50

VI

Her balmy lips encount'ring his,
Their bodies, as their souls, are joined;
Where both in transports unconfined
Extend themselves upon the moss.
Cloris half dead and breathless lay,
Her soft eyes cast a humid light,
Such as divides the day and night,
Or falling stars, whose fires decay;
And now no signs of life she shows
But what in short-breathed sighs returns and goes.   60

VII

He saw how at her length she lay,
He saw her rising bosom bare;
Her loose, thin robes, through which appear
A shape designed for love and play;
Abandoned by her pride and shame
She does her softest joys dispense,
Off'ring her virgin innocence
A victim to love's sacred flame;
While the o'er-ravished shepherd lies
Unable to perform the sacrifice.   70

VIII

Ready to taste a thousand joys,
The too-transported, hapless swain

Found the vast pleasure turned to pain:
Pleasure which too much love destroys.
The willing garments by he laid,
And heaven all opened to his view,
Mad to possess, himself he threw
On the defenceless lovely maid.
But Oh! what envying gods conspire
To snatch his power, yet leave him the desire!   80

IX

Nature's support (without whose aid
She can no human being give)
Itself now wants the art to live:
Faintness its slackened nerves invade.
In vain th' enragèd youth essayed
To call its fleeting vigour back:
No motion 'twill from motion take.
Excess of love his love betrayed:
In vain he toils, in vain commands,
Th' insensible fell weeping in his hands.   90

X

In this so amorous cruel strife
Where love and fate were too severe,
The poor Lysander in despair
Renounced his reason with his life:
Now all the brisk and active fire
That should the nobler part inflame
Served to increase his rage and shame,
And left no spark for new desire:
Not all her naked charms could move
Or calm that rage that had debauched his love.   100

XI

Cloris returning from the trance
Which love and soft desire had bred,
Her timorous hand she gently laid
(Or guided by design, or chance)
Upon that fabulous Priapus*

That potent god—as poets feign;
But never did young shepherdess
Gathering of fern upon the plain,
More nimbly draw her fingers back
Finding beneath the verdant leaves a snake,   110

XII

Than Cloris her fair hand withdrew,
Finding that god of her desires
Disarmed of all his awful fires,
And cold as flow'rs bathed in the morning dew.
Who can the nymph's confusion guess?
The blood forsook the hinder place,
And strewed with blushes all her face,
Which both disdain and shame expressed;
And from Lysander's arms she fled,
Leaving him fainting on the gloomy bed.   120

XIII

Like lightning through the grove she hies,
Or Daphne from the Delphic god,*
No print upon the grassy road
She leaves, t' instruct pursuing eyes.
The wind that wantoned in her hair
And with her ruffled garments played,
Discovered in the flying maid
All that the gods e'er made of fair.
So Venus when her love was slain*
With fear and haste flew o'er the fatal plain.   130

XIV

The nymph's resentments none but I
Can well imagine or condole:
But none can guess Lysander's soul
But those who swayed his destiny.
His silent griefs swell up to storms,
And not one god his fury spares;
He cursed his birth, his fate, his stars,
But more the shepherdess's charms,

> Whose soft bewitching influence
> Had damned him to the hell of impotence. 140

65 [Pepys's Sexual Adventures] from the *Diary*

SAMUEL PEPYS

These brief extracts illustrate two of Pepys's sexual affairs. The first was with the wife of William Bagwell, a ship's carpenter (her name is unknown), who was his mistress for many years; the *Diary* records frequent assignations, mainly in 1664. The second was with his wife's companion Deb Willet (a surname straight out of Restoration comedy), with whom he had a sexual relationship in 1667–8. Pepys's sex life is neatly summarized in the *Diary*, x. 176–80 and the course of these two affairs helpfully indexed in xi. 8, 311–12. Some of the explicit descriptions of the sexual acts are written in Pepys's private language, a mixture of French and Spanish with his own inventions.

15 [November 1664]. That I might not be too fine for the business I intend this day, I did leave off my fine new cloth suit lined with plush and put on my poor black suit; and after office done (where much business but little done), I to the Change; and thence Bagwell's wife with much ado followed me through Moorfields to a blind alehouse, and there I did caress her and eat and drank, and many hard looks and sithes the poor wretch did give me, and I think verily was troubled at what I did; but at last, after many protestings, by degrees I did arrive at what I would, with great pleasure. Then in the evening, it raining, walked to the town to where she knew where she was; and then I took coach and to Whitehall to a Committee of Tangier, where, and everywhere else I thank God, I find myself growing in repute; and so home and late, very late, at business, nobody minding it but myself; and so home to bed—weary and full of thoughts. Businesses grow high between the Dutch and us on every side.

19 [December 1664]. . . . Thence home; and not finding Bagwell's wife as I expected, I to the Change and there walked up and down, and then home; and she being come, I bid her go and stay at Moorgate for me; and after going up to my wife (whose eye is very bad, but she in very good temper to me); and after dinner, I to the place and walked round the fields again and again; but not finding her, I to

the Change and there found her waiting for me and took her away and to an alehouse, and there I made much of her; and then away thence and to another, and endeavoured to caress her; but elle ne vouloit pas,* which did vex me but I think it was chiefly not having a good easy place to do it upon. So we broke up and parted; and I to the office, where we sat hiring of ships an hour or two; and then to my office and thence (with Captain Taylor home to my house) to give him instructions and some notice of what, to his great satisfaction, had happened today—which I do because I hope his coming into this office will a little cross Sir W. Batten and may do me good. He gone, I to supper with my wife, very pleasant; and then a little to my office and to bed—my mind, God forgive me, too much running upon what I can faire avec la femme de Bagwell demain—having promised to go to Deptford and à aller à sa maison avec son mari* when I come thither.

20. Up and walked to Deptford, where after doing something at the yard, I walked, without being observed, with Bagwell home to his house and there was very kindly used, and the poor people did get a dinner for me in their fashion—of which I also eat very well. After dinner I found occasion of sending him abroad; and then alone avec elle je tentoy à faire ce que je voudrais, et contre sa force je le faisoy, bien que pas à mon contentment.* By and by, he coming back again, I took leave and walked home; and then there to dinner, where Dr Fairbrother came to see me, and Luellin; we dined, and I to the office, leaving them—where we sat all the afternoon, and I late at the office. To supper and to the office again very late; then home to bed.

25 [October 1668]. *Lord's day.* Up, and discoursing with my wife about our house and many new things we are doing of; and so to church I, and there find Jack Fen come, and his wife, a pretty black woman; I never saw her before, nor took notice of her now. So home and to dinner; and after dinner, all the afternoon got my wife and boy to read to me. And at night W. Batelier comes and sups with us; and after supper, to have my head combed by Deb, which occasioned the greatest sorrow to me that ever I knew in this world; for my wife, coming up suddenly, did find me embracing the girl con my hand sub su coats; and indeed, I was with my main in her cunny.* I was at a wonderful loss upon it, and the girl also; and I endeavoured to put it off, but my wife was struck mute and grew angry, and as her voice

came to her, grew quite out of order; and I do say little, but to bed; and my wife said little also, but could not sleep all night; but about 2 in the morning waked me and cried, and fell to tell me as a great secret that she was a Roman Catholic* and had received the Holy Sacrament; which troubled me but I took no notice of it, but she went on from one thing to another, till at last it appeared plainly her trouble was at what she saw; but yet I did not know how much she saw and therefore said nothing to her. But after her much crying and reproaching me with inconstancy and preferring a sorry girl before her, I did give her no provocations but did promise all fair usage to her, and love, and forswore any hurt that I did with her—till at last she seemed to be at ease again; [26] and so toward morning, a little sleep; and so I, with some little repose and rest, rose, and up and by water to Whitehall, but with my mind mightily troubled for the poor girl, whom I fear I have undone by this, my [wife] telling me that she would turn her out of door. However, I was obliged to attend the Duke of York, thinking to have had a meeting of Tangier today, but had not; but he did take me and Mr Wren into his closet, and there did press me to prepare what I had to say upon the answers of my fellow-officers to his great letter; which I promised to do against his coming to town again the next week; and so to other discourse, finding plainly that he is in trouble and apprehensions of the reformers, and would be found to do what he can towards reforming himself. And so thence to my Lord Sandwich; where after long stay, he being in talk with others privately, I to him; and there he taking physic and keeping his chamber, I had an hour's talk with him about the ill posture of things at this time, while the King gives countenance to Sir Ch. Sedley and Lord Buckhurst, telling him their late story of running up and down the streets a little while since all night, and their being beaten and clapped up all night by the constable, who is since chid and imprisoned for his pains.

He tells me that he thinks his matters do stand well with the King—and hopes to have despatch to his mind; but I doubt it, and do see that he doth fear it too. He told me my Lady Carteret's trouble about my writing of that letter of the Duke of York's lately to the office; which I did not own, but declared to be of no injury to G. Carteret, and that I would write a letter to him to satisfy him therein. But this I am in pain how to do without doing myself wrong, and the end I had, of preparing a justification to myself hereafter, when the

faults of the Navy come to be found out. However, I will do it in the
best manner I can.

Thence by coach home and to dinner, finding my wife mightily
discontented and the girl sad, and no words from my wife to her. So
after dinner, they out with me about two or three things; and so
home again, I all the evening busy and my wife full of trouble in her
looks; and anon to bed—where about midnight, she wakes me and
there falls foul on me again, affirming that she saw me hug and kiss
the girl; the latter I denied, and truly; the other I confessed and no
more. And upon her pressing me, did offer to give her under my
hand that I would never see Mrs Pierce more, nor Knepp,* but did
promise her particular demonstrations of my true love to her, own-
ing some indiscretion in what I did, but that there was no harm in it.
She at last on these promises was quiet, and very kind we were, and
so to sleep; [27] and in the morning up, but with my mind troubled
for the poor girl, with whom I could not get opportunity to speak;
but to the office, my mind mighty full of sorrow for her, where all the
morning, and to dinner with my people and to the office all the
afternoon; and so at night home and there busy to get some things
ready against tomorrow's meeting of Tangier; and that being done
and my clerks gone, my wife did towards bedtime begin to be in a
mighty rage from some new matter that she had got in her head, and
did most part of the night in bed rant at me in most high terms, of
threats of publishing my shame; and when I offered to rise, would
have rose too, and caused a candle to be lit, to burn by her all night in
the chimney while she ranted; while [I], that knew myself to have
given some grounds for it, did make it my business to appease her all
I could possibly, and by good words and fair promises did make her
very quiet; and so rested all night and rose with perfect good peace,
being heartily afflicted for this folly of mine that did occasion it; but
was forced to be silent about the girl, which I have no mind to part
with, but much less that the poor girl should be undone by my folly.
[28] So up, with mighty kindness from my wife and a thorough
peace; and being up, did by a note advise the girl what I had done and
owned, which note I was in pain for till she told me that she had
burned it. This evening, Mr Spong came and sat late with me, and
first told me of the instrument called Parrallogram, which I must
have one of, showing me his practice thereon by a map of England.

So by coach with Mr Gibson to Chancery Lane, and there made

oath before a Master of Chancery to my Tangier account of fees; and so to Whitehall, where by and by a Committee met; my Lord Sandwich there, but his report was not received, it being late; but only a little business done, about the supplying the place with victuals; but I did get, to my great content, my account allowed of fees, with great applause by my Lord Ashley and Sir W. Penn. Thence home, calling at one or two places, and there about our workmen, who are at work upon my wife's closet and other parts of my house, that we are all in dirt. So after dinner, with Mr Gibson all the afternoon in my closet; and at night to supper and to bed, my wife and I at good peace, but yet with some little grudgings of trouble in her, and more in me, about the poor girl.

12 [January 1669]. Up and to the office, where by occasion of a message from the Treasurers that the Board found fault with Commissioner Middleton, and I went up from the Board to the Lords of the Treasury to meet our Treasurers; and did, and there did dispute the business, it being about the manner of paying a little money to Chatham yard; wherein I find the Treasurers mighty supple, and I believe we shall bring them to reason; though they begin mighty upon us, as if we had no power of directing them, but they us. Thence back presently home to dinner, where I discern my wife to have been in pain where I have been, but said nothing to me; but I believe did send W. Hewer to seek me, but I take no notice of it—but am vexed. So to dinner with my people, and then to the office, where all the afternoon, and did much business and at it late; and so home to supper and to bed.

This day, meeting Mr Pierce at Whitehall, he tells me that his boy hath a great mind to see me, and is going to school again; and Dr Clerke, being by, doth tell me that he is a fine boy; but I durst not answer anything, because I durst not invite him to my house for fear of my wife, and therefore to my great trouble was forced to neglect that discourse. But here Mr Pierce, I asking him whither he was going, he told me as a great secret that he was going to his master's mistress, Mrs Churchhill, [with] some physic; meaning for the pox I suppose, or else that she is got with child; but I suppose the former, by his manner of speaking it.

This evening I observed my wife mighty dull; and I myself was not mighty fond, because of some hard words she did give me at noon, out of a jealousy at my being abroad this morning; when, God knows, it was upon the business of the office unexpectedly; but I to bed, not thinking but she would come after me; but waking by and by out of a slumber, which I usually fall into presently after my coming into the bed, I found she did not prepare to come to bed, but got fresh candles and more wood for her fire, it being mighty cold too. At this being troubled, I after a while prayed her to come to bed, all my people being gone to bed; so after an hour or two, she silent, and I now and then praying her to come to bed, she fell out into a fury, that I was a rogue and false to her; but yet I could perceive that she was to seek what to say; only, she invented, I believe, a business that I was seen in a hackney-coach with the glasses up with Deb, but could not tell the time, nor was sure I was he. I did, as I might truly, deny it, and was mightily troubled; but all would not serve. At last, about one a-clock, she came to my side of the bed and drew my curtain open, and with the tongs, red hot at the ends, made as if she did design to pinch me with them; at which in dismay I rose up, and with a few words she laid them down and did by little and little, very sillily, let all the discourse fall; and about 2, but with much seeming difficulty, came to bed and there lay well all night, and long in bed talking together with much pleasure; it being, I know, nothing but her doubt of my going out yesterday without telling her of my going which did vex her, poor wretch, last night: and I cannot blame her jealousy, though it doth vex me to the heart.

66   *Sigismonda and Guiscardo*

JOHN DRYDEN

A translation from one of the stories in Boccaccio's *Decameron*; printed in *Fables Ancient and Modern* (1700).

> While Norman Tancred in Salerno reigned,
> The title of a gracious prince he gained;
> Till turned a tyrant in his latter days,
> He lost the lustre of his former praise;
> And from the bright meridian where he stood,
> Descending, dipped his hands in lovers' blood.
>   This prince, of Fortune's favour long possessed,

Yet was with one fair daughter only blessed;
And blessed he might have been with her alone,
But oh! how much more happy, had he none! 10
She was his care, his hope, and his delight,
Most in his thought, and ever in his sight:
Next, nay beyond his life, he held her dear;
She lived by him, and now he lived in her.
For this, when ripe for marriage, he delayed
Her nuptial bands, and kept her long a maid,
As envying any else should share a part
Of what was his, and claiming all her heart.
At length, as public decency required,
And all his vassals eagerly desired, 20
With mind averse, he rather underwent
His people's will, than gave his own consent.
So was she torn, as from a lover's side,
And made almost in his despite a bride.

   Short were her marriage joys; for in the prime
Of youth, her lord expired before his time;
And to her father's court, in little space ⎫
Restored anew, she held a higher place, ⎬
More loved, and more exalted into grace. ⎭
This princess fresh, and young, and fair, and wise, 30
The worshipped idol of her father's eyes,
Did all her sex in every grace exceed,
And had more wit beside than women need.

   Youth, health, and ease, and most an amorous mind, ⎫
To second nuptials had her thoughts inclined; ⎬
And former joys had left a secret sting behind. ⎭
But prodigal in every other grant,
Her sire left unsupplied her only want;
And she, betwixt her modesty and pride,
Her wishes, which she could not help, would hide. 40

   Resolved at last to lose no longer time,
And yet to please herself without a crime,
She cast her eyes around the court, to find
A worthy subject suiting to her mind,
To him in holy nuptials to be tied,
A seeming widow, and a secret bride.

Among the train of courtiers, one she found
With all the gifts of bounteous nature crowned,
Of gentle blood, but one whose niggard fate
Had set him far below her high estate: 50
Guiscard his name was called, of blooming age,
Now squire to Tancred, and before his page:
To him, the choice of all the shining crowd,
Her heart the noble Sigismonda vowed.

   Yet hitherto she kept her love concealed,
And with close glances every day beheld
The graceful youth; and every day increased
The raging fire that burned within her breast;
Some secret charm did all his acts attend,
And what his fortune wanted, hers could mend: 60
Till, as the fire will force its outward way,
Or, in the prison pent, consume the prey,
So long her earnest eyes on his were set;
At length their twisted rays together met,*
And he, surprised with humble joy, surveyed
One sweet regard, shot by the royal maid.
Not well assured, while doubtful hopes he nursed,
A second glance came gliding like the first;
And he who saw the sharpness of the dart,
Without defence received it in his heart.   70
In public, though their passion wanted speech,
Yet mutual looks interpreted for each:
Time, ways, and means of meeting were denied,
But all those wants ingenious love supplied.
Th' inventive god, who never fails his part,
Inspires the wit, when once he warms the heart.

   When Guiscard next was in the circle seen,
Where Sigismonda held the place of queen,
A hollow cane within her hand she brought,
But in the concave had enclosed a note;   80
With this she seemed to play, and, as in sport,
Tossed to her love, in presence of the court;
'Take it,' she said; 'and when your needs require,
This little brand will serve to light your fire.'
He took it with a bow, and soon divined

The seeming toy was not for nought designed:
But when retired, so long with curious eyes
He viewed the present, that he found the prize.
Much was in little writ; and all conveyed ⎫
With cautious care, for fear to be betrayed ⎬   90
By some false confidant, or favourite maid. ⎭
The time, the place, the manner how to meet,
Were all in punctual order plainly writ:
But since a trust must be, she thought it best ⎫
To put it out of laymen's power at least, ⎬
And for their solemn vows prepared a priest. ⎭

    Guiscard (her secret purpose understood)
With joy prepared to meet the coming good;
Nor pains nor danger was resolved to spare,
But use the means appointed by the fair.   100

    Near the proud palace of Salerno stood
A mount of rough ascent, and thick with wood;
Through this a cave was dug with vast expense,
The work it seemed of some suspicious prince,
Who, when abusing power with lawless might,
From public justice would secure his flight.
The passage, made by many a winding way,
Reached e'en the room in which the tyrant lay,
Fit for his purpose; on a lower floor.
He lodged, whose issue was an iron door,   110
From whence, by stairs descending to the ground,
In the blind grot a safe retreat he found.
Its outlet ended in a brake o'ergrown
With brambles, choked by time, and now unknown.
A rift there was, which from the mountain's height
Conveyed a glimmering and malignant light,
A breathing-place to draw the damps away,
A twilight of an intercepted day.
The tyrant's den, whose use, though lost to fame,
Was now th' apartment of the royal dame;   120
The cavern only to her father known,
By him was to his darling daughter shown.

    Neglected long she let the secret rest,
Till love recalled it to her labouring breast,

And hinted as the way by heaven designed
The teacher, by the means he taught, to blind.
What will not women do, when need inspires
Their wit, or love their inclination fires!
Though jealousy of state th' invention found,
Yet love refined upon the former ground.   130
That way the tyrant had reserved to fly
Pursuing hate, now served to bring two lovers nigh.

   The dame, who long in vain had kept the key,
Bold by desire, explored the secret way;
Now tried the stairs, and wading through the night,
Searched all the deep recess, and issued into light.
All this her letter had so well explained,
Th' instructed youth might compass what remained:
The cavern mouth alone was hard to find,
Because the path disused was out of mind: 140
But in what quarter of the copse it lay,
His eye by certain level could survey:
Yet (for the wood perplexed with thorns he knew)
A frock of leather o'er his limbs he drew:
And thus provided, searched the brake around,
Till the choked entry of the cave he found.

   Thus, all prepared, the promised hour arrived,
So long expected, and so well contrived:
With love to friend, th' impatient lover went,
Fenced from the thorns, and trod the deep descent.   150
The conscious priest, who was suborned before,
Stood ready posted at the postern door;
The maids in distant rooms were sent to rest,
And nothing wanted but th' invited guest.
He came, and knocking thrice without delay,
The longing lady heard, and turned the key;
At once invaded him with all her charms,
And the first step he made, was in her arms:
The leathern outside, boist'rous as it was,
Gave way, and bent beneath her strict embrace: 160
On either side the kisses flew so thick,
That neither he nor she had breath to speak.
The holy man, amazed at what he saw,

Made haste to sanctify the bliss by law;
And muttered fast the matrimony o'er,
For fear committed sin should get before.
His work performed, he left the pair alone,
Because he knew he could not go too soon;
His presence odious, when his task was done.
What thoughts he had, beseems not me to say, 170
Though some surmise he went to fast and pray,
And needed both, to drive the tempting thoughts away.

 The foe once gone, they took their full delight;
'Twas restless rage and tempest all the night:
For greedy love each moment would employ,
And grudged the shortest pauses of their joy.

 Thus were their loves auspiciously begun,
And thus with secret care were carried on.
The stealth itself did appetite restore,
And looked so like a sin, it pleased the more. 180

 The cave was now become a common way,
The wicket often opened, knew the key.
Love rioted secure, and long enjoyed,
Was ever eager, and was never cloyed.

 But as extremes are short, of ill and good,
And tides at highest mark regorge the flood;
So Fate, that could no more improve their joy,
Took a malicious pleasure to destroy.

 Tancred, who fondly loved, and whose delight
Was placed in his fair daughter's daily sight, 190
Of custom, when his state affairs were done,
Would pass his pleasing hours with her alone:
And, as a father's privilege allowed,
Without attendance of th' officious crowd.

 It happened once, that when in heat of day
He tried to sleep, as was his usual way,
The balmy slumber fled his wakeful eyes,
And forced him, in his own despite, to rise:
Of sleep forsaken, to relieve his care,
He sought the conversation of the fair: 200
But with her train of damsels she was gone,
In shady walks the scorching heat to shun:

He would not violate that sweet recess,
And found besides a welcome heaviness
That seized his eyes; and slumber, which forgot
When called before to come, now came unsought.
From light retired behind his daughter's bed,
He for approaching sleep composed his head;
A chair was ready, for that use designed,
So quilted, that he lay at ease reclined;   210
The curtains closely drawn, the light to screen,
As if he had contrived to lie unseen:
Thus covered with an artificial night,
Sleep did his office soon, and sealed his sight.

   With heaven averse, in this ill-omened hour
Was Guiscard summoned to the secret bower,
And the fair nymph, with expectation fired,
From her attending damsels was retired:
For, true to love, she measured time so right
As not to miss one moment of delight.   220
The garden, seated on the level floor,
She left behind, and locking every door,
Thought all secure; but little did she know,
Blind to her fate, she had enclosed her foe.
Attending Guiscard, in his leathern frock,
Stood ready, with his thrice-repeated knock:
Thrice with a doleful sound the jarring grate
Rung deaf, and hollow, and presaged their fate.
The door unlocked, to known delight they haste,
And panting in each other's arms, embraced;   230
Rush to the conscious bed, a mutual freight,
And heedless press it with their wonted weight.

   The sudden bound awaked the sleeping sire,
And showed a sight no parent can desire:
His opening eyes at once with odious view
The love discovered, and the lover knew:
He would have cried; but hoping that he dreamt,
Amazement tied his tongue, and stopped th' attempt.
Th' ensuing moment all the truth declared, ⎫
But now he stood collected, and prepared; ⎬   240
For malice and revenge had put him on his guard. ⎭

So, like a lion that unheeded lay,
Dissembling sleep, and watchful to betray,
With inward rage he meditates his prey.
The thoughtless pair, indulging their desires,
Alternate kindled and then quenched their fires;
Nor thinking in the shades of death they played,
Full of themselves, themselves alone surveyed,
And, too secure, were by themselves betrayed.
Long time dissolved in pleasure thus they lay, 250
Till nature could no more suffice their play;
Then rose the youth, and through the cave again
Returned; the princess mingled with her train.

Resolved his unripe vengeance to defer,
The royal spy, when now the coast was clear,
Sought not the garden, but retired unseen
To brood in secret on his gathered spleen,
And methodize revenge: to death he grieved;
And, but he saw the crime, had scarce believed.
Th' appointment for th' ensuing night he heard; 260
And therefore in the cavern had prepared
Two brawny yeomen of his trusty guard.

Scarce had unwary Guiscard set his foot
Within the farmost entrance of the grot,
When these in secret ambush ready lay,
And rushing on the sudden seized the prey:
Encumbered with his frock, without defence,
An easy prize, they led the prisoner thence,
And, as commanded, brought before the prince.
The gloomy sire, too sensible of wrong 270
To vent his rage in words, restrained his tongue;
And only said, 'Thus servants are preferred,
And trusted, thus their sovereigns they reward.
Had I not seen, had not these eyes received
Too clear a proof, I could not have believed.'

He paused, and choked the rest. The youth who saw
His forfeit life abandoned to the law,
The judge th' accuser, and th' offence to him
Who had both power and will t' avenge the crime,
No vain defence prepared; but thus replied, 280

'The faults of love by love are justified:
With unresisted might the monarch reigns,
He levels mountains, and he raises plains;
And not regarding difference of degree,
Abased your daughter, and exalted me.'
    This bold return with seeming patience heard,
The prisoner was remitted to the guard.
The sullen tyrant slept not all the night,
But lonely walking by a winking light,
Sobbed, wept, and groaned, and beat his withered breast,   290
But would not violate his daughter's rest;
Who long expecting lay, for bliss prepared,
Listening for noise, and grieved that none she heard;
Oft rose, and oft in vain employed the key,
And oft accused her lover of delay;
And passed the tedious hours in anxious thoughts away.

    The morrow came; and at his usual hour
Old Tancred visited his daughter's bower;
Her cheek (for such his custom was) he kissed,
Then blessed her kneeling, and her maids dismissed.   300
The royal dignity thus far maintained,
Now left in private, he no longer feigned;
But all at once his grief and rage appeared,
And floods of tears ran trickling down his beard.
    'O Sigismonda,' he began to say:
Thrice he began, and thrice was forced to stay,
Till words with often trying found their way:
'I thought, O Sigismonda, (but how blind
Are parents' eyes, their children's faults to find!)
Thy virtue, birth, and breeding were above   310
A mean desire, and vulgar sense of love:
Nor less than sight and hearing could convince
So fond a father, and so just a prince,
Of such an unforeseen, and unbelieved offence.
Then what indignant sorrow must I have,
To see thee lie subjected to my slave!
A man so smelling of the people's lee,
The court received him first for charity;
And since with no degree of honour graced,

But only suffered, where he first was placed: 320
A grovelling insect still; and so designed
By nature's hand, nor born of noble kind:
A thing by neither man nor woman prized,
And scarcely known enough to be despised.
To what has heaven reserved my age? Ah why
Should man, when nature calls, not choose to die,
Rather than stretch the span of life, to find
Such ills as fate has wisely cast behind,
For those to feel, whom fond desire to live
Makes covetous of more than life can give! 330
Each has his share of good, and when 'tis gone,
The guest, though hungry, cannot rise too soon.*
But I, expecting more, in my own wrong
Protracting life, have lived a day too long.
If yesterday could be recalled again,
E'en now would I conclude my happy reign:
But 'tis too late, my glorious race is run,
And a dark cloud o'ertakes my setting sun.
Hadst thou not loved, or loving saved the shame
(If not the sin) by some illustrious name, 340
This little comfort had relieved my mind,
'Twas frailty, not unusual to thy kind:
But thy low fall beneath thy royal blood,
Shows downward appetite to mix with mud:
Thus not the least excuse is left for thee,
Nor the least refuge for unhappy me.
    'For him I have resolved: whom by surprise
I took, and scarce can call it in disguise;
For such was his attire as with intent
Of nature, suited to his mean descent. 350
The harder question yet remains behind: ⎫
What pains a parent and a prince can find ⎬
To punish an offence of this degenerate kind. ⎭
    'As I have loved, and yet I love thee more
Than ever father loved a child before,
So that indulgence draws me to forgive:
Nature, that gave thee life, would have thee live.
But, as a public parent of the state,

My justice, and thy crime, requires thy fate.
Fain would I choose a middle course to steer;   360
Nature's too kind, and justice too severe:
Speak for us both, and to the balance bring
On either side the father and the king.
Heaven knows, my heart is bent to favour thee;
Make it but scanty weight, and leave the rest to me.'*

    Here stopping with a sigh, he poured a flood
Of tears, to make his last expression good.

    She, who had heard him speak, nor saw alone
The secret conduct of her love was known,
But he was taken who her soul possessed,   370
Felt all the pangs of sorrow in her breast;
And little wanted, but a woman's heart*
With cries, and tears, had testified her smart:
But inborn worth, that fortune can control,*
New strung, and stiffer bent her softer soul;
The heroine assumed the woman's place,
Confirmed her mind, and fortified her face:
Why should she beg, or what could she pretend,
When her stern father had condemned her friend!
Her life she might have had; but her despair   380
Of saving his, had put it past her care:
Resolved on fate, she would not lose her breath,
But rather than not die, solicit death.
Fixed on this thought, she, not as women use
Her fault by common frailty would excuse,
But boldly justified her innocence,
And while the fact was owned, denied th' offence:
Then with dry eyes, and with an open look,
She met his glance midway, and thus undaunted spoke:

    'Tancred, I neither am disposed to make   390
Request for life, nor offered life to take:
Much less deny the deed; but least of all
Beneath pretended justice weakly fall.
My words to sacred truth shall be confined,
My deeds shall show the greatness of my mind.
That I have loved, I own; that still I love,
I call to witness all the powers above:

Yet more I own: to Guiscard's love I give
The small remaining time I have to live;
And if beyond this life desire can be,   400
Not fate itself shall set my passion free.

'This first avowed; nor folly warped my mind,
Nor the frail texture of the female kind
Betrayed my virtue: for too well I knew
What honour was, and honour had his due:
Before the holy priest my vows were tied,
So came I not a strumpet, but a bride;
This for my fame, and for the public voice:
Yet more, his merits justified my choice;
Which had they not, the first election thine,   410
That bond dissolved, the next is freely mine:
Or grant I erred, (which yet I must deny)
Had parents power e'en second vows to tie,
Thy little care to mend my widowed nights   ⎫
Has forced me to recourse of marriage rites,   ⎬
To fill an empty side, and follow known delights. ⎭
What have I done in this, deserving blame?
State laws may alter: nature's are the same;
Those are usurped on helpless womankind,
Made without our consent, and wanting power
     to bind.   420

'Thou, Tancred, better shouldst have understood,
That as thy father gave thee flesh and blood,
So gav'st thou me: not from the quarry hewed,
But of a softer mould, with sense endued;
E'en softer than thy own, of suppler kind,
More exquisite of taste, and more than man refined.
Nor need'st thou by thy daughter to be told,
Though now thy sprightly blood with age be cold:
Thou hast been young, and canst remember still,
That when thou hadst the power, thou hadst the will;   430
And from the past experience of thy fires,   ⎫
Canst tell with what a tide our strong desires ⎬
Come rushing on in youth, and what their rage requires. ⎭

'And grant thy youth was exercised in arms,
When love no leisure found for softer charms,

My tender age in luxury was trained,
With idle ease and pageants entertained;
My hours my own, my pleasures unrestrained.
So bred, no wonder if I took the bent
That seemed e'en warranted by thy consent;   440
For, when the father is too fondly kind,
Such seed he sows, such harvest shall he find.
Blame then thyself, as reason's law requires,
(Since nature gave, and thou foment'st my fires;)
If still those appetites continue strong,
Thou mayst consider, I am yet but young:
Consider too, that having been a wife,
I must have tasted of a better life,
And am not to be blamed, if I renew,
By lawful means, the joys which then I knew.   450
Where was the crime, if pleasure I procured,
Young, and a woman, and to bliss inured?
That was my case, and this is my defence:
I pleased myself, I shunned incontinence,
And urged by strong desires, indulged my sense.

  'Left to myself, I must avow, I strove
From public shame to screen my secret love,
And well acquainted with thy native pride,
Endeavoured what I could not help, to hide;
For which a woman's wit an easy way supplied.   460
How this, so well contrived, so closely laid,
Was known to thee, or by what chance betrayed,
Is not my care: to please thy pride alone,
I could have wished it had been still unknown.

  'Nor took I Guiscard by blind fancy led,
Or hasty choice, as many women wed;
But with deliberate care, and ripened thought,
At leisure first designed, before I wrought:
On him I rested, after long debate,
And not without considering, fixed my fate: 470
His flame was equal, though by mine inspired;
(For so the difference of our birth required:)
Had he been born like me, like me his love
Had first begun what mine was forced to move:

But thus beginning, thus we persevere;
Our passions yet continue what they were,
Nor length of trial makes our joys the less sincere.

   'At this my choice, though not by thine allowed,
(Thy judgement herding with the common crowd)
Thou tak'st unjust offence; and, led by them   480
Dost less the merit than the man esteem.
Too sharply, Tancred, by thy pride betrayed,
Hast thou against the laws of kind inveighed;
For all th' offence is in opinion placed,
Which deems high birth by lowly choice debased:
This thought alone with fury fires thy breast,
(For holy marriage justifies the rest)
That I have sunk the glories of the state,
And mixed my blood with a plebeian mate:
In which I wonder thou shouldst oversee   490
Superior causes, or impute to me
The fault of Fortune, or the Fates' decree.
Or call it heaven's imperial power alone,
Which moves on springs of justice, though unknown;
Yet this we see, though ordered for the best,
The bad exalted, and the good oppressed;
Permitted laurels grace the lawless brow,
Th' unworthy raised, the worthy cast below.

   'But leaving that: search we the secret springs,
And backward trace the principles of things;   500
There shall we find, that when the world began,
One common mass composed the mould of man;
One paste of flesh on all degrees bestowed,
And kneaded up alike with moistening blood.
The same almighty power inspired the frame
With kindled life, and formed the souls the same:
The faculties of intellect and will
Dispensed with equal hand, disposed with equal skill,
Like liberty indulged with choice of good or ill.
Thus born alike, from virtue first began   510
The difference that distinguished man from man:
He claimed no title from descent of blood,
But that which made him noble made him good:

Warmed with more particles of heavenly flame, ⎫
He winged his upward flight, and soared to fame; ⎬
The rest remained below, a tribe without a name. ⎭

   'This law, though custom now diverts the course,
As nature's institute, is yet in force;
Uncancelled, though disused: and he whose mind
Is virtuous, is alone of noble kind;   520
Though poor in fortune, of celestial race;
And he commits the crime, who calls him base.

   'Now lay the line, and measure all thy court
By inward virtue, not external port,
And find whom justly to prefer above
The man on whom my judgement placed my love:
So shalt thou see his parts and person shine,
And thus compared, the rest a base degenerate line.
Nor took I, when I first surveyed thy court,
His valour, or his virtues on report;   530
But trusted what I ought to trust alone,
Relying on thy eyes, and not my own;
Thy praise (and thine was then the public voice)
First recommended Guiscard to my choice:
Directed thus by thee, I looked and found
A man I thought deserving to be crowned;
First by my father pointed to my sight,
Nor less conspicuous by his native light:
His mind, his mien, the features of his face,
Excelling all the rest of human race: 540
These were thy thoughts, and thou couldst judge aright,
Till interest made a jaundice in thy sight.

   'Or should I grant thou didst not rightly see;
Then thou wert first deceived, and I deceived by thee.
But if thou shalt allege, through pride of mind,
Thy blood with one of base condition joined,
'Tis false; for 'tis not baseness to be poor;
His poverty augments thy crime the more;
Upbraids thy justice with the scant regard
Of worth: whom princes praise, they should reward.   550
Are these the kings entrusted by the crowd
With wealth to be dispensed for common good?

The people sweat not for their king's delight,
T" enrich a pimp, or raise a parasite;
Theirs is the toil; and he who well has served
His country, has his country's wealth deserved.

'E'en mighty monarchs oft are meanly born,
And kings by birth to lowest rank return;
All subject to the power of giddy chance,
For Fortune can depress, or can advance: 560
But true nobility is of the mind,
Not given by chance, and not to chance resigned.

'For the remaining doubt of thy decree,
What to resolve, and how dispose of me,
Be warned to cast that useless care aside:
Myself alone will for myself provide.
If in thy doting and decrepit age,
Thy soul, a stranger in thy youth to rage,
Begins in cruel deeds to take delight,
Gorge with my blood thy barbarous appetite;   570
For I so little am disposed to pray
For life, I would not cast a wish away.
Such as it is, th' offence is all my own;
And what to Guiscard is already done,
Or to be done, is doomed by thy decree, ⎫
That, if not executed first by thee,   ⎬
Shall on my person be performed by me. ⎭

'Away! with women weep, and leave me here,
Fixed, like a man to die, without a tear;
Or save, or slay us both this present hour,   580
'Tis all that fate has left within thy power.'

She said; nor did her father fail to find,
In all she spoke, the greatness of her mind;
Yet thought she was not obstinate to die,
Nor deemed the death she promised was so nigh:
Secure in this belief, he left the dame,
Resolved to spare her life, and save her shame;
But that detested object to remove,
To wreak his vengeance, and to cure her love.

Intent on this, a secret order signed,   590
The death of Guiscard to his guards enjoined:

Strangling was chosen, and the night the time,
A mute revenge, and blind as was the crime:
His faithful heart, a bloody sacrifice,
Torn from his breast to glut the tyrant's eyes,
Closed the severe command: for (slaves to pay)
What kings decree, the soldier must obey:
Waged against foes; and, when the wars are o'er
Fit only to maintain despotic power:
Dangerous to freedom, and desired alone   600
By kings who seek an arbitrary throne:*
Such were these guards; as ready to have slain
The prince himself, allured with greater gain:
So was the charge performed with better will,
By men inured to blood, and exercised in ill.

   Now, though the sullen sire had eased his mind,
The pomp of his revenge was yet behind,
A pomp prepared to grace the present he designed.
A goblet rich with gems, and rough with gold,
Of depth, and breadth, the precious pledge to hold,   610
With cruel care he chose: the hollow part
Enclosed, the lid concealed the lover's heart:
Then of his trusted mischiefs, one he sent,
And bade him with these words the gift present:
'Thy father sends thee this, to cheer thy breast,
And glad thy sight with what thou lov'st the best;
As thou hast pleased his eyes, and joyed his mind,
With what he loved the most of human kind.'
   Ere this the royal dame, who well had weighed
The consequence of what her sire had said,   620
Fixed on her fate, against th' expected hour,
Procured the means to have it in her power:
For this she had distilled, with early care,
The juice of simples, friendly to despair,
A magazine of death; and thus prepared,
Secure to die, the fatal message heard:
Then smiled severe; nor with a troubled look,
Or trembling hand, the funeral present took;
E'en kept her countenance, when the lid removed,
Disclosed the heart unfortunately loved: 630

She needed not be told within whose breast
It lodged; the message had explained the rest.
Or not amazed, or hiding her surprise,
She sternly on the bearer fixed her eyes:
Then thus: 'Tell Tancred on his daughter's part,
The gold, though precious, equals not the heart:
But he did well to give his best; and I,
Who wished a worthier urn, forgive his poverty.'

At this, she curbed a groan that else had come,
And pausing, viewed the present in the tomb: 640
Then to the heart adored devoutly glued
Her lips, and raising it, her speech renewed:
'E'en from my day of birth to this, the bound
Of my unhappy being, I have found
My father's care and tenderness expressed.
But this last act of love excels the rest:
For this so dear a present, bear him back
The best return that I can live to make.'

The messenger dispatched, again she viewed
The loved remains and, sighing, thus pursued: 650
'Source of my life, and lord of my desires,
In whom I lived, with whom my soul expires;
Poor heart, no more the spring of vital heat,
Cursed be the hands that tore thee from thy seat!
The course is finished which thy Fates decreed,
And thou from thy corporeal prison freed:
Soon hast thou reached the goal with mended pace,
A world of woes dispatched in little space:
Forced by thy worth, thy foe (in death become
Thy friend) has lodged thee in a costly tomb;   660
There yet remained thy funeral exequies,
The weeping tribute of thy widow's eyes;
And those indulgent heaven has found the way
That I, before my death, have leave to pay.
My father e'en in cruelty is kind,
Or heaven has turned the malice of his mind }
To better uses than his hate designed;
And made th' insùlt, which in his gift appears,
The means to mourn thee with my pious tears;

Which I will pay thee down, before I go,   670
And save myself the pains to weep below—
If souls can weep; though once I meant to meet
My fate with face unmoved, and eyes unwet,
Yet since I have thee here in narrow room,
My tears shall set thee first afloat within thy tomb:
Then (as I know thy spirit hovers nigh)
Under thy friendly conduct will I fly
To regions unexplored, secure to share
Thy state; nor hell shall punishment appear,
And heaven is double heaven, if thou art there.'   680
    She said. Her brimful eyes, that ready stood,
And only wanted will to weep a flood,
Released their watery store, and poured amain,
Like clouds low hung, a sober shower of rain;
Mute solemn sorrow, free from female noise,
Such as the majesty of grief destroys:
For, bending o'er the cup, the tears she shed
Seemed by the posture to discharge her head,
O'erfilled before; and oft (her mouth applied
To the cold heart) she kissed at once and cried.   690
Her maids, who stood amazed, nor knew the cause
Of her complaining, nor whose heart it was,
Yet all due measures of her mourning kept,
Did office at the dirge, and by infection wept;
And oft inquired th' occasion of her grief,
(Unanswered but by sighs) and offered vain relief.
At length, her stock of tears already shed,
She wiped her eyes, she raised her drooping head,
And thus pursued: 'O ever-faithful heart,
I have performed the ceremonial part,   700
The decencies of grief. It rests behind,
That as our bodies were, our souls be joined:
To thy whate'er abode, my shade convey,
And as an elder ghost, direct the way.'
She said; and bade the vial to be brought,
Where she before had brewed the deadly draught;
First pouring out the med'cinable bane,
The heart her tears had rinsed she bathed again;

Then down her throat the death securely throws,
And quaffs a long oblivion of her woes.   710
   This done, she mounts the genial bed, and there,
(Her body first composed with honest care,)
Attends the welcome rest. Her hands yet hold
Close to her heart, the monumental gold;
Nor further word she spoke, but closed her sight,
And quiet, sought the covert of the night.
   The damsels, who the while in silence mourned,
Not knowing, nor suspecting death suborned,
Yet, as their duty was, to Tancred sent,
Who, conscious of th' occasion, feared th' event.   720
Alarmed, and with presaging heart he came,
And drew the curtains, and exposed the dame
To loathsome light: then with a late relief
Made vain efforts to mitigate her grief.
She, what she could excluding day, her eyes
Kept firmly sealed, and sternly thus replies:
   'Tancred, restrain thy tears, unsought by me,
And sorrow, unavailing now to thee:
Did ever man before afflict his mind
To see th' effect of what himself designed?   730
Yet, if thou hast remaining in thy heart
Some sense of love, some unextinguished part
Of former kindness, largely once professed,⎤
Let me by that adjure thy hardened breast⎬
Not to deny thy daughter's last request:⎦
The secret love which I so long enjoyed,
And still concealed to gratify thy pride,
Thou hast disjoined; but with my dying breath,
Seek not, I beg thee, to disjoin our death:
Where'er his corpse by thy command is laid,   740
Thither let mine in public be conveyed;
Exposed in open view, and side by side,
Acknowledged as a bridegroom and a bride.'
   The prince's anguish hindered his reply;
And she, who felt her fate approaching nigh,
Seized the cold heart, and heaving to her breast,
'Here, precious pledge,' she said, 'securely rest.'

These accents were her last; the creeping death
Benumbed her senses first, then stopped her breath.

    Thus she for disobedience justly died;   750
The sire was justly punished for his pride:
The youth, least guilty, suffered for th' offence
Of duty violated to his prince;
Who late repenting of his cruel deed,
One common sepulchre for both decreed;
Entombed the wretched pair in royal state,
And on their monument inscribed their fate.

67   From *All for Love*

JOHN DRYDEN

From Act II; published 1678. The Roman general Antony has decided to
end his relationship with the Egyptian Queen Cleopatra, and return to his
military duties in Rome. His Roman friends, including Ventidius, try to
prevent him from seeing Cleopatra, lest his resolution to leave her should
fail. She is fetched by her minion Alexas to meet Antony, for the first time
in the play.

              Enter Cleopatra, Charmion, and Iras

  Antony. Well, Madam, we are met.

  Cleo.   Is this a meeting?
Then we must part?

  Ant.   We must.

  Cleo.   Who says we must?

  Ant. Our own hard fates.

  Cleo.   We make those fates ourselves.

  Ant. Yes, we have made 'em; we have loved each other
Into our mutual ruin.

  Cleo. The gods have seen my joys with envious eyes;
I have no friends in heaven, and all the world,
As 'twere the business of mankind to part us,
Is armed against my love: ev'n you yourself
Join with the rest; you, you are armed against me.   250

Ant. I will be justified in all I do
To late posterity, and therefore hear me.
If I mix a lie
With any truth, reproach me freely with it;
Else favour me with silence.

Cleo.   You command me,
And I am dumb.

Ventidius. I like this well: he shows authority.

Ant. That I derive my ruin
From you alone—

Cleo.   O heavens! I ruin you?

Ant. You promised me your silence, and you break it   260
Ere I have scarce begun.

Cleo.   Well, I obey you.

Ant. When I beheld you first, it was in Egypt,
Ere Caesar saw your eyes. You gave me love,*
And were too young to know it: that I settled
Your father in his throne was for your sake;
I left th' acknowledgement for time to ripen.
Caesar stepped in, and with a greedy hand
Plucked the green fruit ere the first blush of red,
Yet cleaving to the bough. He was my lord,
And was, beside, too great for me to rival,   270
But I deserved you first, though he enjoyed you.
When, after, I beheld you in Cilicia,
An enemy to Rome, I pardoned you.

Cleo. I cleared myself—

Ant.   Again you break your promise.
I loved you still, and took your weak excuses,
Took you into my bosom, stained by Caesar,
And not half mine. I went to Egypt with you,
And hid me from the business of the world,
Shut out enquiring nations from my sight,
To give whole years to you.   280

Vent. aside. Yes, to your shame be't spoken.

Ant.   How I loved,

Witness ye days and nights, and all your hours
That danced away with down upon your feet,
As all your business were to count my passion.
One day passed by, and nothing saw but love;
Another came, and still 'twas only love:
The suns were wearied out with looking on,
And I untired with loving.
I saw you every day, and all the day,
And every day was still but as the first,   290
So eager was I still to see you more.

   Vent. 'Tis all too true.

   Ant.   Fulvia, my wife, grew jealous,
As she indeed had reason; raised a war
In Italy, to call me back.

   Vent.   But yet
You went not.

   Ant.   While within your arms I lay,
The world fell mouldering from my hands each hour,
And left me scarce a grasp: I thank your love for't.

   Vent. Well pushed: that last was home.

   Cleo.   Yet may I speak?

   Ant. If I have urged a falsehood, yes; else, not.
Your silence says I have not. Fulvia died—   300
Pardon, you gods, with my unkindness died.
To set the world at peace I took Octavia,
This Caesar's sister: in her pride of youth
And flower of beauty did I wed that lady,
Whom blushing I must praise, because I left her.
You called; my love obeyed the fatal summons:
This raised the Roman arms; the cause was yours.
I would have fought by land, where I was stronger;
You hindered it, yet when I fought at sea,
Forsook me fighting, and—oh, stain to honour!   310
Oh, lasting shame!—I knew not that I fled,
But fled to follow you.*

   Vent. What haste she made to hoist her purple sails!
And, to appear magnificent in flight,

Drew half our strength away.

Ant. All this you caused,
And would you multiply more ruins on me?
This honest man, my best, my only friend,
Has gathered up the shipwreck of my fortunes.
Twelve legions I have left, my last recruits,
And you have watched the news, and bring your eyes 320
To seize them too. If you have aught to answer,
Now speak, you have free leave.

Alexas aside. She stands confounded.
Despair is in her eyes.

Vent. Now lay a sigh i' th' way to stop his passage;
Prepare a tear, and bid it for his legions:
'Tis like they shall be sold.

Cleo. How shall I plead my cause, when you, my judge,
Already have condemned me? Shall I bring
The love you bore me for my advocate?
That now is turned against me, that destroys me, 330
For love once past is at the best forgotten,
But oftener sours to hate: 'twill please my Lord
To ruin me, and therefore I'll be guilty.
But could I once have thought it would have pleased you,
That you would pry with narrow searching eyes
Into my faults, severe to my destruction,
And watching all advantages with care
That serve to make me wretched? Speak, my Lord,
For I end here. Though I deserve this usage,
Was it like you to give it?

Ant. Oh, you wrong me 340
To think I sought this parting, or desired
To accuse you more than what will clear myself
And justify this breach.

Cleo. Thus low I thank you,
And since my innocence will not offend,
I shall not blush to own it.

Vent. After this,
I think she'll blush at nothing.

Cleo.   You seem grieved
(And therein you are kind), that Caesar first
Enjoyed my love, though you deserved it better:
I grieve for that, my Lord, much more than you,
For had I first been yours, it would have saved   350
My second choice; I never had been his,
And ne'er had been but yours. But Caesar first,
You say, possessed my love. Not so, my Lord:
He first possessed my person, you my love;
Caesar loved me, but I loved Antony.
If I endured him after, 'twas because
I judged it due to the first name of men,
And, half constrained, I gave, as to a tyrant,
What he would take by force.

Vent.   O siren! Siren!
Yet grant that all the love she boasts were true,   360
Has she not ruined you? I still urge that,
The fatal consequence.

Cleo.   The consequence indeed,
For I dare challenge him, my greatest foe,
To say it was designed: 'tis true I loved you,
And kept you far from an uneasy wife:
Such Fulvia was.
Yes, but he'll say you left Octavia for me;
And can you blame me to receive that love
Which quitted such desert for worthless me?
How often have I wished some other Caesar,   370
Great as the first, and as the second young,
Would court my love, to be refused for you!

Vent. Words, words; but Actium, Sir, remember Actium.

Cleo. Ev'n there I dare his malice. True, I counselled
To fight at sea, but I betrayed you not.
I fled, but not to th' enemy. 'Twas fear:
Would I had been a man, not to have feared,
For none would then have envied me your friendship,
Who envy me your love.

Ant.   We're both unhappy.

If nothing else, yet our ill fortune parts us.   380
Speak: would you have me perish by my stay?

 Cleo. If as a friend you ask my judgement, go;
If as a lover, stay. If you must perish—
'Tis a hard word—but stay.

 Vent. See now th' effects of her so boasted love!
She strives to drag you down to ruin with her;
But could she 'scape without you, oh, how soon
Would she let go her hold, and haste to shore,
And never look behind!

 Cleo. Then judge my love by this. (*Giving Antony a writing*)
         Could I have borne   390
A life or death, a happiness or woe
From yours divided, this had given me means.

 Ant. By Hercules, the writing of Octavius!
I know it well; 'tis that proscribing hand,
Young as it was, that led the way to mine,
And left me but the second place in murder.—
See, see, Ventidius! Here he offers Egypt,
And joins all Syria to it as a present,
So, in requital, she forsake my fortunes,
And join her arms with his.

 Cleo.   And yet you leave me!   400
You leave me, Antony, and yet I love you,
Indeed I do. I have refused a kingdom;
That's a trifle:
For I could part with life, with anything
But only you. Oh, let me die but with you!
Is that a hard request?

 Ant.   Next living with you,
'Tis all that Heaven can give.

 Alex. aside.   He melts; we conquer.

 Cleo. No; you shall go. Your interest calls you hence;
Yes, your dear interest pulls too strong for these
Weak arms to hold you here.— (*Takes his hand*)
      Go, leave me, soldier,   410
For you're no more a lover, leave me dying:

Push me all pale and panting from your bosom,
And when your march begins, let one run after,
Breathless almost for joy, and cry, 'She's dead'.
The soldiers shout; you then perhaps may sigh,
And muster all your Roman gravity.
Ventidius chides, and straight your brow clears up,
As I had never been.

 Ant.   Gods, 'tis too much,
Too much for man to bear!

 Cleo.   What is't for me, then,
A weak, forsaken woman, and a lover?—   420
Here let me breathe my last: envy me not
This minute in your arms; I'll die apace,
As fast as e'er I can, and end your trouble.

 Ant. Die? Rather let me perish! Loosened nature
Leap from its hinges; sink the props of heaven,
And fall the skies to crush the nether world!
My eyes, my soul, my all!—   (*Embraces her*)

 Vent.   And what's this toy
In balance with your fortune, honour, fame?

 Ant. What is't, Ventidius? It outweighs 'em all;
Why, we have more than conquered Caesar now.   430
My Queen's not only innocent, but loves me.
This, this is she who drags me down to ruin!
But could she 'scape without me, with what haste
Would she let slip her hold, and make to shore,
And never look behind!
Down on thy knees, blasphemer as thou art,
And ask forgiveness of wronged innocence.

 Vent. I'll rather die than take it. Will you go?

 Ant. Go? Whither? Go from all that's excellent?
Faith, honour, virtue, all good things forbid   440
That I should go from her who sets my love
Above the price of kingdoms. Give, you gods,
Give to your boy, your Caesar,
This rattle of a globe to play withal,
This gewgaw world, and put him cheaply off:
I'll not be pleased with less than Cleopatra.

Cleo. She's wholly yours. My heart's so full of joy
That I shall do some wild extravagance
Of love in public, and the foolish world,
Which knows not tenderness, will think me mad.   450

Vent. O women! Women! Women! All the gods
Have not such power of doing good to man
As you of doing harm.   (*Exit*)

Ant.   Our men are armed.
Unbar the gate that looks to Caesar's camp.
I would revenge the treachery he meant me,
And long security makes conquest easy.
I'm eager to return before I go,
For all the pleasures I have known beat thick
On my remembrance. How I long for night!
   That both the sweets of mutual love may try,   460
   And once triùmph o'er Caesar ere we die.   (*Exeunt*)

68   *Said by a Young Lady to her Child, Taking*
          Something to Destroy it

ANONYMOUS

Previously unpublished. Lines 1, 2, and 16 deviate from the pentameter
pattern; they may be corrupt textually, or intentionally awkward.

Thou that thy life ere thy birth must lose,
   Twixt nothing and a being, mixture of extremes,
Unfinished embryo whom both states refuse,
   As each too perfect or imperfect deems:

Got when my passion honour's laws o'ercame,
   Condemned to death by its severe decree;
Unhappy product of my lawless flame,
   Thou must the victim of my honour be.

Die to prevent thy cruel mother's shame,
   But doing so, forget you e'er were mine;   10
And when returned to chaos, whence you came,
   Tell not the shades the horror of my crime.

To love and honour all mankind's a slave,
   Whose rigid laws none nobly can decline;
Blame love then, who th' imperfect being gave,
   And tyrant honour that doth thy death design.

69   *To my Children*

LUCY HUTCHINSON

Written 1664–71. It is one of two brief character sketches of her husband, Col. John Hutchinson, which precede the main memoir. John Hutchinson had been a prominent military leader on the Parliamentarian side in the Civil War; after the Restoration he was arrested and imprisoned in the Tower of London. In 1664 he was moved to Sandown Castle in Kent, where he died.

They who dote on mortal excellencies, when, by the inevitable fate of all things frail, their adored idols are taken from them, may let loose the winds of passion to bring in a flood of sorrow whose ebbing tides carry away the dear memory of what they have lost; and when comfort is essayed to such mourners, commonly all objects are removed out of their view, which may with their remembrance renew the grief; and in time these remedies succeed, when oblivion's curtain is by degrees drawn over the dead face, and things less lovely are liked, while they are not viewed together with that which was most excellent. But I that am under a command* not to grieve at the common rate of desolate women, while I am studying which way to moderate my woe, and if it were possible to augment my love, can for the present find out none more just to your dear father nor consolatory to myself than the preservation of his memory, which I need not gild with such flattering commendations as the hired preachers do equally give to the truly and titularly honourable. A naked, undressed narrative, speaking the simple truth of him, will deck him with more substantial glory, than all the panegyrics that the best pens could ever consecrate to the virtues of the best men.

   Indeed, that resplendent body of light, which the beginning and ending of his life made up to discover the deformities of this wicked age and to instruct the erring children of this generation, will, through my apprehension and expression, shine as under a very thick cloud, which will obscure much of their lustre; but there is need of this medium to this world's weak eyes, which I fear hath but few people so virtuous in it as can believe (because they find themselves so short) that any other could make so large a progress in the race of piety, honour, and virtue: but I am almost stopped before I set forth to trace his steps, finding the number of them, by which he still outwent himself, more than my imperfect arithmetic can count, and the exact figure of them such as my unskilful pen cannot describe. I fear to injure that memory which I would honour, and to disgrace his name with a poor monument; but when I have beforehand laid this necessary caution, and ingenuously confessed that through my inability either to receive or administer much of that wealthy stock of his glory that I was entrusted with for the benefit of all, and particularly his own posterity, I must withhold a great part from them, I hope I shall be pardoned for drawing an imperfect image of him, especially when even the rudest draft that endeavours to counterfeit him will have much delightful loveliness in it.

What shall I write of him is but a copy of [him]. The original of all excellence is God him[self] and God alone, whose glory was first transcribed [in] the humanity of Christ and [in] that copy left us fair in the written Word, wherein this pious soul exercised himself day and night as the rule of his practice. The power he had to approach it, his delight in transcribing it, and his final perseverance in that laudable delight were all but extracts of Christ drawn upon his spirit by the Spirit of God. If, therefore, while I had a happy enjoyment of him and communication of his gifts and graces during his abode in the flesh, I did not look so far beyond the creature as I ought, delighting more than I ought to have done in the mirror that reflected the Creator's excellence, which I should have always admired in its own fountain, I desire not to pursue that sin, but, while I celebrate the glories of a saint, that I and any for whom I may declare them may give God the first and chiefest glory for all the goodness he gives to the children of men. This excellent person whom I desire to commemorate to you, though one of the best of men, was yet but man, a son of Adam, an inheritor of his corrupted nature, subject to all the sins and miseries that attend it, which is necessary to be considered, that we may the more magnify the riches of God's grace and admirable power, whereby he raised that wretched fallen nature and changed it into such a blessed image of his own glory, making it to enjoy so sweet a communion with himself and to bear so clear a testimony of his grace and truth and holiness before this erring age.

Let not excess of love and delight in the stream make us forget the fountain: he and all his excellencies came from God, and flowed back into their own spring. There let us seek them, thither let us hasten after him; there having found him, let us cease to bewail among the dead that which is risen, or rather was immortal. His soul conversed with God so much when he was here, that it rejoices to be now eternally freed from interruption in that blessed exercise. His virtues were recorded in heaven's annals, and can never perish; by them he yet teaches us and all those to whose knowledge they shall arrive. What have we then lost? His flesh?—No—that is but laid to sleep that it may wake again more vigorous and beautiful. That corruption hath by the power of Christ a seed of incorruption; that mortal shall shortly awake immortal. It is only his fetters, his sins, his infirmities, his diseases that are dead never to revive again, nor would we have them; they were his enemies and ours; by faith in Christ he vanquished them. Our conjunction, if we had any with him, was indissoluble; if we were knit together by one spirit into one body of Christ, we are so still; if we were mutually united in one love of God, good men, and goodness, we are so still. What is it then we wail in his remove? The distance? Faithless fools! 'tis sorrow only makes it. Let us but ascend to God in holy joy for the great grace given his poor servant, and he is there with us. He is only removed from the malice of his enemies, for which we should not express love to him in being afflicted. We may mourn for ourselves that we come so tardily after him; that we want his guide and assistance in our way; and yet if our tears did not put out our eyes we should see him even in heaven, holding forth his flaming lamp of virtuous examples and precepts, to light us through the dark world. It is time that I open the shut [eyes] and let in to your knowledge that splendour which, while it cheers and enlightens your heavy senses, should make us remember to give all his and all our glory to God alone, who is the only father and fountain of all light and excellence.

Desiring, if my treacherous memory have not lost the dearest treasure that ever I committed to its trust, to relate to you his holy, virtuous, honourable life, I would put his picture in the front of his book, but my unskilful hand will injure him. Yet to such of you as have not seen him to remember his person, I leave this:

His Description

He was of a middle stature, of a slender and exactly well-proportioned shape in all parts; his complexion fair; his hair of light brown, very thick set in his youth, softer than the finest silk, curling into loose great rings at the ends; his eyes of a lively grey; well-shaped and full of life and vigour graced with many becoming motions; his visage thin, his mouth well made, and his lips very ruddy and graceful, although the nether chap shut over the upper, yet it was in such a manner as was not unbecoming; his teeth were even and white as the purest ivory; his chin was something long, and the mould of his face; his forehead was not very high; his nose was raised and sharp; but withal he had a most amiable countenance, which carried in it something of magnanimity and majesty mixed with sweetness, that at the same time bespoke love and awe in all that saw him. His eyes had an excellence of beauty, vigour, and cheerfulness, especially when he was well pleased, that conveyed delight to all that beheld them, and if he were angry darted a becoming fire as terrible as bright. His skin was smooth and white, his legs and feet excellently well-made. He was quick in his pace and turns, nimble and active and graceful in all his motions; he was apt for any bodily exercise, and any that he did became him; he could dance admirably well, but neither in youth nor riper years made any practice of it. He had skill in fencing, such as became a gentleman. He had a great love to music, and often diverted himself with a viol, on which he played masterly; and he had an exact ear and judgement in other music. He shot excellently in bows and guns, and much used them for his exercise. He had great judgement in paintings, engraving, sculpture, and all excellent arts, wherein he was much delighted, and had many curiosities of value in all kinds; he took great delight in perspective glasses, and for his other rarities was not so much affected with the antiquity as with the art of the work. He had a great delight in improvements, in planting groves and walks and fruit-trees, in opening springs and making fish-ponds; of country recreations he loved none but hawking, and in that was very eager and much delighted for the time he used it, but soon left it off. He was wonderful neat and cleanly, and genteel in his habit, and had a very good fancy in making good clothes, but he left off very early the wearing of anything that was costly, yet in his plainest negligent habit appeared very much a gentleman. He had more address than force of body, yet the courage of his soul so supplied his members that he never wanted strength when he found occasion to employ it. His conversation was very pleasant, for he was naturally cheerful and had a ready wit and apprehension. He was eager in everything he did, earnest in dispute, but withal very rational, so that he was seldom overcome. Everything that it was necessary for him to do he did with delight, free and unconstrained; he hated ceremonious compliment, but yet had a natural civility and complaisance to all people as made his converse very delightful. He was of a tender constitution, but through the vivacity of his spirit could undergo labours, watchings, and journeys, as well as any of stronger compositions; he was rheumatic, and had a long sickness and distemper occasioned thereby, two or three years after the war ended, but else, for the latter half of his life, was healthy though tender. In his youth and childhood he was sickly, much troubled with weakness and toothaches, but then his spirits carried him through them. He was very patient under sickness of pain, or any common accidents, but yet, upon occasions, though never without just ones, he would be very angry and had, even [in that], such a grace as made him to be feared, yet he was never outrageous in passion. He had a very good faculty in persuading, and would speak very well, pertinently and effectually without premeditation upon the greatest occasions that could be offered, for, indeed, his judgement was so nice that he could never frame any speech beforehand to please himself; but his invention was so ready, and wisdom so habitual in all his speeches, that he never had reason to repent himself of speaking at any time without ranking the words beforehand; he was not talkative, yet free of discourse. He was of a very spare diet and temperate both in meats and drinks, not much given to sleep; an early riser when he was in health, he loved not to go very soon to bed; he never was at any time idle, and hated to see any one else so. In all his natural and ordinary inclinations and composure, there was something extraordinary and tending to virtue, beyond what I can describe, or can be gathered from a bare dead description. There was a life of spirit and power in him that is not to be found in any copy drawn from him. To sum up, therefore, all that can be said of his outward frame and disposition, we must truly conclude that it was a very handsome and well furnished lodging prepared for the reception of that prince* who in the administration of all excellent virtues reigned there a while, till he was called back to the palace of the universal emperor.

His Virtues

To number his virtues is to give the epitome of his life, which was nothing else but a progress from one degree of virtue to another, till in a short time he arrived to that height which many longer lives could never reach; and had I but the power of rightly disposing and relating them, his single example would be more instructive than all the rules of the best moralists, for his practice was of a more divine extraction, drawn from the word of God, and wrought up by the assistance of his Spirit in him. Therefore in the head of all his virtues I shall set that which was the head and spring of them all, his Christianity, for this alone is the true royal blood that runs through the whole body of virtues, and every pretender to that glorious family which hath no tincture of it is an impostor and a spurious brat. This is that sacred fountain which baptizeth all the gentile virtues that so immortalize the names of Cicero, Plutarch, Seneca, and all the old philosophers; herein they are regenerated, and take a new name and nature. Digged up out of the wilderness of nature, and dipped in this living spring, they are planted and flourish in the paradise of God.

By Christianity I intend that universal habit of grace which is wrought in a soul by the regenerating Spirit of God, whereby the whole creature is resigned up into the divine will and love, and all its actions designed to the obedience of that for the glory of its Maker. This began to work very early in him and upon him, and even in his childhood wrought in his heart a reverence of God, a seeking after the knowledge of him, a love and delight in his law, a perfect detestation of sin, with a desire, delight, and endeavour to do well, a belief of eternity and a sense of men's conditions in life [and] death, a sense of natural corruption, a groaning under it and a desire to be freed from it. As he grew [up] he attained a great degree of zeal for God and his honour, and thereupon would be severely angry against professors who walked not according to the Gospel. As soon as he had improved his natural understanding with the acquisition of learning, the first studies he exercised himself in were principles of religion, and the first knowledge he laboured for was the knowledge of God, which by a diligent examination of the Scripture, and the several doctrines of great men pretending that ground, he at length obtained; and for the doctrinal principles of religion was convinced and established much in the way of Mr Calvin,* but not as his way but as the way of God. Afterward, when he had laid a sure and orthodox foundation in the doctrine of the free grace of God given us by Jesus Christ, he began to survey the superstructures, and to discover much of the hay and stubble of men's inventions in God's worship, which the spirit of God burned up in the day of their trial. His faith being established in the truth, he was full of love to God and all his saints. He hated persecution for religion, and was always a champion for all religious people against all their great oppressors. He never did anything without measuring it by the rule of conscience, and for the gain of the whole world would not have committed one sin or omitted one duty against his conscience, that, being persuaded neither his estate, honour, wife, children, nor his own life weighed anything with him in the balance against Christ and his interest, and having often cheerfully set them at the hazard, he at last joyfully parted with them all at God's call and for God's cause. The more God chastened him, the more he loved him, kissing the rod and rejoicing in the scourge that drove him nearer to God. When God turned the great wheel in this nation,* he re-examined all his former ways and actions, and the Lord gave him comfort, confirmation, and great advancement in his love.

He then cast off all other studies and wholly applied himself to the Scriptures, and they were sweet counsellors and refreshment to him in all his adversities; he was never so patient as in the times of his greatest provocation. In every stroke God seemed to give him he more regarded and rejoiced in the mercy than grieved at the cross; yet he was not insensible of the hand of God in all things. No hiding of his face, no seeming frowns, could damp his confidence in God; even in death he retained it, and rejoiced in the salvation of the Lord when he seemed to kill him. He took wonderful notice, and was thankful for all God's mercies; in his greatest straits he renewed his strength and courage by considering former experiences, but his life and joy was most in resignation and submission to God, unfeignedly desiring the fulfilling of his will and glory, though in his own destruction. But he was full of faith that God, who had moulded him into such a submissive frame of spirit, would not finally destroy him. He was very desirous to communicate the grace of God given him, and to instruct others what God had taught him, and neglected not to exhort his children and family to diligence in searching after the knowledge of God, and to prayer and to holiness and watchfulness in this evil day. In short, I that have been the faithful depository of all his secrets must witness for him that in all times his heart was sincere and steadfast to the Lord, and that towards his latter years he grew abundantly in the grace and knowledge of the Lord Jesus Christ and in the love of God, from whom he had many revelations of mercy and loving kindness, which bore him admirably up above all the waves of this tumultuous world, and made him sail on to heaven with great tranquillity, joy and thankfulness, so much as it is not possible for my narrow exp[ression] to describe.

Christianity in him was as the fountain of all his virtues, and diffused itself into every stream. That of his prudence falls into the next mention. He from a child was wise, and sought to by many that might have been his fathers for counsel, which he could excellently give to himself and others; and whatever cross event in any of his affairs may give occasion to fools to overlook the wisdom of the design, yet he had as great a foresight, as strong a judgement, as clear an apprehension of men and things as no man more. He had rather a firm impression than a great memory, yet he was forgetful of nothing but injuries. His own integrity made him credulous of other men's, till reason and experience convinced [him] and as unapt to believe cautions which could not be received without entertaining ill opinions of men; yet he had wisdom enough never to commit himself to a traitor, though he was once wickedly betrayed by friends whom necessity, and not mistake, forced him to trust. He was as ready to hear as to give counsel, and never pertinacious in his will when his reason was convinced. There was no opinion which he was most settled in, either concerning divine or human things, but he would patiently and impartially hear it debated. In matters of faith his reason always submitted to the Word of God, and what he could not comprehend, he would believe because it was written; but in all other things, the greatest names in the world could never lead him without reason. He would deliberate when there was time, but never, by tedious dispute, lost an opportunity of anything that was to be done. He would hear as well as speak, and yet never spoke impertinently or unseasonably.

He very well understood himself, his own advantages, natural parts, gifts and acquirements, yet so as neither to glory of them to others, nor overvalue himself for them; for he had an excellent virtuous modesty, which shut out all vanity of mind, and yet admitted that necessary, true understanding of himself which was requisite for the best improvement of all his talents. He no less understood and was more heedful to remark his defects, imperfections, and disadvantages, but that too only to excite his circumspection concerning them, not to damp his spirit in any noble enterprise. He had a noble spirit of government, both in civil, military and ecumenical administrations, which forced even from unwilling subjects a love and reverence of him, and endeared him to the souls of those rejoiced to be governed by him. He had a native majesty that struck an awe of him into the hearts of men, and a sweet greatness that commanded love. He had a clear discerning of men's spirits, and knew how to give every one their just weight. He contemned none that were not wicked, in whatever low degree of nature or fortune they were otherwise: wherever he saw wisdom, learning, or other virtues in men, he honoured them highly, and admired them to their full rate, but never gave himself blindly up to the conduct of the greatest master. Love itself, which was as powerful in his as in any soul, rather quickened than blinded the eyes of his judgement in discerning the imperfections of those that were most dear to him. His soul ever reigned as king in the internal throne, and never was captive to his sense; religion and reason, its two favoured councillors, took order that all the passions kept within their own just bounds, there did him good service, and furthered the public weal. He found such felicity in that proportion of wisdom that he enjoyed, as he was a great lover of that which advanced it, learning and arts; which he not only honoured [in] others, but had by his industry arrived to be himself a far greater scholar than is absolutely requisite for a gentleman. He had many excellent attainments, but he no less evidenced his wisdom in knowing how to rank and use them, than in gaining them. He had wit enough to have been subtle and cunning, but he so abhorred dissimulation that I cannot say he was either. Greatness of courage would not suffer him to put on a vizard to secure him from any; to retire into the shadow of privacy and silence was all his prudence could effect in him.

It will be as hard to say which was the predominant virtue in him, as which is so in its own nature. He was as excellent in justice as in wisdom; the greatest advantage, nor the greatest danger, nor the dearest interest or friend in the world, could not prevail on him to pervert justice even to an enemy. He never professed the thing he intended not, nor promised what he believed out of his own power, nor failed the performance of anything that was in his power to fulfil. Never fearing anything he could suffer for the truth, he never at any time would refrain a true or give a false witness; he loved truth so much that he hated even sportive lies and gulleries. He was so just to his own honour that he many times forbore things lawful and delightful to him, rather than he would give anyone occasion of scandal. Of all lies he most hated hypocrisy in religion, either to comply with changing governments or persons, without a real persuasion of conscience, or to practise holy things to get the applause of men or any advantage by the reputation of religion. Whatever he practised in religion was neither for faction nor advantage but contrary to it and purely for conscience sake. In his youth the Devil laid the common block in his way to make him fear profession lest walking not to the height of it he should give occasion to the scandal of hypocrisy; but, as he hated outsides in religion, so he could worse endure those apostacies, denials of the Lord and base compliances with his adversaries which timorous men practise under the name of prudent and just condescensions to avoid persecution. He detested all scoffs at any practice of worship, though such a one as he was not persuaded of.

As in religion so in friendship, he never professed love when he had it not, nor disguised hate or aversion, which indeed he never had to any party or person, but to their sins, and loved even his bitterest enemies so well that I am witness how his soul mourned for them, and how heartily he desired their conversion; but their wickedness his righteous soul abhorred. If he were defective in any part of justice, it was when it was in his power to punish those who had injured him, whom I have so often known him to recompense with favours instead of revenge, that his friends used to tell him, if they had any occasion to make him favourably partial to them, they would provoke him by an injury. He was as faithful and constant to his friends as merciful to his enemies: nothing grieved him more than to be obliged where he could not hope to return it. He, that was a rock to all assaults of might and violence, was the gentlest, easiest soul to kindness, that the least warm spark melted him into anything that was not sinful. There never was a man more exactly just in the performance of duties to all relations and to all persons. Honour and obedience and love to his father were so natural and so lasting in him, that it is impossible to imagine a better son than he was; and whoever would pray for a blessing in children to any one, could but wish them such a son as he. He never repined at his father's will in anything, how much soever it were his prejudice, but would praise and defend even his giving away some of his estate, which people thought he should not have, nor would endure to hear anyone say his father was not so kind to him as he might have been, but to his dying day preserved his father's memory with such tender affection and reverence as was admirable, and had that high regard for his mother-in-law and the children she brought his father, that he could not have been more dearly concerned in all their interests if it had been his own mother—which, all things considered, although they were deserving persons, was an example of piety and goodness that will not easily be matched.

For conjugal affection to his wife, it was such in him, as whosoever would draw out a rule of honour, kindness, and religion to be practised in that estate, need no more to but draw out exactly his example. Never man had a greater passion for a woman, nor a more honourable esteem of a wife; yet he was not uxorious, nor remitted not that just rule which it was her honour to obey, but managed the reins of government with such prudence and affection that she who would not delight in such an honourable and advantageable subjection, must have wanted a reasonable soul. He governed by persuasion, which he never employed but to things honourable and profitable for herself. He loved her soul and her honour more than her outside, and yet he had even for her person a constant indulgence, exceeding the common temporary passions of the most uxorious fools. If he esteemed her at a higher rate than she in herself could have deserved, he was the author of that virtue he doted on, while she only reflected his own glories upon him; all that she was, was him while he was here, and all that she is now at best is but his pale shade. So liberal was he to her, and of so generous a temper, that he hated the mention of severed purses, his estate being so much at her disposal that he never would receive an account of anything she expended. So constant was he in his love, that when she ceased to be young and lovely, he began to show more fondness; he loved her at such a kind and generous rate as words cannot express. Yet even this, which was the highest love he or any man could have, was yet bounded by a superior: he loved her in the Lord as his fellow-creature, not his idol, but in such a manner as showed that an affection, bounded in the just rules of duty, far exceeds every way all the irregular passions in the world. He loved God above her, and all the other dear pledges of his heart,* and at his command and for his glory cheerfully resigned them. He was as kind a father, as dear a brother, as good natured a master, and as faithful a friend as the world had, yet in all these relations the greatest indulgence he could have in the world never prevailed on him to indulge vice in the dearest person, but the more dear any were to him, the more was he offended at anything that might take off the lustre of their glory. As he had great severity against errors and follies pertinaciously pursued till any he loved were convinced of them, so he had the most merciful and gentle and compassionate frame of spirit that can be imagined to those who were sensible of their errors and frailties, although they had been never so injurious to himself.

Nor was his soul less shining in honour than in love. Piety still being the bond of all his other virtues, there was nothing he durst not do or suffer, but sin against God; and therefore, as he never regarded his life in any noble and just enterprise, so he never staked it in rash or unwarrantable hazards. He was never surprised nor amazed nor confounded with great difficulties or dangers, which rather served to animate than distract his spirits; he had cast up his accounts with life and death, and fixed his purpose to entertain both honourably, so that no accident ever dismayed him, but he rather rejoiced in such troublesome conflicts as might signalize his generosity. A truer or more lively valour there never was in any man, but in all his actions it ever marched in the same file with wisdom. He understood well, and as well performed when he undertook it, the military art in all parts of it, and naturally loved the employment as it suited with his active temper more than any, receiving a mutual delight in leading those men that loved his conduct. And when he commanded soldiers, never was man more loved and reverenced by all that were under him; for he would never condescend to them in anything they mutinously sought, nor suffer them to seek what it was fit for him to provide, but prevented them by his loving care; and while he exercised his authority no way but in keeping them to their just duty, they joyed as much in his commands as he in their obedience. He was very liberal to them, but ever chose just times and occasions to exercise it. I cannot say whether he were more truly magnanimous or less proud; he never disdained the meanest person, nor flattered the greatest. He had a loving and sweet courtesy to the poorest, and would often employ many spare hours with the commonest soldiers and the poorest labourers, but still so ordering his familiarity as it never raised them to a contempt, but entertained still at the same time reverence with love of him. He ever preserved himself in his own rank, neither being proud of it so as to despise any inferior, nor letting fall that just decorum which his honour obliged him to keep up. He was as far from envy of superiors as from contemning those that were under him. He was above the ambition of vain titles, and so well contented with the even ground of a gentleman, that no invitation could have prevailed upon him to advance one step that way; he loved substantial not airy honour. As he was above seeking or delighting in empty titles for himself, so he neither denied nor envied any man's due precedency, but pitied those that took a glory in that which had no foundation of virtue. As little did he seek after popular applause, or pride himself in it, if at any time it cried up his just [deserts]; he more delighted to do well than to be praised, and never set vulgar commendations at such a rate, as to act contrary to his own conscience or reason for the obtaining them; nor would he forbear a good action which he was bound to, though all the world disliked it, for he ever looked on things as they were in themselves, not through the dim spectacles of vulgar estimation. As he was far from vain affectation of popularity, so he never neglected that just care that an honest man ought to have of his reputation, and was satisfied if his own conscience cleared him from guilt of anything that might blemish it, and was as careful to avoid the appearances of evil as evil itself; but if he were evil spoken of for truth or righteousness sake, he rejoiced in taking up that reproach which all good men that dare bear their testimony against an evil generation must suffer. Though his zeal for truth and virtue caused the wicked, with the sharp razors of their malicious tongues, to attempt to shave off the glories from his head, yet his honour springing from the fast root of virtue did but grow the thicker and more beautiful for all their endeavours to cut it off.

He was as free from avarice as from ambition and pride. Never had any man a more contented and thankful heart for the estate that God had given, but it was a very narrow compass for the exercise of his great heart. He loved hospitality as much as he hated riot; he could contentedly be without things beyond his reach, though he took very much pleasure in all those noble delights that exceeded not his faculties. In things that were of mere pleasure, he loved not to aim at that he could not attain; he would rather wear clothes absolutely plain than pretending to gallantry, and would rather choose to have none than mean jewels or pictures and such things as were not of absolute necessity. He would rather give nothing than a base reward or present, and upon that score lived very much retired, though his nature was very sociable and delighted in going into and receiving company, because his fortune would not allow him to do it in such a noble manner as suited with his mind, but at an expense greater than his prudence judged fit to lay out unnecessarily. When the most noble delights were taken from him, he could bend his mind to recreate itself as well in any or in no diversion as in the richest curiosities. Thus, he that had been master of great variety of as good and excellently engraved agates and other natural and artificial rarities in precious stones, such as none could show a better collection of, yet in his prison as much delighted himself in cockle shells, and employed his little time of recreation as cheerfully in them as in the other, never regretting the want of all his noble and excellent delights, though no man enjoyed them with more pleasure and thankfulness. His virtues come very much sullied out of my hands; and, indeed, he that would commemorate his heroic glory should have a soul equally great to conceive and express that which my dejected and inferior spirit cannot perform. In short, he was so truly magnanimous that prosperity could never lift him up in the least, nor give him any tincture of pride or vain-glory, nor diminish a general affability, courtesy and civility that he always showed to all persons. When he was most exalted he was most merciful and compassionate to those that were humbled. At the same time that he vanquished any enemy, he cast away all his ill-will to him, and entertained thoughts of love and kindness so long as he was not in a posture of opposition. He was as far from meanness as from pride, as truly generous as humble, and showed his noble spirit more in adversity than in his prosperous condition; he vanquished all the spite of his enemies by his manly suffering, and all the contempts they could cast at him were theirs, not his, shame.

When God afflicted him, he fell down at his feet; he cast away his crown before him, humbled himself in dust and ashes, and accepted punishment at his hands. But men, though they crushed the brittle walls he dwelt in, could never conquer him nor deject him. With what an admirable patience and cheerfulness he waited for the salvation of the Lord I have not words to express. Though he fell in the conflict, I am sure he lived and died a conquerer. Innocence armed him with courage that had no false place in it to let in terror or woe for anything that they could do; he feared nothing that could be threatened to him, regretted nothing that they could take from [him], despised all that could be offered to tempt or fright him from his innocence. And though the greatness of his natural courage, which was more clear and truly generous than ever I knew in any man, hath a great share in the bravery of his suffering, and God is to have the glory of that as of all his other goodness, being only streams from the eternal fountain of goodness, yet his support and extraordinary cheerfulness in his last trial in prison was the effect of a more immediate divine supply which the Lord gave his servant in his last extremity, keeping up the stream of his natural affections at their full height, and conducting them through their just bounds till they were all swallowed up in the ocean of divine love.

His whole life was the rule of temperance in meat, drink, apparel, pleasure and all those things that may be lawfully enjoyed; and herein his temperance was more excellent than others', in whom it is not so much a virtue but proceeds from want of appetite or gust of pleasure, as that in him which was a true, wise and religious government of the desire and delight he took in the things he enjoyed. He had a certain activity of spirit which could never endure idleness either in himself nor others, and that made him eager, for the time he indulged it, as well in pleasure as in business. Indeed, though in youth he exercised innocent sports a little while, yet afterwards his business was his pleasure. But how intent soever he were in anything, how much soever it delighted him, he could freely and easily cast it away when God called him to something else. He had as much modesty as could consist with a true virtuous assurance, and hated an impudent person. He was so chaste that neither in youth nor riper age none of the most fair or enticing women could ever draw him so much as into unnecessary familiarity or vain converse with them or any sort of play or dalliance, yet he despised nothing of the female sex but their follies and vanities; wise and virtuous women he loved, and delighted in all pure, holy and unblamable conversation with them, but so as never to excite scandal or temptation. Scurrilous and nasty discourse, even among men, he abhorred, and though he sometimes took pleasure in wit and mirth, yet that which was mixed with impurity he never would endure. The heat of his youth a little inclined him to the passion of anger, and the goodness of his nature to that of love and grief, but reason was never dethroned by them, but continued governess and moderator in his soul.

All this and more is true, but I so much dislike the manner of relating it that I will make another essay.

70   *Baucis and Philemon*

JOHN DRYDEN

A translation from one of the stories in Ovid's *Metamorphoses*, Book VIII; printed in *Fables Ancient and Modern* (1700).

The author pursuing the deeds of Theseus, relates how he, with his friend Pirithous, were invited by Achelous, the river-god, to stay with him till his waters were abated. Achelous entertains them with a relation of his own love to Perimele, who was changed into an island by Neptune, at his request. Pirithous, being an atheist, derides the legend, and denies the power of the gods to work that miracle. Lelex, another companion of Theseus, to confirm the story of Achelous, relates another metamorphosis of Baucis and Philemon into trees; of which he was partly an eye-witness.

> Thus Achelous ends. His audience hear,
> With admiration, and admiring, fear
> The powers of heaven; except Ixion's son*
> Who laughed at all the gods, believed in none.
> He shook his impious head, and thus replies,
> 'These legends are no more than pious lies:
> You attribute too much to heavenly sway
> To think they give us forms, and take away.'
>   The rest, of better minds, their sense declared

Against this doctrine, and with horror heard.   10
Then Lelex rose, an old experienced man,
And thus with sober gravity began:
'Heaven's power is infinite: earth, air, and sea,
The manufacture mass, the making power obey.
By proof to clear your doubt: in Phrygian ground
Two neighbouring trees, with walls encompassed round,
Stand on a moderate rise, with wonder shown,
One a hard oak, a softer linden one:
I saw the place and them, by Pittheus sent
To Phrygian realms, my grandsire's government.   20
Not far from thence is seen a lake, the haunt
Of coots, and of the fishing cormorant.
Here Jove with Hermes came; but in disguise
Of mortal men concealed their deities.
One laid aside his thunder, one his rod;*
And many toilsome steps together trod.
For harbour at a thousand doors they knocked,
Not one of all the thousand but was locked.
At last an hospitable house they found,
A homely shed; the roof not far from ground,   30
Was thatched with reeds and straw together bound.
There Baucis and Philemon lived, and there
Had lived long married, and a happy pair:
Now old in love; though little was their store,
Inured to want, their poverty they bore,
Nor aimed at wealth, professing to be poor.
For master or for servant here to call
Was all alike, when only two were all.
Command was none, where equal love was paid,
Or rather both commanded, both obeyed.   40
    'From lofty roofs the gods repulsed before,
Now stooping, entered through the little door.
The man (their hearty welcome first expressed)
A common settle drew for either guest,
Inviting each his weary limbs to rest.
But ere they sat, officious Baucis lays
Two cushions stuffed with straw, the seat to raise;
Coarse, but the best she had; then rakes the load

Of ashes from the hearth, and spreads abroad
The living coals, and lest they should expire,   50
With leaves and barks she feeds her infant fire.
It smokes, and then with trembling breath she blows,
Till in a cheerful blaze the flames arose.
With brushwood and with chips she strengthens these,
And adds at last the boughs of rotten trees.
The fire thus formed, she sets the kettle on
(Like burnished gold the little seether shone),
Next took the coleworts which her husband got
From his own ground (a small well-watered spot);
She stripped the stalks of all their leaves, the best   60
She culled, and then with handy care she dressed.
High o'er the hearth a chine of bacon hung:
Good old Philemon seized it with a prong,
And from the sooty rafter drew it down;
Then cut a slice, but scarce enough for one;
Yet a large portion of a little store,
Which for their sakes alone he wished were more.
This in the pot he plunged without delay,
To tame the flesh and drain the salt away.
The time between, before the fire they sat,   70
And shortened the delay by pleasing chat.
   'A beam there was, on which a beechen pail
Hung by the handle on a driven nail:
This filled with water, gently warmed, they set ⎫
Before their guests; in this they bathed their feet, ⎬
And after with clean towels dried their sweat: ⎭
This done, the host produced the genial bed, ⎫
Sallow the feet, the borders, and the stead, ⎬
Which with no costly coverlet they spread, ⎭
But coarse old garments; yet such robes as these   80
They laid alone at feasts, on holidays.
The good old housewife, tucking up her gown,
The table sets; th' invited gods lie down.
The trivet table of a foot was lame,
A blot which prudent Baucis overcame,
Who thrusts beneath the limping leg a shard;
So was the mended board exactly reared:

Then rubbed it o'er with newly gathered mint,
A wholesome herb, that breathed a grateful scent.
Pallas began the feast, where first was seen   90
The particoloured olive, black and green:*
Autumnal cornels next in order served,
In lees of wine well pickled, and preserved.
A garden salad was the third supply,
Of endive, radishes and chicory;
Then curds and cream, the flower of country fare,⎫
And new laid eggs, which Baucis' busy care   ⎬
Turned by a gentle fire, and roasted rare.   ⎭
All these in earthen ware were served to board; ⎫
And next in place an earthen pitcher, stored   ⎬   100
With liquor of the best the cottage could afford. ⎭
This was the table's ornament and pride,
With figures wrought: like pages at his side
Stood beechen bowls; and these were shining clean,
Varnished with wax without, and lined within.
By this the boiling kettle had prepared,
And to the table sent the smoking lard;
On which with eager appetite they dine,
A savoury bit, that served to relish wine.
The wine itself was suiting to the rest,   110
Still working in the must, and lately pressed.
The second course succeeds like that before,
Plums, apples, nuts, and of their wintry store
Dry figs, and grapes, and wrinkled dates were set
In canisters, t' enlarge the little treat.
All these a milk-white honeycomb surround,
Which in the midst the country banquet crowned.
But the kind hosts their entertainment grace
With hearty welcome, and an open face.
In all they did, you might discern with ease   120
A willing mind, and a desire to please.
    'Meantime the beechen bowls went round, and still
Though often emptied, were observed to fill;
Filled without hands, and of their own accord
Ran without feet, and danced about the board.
Devotion seized the pair, to see the feast

With wine, and of no common grape, increased;
And up they held their hands, and fell to prayer,
Excusing as they could their country fare.

   'One goose they had, ('twas all they could allow)   130
A wakeful sentry, and on duty now,
Whom to the gods for sacrifice they vow:
Her, with malicious zeal, the couple viewed;
She ran for life, and limping they pursued:
Full well the fowl perceived their bad intent,
And would not make her masters' compliment;
But persecuted, to the powers she flies,
And close between the legs of Jove she lies.
He with a gracious ear the suppliant heard,
And saved her life; then what he was declared,   140
And owned the god. "The neighbourhood", said he,
"Shall justly perish for impiety:
You stand alone exempted; but obey
With speed, and follow where we lead the way;
Leave these accursed; and to the mountain's height
Ascend; nor once look backward in your flight."

   'They haste, and what their tardy feet denied,
The trusty staff (their better leg) supplied.
An arrow's flight they wanted to the top,
And there secure, but spent with travel, stop;   150
Then turn their now no more forbidden eyes:
Lost in a lake the floated level lies;
A watery desert covers all the plains,
Their cot alone, as in an isle, remains.
Wondering with weeping eyes, while they deplore
Their neighbours' fate, and country now no more,
Their little shed, scarce large enough for two,
Seems, from the ground increased, in height and bulk to grow.
A stately temple shoots within the skies;
The crotches of their cot in columns rise;   160
The pavement polished marble they behold,
The gates with sculpture graced, the spires and tiles of gold.

   'Then thus the sire of gods, with look serene:
"Speak thy desire, thou only just of men;
And thou, O woman, only worthy found

To be with such a man in marriage bound."
   'Awhile they whisper; then to Jove addressed,
Philemon thus prefers their joint request:
"We crave to serve before your sacred shrine,
And offer at your altars rites divine;   170
And since not any action of our life
Has been polluted with domestic strife,
We beg one hour of death; that neither she
With widow's tears may live to bury me,
Nor weeping I, with withered arms may bear
My breathless Baucis to the sepulchre."
   'The godheads sign their suit. They run their race
In the same tenor all th' appointed space:
Then, when their hour was come, while they relate
These past adventures at the temple gate,   180
Old Baucis is by old Philemon seen
Sprouting with sudden leaves of sprightly green;
Old Baucis looked where old Philemon stood,
And saw his lengthened arms a sprouting wood.
New roots their fastened feet begin to bind,
Their bodies stiffen in a rising rind:
Then ere the bark above their shoulders grew,
They give and take at once their last adieu.
At once, "Farewell, O faithful spouse," they said;
At once th' encroaching rinds their closing lips invade.   190
E'en yet, an ancient Tyanaean shows
A spreading oak, that near a linden grows;
The neighbourhood confirm the prodigy,
Grave men, not vain of tongue, or like to lie.
I saw myself the garlands on their boughs,
And tablets hung for gifts of granted vows;
And offering fresher up, with pious prayer,
"The good", said I, "are God's peculiar care,
And such as honour heaven, shall heavenly honour share."'

RELIGION AND PHILOSOPHY

71   From *Paradise Lost*, Book XII

JOHN MILTON

After the Fall, Adam is informed by the archangel Raphael as to the future
of the human race: its redemption by Christ, the gift of the Holy Spirit,
the corruption of the Church, and man's attainment of an inner paradise.
In this extract, Adam speaks first.

> 'O goodness infinite, goodness immense!
> That all this good of evil shall produce,*
> And evil turn to good; more wonderful
> Than that which by creation first brought forth
> Light out of darkness! Full of doubt I stand,
> Whether I should repent me now of sin
> By me done and occasioned, or rejoice
> Much more, that much more good thereof shall spring,
> To God more glory, more good will to men
> From God, and over wrath grace shall abound.
> But say, if our deliverer up to heaven
> Must reascend, what will betide the few   480
> His faithful, left among th' unfaithful herd,
> The enemies of truth; who then shall guide
> His people, who defend? Will they not deal
> Worse with his followers than with him they dealt?'
>   'Be sure they will,' said th' angel; 'but from heaven
> He to his own a Comforter will send,*
> The promise of the Father, who shall dwell
> His Spirit within them, and the law of faith
> Working through love, upon their hearts shall write,

To guide them in all truth, and also arm   490
With spiritual armour, able to resist
Satan's assaults, and quench his fiery darts,
What man can do against them, not afraid,
Though to the death, against such cruelties
With inward consolations recompensed,
And oft supported so as shall amaze
Their proudest persecutors: for the Spirit
Poured first on his apostles, whom he sends
T' evangelize the nations, then on all
Baptized, shall them with wondrous gifts endue   500
To speak all tongues, and do all miracles,*
As did their Lord before them. Thus they win
Great numbers of each nation to receive
With joy the tidings brought from heaven: at length
Their ministry performed, and race well run,
Their doctrine and their story written left,
They die; but in their room, as they forewarn,*
Wolves shall succeed for teachers, grievous wolves,
Who all the sacred mysteries of heaven
To their own vile advantages shall turn   510
Of lucre and ambition, and the truth
With superstitions and traditions taint,
Left only in those written records pure,*
Though not but by the Spirit understood.
Then shall they seek t' avail themselves of names,
Places and titles, and with these to join
Secular power, though feigning still to act
By spiritual, to themselves appropriating
The Spirit of God, promised alike and given
To all believers; and from that pretence,   520
Spiritual laws by carnal power shall force
On every conscience; laws which none shall find
Left them enrolled, or what the Spirit within*
Shall on the heart engrave. What will they then
But force the spirit of grace itself, and bind
His consort liberty; what, but unbuild
His living temples, built by faith to stand,
Their own faith not another's: for on earth

Who against faith and conscience can be heard
Infallible? Yet many will presume: 530
Whence heavy persecution shall arise
On all who in the worship persevere
Of spirit and truth; the rest, far greater part,
Well deem in outward rites and specious forms
Religion satisfied; truth shall retire
Bestuck with slanderous darts, and works of faith
Rarely be found: so shall the world go on,
To good malignant, to bad men benign,
Under her own weight groaning till the day
Appear of respiration to the just,   540
And vengeance to the wicked, at return
Of him so lately promised to thy aid
The woman's seed, obscurely then foretold,
Now amplier known thy Saviour and thy Lord,
Last in the clouds from heaven to be revealed
In glory of the Father, to dissolve
Satan with his perverted world, then raise
From the conflagrant mass, purged and refined,
New heavens, new earth, ages of endless date
Founded in righteousness, and peace, and love,   550
To bring forth fruits joy and eternal bliss.'
    He ended; and thus Adam last replied:
'How soon hath thy prediction, seer blest,
Measured this transient world, the race of time,
Till time stand fixed: beyond is all abyss,
Eternity, whose end no eye can reach.
Greatly instructed I shall hence depart,
Greatly in peace of thought, and have my fill
Of knowledge, what this vessel can contain;
Beyond which was my folly to aspire.   560
Henceforth I learn, that to obey is best,
And love with fear the only God, to walk
As in his presence, ever to observe
His providence, and on him sole depend,
Merciful over all his works, with good
Still overcoming evil, and by small
Accomplishing great things, by things deemed weak

Subverting worldly strong, and worldly wise
By simply meek; that suffering for truth's sake
Is fortitude to highest victory,   570
And to the faithful death the gate of life;
Taught this by his example whom I now
Acknowledge my redeemer ever blest.'
    To whom thus also th' angel last replied:
'This having learned, thou hast attained the sum
Of wisdom; hope no higher, though all the stars
Thou knew'st by name, and all th' ethereal powers,
All secrets of the deep, all nature's works,
Or works of God in heaven, air, earth, or sea,
And all the riches of this world enjoyed'st,   580
And all the rule, one empire; only add
Deeds to thy knowledge answerable, add faith,
Add virtue, patience, temperance, add love,
By name to come called charity, the soul
Of all the rest: then wilt thou not be loath
To leave this paradise, but shalt possess
A paradise within thee, happier far.'

72   From *The Third Century*

THOMAS TRAHERNE

Probably written in the early 1670s. The present extract comes from the
five centuries (sets of one hundred) of meditations, and provides a form
of spiritual autobiography, presenting a mystical vision of Traherne's
childhood.

I

Will you see the infancy of this sublime and celestial greatness?
Those pure and virgin apprehensions I had from the womb, and that
divine light wherewith I was born, are the best unto this day, wherein
I can see the universe. By the gift of God they attended me into the
world, and by his special favour I remember them till now. Verily
they seem the greatest gifts his wisdom could bestow, for without
them all other gifts had been dead and vain. They are unattainable by

book, and therefore I will teach them by experience. Pray for them earnestly: for they will make you angelical, and wholly celestial. Certainly Adam in paradise had not more sweet and curious apprehensions of the world, than I when I was a child.

2

All appeared new, and strange at the first, inexpressibly rare, and delightful, and beautiful. I was a little stranger which at my entrance into the world was saluted and surrounded with innumerable joys. My knowledge was divine: I knew by intuition those things which since my apostasy I collected again by the highest reason.* My very ignorance was advantageous. I seemed as one brought into the estate of innocence. All things were spotless, and pure, and glorious: yea, and infinitely mine, and joyful, and precious. I knew not that there were any sins, or complaints, or laws. I dreamed not of poverties, contentions, or vices. All tears and quarrels were hidden from mine eyes. Everything was at rest, free, and immortal. I knew nothing of sickness, or death, or exaction; in the absence of these I was entertained like an angel with the works of God in their splendour and glory; I saw all in the peace of Eden; heaven and earth did sing my Creator's praises, and could not make more melody to Adam, than to me. All time was eternity, and a perpetual Sabbath. Is it not strange, that an infant should be heir of the world, and see those mysteries which the books of the learned never unfold?

3

The corn was orient and immortal wheat, which never should be reaped, nor was ever sown. I thought it had stood from everlasting to everlasting. The dust and stones of the street were as precious as gold. The gates were at first the end of the world, the green trees when I saw them first through one of the gates transported and ravished me; their sweetness and unusual beauty made my heart to leap, and almost mad with ecstasy, they were such strange and wonderful thing[s]. The men! O what venerable and reverend creatures did the aged seem! Immortal cherubims! And young men glittering and sparkling angels, and maids strange seraphic pieces of life and beauty! Boys and girls tumbling in the street, and playing, were moving jewels. I knew not that they were born or should die. But all things abided eternally as they were in their proper places. Eternity was manifest in the light of the day, and some thing infinite behind every thing appeared: which talked with my expectation and moved my desire. The city seemed to stand in Eden, or to be built in heaven. The streets were mine, the temple was mine, the people were mine, their clothes and gold and silver was mine, as much as their sparkling eyes, fair skins, and ruddy faces. The skies were mine, and so were the sun and moon and stars, and all the world was mine, and I the only spectator and enjoyer of it. I knew no churlish proprieties, nor bounds, nor divisions; but all proprieties and divisions were mine: all treasures and the possessors of them. So that with much ado* I was corrupted, and made to learn the dirty devices of this world. Which now I unlearn, and become as it were a little child again, that I may enter into the kingdom of God.*

4

Upon those pure and virgin apprehensions which I had in my infancy, I made this poem.

I

That childish thoughts such joys inspire,
Doth make my wonder, and his glory higher;
   His bounty and my wealth more great:
It shows his kingdom and his work complete;
   In which there is not anything
Not meet to be the joy of cherubim.

2

He in our childhood with us walks,
And with our thoughts mysteriously he talks;
   He often visiteth our minds,
But cold acceptance in us ever finds.   10
   We send him often grieved away,
Who else would show us all his kingdom's joy.

3

O Lord, I wonder at thy love,
Which did my infancy so early move:
   But more at that which did forbear,

And move so long, though slighted many a year:
    But most of all, at last that thou
Thyself shouldst me convert, I scarce know how.

4

    Thy gracious motions oft in vain
Assaulted me: my heart did hard remain   20
    Long time! I sent my God away
Grieved much, that he could not give me his joy.
    I careless was, nor did regard
The end for which he all those thoughts prepared.

5

    But now, with new and open eyes,
I see beneath, as if I were above the skies:
    And as I backward look again
See all his thoughts and mine most clear and plain.
    He did approach, he me did woo:
I wonder that my God this thing would do.   30

6

    From nothing taken first I was;
What wondrous things his glory brought to pass!
    Now in the world I him behold,
And me, envelopèd in precious gold;
    In deep abysses of delights,
In present hidden glorious benefits.

7

    Those thoughts his goodness long before
Prepared as precious and celestial store:
    With curious art in me inlaid,
That childhood might itself alone be said   40
    My tutor, teacher, guide to be,
Instructed then ev'n by the Deity.

5

Our Saviour's meaning, when he said, he must be born again and
become a little child that will enter into the kingdom of heaven, is

deeper far than is generally believed. It is not only in a careless reliance upon divine providence that we are to become little children, or in the feebleness and shortness of our anger and simplicity of our passions: but in the peace and purity of all our soul. Which purity also is a deeper thing than is commonly apprehended, for we must disrobe ourselves of all false colours, and unclothe our souls of evil habits; all our thoughts must be infant-like and clear: the powers of our soul free from the leaven of this world, and disentangled from men's conceits and customs. Grit in the eye or the yellow jaundice will not let a man see those objects truly that are before it. And therefore it is requisite that we should be as very strangers to the thoughts, customs, and opinions of men in this world as if we were but little children. So those things would appear to us only which do to children when they are first born. Ambitions, trades, luxuries, inordinate affections, casual and accidental riches invented since the Fall would be gone, and only those things appear, which did to Adam in paradise, in the same light and in the same colours. God in his works, glory in the light, love in our parents, men, ourselves, and the face of heaven. Every man naturally seeing those things, to the enjoyment of which he is naturally born.

6

Everyone provideth objects, but few prepare senses whereby and light wherein to see them. Since therefore we are born to be a burning and shining light, and whatever men learn of others, they see in the light of others' souls: I will in the light of my soul show you the universe. Perhaps it is celestial, and will teach you how beneficial we may be to each other. I am sure it is a sweet and curious light to me: which had I wanted, I would have given all the gold and silver in all worlds to have purchased. But it was the gift of God, and could not be bought with money. And by what steps and degrees I proceeded to that enjoyment of all eternity which now I possess I will likewise show you. A clear and familiar light it may prove unto you.

7

The first light which shined in my infancy in its primitive and innocent clarity was totally eclipsed: insomuch that I was fain to learn all again. If you ask me how it was eclipsed, truly by the customs and manners of men, which like contrary winds blew it out; by an innumerable company of other objects, rude, vulgar, and worthless things that like so many loads of earth and dung did overwhelm and bury it; by the impetuous torrent of wrong desires in all others whom I saw or knew that carried me away and alienated me from it; by a whole sea of other matters and concernments that covered and drowned it; finally by the evil influence of a bad education that did not foster and cherish it. All men's thoughts and words were about other matters; they all prized new things which I did not dream of. I was a stranger and unacquainted with them; I was little and reverenced their authority; I was weak, and easily guided by their example; ambitious also, and desirous to approve myself unto them. And finding no one syllable in any man's mouth of those things, by degrees they vanished, my thoughts (as indeed what is more fleeting than a thought?) were blotted out. And at last all the celestial, great, and stable treasures to which I was born, as wholly forgotten as if they had never been.

8

Had any man spoken of it, it had been the most easy thing in the world to have taught me, and to have made me believe, that heaven and earth was God's house, and that he gave it me. That the sun was mine, and that men were mine, and that cities and kingdoms were mine also; that earth was better than gold, and that water was, every drop of it, a precious jewel. And that these were great and living treasures; and that all riches whatsoever else was dross in comparison. From whence I clearly find how docible our nature is in natural things, were it rightly entreated. And that our misery proceedeth ten thousand times more from the outward bondage of opinion and custom, than from any inward corruption or depravation of nature; and that it is not our parents' loins, so much as our parents' lives, that enthrals and blinds us.* Yet is all our corruption derived from Adam: inasmuch as all the evil examples and inclinations of the world arise from his sin. But I speak it in the presence of God and of our Lord Jesus Christ, in my pure primitive virgin light, while my apprehensions were natural and unmixed, I cannot remember but that I was ten thousand times more prone to good and excellent things, than evil. But I was quickly tainted and fell by others.

9

It was a difficult matter to persuade me that the tinselled ware upon a hobbyhorse was a fine thing. They did impose upon me, and obtrude their gifts that made me believe a ribbon or a feather curious. I could not see where the curiousness or fineness. And to teach me that a purse of gold was of any value seemed impossible, the art by which it becomes so, and the reasons for which it is accounted so, were so deep and hidden to my inexperience. So that nature is still nearest to natural things, and farthest off from preternatural; and to esteem that the reproach of nature, is an error in them only who are unacquainted with it. Natural things are glorious, and to know them glorious; but to call things preternatural 'natural', monstrous. Yet all they do it, who esteem gold, silver, houses, lands, clothes etc. the riches of nature, which are indeed the riches of invention. Nature knows no such riches, but art and error makes them. Not the God of nature, but sin only was the parent of them. The riches of nature are our souls and bodies, with all their faculties, senses, and endowments. And it had been the easiest thing in the whole world, that all felicity consisted in the enjoyment of all the world, that it was prepared for me before I was born, and that nothing was more divine and beautiful.

10

Thoughts are the most present things to thoughts, and of the most powerful influence. My soul was only apt and disposed to great things; but souls to souls are like apples to apples, one being rotten rots another. When I began to speak and go, nothing began to be present to me, but what was present in their thoughts. Nor was anything present to me any other way, than it was so to them. The glass of imagination was the only mirror wherein anything was represented or appeared to me. All things were absent which they talked not of. So I began among my playfellows to prize a drum, a fine coat, a penny, a gilded book etc. who before never dreamed of any such wealth. Goodly objects to drown all the knowledge of heaven and earth! As for the heavens, and the sun and stars, they disappeared and were no more unto me than the bare walls. So that the strange riches of man's invention quite overcame the riches of nature, being learned more laboriously, and in the second place.

11

By this let nurses, and those parents that desire holy children, learn to make them possessors of heaven and earth betimes, to remove silly objects from before them, to magnify nothing but what is great indeed, and to talk of God to them and of his works and ways before they can either speak or go. For nothing is so easy as to teach the truth because the nature of the thing confirms the doctrine. As when we say the sun is glorious, a man is a beautiful creature, sovereign over beasts and fowls and fishes, the stars minister unto us, the world was made for you, etc. But to say this house is yours, and these lands are another man's, and this bauble is a jewel and this gewgaw a fine thing, this rattle makes music etc. is deadly, barbarous, and uncouth to a little child; and makes him suspect all you say, because the nature of the thing contradicts your words. Yet doth that blot out all noble and divine ideas, dissettle his foundation, render him uncertain in all things, and divide him from God. To teach him those objects are little vanities, and that though God made them by the ministry of man, yet better and more glorious things are more to be esteemed, is natural and easy.

12

By this you may see who are the rude and barbarous Indians. For verily there is no savage nation under the cope of heaven, that is more absurdly barbarous than the Christian world. They that go naked and drink water and live upon roots are like Adam or angels in comparison of us. But they indeed that call beads and glass buttons jewels, and dress themselves with feather, and buy pieces of brass and broken hafts of knives of our merchants are somewhat like us. But we pass them in barbarous opinions and monstrous apprehensions: which we nickname 'civility', and 'the mode', amongst us. I am sure those barbarous people that go naked come nearer to Adam, God, and angels in the simplicity of their wealth, though not in knowledge.

13

You would not think how these barbarous inventions spoil your knowledge. They put grubs and worms in men's heads that are enemies to all pure and true apprehensions, and eat out all their happiness. They make it impossible for them in whom they reign to believe there is any excellency in the works of God, or to taste any sweetness in the nobility of nature, or to prize any common, though never so great a blessing. They alienate men from the life of God, and at last make them to live without God in the world. To live the life of God is to live to all the works of God, and to enjoy them in his image, from which they are wholly diverted that follow fashions. Their fancies are corrupted with other jingles.

14

Being swallowed up therefore in the miserable gulf of idle talk and worthless vanities, thenceforth I lived among shadows, like a prodigal son feeding upon husks with swine.* A comfortless wilderness full of thorns and troubles the world was, or worse: a waste place covered with idleness and play, and shops and markets and taverns. As for churches, they were things I did not understand. And schools were a burden: so that there was nothing in the world worth the having, or enjoying, but my game and sport, which also was a dream and, being passed, wholly forgotten. So that I had utterly forgotten all goodness, bounty, comfort, and glory: which things are the very brightness of the glory of God, for lack of which therefore he was unknown.

15

Yet sometimes in the midst of these dreams, I should come a little to myself so far as to feel I wanted something, secretly to expostulate with God for not giving me riches, to long after an unknown happiness, to grieve that the world was so empty, and to be dissatisfied with my present state because it was vain and forlorn. I had heard of angels, and much admired that here upon earth nothing should be but dirt and streets and gutters; for as for the pleasures that were in great men's houses, I had not seen them; and it was my real happiness they were unknown, for because nothing deluded me, I was the more inquisitive.

16

Once I remember (I think I was about four year old) when I thus reasoned with myself, sitting in a little obscure room in my father's poor house. If there be a God, certainly he must be infinite in goodness. And that I was prompted to by a real whispering instinct of nature. And if he be infinite in goodness, and a perfect being in wisdom and love, certainly he must do most glorious things, and give us infinite riches; how comes it to pass therefore that I am so poor? Of so scanty and narrow a fortune, enjoying few and obscure comforts? I thought I could not believe him a God to me, unless all his power were employed to glorify me. I knew not then my soul, or body; nor did I think of the heavens and the earth, the rivers and the stars, the sun or the seas: all those were lost, and absent from me. But when I found them made out of nothing for me, then I had a God indeed, whom I could praise, and rejoice in.

17

Sometimes I should be alone, and without employment, when suddenly my soul would return to itself, and forgetting all things in the whole world which mine eyes had seen, would be carried away to the ends of the earth; and my thoughts would be deeply engaged with inquiries: How the earth did end? Whether walls did bound it, or sudden precipices, or whether the heavens by degrees did come to touch it; so that the face of the earth and heaven were so near, that a man with difficulty could creep under? Whatever I could imagine was inconvenient, and my reason being posed was quickly wearied. What also upheld the earth (because it was heavy) and kept it from falling; whether pillars, or dark waters? And if any of these, what then upheld those, and what again those, of which I saw there would be no end? Little did I think that the earth was round, and the world so full of beauty, light, and wisdom. When I saw that, I knew by the perfection of the work there was a God, and was satisfied, and rejoiced. People underneath and fields and flowers with another sun and another day pleased me mightily: but more when I knew it was the same sun that served them by night, that served us by day.

18

Sometimes I should soar above the stars and inquire how the heavens ended, and what was beyond them: concerning which by no means could I receive satisfaction. Sometimes my thoughts would carry me to the creation, for I had heard now, that the world which at first I thought was eternal, had a beginning: how therefore that beginning was, and why it was; why it was no sooner, and what was before, I mightily desired to know. By all which I easily perceive that my soul was made to live in communion with God, in all places of his dominion, and to be satisfied with the highest reason in all things. After which it so eagerly aspired, that I thought all the gold and silver in the world but dirt, in comparison of satisfaction in any of these. Sometimes I wondered why men were made no bigger? I would have had a man as big as a giant, a giant as big as a castle, and a castle as big as the heavens. Which yet would not serve: for there was infinite space beyond the heavens, and all was defective and but little in comparison; and for him to be made infinite, I thought it would be to no purpose, and it would be inconvenient. Why also there was not a better sun, and better stars, a better sea and better creatures I much admired. Which thoughts produced that poem upon moderation which afterwards was written. Some part of the verses are these:

19

In making bodies Love could not express
Itself, or Art, unless it made them less.
O what a monster had in man been seen,
Had every thumb or toe a mountain been!
What worlds must he devour when he did eat?
What oceans drink! yet could not all his meat,
Or stature, make him like an angel shine,
Or make his soul in glory more divine.
A soul it is that makes us truly great,
Whose little bodies make us more complete.   10
An understanding that is infinite,
An endless, wide, and everlasting sight,
That can enjoy all things, and nought exclude,
Is the most sacred greatness may be viewed.
'Twas inconvenient that his bulk should be
An endless hill; he nothing then could see;
No figure have, no motion, beauty, place,
No colour, feature, member, light, or grace.
A body like a mountain is but cumber.

An endless body is but idle lumber.   20
It spoils convèrse, and time itself devours,
While meat in vain, in feeding idle powers.
Excessive bulk being most injurious found,
To those conveniences which men have crowned,
His wisdom did his power here repress:
God made man greater while he made him less.

20

The excellencies of the sun I found to be of another kind than that
splendour after which I sought, even in unknown and invisible services; and that God by moderation wisely bounding his almighty
power, had to my eternal amazement and wonder made all bodies far
greater than if they were infinite: there not being a sand nor mote in
the air that is not more excellent than if it were infinite. How rich
and admirable then is the Kingdom of God, where the smallest is
greater than an infinite treasure! Is not this incredible? Certainly to
the placits and doctrines of the schools: till we all consider, that
infinite worth shut up in the limits of a material being, is the only
way to a real infinity. God made nothing infinite in bulk, but everything there where it ought to be. Which, because moderation is a
virtue observing the golden mean,* in some other parts of the former
poem is thus expressed:

21

His power bounded, greater is in might,
Than if let loose, 'twere wholly infinite.
He could have made an endless sea by this,
But then it had not been a sea of bliss.
Did waters from the centre to the skies
Ascend, 'twould drown whatever else we prize.
The ocean bounded in a finite shore,
Is better far because it is no more.
No use nor glory would in that be seen;
His power made it endless in esteem.   10
Had not the sun been bounded in its sphere,
Did all the world in one fair flame appear,
And were that flame a real infinite,

'Twould yield no profit, splendour, nor delight.
Its corpse confined, and beams extended, be
Effects of wisdom in the Deity.
One star made infinite would all exclude;
An earth made infinite could ne'er be viewed.
But one being fashioned for the other's sake,
He bounding all, did all most useful make;   20
And which is best, in profit and delight
Though not in bulk, they all are infinite.

22

These liquid, clear satisfactions were the emanations of the highest
reason, but not achieved till a long time afterwards. In the meantime I was sometimes, though seldom, visited and inspired with
new and more vigorous desires after that bliss which nature whis-
pered and suggested to me. Every new thing quickened my curiosity and raised my expectation. I remember once, the first time I
came into a magnificent or noble dining room, and was left there
alone, I rejoiced to see the gold and state and carved imagery, but
when all was dead, and there was no motion, I was weary of it and
departed dissatisfied. But afterwards, when I saw it full of lords and
ladies and music and dancing, the place which once seemed not to
differ from a solitary den, had now entertainment and nothing of
tediousness but pleasure in it. By which I perceived (upon a reflection made long after) that men and women are (when well understood) a principal part of our true felicity. By this I found also that
nothing that stood still, could by doing so be a part of happiness;
and that affection, though it were invisible, was the best of motions.
But the august and glorious exercise of virtue, was more solemn
and divine, which yet I saw not. And that all men and angels should
appear in heaven.

23

Another time, in a louring and sad evening, being alone in the field,
when all things were dead and quiet, a certain want and horror fell
upon me, beyond imagination. The unprofitableness and silence of
the place dissatisfied me, its wideness terrified me, from the utmost
ends of the earth fears surrounded me. How did I know but dangers

might suddenly arise from the East, and invade me from the
unknown regions beyond the seas? I was a weak and little child, and
had forgotten there was a man alive in the earth. Yet some thing also
of hope and expectation comforted me from every border. This
taught me that I was concerned in all the world; and that in the
remotest borders the causes of peace delight me, and the beauties of
the earth when seen were made to entertain me; that I was made to
hold a communion with the secrets of divine providence in all the
world; that a remembrance of all the joys I had from my birth ought
always to be with me; that the presence of cities, temples, and kingdoms ought to sustain me; and that to be alone in the world was to be
desolate and miserable. The comfort of houses and friends, and the
clear assurance of treasures everywhere, God's care and love, his
goodness, wisdom, and power, his presence and watchfulness in all
the ends of the earth, were my strength and assurance for ever; and
that these things being absent to my eye, were my joys and consolations: as present to my understanding as the wideness and emptiness
of the universe which I saw before me.

73   [*The Pilgrim's Hymn*]

JOHN BUNYAN

From *The Second Part of The Pilgrim's Progress* (1684), where it is a
reflection on Mr Valiant.

>   Who would true valour see,
>   Let him come hither;
>   One here will constant be,
>   Come wind, come weather.
>   There's no discouragement,
>   Shall make him once relent,
>   His first avowed intent
>   To be a pilgrim.
>
>   Who so beset him round
>   With dismal stories,   10
>   Do but themselves confound:
>   His strength the more is.

No lion can him fright,
He'll with a giant fight,
But he will have the right
To be a pilgrim.

Hobgoblin nor foul fiend
Can daunt his spirit:
He knows he at the end
Shall life inherit.   20
Then fancies fly away,
He'll fear not what men say,
He'll labour night and day
To be a pilgrim.

74   From *The Affections of My Soul*

RICHARD LANGHORNE

From 'The Affections of my Soul, after Judgement given against me in a
Court of Justice, upon the Evidence of False Witnesses', a section of *Mr
Langhorn's Memoires, with some Meditations and Devotions of his, During his
Imprisonment* (1679). Langhorne was one of the victims of the Popish Plot
(see headnote to **9**), convicted of treason on the false evidence of Titus
Oates and his crony William Bedloe, and executed in 1679. This prayer is
not in verse, but in cadenced, biblical prose.

x

O Father of mercy,
Behold thy child, who hath been a prodigal;*
Who, having wasted all his goods,
And spent his time in vanity,
Drawn by thy grace and love
Is now returning to thy house,
And humbly begs for pardon at thy hands.
    Alas!
I have lived as without reason,
Since first I had the use of reason;
I have done nothing of myself but evil,
From the time that I first knew what good was.

I have sinned against heaven, and against thee;
I deserve not the title of thy son,
Or to have admittance into thy house.
And though I am wholly innocent
Of the crime for which I am sentenced now to die,
Yet from thy hands I have deserved a death to
All eternity.
But thou hast made me know
That thou canst not cease to be a father
For my having often ceased to comport myself
As thy child.
Thou canst not lose thy goodness
By my having often forgotten my gratitude;
Thou canst not forget to be a father of mercy
By my having become a child of misery.

XI

O my Father,
O thou, the best of all fathers,
Have pity on the most wretched of all thy children:
I was lost, but by thy mercy am now found;
I was dead, but by thy grace am now raised again;
I was gone astray after vanity,
But am now ready to appear before thee.
O my Father,
Come now in mercy and receive thy child;
Give him the kiss of peace,
Remit unto him all his sins,
Clothe him with thy nuptial robe,
Receive him into thy house,
Permit him to have a place at thy feast,
And forgive all those who are guilty of his death.

XII

O Jesu,
The comforter of the afflicted,
The refuge of the oppressed,
The redeemer of the captives,
The hope of the distressed,

Behold, I address unto thee
Who never drivest any from thee
Who approach unto thee with faith, hope, and love:
    My heart tells thee
That it burns with a desire to see thee,
And that for that end it is impatient to die.
Come, sweet Jesu,
    Come quickly,
Draw my soul from this prison,
Recall me from this banishment,
Conduct me to my dear country.
Behold, the just expect me,
My friends reach out their arms towards me.
O how beautiful are thy tabernacles!
O how admirable is thy palace!
O what content shall I have with thee!
What happiness in thy company!
I die with a desire to die.
Come, blessed Jesus,
And receive my spirit
Which languisheth to be with thee.
Into thy hand, O Jesus,
I recommend my spirit.

75   [*My Life*]

ROBERT JAMES

From Leeds University Library, Brotherton Collection, MS Lt 18, dated
29 September 1684; previously unpublished. Since 'marigold' is spelt
'Marygold' in the manuscript, it may be an allusion to the Virgin Mary;
and since 'sun' is spelt 'sonn', that alludes punningly to Christ, the Son of
God (as in Donne's 'Hymn to God the Father') whose resurrection offers
eternal life.

My life is like a bubble, but a blast:
At first God breathed into me, and I live,
And like a bubble I do daily waste,

And am like water poured into a sieve.
Lord, since I was thy bubble, when I die
Like to a bubble let me' ascend on high.

Or if you will, my life is like a flower,
And like a flower for a while I stand:
I am, and am not, in another hour,
For I am gathered by the owner's hand.   10
Since I am so, why am I so corrupt,
That do not know how soon I may be plucked?

But of all flowers, most of all methinks
Resembled in the marigold am I,
And like the marigold that wakes and winks
Still as it sees the sun, am born and die.
But here's my comfort: with that flower when
The sun ariseth, I shall blow again.

76   From *A Narrative of God's Gracious Dealings*

HANNAH ALLEN

From *A Narrative of God's Gracious Dealings with that Choice Christian Mrs Hannah Allen (afterwards married to Mr Hatt), Reciting the great Advantages the Devil made of her Deep Melancholy, and the Triumphant Victories, Rich and Sovereign Graces, God gave her over all his Stratagems and Devices* (1683). Allen relates how, after the death of her husband, from February 1663 onwards she was overcome with the conviction that she was damned and was about to die. This extract takes up the story in May 1664, when she was staying in the country with her aunt, Mrs Wilson. At the end of the text as given here, Allen adds a dozen scriptural quotations which had particularly sustained her. In the original text her thoughts and speech are italicized, and move fluidly between direct and indirect speech; modern conventions, using inverted commas, cannot always represent this smoothly.

One night, I said there was a great clap of thunder, like the shot of a piece of ordnance, came down directly over my bed; and that the same night, a while after, I heard like the voice of two young men singing in the yard, over against my chamber; which I said were devils in the likeness of men, singing for joy that they had overcome me; and in the morning, as I was going to rise, that scripture in the 10th of Heb[rews] and the last words of the 26th verse was suggested to me from heaven (as I thought): 'There remains no more sacrifice for sin'. And this delusion remained with me as an oracle all along: that by this miracle of the thunder, and the voice, and the scripture, God revealed to me that I was damned. When my aunt asked me, 'Do you think God would work a miracle to convince you that you are rejected? It is contrary to the manner of God's proceedings: we do not read of such a thing in all the scripture'; my answer was: 'Therefore my condition is unparalleled; there was never such an one since God made any creature, either angels or men, nor never will be to the end of the world.'

One night as I was sitting by the fire, all of a sudden I said I should die presently; whereupon my aunt was called, to whom I said, 'Aunt, I am just dying; I cannot live an hour if there were no more in the world'. In this opinion I continued a great while, every morning saying I should die before night, and every night, before morning. When I was thus in my dying condition, I often begged earnestly of my aunt to bring up my child strictly, that if it were possible he might be saved, though he had such a mother.

Many places of scripture I would repeat with much terror, applying them to myself: as Jer[emiah] vi 29, 30: 'The bellows are burnt, the lead is consumed of the fire; the founder melteth in vain; reprobate silver shall men call them, because the Lord hath rejected them.' Ezek[iel] xxiv 13: 'In thy filthiness is lewdness, because I have purged thee and thou wast not purged; thou shalt not be purged from thy filthiness any more, till I have caused my fury to rest upon thee'. Luke xiii 24: 'Strive to enter in at the strait gate; for many, I say unto you, will seek to enter in, and shall not be able.' This last scripture I would express with much passionate weeping, saying, 'This is a dreadful scripture; I sought, but not in a right way, for the devil blinded mine eyes; I sought to enter, but was not able.'

When both my inward and outward distempers grew to such a height, my aunt acquainted my friends at London with my condition, for at London I had formerly had four loving uncles, my father's brethren (two whereof were then living), and a brother of my own that was set up in his trade. These advised to send me up to London, there being the best means both for soul and body: in order to which Mrs Wilson sent to entreat my mother to accompany me to London (for at that time she could not leave her family so long); who accordingly came, but she found it a hard work to persuade me to this journey, for I said, 'I should not live to get to the coach, but I must go and die by the way to please my friends'. I went up in the Tamworth coach, so that it was twenty two miles thither. Tuesday was the day we set forwards on, and on that day in particular, the devil had suggested to me (the Friday before) that I must die and be with him. And this the more confirmed me in my fear. My aunt went with me that day's journey, which was first to Tamworth on horse-back, and from thence nine miles farther in the coach to Nuneaton, which was a long journey for one so weak and ill as I was. My aunt complaining of weariness, 'Ah', said I, 'but what must I do, that must have no rest to all eternity!' The next morning I would fain have returned back with my aunt, but there we parted, and I went forward with my mother; and a very sad journey my mother had with me, for every morning she had no small trouble to persuade me to rise to go on my journey: I would earnestly argue against it, and say, 'I shall surely die by the way, and had I not better die in bed? Mother, do you think people will like to have a dead corpse in the coach with them?' But still at last my mother with much patience and importunity prevailed with me. As I passed along the way, if I saw a church, as soon as I cast my eyes upon it, it was presently suggested to me, 'That's a hell house', with a kind of indignation; and this I thought was from myself, and therefore never spoke of it till after my recovery, for I thought if it had been known how vile I was, I must have been put to some horrible death. When I saw any black clouds gather or the wind rise as we went along, I presently concluded that some dreadful thing would fall out to show what an one I was.

When I came to London, I went to my brother's house in Swithun's Lane, where my mother stayed with me about three weeks or a month, in which time I took much physic of one Mr Cocket, a chemist that lived over the way; but still I was (as I thought) always dying; and I yet wearying my mother with such fancies and stories, one evening my mother said to me, 'Well, if you will believe you shall be saved if you die not this night, I will believe all that you say to be true if you do die this night'. To this she* agreed, and in the night about one o'clock (as we thought), the maid being newly gone out of the chamber to bed, but left a watch-light burning, we both heard like the hand of a giant knock four times together on the chamber door, which made a great noise, the door being wainscot. Then said I, 'You see, mother, though I died not tonight, the devil came to let you know that I am damned.' My mother answered, 'But you see he had no power to come into the chamber.'

Soon after this, my mother returned home into the country, and left me in my brother's house, who was a young man, unmarried, and had only a man and a maid; and he much abroad himself about his occasions. And now my opinion of dying suddenly began to leave me, therefore I concluded that God would not suffer me to die a natural death, but that I should commit some fearful abomination, and so be put to some horrible death. One day, my brother going along with me to Doctor Pridgeon, as we came back I saw a company of men with halberds. 'Look, brother,' said I, 'you will see such as these, one of these days, carry me to Newgate.' To prevent which I studied several ways to make away myself, and I being so much alone, and in a large solitary house, had the more liberty to endeavour it. First I thought of taking opium, that I might die in my sleep, and none know but that I died naturally (which I desired, that my child might not be disgraced by my untimely end), and therefore sent the maid to several apothecaries' shops for it: some said they had none, others said it was dangerous and would not sell it her. Once she had got some, and was coming away with it, the master of the shop coming in asked what she had, and when he knew, took it from her (this the maid told me). When I had sent her up and down several days, and saw she could get none, then I got spiders and took one at a time in a pipe with tobacco; but never scarce took it out, for my heart would fail me. But once I thought I had been poisoned: in the night, awaking out of my sleep, I thought I felt death upon me (for I had taken a spider when I went to bed) and called to my brother, and told him so; who presently arose and went to his friend an apothecary, who came and gave me something to expel it. The next day, my uncles and brother (considering the inconveniency of that lonesome house) removed me to Mr Peter Walker's house, a hosier at the Three Crowns in Newgate market (whose wife was my kinswoman) who received me very courteously, though I was at that time but an uncomfortable guest.

In the time I was at my brother's, I had strange apprehensions that the lights that were in neighbouring houses were apparitions of devils, and that those lights were of their making; and if I heard the voice of people talk or read in other houses, I would not be persuaded but that it was devils like men, talking of me, and mocking at my former reading, because I proved such an hypocrite.

*Madam,**

As for the first time I was at my cousin Walker's, I refer your ladyship to them, or any friend else that may assist you; only I have here set down several passages as they came to my mind which passed there, which your ladyship may make use of as you please.

One time while I lay at my cousin Walker's, having promised a friend that was very importunate with me to go to a sermon with her, about two or three days after, the devil began to terrify me for making that promise, and suggested to me that 'I had much better break it than keep it, for I had enough sermons to answer for already'. And sitting in great distress, contriving how I might put off my going, the devil found me out a place on the top of the house, a hole where some boards were laid, and there I crowded in myself and laid a long black scarf upon me, and put the boards as well as I could to hide me from being found; and there intended to lie till I should starve to death; and all the family and others concluded I had stolen out at the door unknown to them, to go lose myself in some wood, which I much talked of. But when I had lain there almost three days, I was so hungry and cold, it being a very sharp season, that I was forced to call as loud as I could, and so was heard and released from that place.

While she was at Mr Walker's house, a minister being desired to come and discourse with her, did come; and finding her in a more dejected state than any he ever saw, did oft visit her, and perceiving little visible good effect of his conferences with her, proposed to preach a sermon to her that might suit her condition, hoping God might bless that ordinance to her, that she might hear the voice of joy and gladness, that so the bones that God had broken might rejoice. She consented to hear his sermon, and when upon the day appointed he came to dispense the word, he found her writing the ensuing lines to dissuade him:

Sir,

This is to beseech you, as you would detract a few scalding drops of the fury of the Almighty from my poor, miserable and ever-to-be-abhorred

soul to all eternity, that you cease your study upon any subject on my
account, and likewise your prayers; and instead of that, pray to God to
rid the world immediately of such a monster, who am not only guilty of
all the sins of the devil, but likewise of such crimes as he is not capable of;
which you will say is incredible, but woe and alas, 'tis true.

This is all she had written: the minister coming in unexpectedly prevented what she further intended to write.

Afterwards, the minister invited her to his house, where she was above a week, but very loath to engage in any duty. The minister's wife did sometimes importune her to pray with her, but could not prevail, she always excusing herself from her unfitness to take the holy and reverend name of God within her polluted lips. 'Dead dog, damned wretch, she dare to speak to the great God!' She expressed so great an awe and dread of the glorious and fearful name of God as discovered much grace in her most desponding state to them that conversed with her. Some years after her recovery, she returning to London came to the aforesaid minister and his wife, declaring to them God's great goodness to her in manifesting himself to her soul, and returned hearty thanks to them for their tenderness to her in her dejected state. From his observation of the ground of her trouble, he advises all Christians to mortify inordinate affection to lawful things: Col[ossians] iii 5.*

I would say that Pashur's* doom belonged to me, that I was Magor-missabib, a terror to myself and all my friends (Jerem[iah] xx 3); that I was a hell upon earth, and a devil incarnate; for that which I prayed against in hypocrisy, God had brought upon me in reality. For I used to have frequently in my prayers such an expression as this (apprehending the vileness of my nature): 'If God should leave me to myself, I should be an hell upon earth, a terror to myself and all my friends'; and because this was in hypocrisy, therefore God had brought it on me in reality.

Sometimes when they had told me I had been prayed for, I would say, 'They did not pray for me, for I was not to be prayed for; for the scripture said, "That they who had sinned the sin unto death, were not to be prayed for"'.* And when a good friend of mine, Mr Blake, came daily and unweariedly to see me, I would ask him, 'Why he yet came, seeing I rejected his counsel?'; and, 'Christ bid his messengers shake the dust of their feet off against such'. I would say, 'Because I have built my fabric upon the sand so high, therefore my fall is so dreadful.'* When I was told of some that were possessed with the devil, and were by prayer dispossessed, I would reply, 'What tell you me of possession? I cared not if I were possessed with a thousand devils, so I were not a devil to myself.' When some had told me that I had been prayed for, I would answer, 'I was the less beholding to them, for it would but sink me the deeper into hell.' I would often say, 'I was a thousand times worse than the devil, for the devil had never committed such sins as I had; for I had committed worse sins than the sin against the Holy Ghost'.* Some would answer, 'The scripture speaks not of worse sins, and can you be guilty of greater sins than the scripture mentions?' 'Yes,' said I, 'my sins are so great, that if all the sins of all the devils and damned in hell, and all the reprobates on earth were comprehended in one man, mine are greater. There is no word comes so near the comprehension of the dreadfulness of my condition, as that I am the monster of the creation.' In this word I much delighted.

I would say, 'Let him that thinks he stands, take heed lest he fall: I once thought myself to stand, but am miserably fallen.'

When I was forced to be present at duty, I would often stop my ears, my carriage was very rugged and cross, contrary to my natural temper. Here I practised many devices to make away myself, sometimes by spiders (as before), sometimes endeavouring to let myself blood with a pair of sharp scissors, and so bleed to death: once when the surgeon had let me blood, I went up into a chamber and bolted the door to me, and took off the plaster and tied my arm, and set the vein a-bleeding again; which Mrs Walker fearing, ran upstairs and got into the chamber to me; I seeing her come in, ran into the leads, and there my arm bled upon the wall. 'Now,' said I, 'you may see there is the blood of a cursed reprobate.'

I pleased myself, often, with contriving how to get into a wood and die there; and one morning I cunningly got out from my cousins and went into Smithfield, where I walked up and down a great while, and knew not what to do. At last, I tried to hire a coach, but liked not the men there; then I went into Aldersgate Street, and asked a coachman what he would take to carry me to Barnet (for then I meant to go into a wood) but the man upon some small occasion sadly cursed and swore, which struck some terror into me. 'What,' thought I, 'must such as this be my companions for ever?', and so went away from him, and found one with a good honest look, and with him I agreed; and was to give him eight shillings; who carried me a good way beyond Highgate. And as I went along, I thought, 'Am I now going to converse with devils?' With suchlike thoughts as these I was discouraged from going on, and called to the coachman, and prayed him to drive back again, and told him it was only a melancholy fancy. By these and several other ways I thought to put an end to my life, but the watchful eye of the Lord always graciously prevented me.

When I heard any dreadful thing cried about the street in books, I would say, 'Oh, what fearful things will be put out of me ere long in books!' I would say, 'I should be called Allen that cursed apostate.' When I had tried many ways to make away myself, and still saw God prevented my designs, I would say to myself, 'Well, I see it cannot be, it must not be; God will have me come to some fearful end, and it's fit it should be so, that God may glorify himself upon such a wretched creature.'

As I was going along the streets, a godly minister passing by me, 'Oh,' thought I, 'with what horror shall I see that face at the great day!' So would I think by many others of God's people that I knew, either relations or otherwise. I said, 'I exceedingly wondered that such a pious man as I heard my father was, should have such a child.'

I used to say, 'I would change conditions with Julian,* and that he was a saint in comparison with me. Nay, that the devil himself was a saint compared with me.' I would say that 'the hottest place in hell must be mine; nay, did you know me, you would say it were too good for me, though I, poor creature, cannot think so.'

When I complained of those dreadful sins I said I was guilty of, some would ask me, 'If I would be glad to be rid of 'em, and to be in another condition?' 'Yes,' said I, 'so had the devils; who do you think would not be happy? But I cannot desire it upon any other account.' I would say, 'I now saw that my faith was only a fancy, and that according to an expression of Mr Baxter's* in a book of his, that the love I formerly had to God was carnal and diabolical.'

I would say to my cousin Walker, 'Though I am a damned reprobate, yet from me believe (for sometimes the devil speaks truth) that there is a God, and that his word is true, and that there is a devil, and that there is an hell, which I must find by woeful experience.'

I would often ask my cousin Walker, 'What those that came to visit me, thought of my condition?' He would answer, 'Very well.' I much wondered at it, and would do what I could to discourage 'em from coming; yet if at any time I thought they neglected me, I would be secretly troubled, as afterward I said.

I was wont earnestly to enquire whether it was possible that the child of such a mother as I could be saved; yet I would say I was without natural affection, that I loved neither God nor man, and that I was given up to work all manner of wickedness with greediness. 'We see no such thing by you,' would some say; I would answer, 'Ay, but it is in my heart.' 'Why doth it not break out in act?' say they. 'It will do ere long,' said I.

The devil would bring many places of scripture to my mind, especially promises; as I said, to jeer me with them, because once I thought I delighted in them, but was miserably mistaken; which did much terrify me.

I would with dread think with myself, if the men of Beth-shemesh were so destroyed (1 Sam[uel] vi 19) but for looking into the ark, what will be my condemnation that have so often meddled with the holy ordinances of God, as the word and sacraments; and now proved to be only a cursed hypocrite, and nothing to do with them. I thought with myself then, I would not partake of the sacrament of the Lord's Supper for a thousand worlds.

When any friend desired me to go to hear the word of God, I would earnestly beg of them to let me alone, saying I had sermons enough to answer for already, and that it would add to my great account. If they offered to compel me to go, I would desire them to let me alone, and I would go with them the next time, if I lived till then; but my aim was to make away myself just before the time came, for I thought I had better go to hell sooner, than hear the word still, and thereby increase my torment, and heap up wrath against the day of wrath, as I often expressed it.

I would sometimes say to my cousin Walker, 'Will you not pity me, that must, as sure as that there is a God, for ever burn in hell? I must confess I am not to be pitied, for did you know me, you would abhor me, and say hell was too good for me; yet, however, pity me as I am your fellow-creature, and once thought myself not only a woman but a Christian; and though I was such a dreadful wretch as now it appears, yet I did not know it, I verily thought myself in a good condition; and when you see me come to my horrible end, which I am sure will be ere long, though you must loathe me, yet, I say, pity me.'

'Yes,' he would say, 'if I thought it was true, I would pity you, but I do not believe it.' I used to say God could not save me, and the reason I gave was, that God could not deny himself.

I found within myself (as I apprehended) a scorning and jeering at religion, and them that professed it, and a despising of 'em. When I came to the height of my distemper, the struggling and fighting that was in me continually at first (while I combatted with Satan) left me. When I complained how vile I was, my friends would tell me, 'It was not I, but the devil's temptations;' I would answer, 'No, it is from myself; I am the devil now, the devil hath now done his work, he hath done tempting of me, he hath utterly overcome me.' 'Then why are you so troubled?' would some say. I would answer, 'Have I not cause to be troubled, think you, that am assuredly given up to the devil and eternally damned?' I would write in several places on the walls with the point of my scissors, 'Woe, woe, and alas to all eternity! I am undone, undone for ever, so as never any was before me.'

Upon some sudden occasion I would sometimes smile, but when I did, I would exceedingly check myself, and be the more troubled afterwards.

Mr Walker endeavoured to get Mr Baxter to come to me, but he still missed of him when he came to town. 'No,' said I, 'God will not let Mr Baxter come to such a wretch as I am.' But I had then a secret desire to see him, rather than anyone else. And to my best remembrance, my cousin Walker told me that he asked me if I would believe better of myself if Mr Baxter told me my condition was safe, and that I answered yes.

When another Christian friend, Mr Mason, brought me acquainted with any of God's people, I would say, 'Alas, Mr Mason, you'll dearly repent this; and how must I curse you in hell for all that you did in kindness to me!'

What is here writ of Mr Blake and Mr Mason is but to hint what may be said of my carriage towards them.

The next spring, which was in May 1665, my aunt Wilson came up to London, being restless in her mind till she saw me. When I heard that my aunt was come to Highgate to her brother's house, and did not come to London till Monday, I often said, 'I hoped to have seen my aunt before I died, but now I shall not: this fire within me will kindle and burn me before Monday.' On Monday my aunt came;

I, being taken with the first sight of her, went with her to dinner to a friend's house in the Old Jewry (Mr Hatt's house, who afterwards married her*), but was at my old language still every day, that the fire would kindle within me and burn me. The sickness then increasing, my aunt resolved to take me down again into the country, which I was very glad of; for there I thought I should live more privately, and be less disturbed (for so I accounted of the kind visits of friends). A week before midsummer, we set forward toward Derbyshire, and an uncomfortable journey we had, for by the way I would not eat sufficient to support nature. When I was come to Snelston again, I was where I would be, for there I could do what I pleased with little opposition; there I shunned all company, though they were my near relations, nor could I endure to be present at prayer, or any other part of God's worship, nor to hear the sound of reading, nor the sight of a book or paper, though it were but a letter or an almanac.

The Lady Baker was pleased to write me several letters which I would not so much as look on, nor hear read by others: one being brought me, and I pressed much to receive it, tore it in pieces. Nay, I would strike the horn-book out of my child's hand, but that would trouble me as soon as I had done it. I would wish I had never seen book or learned letter; I would say it had been happy for me if I had been born blind, daily repeating my accustomed language, that I was a cursed reprobate, and the monster of the creation.

One sabbath day, being disturbed about some small trifle, I fell into violent passion, weeping even to roaring, and cried out, 'I was made to be damned: God made me to that very end, to show the power of his justice more in me than in any other creature.'

My aunt sometimes would tell me that my expressions were so dreadful she knew not how to bear them. I would answer roundly, 'But what must I do, then, that must feel them?' I would often say to my aunt, 'Oh, you little know what a dismal, dark condition I am in! Methinks I am as dark as hell itself.' My aunt would say, 'Cousin, would you but believe you were melancholy, it might be a great means to bring you out of this condition.' 'Melancholy?' would I say, 'I have cause to be melancholy, that am as assuredly damned as that there is a God, and no more hopes of me than of the devils! I have more cause to be melancholy than they have; it's a fearful thing to fall into the hands of the living God' (Heb[rews] x verse 31).

My aunt would persuade me to seek God in the use of means,

from that argument of the resolution of the four lepers in the 2 Kings vii 4. I would answer with scorn, 'I have heard that often enough.'

One fit my humour was such that when friends would have argued with me about my condition, I would not speak, but only give them some short, scornful answer and no more; but I would be sometimes in one temper and sometimes in another; my aunt would take the advantage of my best humour to talk with me then, and the main thing she designed in most of her arguments with me was to convince me of the fallacy and delusion that was in my opinion that it was so infallibly revealed to me that I was damned; but alas, all took no place with me, but when she began to speak with me of such things, I would generally fling away in a great fume, and say, 'Will you not let me alone yet? Methinks you might let me have a little quiet while I am out of hell.' This was almost my daily practice while I was with my aunt. I was usually very nimble in my answers, and peevishly pertinacious to please my own cross humour.

My aunt told me she believed God would not have exercised me so with afflictions from my childhood if he intended to reject me at last. I answered, 'Do you not remember what Mr Calamy* used to say, that unsanctified afflictions parboil the soul for hell? Oh,' said I, 'that I had gone to hell as soon as I had been born, seeing I was born to be damned, and then I had not had so many sins to have answered for, then I should not have lived to be a terror to myself and all that know me, and my torments in hell would have been far less.'

When my grandmother had told me of the depths of the mercy of God in Christ, I would answer with indignation, 'What do you tell me of a Christ? It had been better for me if there had never been a saviour: then I should have gone to hell at a cheaper rate.'

Towards winter I grew to eat very little (much less than I did before) so that I was exceeding lean, and at last nothing but skin and bones. A neighbouring gentlewoman, a very discreet person that had a great desire to see me, came in at the back door of the house unawares, and found me in the kitchen; who after she had seen me, said to Mrs Wilson, 'She cannot live, she hath death in her face.' I would say still that every bit I did eat hastened my ruin, and that I had it with a dreadful curse; and what I ate increased the fire within me, which would at last burn me up; and I would now willingly live out of hell as long as I could.

Thus sadly I passed that winter, and towards spring I began to eat a little better.

This spring, in April 1666, my good friends Mr Shorthose and his wife, whose company formerly I much delighted in, came over; and when I heard they were come and were at their brother's house half a mile off, and would come thither the Friday after, 'Ah,' says I, 'that I dreaded; I cannot endure to see him, nor hear his voice; I have told him so many dreadful lies' (meaning what I had formerly told him of my experiences, and, as I thought, infallible evidences of the love of God towards me; and now believed myself to be the vilest creature upon earth); 'I cannot see his face,' and wept tenderly. Wherewith my aunt was much affected, and promised that when he came he should not see me. (I would have seen neither of them, but especially my he-cousin.) On the Friday, soon after they came in, they asked for me, but my aunt put them off till after dinner, and then told them she had engaged her word they should not see me, and that if she once broke her promise with me, I would not believe her hereafter. With such persuasions she kept them from seeing me, but not satisfied them; for that night Mr Shorthose was much troubled, and told his wife if he had thought they must not have seen me, he would scarce have gone to Snelston. The next day they supped at Mr Robert Archer's house (Mrs Wilson's brother, that then lived in the same town) where my aunt supped with them. At the table something was said of their not seeing Mrs Allen, but after supper Mr Shorthose and his wife stole away from the company to Mrs Wilson's, where they came in at the back side of the house suddenly into the kitchen where I was. But as soon as I saw them, I cried out in a violent manner several times, 'Ah, aunt Wilson, hast thou served me so!', and ran into the chimney and took up the tongs. 'No,' said they, 'Your aunt knows not of our coming.' 'What do you do here?' said I. 'We have something to say to you,' said they. 'But I have nothing to say to you,' said I. Mr Shorthose took me by the hand, and said, 'Come, come, lay down those tongs and go with us into the parlour;' which I did, and there they discoursed with me till they had brought me to so calm and friendly a temper that when they went I accompanied them to the door and said, 'Methinks I am loath to part with them.' Mr Short-hose, having so good encouragement, came the next day again, being sabbath day, after dinner, and prevailed with me to walk with him into an arbour in the orchard; where he had much discourse with me; and amongst the rest he entreated me to go home with him, which after long persuasions both from him and my aunt, I consented to; upon this condition, that he promised me he would not compel me to anything of the worship of God, but what he could do by persuasion. And that week I went with them, where I spent that summer; in which time it pleased God by Mr Shorthose's means to do me much good, both in soul and body. He had some skill in physic himself, and also consulted with physicians about me; he kept me to a course of physic most part of the summer, except when the great heat of the weather prevented. I began much to leave my dreadful expressions concerning my condition, and was present with them at duty; and at last they prevailed with me to go with them to the public ordinance, and to walk with them to visit friends, and was much altered for the better.

A fortnight after Michaelmas my aunt fetched me home again to Snelston, where I passed that winter much better than formerly, and was pretty conformable and orderly in the family; and the next summer was much after the same manner, but grew still something better; and the next winter likewise still mending though but slowly, till the spring began, and then I changed much from my retiredness, and delighted to walk with friends abroad.

And this spring it pleased God to provide a very suitable match for me, one Mr Charles Hatt, a widower living in Warwickshire, with whom I live very comfortably, both as to my inward and outward man; my husband being one that truly fears God.

As my melancholy came by degrees, so it wore off by degrees, and as my dark melancholy bodily distempers abated, so did my spiritual maladies also; and God convinced me by degrees that all this was from Satan, his delusions and temptations working in those dark and black humours, and not from myself; and this God cleared up to me more and more, and accordingly my love to and delight in religion increased. And it is my desire that, lest this great affliction should be a stumbling block to any, it may be known (seeing my case is published) that I evidently perceive that God did it in much mercy and faithfulness to my soul; and though for the present it was a bitter cup, yet that it was but what the only wise God saw I had need of according to that place 1 Pet[er] i 6: 'Though now for a season, if need be, ye are in heaviness through manifold temptations.' Which scripture did much comfort me under my former afflictions in my first husband's days.

77   From *The Hind and the Panther*

JOHN DRYDEN

First published 1687, this long allegorical poem is a defence of the Roman
Catholic Church (in the figure of the Hind) against the Church of England (the Panther) and Nonconformist sects (various animals). In the
present extract, from Book I, the poet speaks in his own voice to acknowledge his past errors and to affirm his discovery of the true faith and
true Church, which is the 'unerring guide' of line 65 and the 'director' of
line 70.

> What weight of ancient witness can prevail
> If private reason hold the public scale?
> But, gracious God, how well dost thou provide
> For erring judgements an unerring guide!
> Thy throne is darkness in th' abyss of light,
> A blaze of glory that forbids the sight;
> O teach me to believe thee thus concealed,
> And search no farther than thyself revealed;
> But her alone for my director take   70
> Whom thou hast promised never to forsake!
> My thoughtless youth was winged with vain desires,
> My manhood, long misled by wandering fires,
> Followed false lights; and when their glimpse was gone,
> My pride struck out new sparkles of her own.
> Such was I, such by nature still I am,
> Be thine the glory, and be mine the shame.

78   From *The Indian Emperor*

JOHN DRYDEN

Staged 1665, printed 1667. The play tells of the conquest of Mexico by
the Spaniards, led by Cortez. This scene (v. ii. 1–137) dramatizes the
clash of Spanish Catholic Christianity and American 'Indian' religion.
Montezuma is the Mexican king; Cortez is by now in love with his
daughter.

A Prison

Montezuma, Indian High Priest bound, Pizarro, Spaniards with swords drawn, a Christian Priest.

Piz. Thou hast not yet discovered all thy store.

Mont. I neither can nor will discover more:
The gods will punish you, if they be just;
The gods will plague your sacrilegious lust.

Chr. Priest. Mark how this impious heathen justifies
His own false gods, and our true God denies:
How wickedly he has refused his wealth,
And hid his gold from Christian hands by stealth:
Down with him, kill him, merit heaven thereby.

Ind. High Pr. Can heaven be author of such cruelty?   10

Piz. Since neither threats nor kindness will prevail,
We must by other means your minds assail;
Fasten the engines; stretch 'um at their length,
And pull the straitened cords with all your strength.
                    [*They fasten them to the racks, and then pull them.*

Mont. The gods, who made me once a king, shall know
I still am worthy to continue so:
Though now the subject of your tyranny,
I'll plague you worse than you can punish me.
Know I have gold which you shall never find,
No pains, no tortures shall unlock my mind.   20

Chr. Pr. Pull harder yet; he does not feel the rack.

Mont. Pull till my veins break, and my sinews crack.

Ind. High Pr. When will you end your barb'rous cruelty?
I beg not to escape, I beg to die.

Mont. Shame on thy priesthood that such prayers can bring:
Is it not brave to suffer with thy king?
When monarchs suffer, gods themselves bear part;
Then well may'st thou, who but my vassal art:
I charge thee dare not groan, nor show one sign
Thou at thy torments dost the least repine.   30

Ind. High Pr. You took an oath when you received your crown,
The heavens should pour their usual blessings down;
The sun should shine, the earth its fruits produce,

And nought be wanting to your subjects' use:
Yet we with famine were oppressed, and now
Must to the yoke of cruel masters bow.

   Mont. If those above, who made the world, could be
Forgetful of it, why then blam'st thou me?

   Chr. Pr. Those pains, O Prince, thou sufferest now
     are light
Compared to those which, when thy soul takes flight,   40
Immortal, endless, thou must then endure:
Which death begins, and time can never cure.

   Mont. Thou art deceived: for whensoe'er I die,
The sun my father bears my soul on high:
He lets me down a beam, and mounted there,
He draws it back, and pulls me through the air:
I in the eastern parts, and rising sky,
You in heaven's downfall, and the west must lie.

   Chr. Pr. Fond man, by heathen ignorance misled,
Thy soul destroying when thy body's dead: 50
Change yet thy faith, and buy eternal rest.

   Ind. High Pr. Die in your own: for our belief is best.

   Mont. In seeking happiness you both agree,
But in the search, the paths so different be
That all religions with each other fight,
While only one can lead us in the right.
But till that one hath some more certain mark,
Poor human kind must wander in the dark,
And suffer pains eternally below,
For that which here we cannot come to know.   60

   Chr. Pr. That which we worship, and which you believe,
From nature's common hand we both receive:
All under various names adore and love
One power immense, which ever rules above.
Vice to abhor, and virtue to pursue,
Is both believed and taught by us and you:
But here our worship takes another way.

   Mont. Where both agree 'tis there most safe to stay:
For what's more vain than public light to shun,
And set up tapers while we see the sun?   70

Chr. Pr. Though nature teaches whom we should adore,
By heavenly beams we still discover more.

Mont. Or this must be enough, or to mankind
One equal way to bliss is not designed.
For though some more may know, and some know less,
Yet all must know enough for happiness.

Chr. Pr. If in this middle way you still pretend
To stay, your journey never will have end.

Mont. Howe'er, 'tis better in the midst to stay,
Than wander farther in uncertain way.   80

Chr. Pr. But we by martyrdom our faith avow.

Mont. You do no more than I for ours do now.
To prove religion true——
If either wit or suff'rings would suffice,
All faiths afford the constant and the wise:
And yet ev'n they, by education swayed,
In age defend what infancy obeyed.

Chr. Pr. Since age by erring childhood is misled,
Refer yourself to our unerring head.

Mont. Man and not err! What reason can you give?   90

Chr. Pr. Renounce that carnal reason, and believe.

Mont. The light of nature should I thus betray,
'Twere to wink hard that I might see the day.

Chr. Pr. Condemn not yet the way you do not know;
I'll make your reason judge what way to go.

Mont. 'Tis much too late for me new ways to take,
Who have but one short step of life to make.

Piz. Increase their pains, the cords are yet too slack.

Chr. Pr. I must by force convert him on the rack.

Ind. High Pr. I faint away, and find I can no more: 100
Give leave, O King, I may reveal thy store,
And free myself from pains I cannot bear.

Mont. Think'st thou I lie on beds of roses here,
Or in a wanton bath stretched at my ease?
Die, slave, and with thee die such thoughts as these.

[*High Priest turns aside and dies.*

Enter Cortez attended by Spaniards, he speaks entering.

 Cort. On pain of death, kill none but those who fight;
I much repent me of this bloody night:
Slaughter grows murder when it goes too far,
And makes a massacre what was a war:
Sheathe all your weapons, and in silence move,   110
'Tis sacred here to beauty and to love.
Ha——   *[Sees Montezuma.*
What dismal sight is this, which takes from me
All the delight that waits on victory!

        [Runs to take him off the rack.
Make haste: how now, Religion, do you frown?
Haste, holy Avarice, and help him down.
Ah father, father, what do I endure *[Embracing Montezuma.*
To see these wounds my pity cannot cure!

 Mont. Am I so low that you should pity bring,
And give an infant's comfort to a king?   120
Ask these if I have once unmanly groaned;
Or ought have done deserving to be moaned.

 Cort. Did I not charge thou should'st not stir from hence?

           [To Pizarro.
But martial law shall punish thy offence.
And you,——   *[To the Chr. Priest.*
Who saucily teach monarchs to obey,
And the wide world in narrow cloisters sway;
Set up by kings as humble aids of power,
You that which bred you, viper-like devour,
You enemies of crowns——   130

 Chr. Pr.   Come, let's away,
We but provoke his fury by our stay.

 Cort. If this go free, farewell that discipline
Which did in Spanish camps severely shine:
Accursed gold, 'tis thou hast caused these crimes;
Thou turn'st our steel against thy parent climes!
And into Spain wilt fatally be brought,
Since with the price of blood thou here art bought.

        [Exeunt Priest and Pizarro.

79 *Horace: Odes III. xxix*

JOHN DRYDEN

One of the outstanding translations from classical poetry printed in the miscellany *Sylvae* (1685); see also 24, 51, and 81. As the subtitle, 'Paraphrased in Pindaric Verse and Inscribed to the Right Honourable Laurence, Earl of Rochester', states, this is a free paraphrase of Horace's original.

I

Descended of an ancient line
That long the Tuscan sceptre swayed,
Make haste to meet the generous wine
Whose piercing is for thee delayed:
The rosy wreath is ready made,
 And artful hands prepare
The fragrant Syrian oil that shall perfume thy hair.

II

When the wine sparkles from afar,
And the well-natured friend cries, 'Come away',
Make haste, and leave thy business and thy care; 10
No mortal interest can be worth thy stay.

III

Leave for a while thy costly country seat,
 And, to be great indeed, forget
The nauseous pleasures of the great:
  Make haste and come;
Come and forsake thy cloying store,
Thy turret that surveys from high
The smoke, and wealth and noise of Rome,
And all the busy pageantry
That wise men scorn, and fools adore: 20
Come, give thy soul a loose, and taste the pleasures
  of the poor.

IV

Sometimes 'tis grateful to the rich to try
A short vicissitude, and fit of poverty;
  A savoury dish, a homely treat,
  Where all is plain, where all is neat,
  Without the stately spacious room,
The Persian carpet, or the Tyrian loom,
Clear up the cloudy foreheads of the great.

V

The sun is in the lion mounted high;
   The Sirian star
   Barks from afar,
And with his sultry breath infects the sky;
The ground below is parched, the heavens above us fry.
  The shepherd drives his fainting flock
  Beneath the covert of a rock;
  And seeks refreshing rivulets nigh:
  The Sylvans to their shades retire,
Those very shades and streams, new shades and streams
    require,
And want a cooling breeze of wind to fan the raging fire.

VI

  Thou, what befits the new Lord Mayor,
  And what the City faction dare,
  And what the Gallic arms will do,
  And what the quiver-bearing foe,*
Art anxiously inquisitive to know;
But God has wisely hid from human sight
  The dark decrees of future fate,
  And sown their seeds in depth of night;
He laughs at all the giddy turns of state,
When mortals search too soon, and fear too late.

VII

  Enjoy the present smiling hour,
  And put it out of Fortune's power.
The tide of business, like the running stream,

30

40

50

Is sometimes high, and sometimes low,
A quiet ebb, or a tempestuous flow,
And always in extreme:
Now with a noiseless, gentle course
It keeps within the middle bed;
Anon it lifts aloft the head,
And bears down all before it with impetuous force,
And trunks of trees come rolling down,   60
Sheep and their folds together drown;
Both house and homestead into seas are borne,
And rocks are from their old foundations torn,
And woods made thin with winds their scattered
honours mourn.

VIII

Happy the man, and happy he alone,
He who can call today his own:
He who secure within can say,
'Tomorrow do thy worst, for I have lived today.
Be fair, or foul, or rain, or shine,
The joys I have possessed, in spite of Fate, are mine: 70
Not heaven itself upon the past has power,
But what has been has been, and I have had my hour.'

IX

Fortune, that with malicious joy
Does man her slave oppress,
Proud of her office to destroy
Is seldom pleased to bless;
Still various and unconstant still,
But with an inclination to be ill,
Promotes, degrades, delights in strife,
And makes a lottery of life.   80
I can enjoy her while she's kind,
But when she dances in the wind
And shakes her wings, and will not stay,
I puff the prostitute away:
The little or the much she gave is quietly resigned;
Content with poverty, my soul I arm,
And virtue, though in rags, will keep me warm.

X

What is't to me,
Who never sail in her unfaithful sea,
  If storms arise, and clouds grow black;   90
  If the mast split and threaten wrack,
  Then let the greedy merchant fear
    For his ill-gotten gain,
  And pray to gods that will not hear,
While the debating winds and billows bear
    His wealth into the main.
  For me, secure from Fortune's blows
  (Secure of what I cannot lose),
  In my small pinnace I can sail,
  Contemning all the blustering roar,   100
  And running with a merry gale,
  With friendly stars my safety seek
  Within some little winding creek,
    And see the storm ashore.

80   From *Aureng-Zebe*

JOHN DRYDEN

The last of Dryden's rhymed heroic plays, performed 1675, printed 1676.
This speech is from IV. i. 33–44.

  Aureng-Zebe. When I consider life, 'tis all a cheat;
Yet, fooled with hope, men favour the deceit;
Trust on, and think tomorrow will repay:
Tomorrow's falser than the former day;
Lies worse; and while it says, 'We shall be blessed
With some new joys', cuts off what we possessed.
Strange coz'nage! None would live past years again,
Yet all hope pleasure in what yet remain;   40
And from the dregs of life think to receive
What the first sprightly running could not give.
I'm tired with waiting for this chymic gold
Which fools us young, and beggars us when old.

81   *Lucretius: Against the Fear of Death*

JOHN DRYDEN

Printed in *Sylvae* (1685): see headnote to **79**. The Roman poet Lucretius
(1st cent. BCE) was the author of *De rerum natura* ('On the nature of
things'), an account of the Epicurean philosophy. Epicurus (Greek philosopher, 341–270 BCE) taught that the world was made up of atoms in
random motion, without spirit; if there are gods, they take no interest in
human life. He advocated the pursuit of pleasure—by which he meant not
sensual indulgence but freedom from pain and anxiety. Lucretius was
widely read in the Restoration period; Thomas Creech published a complete verse translation in 1682; Rochester translated two passages; and
Dryden translated five extracts in *Sylvae*. The present passage from Book
III consoles those who fear death, by arguing that since our bodies dissolve into atoms, there will be no 'we' existing after our death: hence no
'we' to feel pleasure or pain.

> What has this bugbear death to frighten man,
> If souls can die, as well as bodies can?
> For, as before our birth we felt no pain
> When Punic arms infested land and main,*
> When heaven and earth were in confusion hurled
> For the debated empire of the world,
> Which awed with dreadful expectation lay,
> Sure to be slaves, uncertain who should sway:
> So, when our mortal frame shall be disjoined,
> The lifeless lump uncoupled from the mind,   10
> From sense of grief and pain we shall be free;
> We shall not feel, because we shall not *be*.
> Though earth in seas, and seas in heaven were lost,
> We should not move, we only should be tossed.
> Nay, ev'n suppose when we have suffered fate,
> The soul could feel in her divided state,
> What's that to us? for we are only we
> While souls and bodies in one frame agree.
> Nay, though our atoms should revolve by chance,
> And matter leap into the former dance;   20
> Though time our life and motion could restore,
> And make our bodies what they were before,

What gain to us would all this bustle bring?
The new-made man would be another thing;
When once an interrupting pause is made,
That individual being is decayed.
We, who are dead and gone, shall bear no part
In all the pleasures, nor shall feel the smart,
Which to that other mortal shall accrue,
Whom of our matter time shall mould anew.   30
For backward if you look on that long space
Of ages past, and view the changing face
Of matter, tossed and variously combined
In sundry shapes, 'tis easy for the mind
From thence t' infer, that seeds of things have been
In the same order as they now are seen:
Which yet our dark remembrance cannot trace,
Because a pause of life, a gaping space
Has come betwixt, where memory lies dead,
And all the wandering motions from the sense
  are fled.   40
For whosoe'er shall in misfortunes live
Must *be* when those misfortunes shall arrive;
And since the man who *is* not, feels not woe
(For death exempts him, and wards off the blow,
Which we the living only feel and bear),
What is there left for us in death to fear?
When once that pause of life has come between,
'Tis just the same as we had never been.
And therefore if a man bemoan his lot,
That after death his mouldering limbs shall rot,   50
Or flames, or jaws of beasts devour his mass,
Know he's an unsincere, unthinking ass.
A secret sting remains within his mind,
The fool is to his own cast offals kind;
He boasts no sense can after death remain, ⎫
Yet makes himself a part of life again: ⎬
As if some other he could feel the pain.   ⎭
If while he live this thought molest his head,
'What wolf or vulture shall devour me dead?',
He wastes his days in idle grief, nor can   60

Distinguish 'twixt the body and the man;
But thinks himself can still himself survive,
And what when dead he feels not, feels alive.
Then he repines that he was born to die,
Nor knows in death there is no other he;
No living he remains his grief to vent,
And o'er his senseless carcass to lament.
If after death 'tis painful to be torn
By birds and beasts, then why not so to burn,
Or drenched in floods of honey to be soaked,   70
Embalmed to be at once preserved and choked;
Or on an airy mountain's top to lie
Exposed to cold and heaven's inclemency,
Or crowded in a tomb to be oppressed
With monumental marble on thy breast?
But to be snatched from all thy household joys,
From thy chaste wife, and thy dear prattling boys,
Whose little arms about thy legs are cast,
And climbing for a kiss prevent their mother's haste,
Inspiring secret pleasure through thy breast;   80
All these shall be no more: thy friends oppressed
Thy care and courage now no more shall free:
'Ah wretch', thou criest, 'ah! miserable me,
One woeful day sweeps children, friends, and wife,
And all the brittle blessings of my life!'
Add one thing more, and all thou say'st is true:
Thy want and wish of them is vanished too,
Which well considered were a quick relief
To all thy vain imaginary grief.
For thou shalt sleep and never wake again,   90
And quitting life, shall quit thy living pain.
But we thy friends shall all those sorrows find ⎫
Which in forgetful death thou leav'st behind;   ⎬
No time shall dry our tears, nor drive thee from our mind. ⎭
The worst that can befall thee, measured right,
Is a sound slumber, and a long good night.
Yet thus the fools, that would be thought the wits,
Disturb their mirth with melancholy fits,
When healths go round, and kindly brimmers flow,

Till the fresh garlands on their foreheads glow,   100
They whine, and cry, 'Let us make haste to live,
Short are the joys that human life can give'.
Eternal preachers, that corrupt the draught,
And pall the god that never thinks with thought;*
Idiots with all that thought, to whom the worst
Of death is want of drink, and endless thirst,
Or any fond desire as vain as these.
For ev'n in sleep, the body wrapped in ease
Supinely lies, as in the peaceful grave,
And wanting nothing, nothing can it crave.   110
Were that sound sleep eternal, it were death;
Yet the first atoms then, the seeds of breath
Are moving near to sense, we do but shake
And rouse that sense, and straight we are awake.
Then death to us, and death's anxiety
Is less than nothing, if a less could be.
For then our atoms, which in order lay,
Are scattered from their heap, and puffed away,
And never can return into their place,
When once the pause of life has left an empty space.   120
And last, suppose great Nature's voice should call
To thee, or me, or any of us all,
'What dost thou mean, ungrateful wretch, thou vain,
Thou mortal thing, thus idly to complain,
And sigh and sob, that thou shalt be no more?
For if thy life were pleasant heretofore,
If all the bounteous blessings I could give ⎫
Thou hast enjoyed, if thou hast known to live, ⎬
And pleasure not leaked through thee like a sieve, ⎭
Why dost thou not give thanks as at a plenteous feast,   130
Crammed to the throat with life, and rise and take
    thy rest?
But if my blessings thou hast thrown away,
If indigested joys passed through and would not stay,
Why dost thou wish for more to squander still?
If life be grown a load, a real ill,
And I would all thy cares and labours end,
Lay down thy burden, fool, and know thy friend.

To please thee I have emptied all my store, ⎫
I can invent, and can supply no more, ⎬
But run the round again, the round I ran before. ⎭   140
Suppose thou art not broken yet with years,
Yet still the self-same scene of things appears,
And would be ever, could'st thou ever live;
For life is still but life, there's nothing new to give.'
What can we plead against so just a bill?
We stand convicted, and our cause goes ill.
But if a wretch, a man oppressed by fate,
Should beg of Nature to prolong his date,
She speaks aloud to him with more disdain,
'Be still thou martyr fool, thou covetous of pain.'   150
But if an old decrepit sot lament,
'What thou', she cries, 'who hast outlived content!
Dost thou complain, who hast enjoyed my store?
But this is still th' effect of wishing more!
Unsatisfied with all that Nature brings,
Loathing the present, liking absent things;
From hence it comes thy vain desires at strife
Within themselves, have tantalized thy life,
And ghastly death appeared before thy sight
Ere thou had'st gorged thy soul and senses with delight.   160
Now leave those joys unsuiting to thy age
To a fresh comer, and resign the stage.'
Is Nature to be blamed if thus she chide?
No, sure; for 'tis her business to provide,
Against this ever-changing frame's decay,
New things to come, and old to pass away.
One being worn, another being makes,
Changed but not lost; for Nature gives and takes:
New matter must be found for things to come,
And these must waste like those, and follow Nature's doom.   170
All things, like thee, have time to rise and rot,
And from each other's ruin are begot;
For life is not confined to him or thee—
'Tis giv'n to all for use, to none for property.
Consider former ages past and gone,
Whose circles ended long ere thine begun,

Then tell me fool, what part in them thou hast?
Thus may'st thou judge the future by the past.
What horror seest thou in that quiet state,
What bugbear dreams to fright thee after fate?   180
No ghost, no goblins that still passage keep,
But all is there serene in that eternal sleep.
For all the dismal tales that poets tell
Are verified on earth, and not in hell.
No Tantalus looks up with fearful eye,
Or dreads th' impending rock to crush him from on high:*
But fear of chance on earth disturbs our easy hours,
Or vain imagined wrath, of vain imagined powers.
No Tityus torn by vultures lies in hell,*
Nor could the lobes of his rank liver swell   190
To that prodigious mass for their eternal meal;
Not though his monstrous bulk had covered o'er
Nine spreading acres, or nine thousand more;
Not though the globe of earth had been the giant's floor;
Nor in eternal torments could he lie,
Nor could his corpse sufficient food supply.
But he's the Tityus, who by love oppressed,
Or tyrant passion preying on his breast,
And ever-anxious thoughts is robbed of rest.
The Sisyphus is he, whom noise and strife*   200
Seduce from all the soft retreats of life,
To vex the government, disturb the laws,
Drunk with the fumes of popular applause;
He courts the giddy crowd to make him great,
And sweats and toils in vain to mount the sovereign seat.
For still to aim at power, and still to fail,
Ever to strive and never to prevail,
What is it, but in reason's true account
To heave the stone against the rising mount;
Which urged, and laboured, and forced up with pain,   210
Recoils and rolls impetuous down, and smokes along the plain?
Then still to treat thy ever-craving mind
With every blessing, and of every kind,
Yet never fill thy ravening appetite,
Though years and seasons vary thy delight,

Yet nothing to be seen of all the store,
But still the wolf within thee barks for more:
This is the fable's moral which they tell
Of fifty foolish virgins damned in hell
To leaky vessels, which the liquor spill—   220
To vessels of their sex, which none could ever fill.*
As for the dog, the Furies, and their snakes,*
The gloomy caverns, and the burning lakes,
And all the vain infernal trumpery,
They neither are, nor were, nor e'er can be.
But here on earth the guilty have in view
The mighty pains to mighty mischiefs due:
Racks, prisons, poisons, the Tarpeian rock,*
Stripes, hangmen, pitch, and suffocating smoke,
And last, and most, if these were cast behind,   230
Th' avenging horror of a conscious mind,
Whose deadly fear anticipates the blow,
And sees no end of punishment and woe,
But looks for more, at the last gasp of breath:
This makes an hell on earth, and life a death.
Meantime, when thoughts of death disturb thy head,
Consider, Ancus great and good is dead;*
Ancus, thy better far, was born to die,
And thou, dost thou bewail mortality?
So many monarchs with their mighty state,   240
Who ruled the world, were overruled by fate.
That haughty king, who lorded o'er the main,*
And whose stupendous bridge did the wild waves restrain
(In vain they foamed, in vain they threatened wreck,
While his proud legions marched upon their back),
Him death, a greater monarch, overcame,
Nor spared his guards the more, for their immortal name.
The Roman chief, the Carthaginian dread,   ⎫
Scipio, the thunderbolt of war is dead,*   ⎬
And like a common slave by Fate in triumph led. ⎭   250
The founders of invented arts are lost,
And wits who made eternity their boast;
Where now is Homer who possessed the throne?
Th' immortal work remains, the mortal author's gone.

Democritus perceiving age invade,*
His body weakened, and his mind decayed,
Obeyed the summons with a cheerful face,
Made haste to welcome death, and met him half the race.
That stroke ev'n Epicurus could not bar,*
Though he in wit surpassed mankind as far   260
As does the midday sun the midnight star.
And thou, dost thou disdain to yield thy breath,
Whose very life is little more than death?
More than one half by lazy sleep possessed,
And when awake, thy soul but nods at best,
Day-dreams and sickly thoughts revolving in thy breast.
Eternal troubles haunt thy anxious mind,
Whose cause and cure thou never hop'st to find;
But still uncertain, with thyself at strife,
Thou wander'st in the labyrinth of life.   270
O, if the foolish race of man, who find
A weight of cares still pressing on their mind,
Could find as well the cause of this unrest,
And all this burden lodged within the breast,
Sure they would change their course, nor live as now,
Uncertain what to wish or what to vow.
Uneasy both in country and in town,
They search a place to lay their burden down.
One restless in his palace walks abroad,
And vainly thinks to leave behind the load;   280
But straight returns, for he's as restless there,
And finds there's no relief in open air.
Another to his villa would retire,
And spurs as hard as if it were on fire;
No sooner entered at his country door,
But he begins to stretch, and yawn, and snore,
Or seeks the city which he left before.
Thus every man o'erworks his weary will
To shun himself, and to shake off his ill;
The shaking fit returns and hangs upon him still.   290
No prospect of repose, nor hope of ease,
The wretch is ignorant of his disease,
Which known would all his fruitless trouble spare,

For he would know the world not worth his care:
Then would he search more deeply for the cause,
And study nature well, and nature's laws:
For in this moment lies not the debate,
But on our future, fixed, eternal state,
That never-changing state which all must keep
Whom Death has doomed to everlasting sleep.   300
Why are we then so fond of mortal life,
Beset with dangers and maintained with strife?
A life which all our care can never save;
One fate attends us, and one common grave.
Besides we tread but a perpetual round,
We ne'er strike out, but beat the former ground,
And the same mawkish joys in the same track are found.
For still we think an absent blessing best,
Which cloys, and is no blessing when possessed;
A new arising wish expels it from the breast.   310
The feverish thirst of life increases still,
We call for more and more, and never have our fill;
Yet know not what tomorrow we shall try,
What dregs of life in the last draught may lie.
Nor, by the longest life we can attain,
One moment from the length of death we gain;
For all behind belongs to his eternal reign.
When once the Fates have cut the mortal thread,*
The man as much to all intents is dead
Who dies today, and will as long be so,   320
As he who died a thousand years ago.

82   *A Kind of Translation*

SIR PHILIP WODEHOUSE

Translated from the Roman poet Claudian's invective *In Rufinum*, against
Flavius Rufinus, the Roman administrator killed in 395 CE.

Oft have I been divided in my thought,
Whether the gods take care of earth, or, nought

Regarding us poor mortal wights below,
Let all things here in loose disorder flow?
For when I view the harmony of things,
The sea-set bounds, the year's returning rings,
Vicissitude of night and day, then I
Judged all things fixed by God's economy:
Who made the stars move regular, the earth
Her fruits in their due seasons to bring forth;   10
Who made the constant-ever-changing moon
Be filled with the sun's light, he with his own;
The shores alongst the waters co-extends;
Upon the middle axis earth appends.
But when I find affairs enveloped, so
The wicked flourish, virtuous live in woe,
Then my religion staggers, and my faith
Falters, as fall'n into a sect which saith*
The seminal forms in idle motion dance,
New species through vast emptiness by chance,   20
Not art, are ruled; and for the deities,
That either there is none, or us defies.
Great Rufin's downfall does at length dissolve
The tumult of my doubts, and God absolve.
Nor will I murmur, 'Miscreants are hoist
To height of power': they are but higher raised
To take the deeper fall.

83   *A Satire against Reason and Mankind*

JOHN WILMOT, EARL OF ROCHESTER

Probably written in 1674; circulated widely in manuscript and in a printed broadside (1679). Lines 174–225 were probably added after the poem had begun to circulate, perhaps in response to Stillingfleet's sermon (see note on p. 412). The satire is indebted to Boileau's *Satire VIII*, but also draws upon many commonplaces of sceptical philosophy: see the notes in the editions by Hammond and Love. Restoration theology was placing increasing stress on the use of reason in the interpretation of religious beliefs. Rochester's poem queries man's rationality, arguing that true reason consists in the satisfaction of bodily needs, and that much of human behaviour is driven by (often unacknowledged) desires and fears. The poem takes the form of a dialogue between the speaker (not necessarily Rochester's own voice) and a clerical opponent.

> Were I (who to my cost already am
> One of those strange, prodigious creatures, man)
> A spirit free to choose for my own share ⎫
> What case of flesh and blood I pleased to wear, ⎬
> I'd be a dog, a monkey, or a bear, ⎭
> Or anything but that vain animal
> Who is so proud of being rational.
> The senses are too gross, and he'll contrive
> A sixth, to contradict the other five,
> And before certain instinct, will prefer　　　　　　　10
> Reason, which fifty times for one does err.
> Reason, an *ignis fatuus* in the mind,
> Which leaving light of nature, sense, behind,*
> Pathless and dangerous wandering ways it takes,
> Through error's fenny bogs, and thorny brakes;
> Whilst the misguided follower climbs with pain
> Mountains of whimsies, heaped in his own brain:
> Stumbling from thought to thought, falls headlong down
> Into doubt's boundless sea, where like to drown,
> Books bear him up awhile, and make him try　　　　20
> To swim with bladders of philosophy,
> In hopes still to o'ertake th' escaping light: ⎫
> The vapour dances in his dazzling sight, ⎬
> Till spent, it leaves him to eternal night. ⎭
> Then old age, and experience, hand in hand,
> Lead him to death, and make him understand,
> After a search so painful, and so long,
> That all his life he has been in the wrong;
> Huddled in dirt the reasoning engine lies,
> Who was so proud, so witty, and so wise.　　　　　30
> Pride drew him in, as cheats their bubbles catch,
> And makes him venture, to be made a wretch.
> His wisdom did his happiness destroy,
> Aiming to know that world he should enjoy;
> And wit was his vain, frivolous pretence

Of pleasing others, at his own expense:
For wits are treated just like common whores,
First they're enjoyed, and then kicked out of doors.
The pleasure past, a threatening doubt remains,
That frights th' enjoyer with succeeding pains: 40
Women and men of wit are dangerous tools,
And ever fatal to admiring fools.
Pleasure allures, and when the fops escape, ⎫
'Tis not that they're beloved, but fortunate, ⎬
And therefore what they fear, at heart they hate. ⎭

But now methinks some formal band and beard
Takes me to task; come on Sir, I'm prepared.

'Then by your favour, anything that's writ
Against this gibing, jingling knack called wit
Likes me abundantly, but you take care,   50
Upon this point, not to be too severe.
Perhaps my Muse were fitter for this part, ⎫
For I profess, I can be very smart ⎬
On wit, which I abhor with all my heart: ⎭
I long to lash it in some sharp essày, ⎫
But your grand indiscretion bids me stay, ⎬
And turns my tide of ink another way. ⎭
What rage ferments in your degenerate mind,
To make you rail at reason, and mankind?
Blessed, glorious man! to whom alone kind heaven   60
An everlasting soul has freely given;
Whom his great Maker took such care to make,
That from himself he did the image take,*
And this fair frame in shining reason dressed,
To dignify his nature above beast.
Reason, by whose aspiring influence
We take a flight beyond material sense;
Dive into mysteries, then soaring pierce
The flaming limits of the universe;
Search heaven and hell, find out what's acted there,   70
And give the world true grounds of hope and fear!'

Hold, mighty man, I cry, all this we know
From the pathetic pen of Ingelo;*
From Patrick's *Pilgrim*, Stillingfleet's *Replies*,*

And 'tis this very reason I despise.
This supernatural gift, that makes a mite
Think he's the image of the infinite:
Comparing his short life, void of all rest,
To the Eternal, and the ever-blessed.
This busy, puzzling, stirrer-up of doubt,   80
That frames deep mysteries, then finds 'em out;
Filling with frantic crowds of thinking fools
Those reverend bedlams, colleges and schools;
Borne on whose wings each heavy sot can pierce
The limits of the boundless universe.
So charming ointments make an old witch fly,
And bear a crippled carcass through the sky.
'Tis this exalted power, whose business lies
In nonsense, and impossibilities,
This made a whimsical philosopher*   90
Before the spacious world his tub prefer;
And we have modern cloistered coxcombs who
Retire to think, 'cause they have nought to do.
But thoughts are given for actions' government:
Where action ceases, thought's impertinent:
Our sphere of action is life's happiness,
And he who thinks beyond, thinks like an ass.
Thus, whilst against false reasoning I inveigh,
I own right reason, which I would obey:*
That reason that distinguishes by sense,   100
And gives us rules of good and ill from thence:
That bounds desires with a reforming will,
To keep 'em more in vigour, not to kill.
Your reason hinders, mine helps to enjoy,
Renewing appetites yours would destroy.
My reason is my friend, yours is a cheat;
Hunger calls out, my reason bids me eat;
Perversely, yours your appetite does mock,
This asks for food, that answers, 'What's o' clock?'
This plain distinction, Sir, your doubt secures: 110
'Tis not true reason I despise, but yours.
Thus I think reason righted; but for man,
I'll ne'er recant; defend him if you can.

For all his pride, and his philosophy,
'Tis evident, beasts are in their degree
As wise at least, and better far than he.
Those creatures are the wisest who attain,
By surest means, the ends at which they aim.
If therefore Jowler finds and kills his hares,*
Better than Meres supplies committee chairs,* 120
Though one's a statesman, th' other but a hound,
Jowler, in justice, would be wiser found.
You see how far man's wisdom here extends;
Look next, if human nature makes amends,
Whose principles most generous are, and just,
And to whose morals you would sooner trust.
Be judge yourself, I'll bring it to the test:
Which is the basest creature: man, or beast?
Birds feed on birds, beasts on each other prey,
But savage man alone does man betray: 130
Pressed by necessity, they kill for food,
Man undoes man to do himself no good.
With teeth and claws by Nature armed they hunt
Nature's allowance to supply their want.
But man, with smiles, embraces, friendships, praise,
Unhumanly his fellow's life betrays;
With voluntary pains works his distress,
Not through necessity, but wantonness.
For hunger, or for love, they fight or tear,
Whilst wretched man is still in arms for fear; 140
For fear he arms, and is of arms afraid,
By fear to fear successively betrayed:
Base fear, the source whence his best passions came,
His boasted honour, and his dear-bought fame.
That lust of power, to which he's such a slave,
And for the which alone he dares be brave;
To which his various projects are designed,
Which makes him generous, affable, and kind:
For which he takes such pains to be thought wise,
And screws his actions in a forced disguise; 150
Leading a tedious life in misery,
Under laborious, mean hypocrisy:

Look to the bottom of his vast design,
Wherein man's wisdom, power, and glory join;
The good he acts, the ill he does endure,
'Tis all for fear, to make himself secure.
Merely for safety after fame we thirst,
For all men would be cowards if they durst.
And honesty's against all common sense:
Men must be knaves, 'tis in their own defence.   160
Mankind's dishonest; if you think it fair,
Amongst known cheats, to play upon the square,
You'll be undone——
Nor can weak truth your reputation save:
The knaves will all agree to call you knave.
Wronged shall he live, insulted o'er, oppressed,
Who dares be less a villain than the rest.
Thus, Sir, you see what human nature craves,
Most men are cowards, all men should be knaves:
The difference lies (as far as I can see)   170
Not in the thing itself, but the degree;
And all the subject matter of debate,
Is only, who's a knave of the first rate?

All this with indignation have I hurled
At the pretending part of the proud world;
Who, swoll'n with selfish vanity, devise ⎫
False freedoms, holy cheats, and formal lies ⎬
Over their fellow slaves to tyrannize. ⎭
But if in court so just a man there be,
(In court a just man, yet unknown to me)   180
Who does his needful flattery direct
Not to oppress and ruin, but protect—
Since flattery, which way so ever laid,
Is still a tax on that unhappy trade—
If so upright a statesman you can find,
Whose passions bend to his unbiased mind,*
Who does his arts and policies apply
To raise his country, not his family;
Nor while his pride owned avarice withstands,*
Receives close bribes from friends' corrupted hands.   190

Is there a churchman who on God relies?
Whose life his faith and doctrine justifies?*
Not one blown up with vain prelatic pride,
Who for reproof of sins does man deride;*
Whose envious heart makes preaching a pretence,⎫
With his obstreperous, saucy eloquence,   ⎬
To chide at kings, and rail at men of sense; ⎭
Who from his pulpit vents more peevish lies,
More bitter railings, scandals, calumnies,
Than at a gossiping are thrown about,   200
When the good wives get drunk, and then fall out:
None of that sensual tribe, whose talents lie
In avarice, pride, sloth, and gluttony;
Who hunt good livings, but abhor good lives,⎫ *
Whose lust exalted to that height arrives   ⎬
They act adultery with their own wives;   ⎭
And ere a score of years completed be,⎫
Can from the lofty pulpit proudly see ⎬
Half a large parish their own progeny: ⎭
Nor doting bishop who would be adored   210
For domineering at the council board;
A greater fop in business at fourscore,
Fonder of serious toys, affected more
Than the gay, glittering fool at twenty proves,
With all his noise, his tawdry clothes, and loves:
But a meek, humble man, of modest sense,
Who preaching peace, does practise continence;
Whose pious life's a proof he does believe
Mysterious truths, which no man can conceive:*
If upon earth there dwell such Godlike men,   220
I'll here recant my paradox to them,*
Adore those shrines of virtue, homage pay,
And with the rabble world their laws obey.
If such there are, yet grant me this at least,
Man differs more from man, than man from beast.

84 *Upon Nothing*

JOHN WILMOT, EARL OF ROCHESTER

Written before 1678. The capitalization of this text attempts to signal the personifications which are implicit in some (but not all) of Rochester's abstract nouns.

1

Nothing, thou elder brother ev'n to Shade,
Thou hadst a being ere the world was made,
And, well fixed, art alone of ending not afraid.

2

Ere Time and Place were, Time and Place were not,
When primitive Nothing Something straight begot,
Then all proceeded from the great united What.

3

Something, the general attribute of all,
Severed from thee, its sole original,
Into thy boundless self must undistinguished fall.

4

Yet Something did thy mighty power command,   10
And from thy fruitful emptiness's hand
Snatched men, beasts, birds, fire, water, air and land.

5

Matter, the wicked'st offspring of thy race,
By Form assisted, flew from thy embrace,
And rebel Light obscured thy reverend dusky face.

6

With Form and Matter, Time and Place did join,
Body, thy foe, with these did leagues combine,
To spoil thy peaceful realm, and ruin all thy line.

7

But turncoat Time assists the foe in vain,
And bribed by thee destroys their short-lived reign,   20
And to thy hungry womb drives back thy slaves again.

8

Though mysteries are barred from laic eyes,
And the divine alone with warrant pries
Into thy bosom, where thy truth in private lies;

9

Yet this of thee the wise may freely say:
Thou from the virtuous nothing tak'st away,
And to be part of thee the wicked wisely pray.

10

Great Negative, how vainly would the wise
Enquire, define, distinguish, teach, devise,
Didst thou not stand to point their dull philosophies.   30

11

Is, or Is Not, the two great ends of Fate,
And true or false, the subject of debate,
That pèrfect or destroy the vast designs of state;

12

When they have racked the politician's breast,
Within thy bosom most securely rest,
And when reduced to thee are least unsafe, and best.

13

But, Nothing, why does Something still permit
That sacred monarchs should at council sit
With persons highly thought, at best, for nothing fit;

14

Whilst weighty something modestly abstains   40
From princes' coffers, and from statesmen's brains,
And nothing there, like stately Nothing, reigns?

15

Nothing, who dwell'st with fools in grave disguise,
For whom they reverend shapes and forms devise,
Lawn-sleeves, and furs, and gowns, when they like
   thee look wise.*

16

French truth, Dutch prowess, British policy,
Hibernian learning, Scotch civility,
Spaniards' dispatch, Danes' wit, are mainly seen in thee.

17

The great man's gratitude to his best friend,
Kings' promises, whores' vows, towards thee they bend,   50
Flow swiftly into thee, and in thee ever end.

85   *From Seneca, Troades, Act II, Chorus*

JOHN WILMOT, EARL OF ROCHESTER

Written before 1675. Rochester translates ll. 397–408 of Seneca's play
Troades.

After death, nothing is, and nothing death,*
The utmost limits of a gasp of breath:
Let the ambitious zealot lay aside
His hopes of heaven (whose faith is but his pride);
   Let slavish souls lay by their fear,
   Nor be concerned which way, nor where,
   After this life they shall be hurled;
Dead, we become the lumber of the world,
And to that mass of matter shall be swept,
Where things destroyed with things unborn are kept.   10
   Devouring time swallows us whole,
Impartial death confounds body and soul.
   For hell, and the foul fiend that rules
   God's everlasting fiery gaols,
   Devised by rogues, dreaded by fools,

With his grim, grisly dog that keeps the door,*
   Are senseless stories, idle tales,
   Dreams, whimsies, and no more.

86   From *Palamon and Arcite*, Book III

JOHN DRYDEN

This is Dryden's free translation of Chaucer's *The Knight's Tale*, published in *Fables Ancient and Modern* (1700). Arcite has defeated his friend
Palamon in a tournament held to decide which of them should marry
Emily, but he is immediately killed in an accident. In the present passage,
near the end of the poem, King Theseus offers a consolatory vision of
universal harmony, and ends by proposing that the grief of Palamon and
Emily be assuaged by their marriage. The passage expands considerably
on Chaucer's original.

The cause and spring of motion, from above*
Hung down on earth the golden chain of love;
Great was th' effect, and high was his intent,
When peace among the jarring seeds he sent:
Fire, flood, and earth, and air, by this were bound,
And love, the common link, the new creation crowned.
The chain still holds; for, though the forms decay,   1030
Eternal matter never wears away:
The same first mover certain bounds has placed,
How long those perishable forms shall last;
Nor can they last beyond the time assigned
By that all-seeing, and all-making mind:
Shorten their hours they may, for will is free,
But never pass th' appointed destiny.
So men oppressed, when weary of their breath,
Throw off the burden, and suborn their death.
Then, since those forms begin and have their end,   1040
On some unaltered cause they sure depend:
Parts of the whole are we, but God the whole,
Who gives us life, and animating soul.
For nature cannot from a part derive
That being, which the whole can only give:

He, perfect, stable; but imperfect we,
Subject to change, and different in degree:
Plants, beasts, and man; and, as our organs are,
We more or less of his perfection share.
But by a long descent the ethereal fire   1050
Corrupts; and forms, the mortal part, expire.
As he withdraws his virtue, so they pass,
And the same matter makes another mass.
This law th' omniscient power was pleased to give,
That every kind should by succession live;
That individuals die his will ordains;
The propagated species still remains.
The monarch oak, the patriarch of the trees,
Shoots rising up, and spreads by slow degrees;
Three centuries he grows, and three he stays,   1060
Supreme in state, and in three more decays:
So wears the paving pebble in the street,
And towns and towers their fatal periods meet.
So rivers, rapid once, now naked lie,
Forsaken of their springs, and leave their channels dry:
So man, at first a drop, dilates with heat,
Then formed, the little heart begins to beat;
Secret he feeds, unknowing in the cell;
At length, for hatching ripe, he breaks the shell,
And struggles into breath, and cries for aid;   1070
Then helpless in his mother's lap is laid.
He creeps, he walks, and issuing into man,
Grudges their life from whence his own began.
Reckless of laws, affects to rule alone,
Anxious to reign, and restless on the throne;
First vegetive, then feels, and reasons last;
Rich of three souls, and lives all three to waste.*
Some thus, but thousands more in flower of age,*
For few arrive to run the latter stage.
Sunk in the first, in battle some are slain,   1080
And others whelmed beneath the stormy main.
What makes all this, but Jupiter the king,
At whose command we perish, and we spring?
Then 'tis our best, since thus ordained to die,

To make a virtue of necessity;
Take what he gives, since to rebel is vain:
The bad grows better, which we well sustain.
And could we choose the time, and choose aright,
'Tis best to die, our honour at the height,
When we have done our ancestors no shame,   1090
But served our friends, and well secured our fame:
Then should we wish our happy life to close,
And leave no more for Fortune to dispose.
So should we make our death a glad relief
From future shame, from sickness, and from grief;
Enjoying while we live the present hour,
And dying in our excellence and flower.
Then round our deathbed every friend should run,
And joy us of our conquest early won;
While the malicious world, with envious tears,   1100
Should grudge our happy end, and wish it theirs.
Since then our Arcite is with honour dead,
Why should we mourn that he so soon is freed,
Or call untimely what the gods decreed?
With grief as just a friend may be deplored
From a foul prison to free air restored.
Ought he to thank his kinsman or his wife,
Could tears recall him into wretched life?
Their sorrow hurts themselves, on him is lost,
And, worse than both, offends his happy ghost.   1110
What then remains, but after past annoy,
To take the good vicissitude of joy;
To thank the gracious gods for what they give,
Possess our souls, and while we live, to live?
Ordain we then two sorrows to combine,
And in one point th' extremes of grief to join;
That thence resulting joy may be renewed,
As jarring notes in harmony conclude.

EXPLANATORY NOTES

7 *Edward Hyde, Earl of Clarendon, From 'The History of the Rebellion and Civil Wars in England' and 'The Life of Edward, Earl of Clarendon'*: other contemporary views of Charles I (1600–49) and Oliver Cromwell (1599–1658) are collected in *Characters from the Histories and Memoirs of the Seventeenth Century*, ed. David Nichol Smith (1918). Text from *Selections from Clarendon*, ed. G. Huehns (1995).

8 *archbishop of Canterbury . . . Mr Chillingworth*: William Laud (1573–1645), archbishop from 1633, promoter of ecclesiastical discipline and High Church liturgical reform; executed by Parliament. William Chillingworth (1602–44), friend of Clarendon, author of *The Religion of Protestants a Safe Way to Salvation* (1638).

9 *Pericles*: (*c.*495–429 BCE), Athenian statesman.

Nerva: Marcus Cocceius Nerva (*c.*35–98 CE), Roman Emperor 96–8 CE. Tacitus (*Agricola* 3) remarked that his rule combined two incompatible elements, *imperium et libertas*, 'imperial rule and liberty'.

10 *O fortunati . . . norint!*: 'O excessively happy, if only they knew their blessings!' (Virgil, *Georgics*, ii. 458).

15 *quos . . . laudent*: 'whom even his enemies could not criticize unless they also praised him' (Pliny, *Epistles*, III. xii. 4).

ausum . . . possent: 'he dared what no good man would dare to do; he accomplished what could be accomplished by no one except the strongest' (Velleius Paterculus, ii. 24).

17 *Machiavel's method*: set out by the Florentine statesman Niccolò dei Machiavelli (1469–1527) in *Il Principe*.

18 *Samuel Pepys, [The Return of Charles II] from the 'Diary'*: Pepys's account of Charles II's escape after the Battle of Worcester (1651), from a narrative dictated to him by the King in 1680, was edited by W. Matthews in *Charles II's Escape* (1966).

23 *et mirabile in oculis nostris*: 'and marvellous in our eyes' (Matthew 21: 42).

Iam . . . regna: 'now the virgin [Astraea] returns, the kingdom of Saturn returns' (Virgil, *Eclogue* iv. 6).

24 *ambitious Swede*: Charles X had invaded Poland and Denmark; he died in February 1660, leaving his country in the hands of a minor.

France and Spain: the war between France and Spain had ended in 1659, and peace was sealed by the wedding of Louis XIV to Maria Theresa in June 1660.

sacred purple . . . scarlet gown: dress of bishops and peers.

sanguine dye to elephants: blood-red juice provokes elephants to fight in Maccabees 6: 34.

24 *Typhoeus*: when he attacked Mount Olympus the gods fled to Egypt.

Cyclops: one-eyed monster blinded by Odysseus (Homer, *Odyssey*, ix. 375–97).

25 *Otho*: Galba, Emperor of Rome 68–9 CE, adopted Piso as his heir instead of the effeminate Otho. Otho revolted, had Galba and Piso murdered, and briefly gained power before being defeated and committing suicide.

Worcester: Charles II had been defeated at the Battle of Worcester in 1651 in an attempt to gain the throne.

banished David: see 2 Samuel 15–21. For the comparison of Charles II with the biblical King David see Dryden's *Absalom and Achitophel* (8).

26 *grandsire*: Henri IV of France (1553–1610), who extended the powers of the crown, and restored prosperity to the country. A Protestant, he was opposed by the Catholic League. Dryden suggests a parallel with the Puritan Solemn League and Covenant (1643).

chronicles: a perfect rhyme with 'ease' in Restoration pronunciation.

Portunus: the Roman god of harbours.

27 *Prince of Peace*: title for the Messiah from Isaiah 9: 6.

Booth: Sir George Booth led an abortive rising for Charles in 1659.

Monck: General George Monck (1608–70), later Duke of Albemarle, was instrumental in effecting the Restoration by leading the republic's army from Scotland to London in January 1660; he recalled Parliament, which proclaimed Charles King on 8 May.

28 *Legion*: the devil in Luke 8: 26–36.

Sforza: Lodovico Sforza (1451–1508) poisoned his nephew and succeeded him as Duke of Milan, but was betrayed by his own mercenaries to Louis XII of France, and died a prisoner.

29 *helots*: the Spartans would sometimes make their slaves (helots) drunk and exhibit them to their young men to show them the evil of drunkenness.

Batavia: Holland.

Scheveline: Charles embarked from Sheveling (now Scheveningen) near The Hague.

Naseby: the ships' republican names were replaced with royalist ones: see 4.

halcyon: legend says that for the seven days in winter when these birds nest at sea, the winds are still.

30 *Amphitrite*: wife of Neptune, and goddess of the sea (four syllables).

submitted fasces: fasces were bundles of axes and rods carried by the Roman lictors as symbols of office; when the consul Publius Valerius appeared before the people he told the lictors to walk with lowered fasces (*submissis fascibus*: Livy ii. 7) to acknowledge their superior authority.

to Moses: Exodus 33: 19–34: 10.

32 *Andrew Marvell, From 'Last Instructions to a Painter'*: first printed in *Poems on Affairs of State*, Part III (1689). Text from Bodleian Library MS Eng. Poet. d. 49.

33 *Aeolus*: god of the winds.

Spragge: Vice-Admiral Sir Edward Spragge, in command at Sheerness.

Chatham: where the naval arsenal was located.

34 *chain*: a defensive chain had been stretched across the river.

Monck: General George Monck, Duke of Albemarle (see n. to p. 27).

Cornbury: Henry Hyde, Lord Cornbury, son of Edward Hyde, Earl of Clarendon.

Duncombe ... Legge: Sir John Duncombe, Commissioner of the Ordnance; William Legge, Lieutenant-General of the Ordnance.

Royal Charles: the flagship ('admiral': l. 615) of the English fleet, which had carried Charles II from Holland in 1660 (see 3); she had been captured by the Dutch.

35 *Daniel*: Sir Thomas Daniel, in charge of the defences.

Shadrack, Meschack, and Abednego: see Daniel 3.

37 *Oeta and Alcides*: Hercules ('Alcides') intended to immolate himself on a pyre on top of Mt. Oeta, but was taken up to heaven.

Gambo: Gambia, the west coast of Africa, known as the 'gold coast'.

Ruperts: Prince Rupert was one of the naval commanders.

38 *the feared Hebrew*: Samson.

John Wilmot, Earl of Rochester, [A Satire on Charles II]: the manuscripts preserve widely different versions of the poem, in which the wording and order of the lines vary; this was probably due in part to the poem being memorized and passed on orally, since the possession of written copies could have been dangerous. Five representative versions are printed in *Works*, ed. Harold Love (1999), 85–90. Text from *Selected Poems*, ed. Paul Hammond (1982), based on Bodleian MS Rawl. D. 924.

40 *John Dryden, 'Absalom and Achitophel'*: full annotation for this richly allusive poem is provided in *The Poems of John Dryden*, ed. Paul Hammond and David Hopkins (1995–), i. 444–532. Text from the first edition (1681), but incorporating within square brackets minor revisions and two additional passages (ll. 180–91 and 957–60, softening the satire on Shaftesbury and Monmouth) which Dryden included in the second edition later that year.

Israel's monarch: King David, here Charles II. Charles had fourteen acknowledged illegitimate children by several mistresses, but no legitimate offspring.

Michal: Charles's queen, Catharine of Braganza.

41 *Annabel*: Anne, Countess of Buccleuch, married Monmouth in 1663.

41 *Amnon's murder*: either the murder of a beadle by Monmouth and others in a brothel in 1671, or a non-fatal attack by Monmouth's horseguards in 1670 on Sir John Coventry, who had referred in the Commons to the king's sexual interest in actresses.

42 *Saul . . . Ishbosheth*: Oliver Cromwell and his son Richard, who briefly succeeded him.

Good Old Cause: the Commonwealth.

Jebusites: Roman Catholics.

43 *Jewish rabbins*: Anglican theologians.

plot: the Popish Plot: see 9.

Egyptian: French Catholic. The subsequent allusion is to the Roman Catholic doctrine of transubstantiation (that the bread and wine in the mass are turned into the actual physical body and blood of Christ, rather than being symbols of his presence); this was the single most important doctrinal difference between Catholics and Protestants at this period.

45 *triple bond*: the Triple Alliance between England, Holland, and Sweden, formed in 1668 and ended in 1670 by the secret Treaty of Dover, which allied England with France.

patriot: the rhetoric of patriotism was deployed by the Whigs in their claim to be defending the country against Catholic subversion and arbitrary government. Dryden regards this language as specious, here and at ll. 965–73.

46 *cloudy pillar . . . guardian fire*: the Israelites were led through the wilderness by a pillar of cloud by day and fire by night; when they came to the Red Sea, Moses held up his rod and divided the waters (Exodus 13–14).

47 *Pharaoh*: Louis XIV (1638–1715), King of France ('Egypt' in l. 283).

49 *arbitrary sway*: the Whigs alleged that Charles was intending to introduce 'arbitrary' (i.e. autocratic, absolutist) rule along the lines of Louis XIV's government—and perhaps with his military assistance.

50 *Sanhedrin*: the highest court of justice in Jerusalem; here, Parliament.

51 *when resumed . . . . just*: i.e. when the people take back the power which they had entrusted to a ruler, he no longer has any just claim to it.

52 *Perhaps his fear . . . control*: i.e. perhaps Charles's fear of James may be restraining the natural affection arising from his kinship to Monmouth.

53 *Solymæan rout*: London rabble (*Solymæan* means 'of Jerusalem'). The Whigs were skilful at manipulating popular demonstrations, and crowds were important elements in the politics of the Popish Plot and Exclusion Crisis.

Levites: Jewish priests (descendants of Aaron: l. 525); here, the Nonconformist clergy.

54 *dominion . . . grace*: these radical Protestant ministers seek to gain power by claiming that they alone possess 'grace'—the power of the Holy Spirit—which authorizes their actions.

Zimri: George Villiers, Duke of Buckingham (1628–87); former chief minister after the fall of Clarendon; minor poet; author of the play *The Rehearsal* (1671) which satirized Dryden's heroic plays. There are two biblical Zimris: (*a*) in Numbers 25 Zimri takes a Midianite mistress (cf. Buckingham's notorious affair with the Countess of Shrewsbury); (*b*) in 1 Kings 16 Zimri is the king's servant, but rebels and kills him.

55 *Balaam ... Caleb*: the Earl of Huntingdon, and either the Earl of Essex or Lord Grey of Warke.

Nadab: Lord Howard of Escrick. Imprisoned in the Tower for sedition, he is said to have taken the sacrament in lamb's wool (hot ale mixed with roasted apples) instead of wine.

Jonas: Sir William Jones, who as an MP promoted the Exclusion Bills.

Shimei: Slingsby Bethel (1617–97), merchant and London sheriff. Sheriffs were responsible for selecting juries, and during the Exclusion Crisis this was often done with a political bias (see ll. 606–9). The biblical Shimei cursed King David (2 Samuel 16).

sons of Belial: biblical term for rebels and false witnesses.

56 *Rechabite*: the Rechabites drank no wine (Jeremiah 35).

Corah: Titus Oates, whose false allegations in the Popish Plot had condemned many innocent men to death (see 9 and 74). The biblical Corah rebelled against the authority of Moses and Aaron, and the earth swallowed him (Numbers 16). Unfortunately the parallel is incomplete in that respect.

57 *Agag's murder*: probably alluding to reports that Oates had called the Duke of York a traitor who should be hanged. The biblical reference is to 1 Samuel 15.

58 *Hybla*: town in Sicily, famous for its honey.

Egypt and Tyrus: France and Holland.

Bathsheba: Louise de Keroualle, mistress of Charles II.

59 *From east to west*: Monmouth made a triumphal progress from London through the West Country in July and August 1680, in defiance of Charles's orders. He was entertained by Thomas Thynne of Longleat, Wiltshire, a wealthy Whig ('Issachar' in l. 738).

60 *What shall we think?*: in this passage, Dryden examines the principal political theories underlying the Exclusion Crisis:

ll. 759–64: the Whig claim that the rights of the people need to be safeguarded against the threat of arbitrary government represented by James.

ll. 765–76: the Whig argument that kings are only entrusted with power by the people, who may resume it at will; Dryden argues that all succeeding generations are bound by the original establishment of government as inexorably as they are implicated in the original sin of Adam.

ll. 777–94: the Whig argument that no man can be secure and free in a system where sovereign power is the birthright of one man; Dryden counters that if the king can be deprived of his right, then no man's rights are secure.

ll. 795–810: Dryden appeals for peace: to change a settled mode of government risks destroying it completely.

60 *Which flowing . . . out*: i.e. which fluctuates like the tides.

mark: high-water mark.

61 *ark*: the ark of the covenant, containing the stone tablets of the law; it was death to touch it (1 Chronicles 13).

Barzillai: James Butler, Duke of Ormonde (1610–88), Lord Lieutenant of Ireland under both Charles I and Charles II. Seven of his eight sons had died by this date (ll. 829–30), including his eldest, Thomas, Earl of Ossory (ll. 831–53), who had fought for the Dutch against France (ll. 842–3).

62 *Zadok*: William Sancroft (1617–93), Archbishop of Canterbury. See 2 Samuel 15.

Sagan: Jewish high priest's deputy; here, Henry Compton, Bishop of London, son of the Earl of Northampton.

63 *Adriel*: John Sheffield, Earl of Mulgrave (1648–1721), minor poet, and literary patron of Dryden, amongst others.

Jotham: George Saville, Marquis of Halifax (1633–95), a former associate of Shaftesbury, who opposed the Exclusion Bill in the Lords.

Hushai: Laurence Hyde, Earl of Rochester of the second creation; son of the Earl of Clarendon; First Lord of the Treasury.

Amiel: Edward Seymour, descendant of the first Duke of Somerset; as Speaker of the House of Commons 1673–8 he managed business to the advantage of the court, unlike his successor William Williams, Speaker 1680–1 (ll. 908–11).

unequal ruler: Phaëton, son of Apollo, persuaded his father to let him drive the chariot of the sun across the sky for one day. He was unable to control it, and was on the verge of destroying the earth when Jupiter killed him with a thunderbolt.

65 *Samson*: Monmouth. See Judges 16.

Esau . . . Jacob: Jacob tricked his blind father Isaac into giving him the blessing and birthright due to his brother Esau, by covering his hands and neck with goatskin to make them feel like Esau's hairy skin: Genesis 27.

66 *look on grace . . . die*: Moses was allowed to see only the back of God, not his face: Exodus 33.

viper-like: the viper's young were thought to eat their way out of their mother's belly.

67 *cropped*: criminals sometimes had their ears cropped in the pillory.

tongue: alluding to his crony Israel Tongue, who made the earliest allegations in the Popish Plot.

68 *b——y*: readers might interpret this variously as 'blasphemy', 'bawdy', or 'buggery'.

B——l's: unidentified. Bethel? Belial? (For these see notes to p. 55.)

library: an eclectic collection: chapbooks recounting the adventures of notorious rogues; the works of Whig publishers of propaganda; and Hobbes's *Leviathan* (1651), included here probably as a supposedly atheistic text.

c——: probably 'city', since London was a Whig stronghold.

marks of the beast: see Revelation 13–14; the beast was identified by Protestants with the papacy.

69 *Gargantua ... Pantagruel*: grotesque characters in Rabelais's books (1532–4).

New Troy: a medieval name for London.

Bridewell ... Newgate ... King's College: London prisons (the latter being King's Bench), as is 'the Counter' later.

70 *party per pale*: divided down the middle (heraldic term).

save the parish harmless: make sure that the parish will not have to foot the bill for the orphan.

71 *Hungarian*: alluding to the Hungarian Count Teckely, supposed to be a hero of the Whigs for his revolt against the Austrian government which was persecuting his fellow-Protestants.

Multa cadunt: many things fall.

the Observator: a Tory paper published by Sir Roger L' Estrange.

Latona: Roman goddess of childbirth.

Cellier: Elizabeth Cellier, a midwife who visited prisoners in Newgate; she was tried and acquitted for alleged involvement in the Popish Plot.

Sir Thomas: Sir Thomas Player, chamberlain of London and MP; he inflamed fears of a Popish Plot by saying that citizens might expect to wake in the morning and find their throats cut.

Minerva ... Jupiter: Minerva was born from the head of Jupiter.

73 *Portsmouth, Cleveland, and Mazarin*: the king's mistresses, Louise de Keroualle, Duchess of Portsmouth; Barbara Villiers, Duchess of Cleveland; and Hortense, Duchess Mazarin.

Arthur Mainwaring, 'Tarquin and Tullia': text based on British Library MS Add. 29497.

like vipers: see note to p. 66.

74 *pagan priest*: Gilbert Burnet (1643–1715), confidant of William of Orange in Holland before his invasion of England; rewarded with the see of

Salisbury. Dryden draws a composite portrait of Burnet and William as 'the Buzzard' in *The Hind and the Panther* (1687), iii. 1121–33.

74 *passive*: advocating passive obedience (i.e. non-resistance) to the king.

poisoned . . . abroad: alluding to rumours that James II had poisoned his brother Charles II, and was plotting to establish Catholicism in England with foreign military assistance.

son: James II's son, Prince James Francis Edward (1688–1766), was suspected by Whigs to be supposititious.

75 *captain of the guards*: John Churchill, later Duke of Marlborough (1650–1722), was captain of James's horseguards. His wife, Sarah, was a confidante of James's daughter Princess Anne ('the younger Tullia').

79 *thy vaunted sire*: Achilles, who had killed Priam's son Hector.

80 *Marcellus*: Marcus Claudius Marcellus (d. 208 BCE), a distinguished Roman general who served in the first Punic War against Carthage. He also campaigned against the Gauls, and killed their leader in single combat; arms captured in this way were dedicated to Jupiter Feretrius. The youth whom Aeneas sees next is Marcus Claudius Marcellus (42–23 BCE), potential heir to Augustus, whose premature death was widely mourned. Dryden compares Oldham with Marcellus in 33.

83 *those gardens . . . spouse*: the gardens of Adonis (Spenser, *The Faerie Queene*, III. vi); of Alcinous, who was host to Odysseus, son of Laertes (Homer, *Odyssey*, vii); and of Solomon, where he entertained the Queen of Sheba (Song of Solomon 6: 2).

88 *John Oldham, 'A Satire in Imitation of the Third of Juvenal'*: text from *Poems*, ed. Brooks and Selden.

Hundreds: an unhealthy coastal area of Essex.

89 *Mile End*: in the east end of London, where the Whigs had held a provocative banquet in April 1682.

Timon: the misanthrope of Shakespeare's *Timon of Athens*, adapted by Shadwell in 1678; also featured in a satire of that name (1674) sometimes attributed to Rochester.

Morecraft: the money-lender in Beaumont and Fletcher's *The Scornful Lady* (1616).

90 *Sir Sidrophel*: the astrologer in Samuel Butler's poem *Hudibras* (1662–78).

Gadbury: John Gadbury, a contemporary astrologer and writer of almanacs.

Scotch voyage: the Duke of York had lost £30,000 worth of furniture and plate when the *Gloucester*, in which he was sailing to Edinburgh, sank in May 1682.

91 *great Harry*: Henry V, who defeated the French at Agincourt.

Chedreux perruques: periwigs by Chedreux of Paris.

either Haynes: Jo Haynes the comic actor; Brian Haynes, the Irish witness who gave perjured evidence in the Popish Plot trials, changing sides according to who paid him.

pyramid . . . Aston: obscure, but Harold Brooks suggests a reference to a project involving Francis Aston (Secretary of the Royal Society) and the Monument to the Fire of London, sometimes known as the pyramid.

92 *statute*: private Act of Parliament naturalizing an alien.

Sir Martin Mar-all: in Dryden's play of that name (1668) the protagonist 'sings like a screech owl', and so when he wishes to serenade his mistress he has his servant sing from a concealed position while he mimes the song. The ruse fails when Mar-all continues miming after the music finishes.

Prynne . . . Vicars: William Prynne and John Vicars, Puritan versifiers.

eighty: eighty degrees north, the latitude of northern Greenland.

93 *silk weavers' mutiny*: in August 1681 English silk weavers attacked French weavers in London, broke up their equipment, and vandalized their houses. The French weavers were refugees who had fled the increasing persecution of Huguenots (Protestants) in France.

94 *he . . . Or t' other*: Noah (Genesis 6–9) and Lot (Genesis 19).

at prison-grates hung out: hung out of the bars of a cell in order to collect alms.

proverb: bastards were proverbially associated with prosperity and pride.

95 *leather buckets*: leather buckets for use in fire-fighting were commonly kept in churches.

wear woollen in the grave: to help the wool industry, it was a legal requirement for bodies to be buried in woollen shrouds.

96 *tombs and Tower*: the royal tombs in Westminster Abbey, and the menagerie at the Tower of London.

old Noll: the death of Cromwell in September 1658 coincided with a storm.

bells rung backward: as an alarm signal (starting with the deepest bell and ending with the highest).

Pordage: Samuel Pordage, unsuccessful playwright and poet.

Vatican: Vatican Library, probably the largest library at this date.

97 *Act, Commencement*: Ceremonies at Oxford and Cambridge respectively for the conferment of master's and doctor's degrees.

term: law term.

Mortlake: where tapestries were manufactured.

98 *College . . . bills*: the College of Physicians, and the weekly bills of mortality, listing deaths from various causes.

Archer: probably John Archer, justice of Common Pleas, who disliked long trials.

99 *Preston*: Brooks identifies him as Christopher Preston, keeper of a bear-garden.

100 *Heptarchy*: seven kingdoms into which the country was thought to have been divided in Saxon times.

Tyburn: where the gallows stood.

101 *John Wilmot, Earl of Rochester, 'A Letter from Artemisa in the Town to Chloe in the Country'*: text from *Selected Poems*, ed. Hammond, based on Bodleian Library MS Don. b. 8.

Bedlam has many mansions: Bedlam was the London lunatic asylum; the phrasing alludes to John 14: 2.

stand on thorns: proverbial expression for impatience.

102 *hate restraint . . . infamy*: i.e. 'hate chastity, if only because they wish to be infamous'.

Fashions . . . strike: i.e. 'fashions come to replace true taste, and people go for appearance rather than substance'.

103 *Bovey*: Sir Ralph Bovey, notoriously ugly.

Embarrassée: like the French words in the following lines, this was a recent import into English. The use of French terms was a hallmark of fashionable discourse: Melantha in Dryden's *Marriage A-la-Mode* (1673) collects French vocabulary.

Indian Queen: alluding to the play *The Indian Queen* (1665) by Dryden and Sir Robert Howard.

104 *Japan*: the source of the most remote luxuries.

105 *fond to be thought lewd*: foolishly eager to acquire a reputation as a rake.

Foster . . . Nokes: Foster was a woman who passed herself off as one of high social station (see Rochester, *Letters*, p. 71). A 'Nokes' was a fool, a name derived from the comic actor James Nokes.

Betty Morris: a prostitute.

106 *Mantua gown*: a loose upper garment.

107 *libels none*: many verse libels or lampoons did circulate, denouncing women who had been 'kind' (sexually available); some are collected in *Court Satires of the Restoration*, ed. John Harold Wilson (1976).

Then . . . health: it is not clear whether ll. 236–9 report the squire's words to Corinna, or hers to him.

108 *John Wilmot, Earl of Rochester, 'To the Postboy'*: text from *Selected Poems*, ed. Hammond, based on British Library MS Harley 6914.

Bacchus: god of wine.

And bravely left . . . dead: alluding to a brawl at Epsom on 17 June 1676 when Rochester and his companions tossed in a blanket some fiddlers who refused to play for them. In the following skirmish with the watch, Rochester drew his sword on a constable; his friend Capt. Downs who tried to stop him was run through by a pike and killed. Rochester and his companions ran off.

Anonymous, 'Régime de vivre': text from *Poems on Several Occasions by . . . the E. of R——* (1680).

Régime de vivre: rule of life (French). Title taken from manuscript copies; the 1680 edition calls it 'Song'.

109 *Sir Philip Wodehouse, 'A Satirical Flash'*: text from Leeds University Library, Brotherton Collection, MS Lt 40, previously unpublished. The present text selects from amongst several revisions and alternative readings.

Facit indignatio versum: 'Indignation makes verse' (Juvenal, *Satire* i. 790).

O tempora! O mores!: 'O times! O manners!' (Cicero, *In Catilinam*, i. 1).

110 *bard of Malmesbury*: Thomas Hobbes (1588–1679), born in Malmesbury. His materialist and mechanist philosophy (set out most clearly in *Leviathan* (1651)) was often said in the Restoration period to be an encouragement or pretext for atheism and libertinism.

Galateus: sixteenth-century Italian treatise on morals and manners by J. Casa, translated into English in 1701.

Rhadamanth: Rhadamanthus was the ruler of the classical underworld or hell.

111 *John Bunyan, [Vanity Fair] from 'The Pilgrim's Progress'*: the present text omits the marginal notes, which are mostly summaries of the narrative and biblical references.

Beelzebub, Apollyon, and Legion: names of devils.

112 *The Prince . . . through the town*: Matthew 4: 1–10.

they . . . spoke the language of Canaan: i.e. the pilgrims spoke the language of the Promised Land.

113 *Turn . . . vanity*: Psalm 119: 37.

117 *There was also an Act made . . . lions' den*: see Exodus 1: 22, Daniel 3 and 6.

119 *Mitchell*: Betty Mitchell, with whom Pepys enjoyed an amorous relationship.

123 *Mercer*: Mary Mercer, companion to Pepys's wife Elizabeth.

125 *gates*: of Woolwich dockyard.

128 *Bullen . . . St Ellen's*: Boulogne; St Helen's road, off the Isle of Wight.

General: George Monck, Duke of Albemarle (see note to p. 27).

first time: since the start of the fire.

129 *the simplicity of my Lord Mayor*: Sir Thomas Bludworth, Lord Mayor of London 1665–6, initially underestimated the severity of the fire, refusing to order the destruction of houses to check its spread, and saying that 'a woman might piss it out' (Pepys, *Diary*, vii. 280n).

Each element . . . down: i.e. England, victorious on water, is now laid low by fire. Fire, air, earth, and water were thought to be the four elements.

129 *Cum mare . . . OVID*: Jove, about to hurl his thunderbolts at the world, remembers that it is fated that a time will come 'when sea and land, the royal palace of heaven will catch fire and burn' (Ovid, *Metamorphoses*, i. 257–8).

131 *Like crafty . . . accenderet*: 'She handled the longing man with skill, so as to fire his heart by his failure' (Terence, *Heautontimorumenos*, ll. 366–7).

   The ghosts of traitors . . : the heads of traitors were impaled on the Southwark gate tower of London bridge.

   fanatic spectres: Fifth-monarchy men and other radical rebels executed in 1661–2.

   sabbath: associating the witches' sabbath with the puritans, who observed the sabbath as the Lord's Day.

132 *Sigaea igni . . . VIRG.*: 'the straits of Sigaeum light up far and wide' (Virgil, *Aeneid*, ii. 312); associating the Fire of London with the destruction of Troy.

133 *Simois*: the river Simois, near Troy, tried to drown Achilles, and was attacked by the god Hephaestus with fire, tormenting the fish (Homer, *Iliad*, xxi. 305–82).

136 *Vestal fire*: Vesta was the Roman goddess of the home and hearth.

138 *spotted deaths*: the plague which afflicted London in 1665.

139 *poets' songs*: Edmund Waller had written a poem on the repair of St Paul's Cathedral by Charles I. In Greek legend, Amphion built the walls of Thebes by drawing stones after him by the music of his lyre.

   thrones . . . dominions: orders of angels, according to Colossians 1: 16.

140 *laugh*: adapting the Latin *laetus* ('joyful'), used of crops and fields in the sense 'abundant, fertile'.

141 *the Jews . . . went*: see Ezra 1–3.

   Jove: the planet Jupiter, a propitious planet in astrology.

145 *Exchange*: built by Sir Thomas Gresham 1566–8, this was a fashionable area for promenading and assignations; it was destroyed in the Fire of London.

   Spring Garden: at the eastern corner of St James's Park.

147 *virgin honey*: the best honey, made from the whitest combs.

   Priapus: god of procreation, gardens, and vineyards.

   Sylvanus: god of the woods.

148 *Sabine . . . Apulian*: the Sabines lived north-east of Rome, where Horace had his farm, and the Apulians in south-east Italy.

   Lucrine lake: a lagoon off the Bay of Naples, famous for oysters.

   Phasis: area east of the Black Sea, noted for pheasants.

   Ionia: part of Asia Minor on the Aegean Sea.

> *guardian*: Terminus, god of boundaries.

149 *Morecraft*: see note to p. 89.

150 *Phoebus*: the sun-god.

Thetis: a sea nymph.

151 *Mortlake*: see note to p. 97.

Cynthia: goddess of the moon.

152 *the palm, the oak, or bays*: wreaths for military, civic, and poetic achievement respectively.

if here below: i.e. if they grow at all on earth.

To: i.e. compared to.

153 *Apollo . . . reed*: Apollo pursued Daphne, who turned into a laurel as she fled from him; Pan pursued Syrinx, who turned into a reed (from which he made Pan-pipes).

in this: i.e. in this garden. Some editors print 'is this'.

from pleasure less: perhaps (i) retiring from lesser pleasure; (ii) made lesser by such pleasure. Some editors print 'pleasures'.

The mind, that ocean . . . find: referring to the idea that each creature and plant on land had its counterpart in the sea.

My soul . . . glide: Using the idea that the body is merely the clothing ('vest') of the soul, which it discards when it takes flight in contemplation.

155 *The present moment's . . . allow*: an echo of Rochester: see 57.

156 *Sweets . . . spring*: in his *Poems upon Several Occasions* (1710) Congreve revised this line to read: 'The flowers that flourish in the spring'.

Love . . . boy: Cupid.

John Dryden, From 'The Georgics', Book II: the present text incorporates some changes of wording made for the second edition in 1698.

157 *Astræa*: the goddess of justice, who forsook the earth when men grew corrupt (cf. 5).

158 *contending kindred tear the crown*: a brief allusion to the Revolution of 1688–9, when James II was deposed by his son-in-law and daughter, William and Mary. Lines 718, 722–4, and 730–5 are similarly capable of a contemporary political interpretation.

160 *Sabines . . . Remus . . . Etrurian*: names which evoke the ancient inhabitants of Rome and its environs, signifying simplicity and innocence: the Sabines lived north-east of Rome; Remus and Romulus (the legendary founder of Rome) were twins, and both were deified; Etruria is the area inhabited by the Etruscans, predecessors of the Romans.

Saturn's rebel son: Saturn (the 'good old god' of l. 791) was said to have presided over the golden age, until he was deposed by his son Jupiter, who was born in Crete (l. 787).

160 *for sacrifice*: i.e. not for food: vegetarianism is often associated with the golden age.

162 *Jacob*: see Genesis 27–28.

Ceres: Roman goddess of the crops.

feed with manna: see Exodus 16.

163 *Pity . . . truths*: i.e. 'pity for their fellow-men moves the noble-hearted race of doctors to give their care and attention to the search for hidden truth'.

Gibbons . . . Milbourne: William Gibbons was one of Dryden's doctors. Maurus is a classical name for Sir Richard Blackmore, court physician and author of the epic *Prince Arthur* (1695) which included a spiteful attack on Dryden as 'Laurus'. Blackmore had 'robbed and murdered' Virgil (Publius Virgilius Maro) by producing a bad heroic poem. Luke Milbourne was a clergyman who published a bitter attack on Dryden's translation of Virgil in 1698.

164 *Garth*: Sir Samuel Garth (1661–1719), physician and poet.

Münster: in 1665 England paid the Bishop of Münster to invade Holland; he did so, but then made peace unilaterally.

peace: the war against France was ended by the Peace of Ryswick (1697).

165 *Namur*: Namur had been captured by William III's army in 1695.

the Persian king . . . rest: After defeating the Persian king Darius, Alexander the Great (who thought himself the son of Zeus ('Jove' to the Romans)) led his troops into India, but they were reluctant to continue the expedition and wished to return home.

Hannibal . . . his own: the Carthaginian general Hannibal invaded Italy and came close to destroying Rome; he was recalled to Africa to defend Carthage, but only after the war in Italy had turned against him.

166 *grandsire*: Sir Erasmus Driden, grandfather of the poet and of his cousin, was imprisoned for refusing the forced loan demanded by Charles I.

167 *Or . . . unblamed*: i.e. 'or may I, without committing a theological error ['unblamed'], describe you ['holy light'] as the radiance ['beam'] which proceeds from God himself ['of the eternal'] and is eternal along with him ['co-eternal']'.

Bright . . . increate: heavenly light is the bright radiance ('effluence') which proceeds from the bright uncreated essence of God.

Orphean lyre: Orpheus, the archetypal poet and musician of Greek legend, visited the underworld to rescue his wife Eurydice, but lost her when, on the way back up to the daylight, he turned to look at her.

168 *drop serene*: *gutta serena*, the form of blindness from which Milton suffered.

Thamyris . . . Phineus: in Greek legend Thamyris challenged the Muses to a contest in which the winner was to take whatever he wanted; the Muses won, and took his eyes and his lyre. Maeonides is the surname of Homer, reputedly blind. Tiresias was a blind prophet in Greek legend. The Thracian king Phineus was said to have lost his sight because he became too good a prophet and was revealing the secrets of the gods.

the wakeful bird: the nightingale.

169 *God's reconciled decree*: God's decree that man's sins will be atoned for by the incarnation and crucifixion of Christ; 'reconciled' (brought into harmony) alludes to 2 Corinthians 5: 18: 'God . . . hath reconciled us to himself by Jesus Christ'.

Samson . . . sight: see Judges 16, and Milton's *Samson Agonistes* (1671).

in a play: alluding to Dryden's opera *The State of Innocence*, based (with Milton's permission) on *Paradise Lost*, which was written in 1674 but not staged because of the expense.

170 *Town Bays*: Dryden, who had been satirized as Mr Bays in Buckingham's play *The Rehearsal* (performed 1671).

John Oldham, 'A Letter from the Country to a Friend in Town, Giving an Account of the Author's Inclinations to Poetry': text from *Poems*, ed. Brooks and Selden.

that poet: Ovid (43 BCE–17 CE), exiled by Augustus to Tomis on the Black Sea in 8 CE because of some (now unknown) indiscretion which he had committed at Rome. He describes his exile in his poems *Tristia* and *Ex Ponto*. *Scythia* was used vaguely by the Romans to indicate the area north of the Caucasus, and (proverbially) for a wild and uncivilized place. Oldham wrote his poem while working as a schoolmaster in Croydon.

173 *That fabulous wretch*: Midas, whose touch turned everything to gold.

Stagyrite: the philosopher Aristotle (384–322 BCE), born in Stagira, Greece. As ll. 107–10 recall, he wrote a treatise on *Poetics*, and an ode on Hermias which Oldham translated.

177 *Nisus . . . race*: for the story of Nisus and Euryalus, see 51.

178 *Marcellus*: see n. to p. 80 above.

with ivy, and with laurels: in antiquity laurel wreaths denoted conquest, and ivy immortality. Both were later associated with poetry and learning.

John Wilmot, Earl of Rochester, 'An Allusion to Horace': text from *Selected Poems*, ed. Hammond, based on *Poems on Several Occasions* (1680).

foolish patron: John Sheffield, Earl of Mulgrave (1648–1721), Dryden's patron and Rochester's enemy.

Crowne: John Crowne (1640–1712), playwright, whose masque *Calisto* was performed at court in 1675 to general dissatisfaction (including the author's).

Settle: Elkanah Settle (1648–1724), playwright; satirized as Doeg by Dryden in 42. His recent plays had failed to repeat the popular success of his *The Empress of Morocco* (1673).

178 *Otway*: Thomas Otway (1652–85); at this date he had written only his clumsy first play *Alcibiades* (1675), but important comedies and tragedies were to follow, notably *Venice Preserv'd* (1682).

179 *Etherege*: Sir George Etherege (1635–91), playwright, author of three comedies including *The Man of Mode* (1676).

Flatman: The *Poems and Songs* (1674) of Thomas Flatman (1637–88) included pindaric odes, a form which Cowley had popularized.

Lee: Nathaniel Lee (1653–92), playwright, author of the bombastic heroic drama *Sophonisba, or Hannibal's Overthrow* (1675).

Busby: Richard Busby (1606–95), headmaster of Westminster School; famous for his classical learning and ready use of the rod.

hasty Shadwell, and slow Wycherley: see the biographical notes. Shadwell had written nine plays between 1668 and 1675, and acknowledged in his prefaces that they were composed hastily (e.g. **40**). Wycherley had had three plays performed between 1671 and 1675, but they had apparently been composed in the 1660s.

Waller: Edmund Waller (1606–87), poet, author mostly of love poems and some occasional pieces on topical subjects; renowned for his smoothness of metre and clarity of diction. His panegyrics included praise of Charles I, Cromwell, and Charles II.

180 *Buckhurst*: Charles Sackville, Lord Buckhurst, the future Earl of Dorset (1638–1706), poet; his contemporary reputation as a satirist was considerable, but his known œuvre now appears slim; he was an important literary patron, whose clients included Dryden.

Sedley: Sir Charles Sedley (1639–1701), poet and playwright.

But does not Dryden . . . Stiff and affected: for Dryden's critique of Shakespeare, Jonson, Beaumont, and Fletcher, see **39**, and his 'Defence of the Epilogue' (*Works*, xi. 201–18), in which he argues that Jacobean dramatic language and wit were relatively coarse, and that these playwrights did not have the advantage of the greater sophistication of the Restoration court and audience.

Mustapha, The English Princess: the former was a rhymed tragedy by the Earl of Orrery, the latter a tragedy by John Caryll.

181 *Betty Morris*: a prostitute.

Bulkeley: Henry Bulkeley, Master of Charles II's household.

the purblind knight: Sir Car Scroope (1649–80), minor poet and wit, whose poor sight was the subject of contemporary mockery.

Shepherd: Sir Fleetwood Shepherd (1634–98), courtier, wit, and minor poet; associate of Rochester.

Godolphin: Sidney Godolphin (1645–1712), statesman.

Butler: probably Lord John Butler, son of the Duke of Ormonde, but possibly Samuel Butler (1612–80), poet, author of the comic poem *Hudibras*.

Buckingham: George Villiers, Duke of Buckingham: see *Absalom and Achitophel* (8), ll. 544–68.

Anne Wharton, 'An Elegy on the Earl of Rochester': text from *Examen Miscellaneum* (1702), with emendations from *Surviving Works*, ed. G. Greer and S. Hastings (1997).

182 *Daphne*: symbolizing poetry: see n. to p. 153.

his likeness: i.e. man (from Genesis 1: 26).

184 *Anonymous, 'The Miseries of Visits'*: printed by Paul Hammond in *The Seventeenth Century*, 8 (1993), 161–3, from Leeds University Library Brotherton Collection MS Lt 87; and by Harold Love in *Scribal Publication in Seventeenth-Century England* (1993), 257–8, from Lincolnshire Archives Office MS Anc 15/B/4. Text from Hammond's edition.

Nelly, Portsmouth: Nell Gwyn, and Louise de Keroualle, Duchess of Portsmouth; two of Charles II's mistresses.

Car: Sir Car Scroope: see n. to p. 181.

Pembroke: Philip Herbert, Earl of Pembroke (1653–83), who was said to have drunk himself mad; notorious for his bestial and murderous behaviour; 'addicted to field sports', according to John Aubrey.

Behen: Aphra Behn (see biographical notes); her name was variously spelt and pronounced: here it has two syllables.

Mulgrave: see n. to p. 178. The *Essay on Satire* (circulating in manuscript, 1679) which contained satirical portraits of the King, his mistresses, and several courtiers, was probably written by Mulgrave, but was also attributed by contemporaries to Dryden. This was probably the occasion for the attack on Dryden in Rose Alley on 18 December 1679, when the poet was badly beaten. A notice appealing for information and offering a reward of £50 appeared in *The London Gazette* (cf. ll. 34–5).

185 *log*: the fable of the frogs and the stork, representing Charles II as the senseless 'King Log', was used in several Restoration satires (see *Yale POAS*, ii. 343).

187 *Richard Flecknoe, [A Critique of Shakespeare and his Contemporaries]*: full text of 'A Short Discourse of the English Stage' in *Critical Essays of the Seventeenth Century*, ed. J. E. Spingarn, 3 vols. (1908), ii. 91–6.

188 *Suckling*: Sir John Suckling (1609–42), cavalier poet and dramatist; his works included the play *Aglaura* (1638).

189 *to have wanted learning*: Ben Jonson, in his memorial poem prefixed to the First Folio (1623), says that Shakespeare had 'small Latin and less Greek'.

quantum . . . cupressi: 'as cypress trees often do among bending osiers' (Virgil, *Eclogues*, i. 25).

Mr Hales of Eton: John Hales (1584–1656), scholar.

190 *Sir John Suckling*: see n. to p. 188.

190 *verses he writ to him*: Jonson's *Epigrams*, 55.

191 *Discoveries*: Jonson's prose miscellany of moral and critical observations.

192 *Cob . . . Otter*: Cob is a water-carrier in Jonson's *Every Man in his Humour*, and the *tankard* is the large vessel in which he carries the water. Otter is a captain in *Epicoene*.

193 *Longinus*: name traditionally assigned to the author of the Greek treatise *On the Sublime* (first cent. CE); he makes this point in ch. 32.

194 *move*: the 1679 text reads 'meant', which is a misprint for 'move' introduced in the Third Folio edition of Shakespeare (1663), the text used by Dryden.

Out, out . . . passion in the gods: *Hamlet*, II. ii. 489–514, from the Player's speech on the fall of Troy. Scholars no longer think this a quotation from another playwright.

scene between Brutus and Cassius: their quarrel in *Julius Caesar* IV. iii, praised by Dryden in more detail earlier (*Works*, xiii. 227–80).

195 *As in . . . pitied him*: *Richard II*, V. ii. 23–36.

196 *Thomas Shadwell, Preface to 'The Sullen Lovers'*: the documents mentioned in the headnote, concerning the debate between Dryden and Shadwell, are reproduced in facsimile in *Dryden and Shadwell*, ed. Richard L. Oden (1977).

197 *Molière*: pseudonym of Jean-Baptiste Poquelin (1622–73), French comic dramatist.

198 *scenes unbroken*: the practice of *liaison des scènes*, in which scenes within a single Act are linked by the presence of the same characters on stage.

sit quod vis . . . et sibi constet: 'Let it be what you will, let it at least be simple and uniform . . . If you entrust an untried subject to the stage, and if you boldly fashion a new character, maintain it to the end just as it appeared at the outset, and make it self-consistent' (Horace, *De arte poetica*, ll. 23, 125–7).

199 *Bray . . . folly*: Proverbs 27: 22.

200 *John Dryden, 'Mac Flecknoe'*: for Dryden's intricate use of vocabulary and images from the work of Flecknoe and Shadwell, see *Poems*, ed. Hammond and Hopkins, i. 305–36.

Augustus: Gaius Octavius (63 BCE–14 CE), first Roman Emperor, whose leading role in Rome began with his appointment as consul in 43 BCE.

201 *Heywood and Shirley*: Thomas Heywood (*c.*1574–1641), prolific writer of plays and of pageants for the Lord Mayor's Show; James Shirley (1596–1666), prolific dramatist, esp. in comedy.

tautology: cf. Shadwell's discussion of his repetitions in 40.

to prepare thy way: like John the Baptist for Christ (Matthew 3: 3).

King John of Portugal: Flecknoe describes his musical success at the court of Portugal in *A Relation of Ten Years Travels* (1656).

before the royal barge: this occasion is unknown, but appears to involve Shadwell in a barge on the Thames serenading Queen Catharine (who was Portuguese).

in Epsom blankets tossed: see n. to p. 108.

Arion: in Greek legend an expert on the lyre; on returning from a music festival, his prizes excited the greed of the sailors, who tried to throw him overboard, but his singing attracted some dolphins, one of which carried him ashore.

Pissing Alley: running from the Strand to the Thames.

Aston Hall: unidentified.

St André: a French dancing-master who had arranged dances for Shadwell's opera *Psyche* (1675).

202 *Singleton*: John Singleton (d. 1686), one of the King's musicians, frequently employed in the theatre.

Villerius: a character in Davenant's *The Siege of Rhodes* (1656, recently restaged at Whitehall).

Augusta: ancient name for London.

nursery: theatre for the training of young actors, opened 1671.

Maximin: the ranting, atheist emperor in Dryden's *Tyrannic Love* (1670).

Simkin: a clown in *The Humours of Simpkin* (1672).

Panton: Capt. Edward Panton, who planned an academy at Chelsea for the sons of the nobility.

Dekker: Thomas Dekker (*c*.1572–1632) dramatist and City of London poet.

203 *Psyches . . . Bruce*: Shadwell's plays *Psyche* (1675), *The Miser* (1672, based on Molière's *L'Avare*), *The Hypocrite* (lost, presumably based on Molière's *Tartuffe*), and *The Humourists* (1671). Raymond and Bruce are wits in *The Humourists* and *The Virtuoso* (1676) respectively.

Bunhill: near Cripplegate, a burial ground for Nonconformists.

Watling Street: in the heart of the City of London.

Martyrs . . . bum: pages of unsold books were used for lining pie dishes, and as toilet paper.

Ogilby: John Ogilby (1600–76), translator of Virgil and Homer; publisher of atlases; author of a description of Charles II's coronation.

Herringman: Henry Herringman, currently publisher of both Dryden and Shadwell. He had also published one of Flecknoe's works.

High on a throne: echoes *Paradise Lost*, ii. 1 (see 1).

At his right hand . . . face: echoes Virgil, *Aeneid*, xii. 168 and ii. 682–4, describing Aeneas' son Ascanius; the flame seen around the boy's head is a sign of divine approval of the heir.

Hannibal . . . foe to Rome: when the future Carthaginian general Hannibal was about 9 years old, his father Hamilcar took him to an altar, and made him swear that he would become an enemy to Rome (Livy, xxi. 1).

203 *Love's Kingdom*: Flecknoe's play (see 38).

Romulus . . . twice six vultures took: Romulus and Remus agreed to settle a dispute about the site of Rome by observing the flight of birds of omen; Remus saw six vultures, and Romulus twelve.

204 *gentle George . . . wit*: Sir George Etherege (1635–91), and five characters from his plays.

Sedley . . . Epsom: it was rumoured that *Epsom Wells* was not Shadwell's unaided work. Sir Charles Sedley wrote a prologue for it, and later corrected Shadwell's *A True Widow* (1679) for him.

Sir Formal . . . northern dedications: Sir Formal Trifle in Shadwell's *The Virtuoso* speaks in a highly rhetorical manner. Shadwell dedicated this play, and three others, to the Duke of Newcastle, who had also been Flecknoe's patron.

205 *Nicander*: a character in *Psyche* who courts the heroine in a highly rhetorical fashion.

Where . . . arse: i.e. 'Where did Jonson use coarse repartee such as "whip-stitch, kiss my arse"?' (Actually, *The Alchemist* begins: 'Believe't, I will.— Thy worst. I fart at thee', and continues in scatological mode for several lines.) To sell someone bargains was to make a fool of them with a coarse reply to a question. Sir Samuel Hearty in *The Virtuoso* uses the phrase 'whip-stitch, kiss my arse'. 'Whip-stitch' (from a stitch in needlework) meant 'suddenly'.

Eth'rege dost transfuse: characters and plot-motifs from Etherege's *She wou'd if she cou'd* (1668) are used in *Epsom Wells* and *The Virtuoso*.

mountain belly: Jonson refers to his 'mountain belly' in 'My Picture left in Scotland'.

Irish pen: despite the title of the poem, Shadwell had no Irish connections. The reference here is probably to St Patrick having banished snakes from Ireland.

wings . . . and altars: poems in the shape of wings and altars (and other objects) were common in the Renaissance (George Herbert wrote two) but were now out of fashion.

206 *Bruce and Longvil . . . bard*: in *The Virtuoso* Bruce and Longvil dispose of Sir Formal through a trapdoor while he is in the middle of a flight of oratory.

young prophet . . . father's art: Elisha inherited a double portion of Elijah's spirit, along with his mantle, when the latter was taken up into heaven in a chariot (2 Kings 2: 9–13).

207 *almonds*: proverbially rewards given to parrots for speaking.

cry 'whore' to his own mother: when threatened with a duel for attacking Otway in *A Session of the Poets*, Settle acknowledged that he was 'the Son of a Whore' for writing it.

makes . . . key: a quotation from *Absalom Senior*.

four and twenty letters: i/j and u/v were then variant forms of the same letter.

208 *psalm . . . be thy last*: a chaplain might read Psalm 23 to a condemned man on the scaffold.

209 *our sires . . . the giant race before the flood*: Dryden compares the Jacobean and Caroline dramatists with the giants who were said to have inhabited the earth before the flood (Genesis 6: 4), which here signifies the civil war and Commonwealth.

Janus: the god of new beginnings (hence 'January', the first month). He received Saturn after he had been expelled by Jupiter from Crete. Saturn then taught the Italians agriculture and civilization.

The second temple . . . grace: the temple of Jerusalem (which was said to have used the classical orders of architecture) was destroyed by the Babylonians; when it was rebuilt, the second temple was said to be much less impressive than the first. Vitruvius Pollio was a Roman architect who worked during the reign of Augustus; his treatise on architecture is the only one extant from the ancient world, and was influential on Renaissance design. In classical architecture the Doric order has strong columns with plain circular capitals; the Corinthian uses taller and more slender columns, and has capitals decorated with acanthus leaves.

210 *for the study*: Jonson published his plays with theoretical prefaces, and notes detailing his classical sources.

Southerne: Thomas Southerne (1659–1746), playwright, who assisted Dryden in completing *Cleomenes* (1692). Dryden wrote prologues for two of his plays, and commendatory verses for *The Wives' Excuse* (1692).

Fabius: after the Romans were defeated by Hannibal at Cannae in 216 BCE, Fabius Maximus used the strategy of harassing rather than confronting him, and opposed the plans of Scipio to invade Africa, Hannibal's homeland. Scipio's plans were implemented, and were ultimately successful.

Romano . . . Raphael: Giulio Romano (1499–1546) was actually the pupil of Raphael (1483–1520), rather than vice versa.

Edward . . . Edward: Edward II was deposed in 1327 and succeeded by his warrior son Edward III.

my patron: the Earl of Dorset (see n. to p. 180), who assisted both Shadwell and Dryden.

Thy first attempt: *The Old Batchelor* (1693).

214 *Morecraft*: see n. to p. 89.

room, and couch: the provision of a private room with a couch was a much-appreciated feature of the masquerades which were popular in the winters of 1671–3.

216 *first and second days*: the playwright's remuneration consisted of the net receipts for the third day's performance.

217 *afternoon*: performances generally began at three o'clock in the afternoon, and the audience might assemble two or three hours beforehand, especially at a première.

218 *there goes more to*: 'more is needed for the making of'.

As . . . kind: 'as if he took pains to graft new accomplishments on to what nature gave him'.

219 *chanced to please us*: with *The Rover* the previous year.

220 *action, time, and place*: the unities of time, place, and action espoused by neo-classical dramatists, according to which the story represented by a play should take place within a period of 24 hours, within a single location, and without discontinuities of action within each Act.

Anonymous, 'Prologue to Fools have Fortune': printed from Huntington Library MS Ellesmere 8924 by Judith Milhouse and Robert D. Hume in *Huntington Library Quarterly*, 43 (1980), 313–21, and by Pierre Danchin, *The Prologues and Epilogues of the Restoration 1660–1700*, 7 vols. (Nancy, 1981–8), no. A278.

three weak nations: poets, players, critics; the three kingdoms of England, Scotland, and Ireland; perhaps also the three areas of the playhouse—pit, gallery, and boxes—which approximately coincided with the social divisions amongst the audience: the 'town' (lawyers, soldiers, wits, and beaux) in the pit, the 'city' (merchants and their families) in the gallery, and the establishment centred on the royal court in the boxes.

Protestant Intelligences: there were several Whig newspapers with variations on this title, and in the Exclusion Crisis the role of such partisan journals was crucial in shaping public opinion.

Nokes . . . Leigh: James Nokes and Anthony Leigh, leading comic actors with the Duke's Company.

222 *when it swore*: Oates's false testimony, sworn on oath, sent many men to the gallows for treason.

Ananias: the cheat and liar in Acts 5: 1–6.

223 *Bow Street*: a street east of Covent Garden.

Whitehall: where the courtiers lived.

Temple: where the lawyers lived.

Covent Garden: the principal London market, adjacent to the theatres.

Bridges Street: the chocolate house in Bridges Street had a reputation as a place where men could met prostitutes.

224 *town and city*: for the distinction, see n. to p. 220.

My overplus . . . for you: i.e. when she is married, her husband would allow her to have love affairs with members of the audience.

227 *Historia . . . illustrata*: 'History is not yet exemplified in the Latin language' (Cicero, *Brutus* 64).

229 *it . . . enemy*: either (i) the Society is the enemy of extravagant rhetoric; or (ii) extravagant rhetoric is the enemy of natural philosophy.

231 *rites | Mysterious*: 'mysterious' here means 'symbolic': the physical union of man and wife is a symbol of the union between Christ and the Church, according to St Paul in Ephesians 5: 31–2.

232 *our destroyer*: Satan.

233 *Jane Barker, 'A Virgin Life'*: for a manuscript text which probably incorporates revisions, see *Kissing the Rod*, ed. Germaine Greer *et al.* (1988), 360–1.

pristine days: either the days of the early Church, or the time before the Fall.

234 *chariot . . . double portion*: Elisha inherited a double portion of Elijah's spirit, along with his mantle, when the latter was taken up into heaven in a chariot (2 Kings 2: 9–13).

238 *heaven-born hero*: Aeneas, son of the goddess Venus.

240 *Ascanius*: son of Aeneas.

241 *Vesta*: Roman goddess of the hearth.

Sidonian Dido: Dido, Queen of Carthage, daughter of the King of Tyre, a city south of Sidon on the coast of Phoenicia (now Lebanon). She had fallen in love with Aeneas during his stay at Carthage.

242 *ignorant of this . . . danger*: i.e. 'not knowing what danger I may be in'.

paternal piety: reverence for the gods, nation, and family, characteristic of Ascanius' father Aeneas.

Creusa: (three syllables) Ascanius' mother.

what returning . . . thyself prepare: i.e. 'those rewards which I prepare for your successful return home'.

246 *Queen*: Diana, the moon, and goddess of hunting.

247 *his gaping mouth . . . his breath*: i.e. Volscens' mouth and breath.

Capitol: the national temple of the Romans, dedicated to Jupiter.

250 *John Wilmot, Earl of Rochester, 'The Mistress: A Song'*: text from *Selected Poems*, ed. Hammond, based on *Poems* (1691).

251 *John Wilmot, Earl of Rochester, 'Against Constancy'*: text from *Selected Poems*, ed. Hammond, based on *A New Collection of the Choicest Songs* (1676).

252 *John Wilmot, Earl of Rochester, 'Upon his Leaving his Mistress'*: text from *Selected Poems*, ed. Hammond, based on *Poems on Several Occasions* (1680).

253 *John Wilmot, Earl of Rochester, 'Song' ('Absent from thee . . .')*: text from *Selected Poems*, ed. Hammond, based on *Poems* (1691).

253 *John Wilmot, Earl of Rochester, 'Love and Life: A Song'*: text from *Selected Poems*, ed. Hammond, based on *Poems on Several Occasions* (1680).

254 *John Wilmot, Earl of Rochester, 'A Song of a Young Lady to her Ancient Lover'*: text from *Selected Poems*, ed. Hammond, based on *Poems* (1691).

255 *John Wilmot, Earl of Rochester, 'Song' ('Love a woman!')*: text from *Selected Poems*, ed. Hammond, based on *Poems on Several Occasions* (1680); the 1691 edition removes the homosexual interest by cutting the final stanza.

John Wilmot, Earl of Rochester, 'The Fall: A Song': text from *Selected Poems*, ed. Hammond, based on *Poems on Several Occasions* (1680).

256 *John Wilmot, Earl of Rochester, 'The Imperfect Enjoyment'*: text from *Selected Poems*, ed. Hammond, based on *Poems on Several Occasions* (1680).

257 *Woman or man*: emended from manuscript sources; *Poems on Several Occasions* (1680) reads 'woman or boy'.

258 *John Wilmot, Earl of Rochester, 'Song' ('Fair Chloris in a pigsty lay')*: text from *Selected Poems*, ed. Hammond, based on Royal Library, Stockholm, MS Vu. 69.

259 *John Wilmot, Earl of Rochester, 'To a Lady, in a Letter'*: text from *Selected Poems*, ed. Hammond, based on *Poems* (1691).

263 *Priapus*: Greek god of reproduction, represented with a prominent phallus.

264 *Daphne from the Delphic god*: Apollo (whose oracle was at Delphi) fell in love with Daphne, and pursued her until she turned into a tree.

Venus: she fell in love with Adonis, who was killed by a boar.

266 *elle ne vouloit pas*: 'she was not willing'.

faire avec la femme de Bagwell demain . . . à aller à sa maison avec son mari: 'do with Bagwell's wife tomorrow . . . to go to his/her house with her husband'.

avec elle . . . contentment: 'with her I tried to do what I wanted, and against her resistance I did, though not to my satisfaction'.

con my hand sub su coats . . . with my main in her cunny: 'with my hand under her clothes . . . with my hand in her cunt'.

267 *was a Roman Catholic*: Elizabeth Pepys threatened on more than one occasion to become a Roman Catholic, but never did.

268 *Mrs Pierce . . . Knepp*: Elizabeth Pierce (or Pearse), wife of James, the Surgeon-General to the Fleet; and Elizabeth Knepp the actress; both ladies were friends of Pepys and occasioned jealous accusations from his wife.

272 *their twisted rays together met*: Renaissance physiology entertained two theories of sight: either that the eyes received rays emitted from an object, or (as here) that they sent out rays which connected with the object.

279 *Ah why . . . cannot rise too soon*: cf. 'Lucretius: Against the Fear of Death' (81), ll. 121–31.

280 *Make it but scanty weight*: 'add only a little weight [to the scale in which my heart lies, and that will be enough to forgive you]'.

And little wanted, but a woman's heart: 'it would have taken little for her woman's heart [to make its feelings known]'.

that fortune can control: 'that can overcome fortune'.

286 *Waged against foes . . . arbitrary throne*: alluding to the fears that after his wars on the Continent, William III would seek to maintain a standing army for domestic repression.

291 *Caesar*: Julius Caesar (100–44 BCE); he and Cleopatra supposedly had a son, Caesarion. 'This Caesar' in l. 303 is Octavius Caesar, known as Augustus (63 BCE–14 CE), sometime ally and now opponent of Antony.

292 *fled to follow you*: at the naval battle of Actium against Octavius Caesar, Cleopatra quickly fled with her ships, and Antony followed, leading to ignominious defeat.

297 *Anonymous, 'Said by a Young Lady to her Child, Taking Something to Destroy it'*: text from Leeds University Library Brotherton Collection, MS Lt 10.

298 *Lucy Hutchinson, 'To my Children'*: edited by Neil Keeble from the manuscript in the Brewhouse Yard Museum, Nottingham, and reproduced from his edition.

command: from her husband on his deathbed, as she says in the *Memoirs*, p. 330.

302 *that prince*: his soul.

304 *in the way of Mr Calvin*: Jean Calvin (1509–64) taught that all human beings were irrevocably predestined by God (before their birth) to eternal salvation or damnation. Calvinism was the dominant theology of the Church of England in the late sixteenth and early seventeenth century, but by the Restoration had become characteristic mainly of Nonconformist sects.

turned the great wheel in this nation: i.e. at the Restoration.

309 *dear pledges of his heart*: i.e. his children.

313 *Ixion's son*: Pirithous.

314 *his rod*: the caduceus, the wand carried by Hermes ('Mercury' to the Romans) as the messenger of the gods.

316 *Pallas . . . black and green*: olives were associated with Pallas Athene.

319 *good of evil shall produce*: [God's goodness] will bring forth ['produce']: good from evil.

Comforter: the Holy Spirit (a title from John 14: 16).

320 *To speak all tongues*: as in Acts 2: 4.

320 *as they forewarn*: in Acts 20: 29.

 superstitions . . . written records pure: Protestantism insisted that Christian
 doctrine was found in, and founded upon, the Bible alone, which preserved the word of God in pure form; this was to be interpreted by all
 believers with the guidance of the Holy Spirit (ll. 514, 519–20). The
 Roman Catholic Church placed more reliance on ecclesiastical tradition
 and papal authority, which Milton, in common with other Protestants,
 regarded as false and superstitious accretions to pure Christian teaching.

 laws . . . enrolled: laws written in Scripture.

322 *Thomas Traherne, From 'The Third Century'*: text from the edition by
 Margoliouth. Most of Traherne's poems and prose meditations were left
 in manuscript at his death, and rediscovered piecemeal in the twentieth
 century; some are still unpublished.

323 *apostasy . . . highest reason*: i.e. as a child, Traherne knew divine truths by
 intuition; as he grew older, and experienced sin ('apostasy', or falling
 away from a state of grace), this knowledge faded, and was only recovered
 eventually by his contemplative meditations ('highest reason').

324 *with much ado*: with great difficulty.

 a little child . . . the kingdom of God: as Jesus said in Matthew 18: 3.

327 *not our parents' loins . . . that . . . blinds us*: i.e. we are corrupted less by
 original sin (inherited from Adam, and so from our parents at our birth)
 than by the evil environment in which we are reared.

330 *prodigal son . . . swine*: Luke 15: 11–32.

333 *moderation . . . golden mean*: Aristotle taught that moral virtue lay in
 observing the golden mean (or mid-point) between two vices
 (*Nicomachean Ethics*, 1109^a).

336 *prodigal*: see Luke 15: 11–32.

341 *she*: i.e. Hannah herself: this is one of several points where the narrative
 moves for a while into the third person, perhaps reflecting a different
 layer of composition.

343 *Madam*: this letter is perhaps addressed to the Lady Baker whose
 correspondence with Hannah is mentioned later.

344 *Col[ossians]*: iii 5: here St Paul warns the Colossians against 'fornication,
 uncleanness, inordinate affection, evil concupiscence, and covetousness',
 which suggests that the minister thought that 'the ground of her trouble'
 was sexual.

 Pashur: he put Jeremiah in the stocks; for this he was called Magor-
 missabib, 'a terror to thyself, and to all thy friends'.

 scripture said . . . prayed for: 1 John 5: 16.

345 *Christ bid . . . is so dreadful*: Matthew 10: 14 and 7: 26–7.

 the sin against the Holy Ghost: in Mark 3: 28–30 Christ says that anyone
 who blasphemes against the Holy Ghost will never be forgiven.

346 *Julian*: Julian the Apostate, nephew of Constantine the Great, Roman Emperor 361–3 CE. He reversed his uncle's establishment of Christianity as the imperial religion, persecuted believers, and promoted classical philosophy and the worship of the Roman gods.

Mr Baxter: Richard Baxter (1615–91), Nonconformist divine.

349 *her*: i.e. Hannah Allen (not her aunt).

350 *Mr Calamy*: Edmund Calamy (1600–66), Nonconformist divine.

359 *Lord Mayor . . . quiver-bearing foe*: Dryden provides contemporary versions of the political anxieties in Horace's poem: the contested elections for Lord Mayor of London, masterminded by Whig factions; the wars of Louis XIV against Spain and the Holy Roman Empire; and the Turkish invasion of Europe, halted at the gates of Vienna in 1683.

362 *Punic arms*: the three Punic wars in which Rome and Carthage contended for supremacy in the Mediterranean (264–241, 218–201, and 149–146 BCE).

365 *the god*: Bacchus, god of wine.

367 *Tantalus . . . on high*: Lucretius follows the version of the legend in which Tantalus was punished for stealing the gods' nectar and ambrosia by having a large stone suspended over him, for fear of which he dared not drink.

Tityus: two vultures fed eternally on the liver of Tityos, who had tried to rape Leto.

Sisyphus: he had attempted to cheat death, and was condemned to roll a stone uphill, which rolled back each time it reached the top.

368 *fifty foolish virgins . . . could ever fill*: the Danaids murdered their husbands on their wedding night, and were condemned to carry water in perforated vessels.

dog: Cerberus, who guarded the entrance to the underworld.

Furies . . . snakes: the Furies, female figures who avenged crimes, were often depicted with snakes.

Tarpeian rock: a cliff in Rome from which murderers and traitors were thrown to their deaths.

Ancus: legendary fourth king of Rome.

That haughty king: Xerxes, King of Persia, who in 480 BCE built a wooden bridge across the Hellespont to attack Greece.

Scipio: Roman general (236–184/3 BCE) who defeated the Carthaginians.

369 *Democritus*: Greek philosopher (fifth cent. BCE); early proponent of the atomic theory of the universe; advocated living cheerfully within one's limitations.

Epicurus: see headnote (p. 362).

370 *Fates*: the Fates were often represented as three females who spun and cut off the thread of life.

370 *Sir Philip Wodehouse, 'A Kind of Translation'*: text from Leeds University Library, Brotherton Collection, MS Lt 40, previously unpublished. The present text selects from amongst several revisions and alternative readings.

371 *a sect*: the Epicureans: see headnote to 81 (p. 362).

John Wilmot, Earl of Rochester, 'A Satire against Reason and Mankind': text from *Selected Poems*, ed. Hammond, based on *Poems on Several Occasions* (1680).

372 *light of nature, sense*: as Harold Love points out, light is normally used in this period as a metaphor for reason, or for divine illumination of the soul. Rochester, however, gives priority to sense, i.e. the physical sensations of the body, as Hobbes had done in his philosophy (e.g. *Leviathan* (1651), ch. 1), which stressed that the world (including the human body) is entirely constituted by matter in motion, without spirit.

373 *That from himself*: according to Genesis 1: 26.

Ingelo: Nathaniel Ingelo (?1621–1683), author of the religious allegorical romance *Bentivolio and Urania* (1660).

Patrick: Simon Patrick (1626–1707), Anglican bishop, author of *The Parable of the Pilgrim* (1665).

Stillingfleet: Edward Stillingfleet (1635–99), prominent Anglican divine, scholar, and controversialist; he attacked Rochester's poem in a sermon at court on 24 February 1675, and the present reading is probably a revision to allude to that sermon.

374 *a whimsical philosopher*: Diogenes the Cynic (fifth cent. BCE), who lived in a tub, taught that virtue consists in the avoidance of physical pleasure, and that pain and hunger are helpful to the pursuit of goodness.

right reason: this term was normally used in the period for reason which was properly informed; specifically, for that reason which was imparted by God to all mankind as part of their nature, and so provided a secure ground for deduction. Rochester, by contrast, uses the term for reason grounded upon sense-impressions.

375 *Jowler*: name for a heavy-jawed dog.

Meres: Sir Thomas Meres (1635–1715), MP for Lincoln; often chaired parliamentary committees.

376 *bend . . . unbiased mind*: the metaphor is from the bias in a bowl: the mind is not bent out of its proper course by the passions, but instead the passions bend to the mind's direction.

owned avarice withstands: i.e. resists open and acknowledged bribery (but takes bribes in secret).

377 *life . . . justifies*: i.e. whose life testifies to the truth of the beliefs which he professes. Rochester plays on St Paul's assertion (e.g. Romans 5) that Christians are justified (i.e. saved) by faith.

for reproof . . . deride: i.e. who, in the course of condemning sins, condemns human nature itself as utterly corrupt.

good livings: well-endowed parishes: a vicar's income would depend on the revenues accruing from his parish, not on a fixed salary.

which no man can conceive: i.e. which no merely human mind could invent, and are therefore of divine origin; or, which no rational man can understand, and are therefore nonsensical.

my paradox: i.e. Rochester's paradoxical preference for animals over men.

378 *John Wilmot, Earl of Rochester, 'Upon Nothing'*: text from *Selected Poems*, ed. Hammond, based on *Poems on Several Occasions* (1680).

380 *Lawn-sleeves, and furs, and gowns*: the dress respectively of bishops, judges, and scholars.

John Wilmot, Earl of Rochester, 'From Seneca, "Troades", Act II, Chorus': text from *Selected Poems*, ed. Hammond, based on *Poems on Several Occasions* (1680).

and nothing death: i.e. and death itself is nothing.

381 *dog*: Cerberus.

cause and spring of motion: God, the first mover of the universe.

382 *three souls*: Renaissance philosophy, drawing on Aristotle, taught that the soul had three faculties: vegetal (in plants), sensitive (in animals), and rational (in man), each faculty including the lower one, so that man alone possesses all three.

Some thus . . . age: i.e. some die thus, in old age, when all the faculties have decayed; but more die in their prime.

BIOGRAPHICAL NOTES

ALLEN, HANNAH (*c.*1635–after 1683) Author of spiritual autobiography *A Narrative of God's Gracious Dealings* (1683).
    Editions: in *Voices of Madness*, ed. Allan Ingram (Stroud, 1997), and in *Life Writings: Volume 2*, ed. Elizabeth Skerpan-Wheeler (Burlington, Vt., 2000).

BARKER, JANE (1652–*c.*1726) Roman Catholic and Jacobite; poet and novelist.
    Edition: The Galesia Trilogy and Selected Manuscript Poems, ed. Carol Shiner Wilson (New York, 1997). *Biography:* Kathryn King, *Jane Barker: Exile* (Oxford, 2000).

BEHN, APHRA (*c.*1640–1689) The first woman to write extensively for the professional stage; also poet, novelist (noted especially for her slavery narrative *Oroonoko*), and government agent.
    Edition: Works, ed. Janet Todd, 7 vols. (London, 1992). *Biography*: Janet Todd, *The Secret Life of Aphra Behn* (London, 1996). *Criticism:* Janet Todd (ed.), *Aphra Behn Studies* (Cambridge, 1996).

BUNYAN, JOHN (1628–88) Nonconformist writer and preacher; imprisoned 1661–72 and 1677 for illegal preaching; author of *Grace Abounding* (1666) and *The Pilgrim's Progress* (Part I, 1678; Part II, 1684), and some sixty other works.
    Editions: Grace Abounding (Oxford, 1962) and *The Pilgrim's Progress* (Oxford, 1960), both ed. Roger Sharrock; *Miscellaneous Works*, ed. Roger Sharrock *et al.*, 13 vols. (Oxford, 1976–94). *Biographies:* Henri Talon, *John Bunyan* (London, 1951); Christopher Hill, *A Turbulent, Seditious, and Factious People* (Oxford, 1988). *Criticism:* N. H. Keeble (ed.), *John Bunyan: Conventicle and Parnassus* (Oxford, 1988).

CAVENDISH, MARGARET, DUCHESS OF NEWCASTLE (1624–75) Amateur dramatist, prolific lady of letters, and enthusiastic philosopher and scientist.

CONGREVE, WILLIAM (1670–1729) Poet and playwright. Author of several comedies, including *The Double Dealer* (1694), *Love for Love* (1695), and *The Way of the World* (1700).
    Edition: Comedies and *The Mourning Bride, Poems, and Miscellanies*, ed.

Bonamy Dobrée (Oxford, 1925–8). *Biography: William Congreve: Letters and Documents*, ed. John C. Hodges (London, 1964). *Criticism:* Harold Love, *Congreve* (Oxford, 1974).

COWLEY, ABRAHAM (1618–67) Poet and essayist. Author of love poems (*The Mistress*, 1647), pindaric odes, a biblical epic *The Davideis* (both in *Poems*, 1656), and essays on moral themes which mix prose and verse (in *Works*, 1668).

  Editions: Poems (Cambridge, 1905) and *Essays* (Cambridge, 1906), both ed. A. R. Waller; *Collected Works*, ed. Thomas O. Calhoun *et al.*, in progress (Newark, NJ, 1989–); *Selected Poems*, ed. David Hopkins and Tom Mason (Manchester, 1994).

DRYDEN, JOHN (1631–1700) Served alongside Milton and Marvell in Cromwell's government, and wrote *Heroic Stanzas* on the Protector's death. After the Restoration established a literary career, being Poet Laureate and Historiographer Royal to Charles II and James II, but losing these offices at the Revolution in 1689, since he was a Catholic and Jacobite. Author of political poems in defence of the Stuart kings' interests; of poetic apologias for his religious positions (*Religio Laici* (1682) for Anglicanism, *The Hind and the Panther* (1687) for Catholicism after his conversion *c.*1685); literary panegyric and satire; extensive translations (including Juvenal and Persius (1693), the whole of Virgil (1697), and the *Fables Ancient and Modern* (1700) from Chaucer, Ovid, Boccaccio, and Homer); major critical essays; and 27 plays.

  Editions: Poems, ed. James Kinsley, 4 vols. (Oxford, 1958); *Works*, ed. H. T. Swedenberg *et al.*, in progress (Berkeley, 1956–); *Poems*, ed. Paul Hammond and David Hopkins, in progress (London, 1995–). *Biographies:* James Anderson Winn, *John Dryden and his World* (New Haven, 1987); Paul Hammond, *John Dryden: A Literary Life* (Basingstoke, 1991). *Criticism:* Paul Hammond, *Dryden and the Traces of Classical Rome* (Oxford, 1999); Paul Hammond and David Hopkins (eds.), *John Dryden: Tercentenary Essays* (Oxford, 2000); Phillip Harth, *Contexts of Dryden's Thought* (Chicago, 1968) and *Pen for a Party* (Princeton, 1993); David Hopkins, *John Dryden* (Cambridge, 1986); James and Helen Kinsley (eds.), *Dryden: The Critical Heritage* (London, 1971); Cedric D. Reverand II, *Dryden's Final Poetic Mode: The 'Fables'* (Philadelphia, 1988).

EVELYN, JOHN (1620–1706) Man of letters, horticulturist, diarist from 1641.

  Edition: Diary, ed. E. S. de Beer, 6 vols. (Oxford, 1955).

FLECKNOE, RICHARD (*c*.1605–*c*.1677) Roman Catholic priest, traveller, and prolific writer, especially of epigrams and travel narratives, often recycled in new editions. Satirized by Dryden in *Mac Flecknoe* (41).

HUTCHINSON, LUCY (1620–81) Wife of Col. John Hutchinson, Parliamentarian leader, and author of a memoir of him; writer of political, religious, and domestic poetry; translator of Lucretius.
   Editions: Memoirs of the Life of Colonel Hutchinson, ed. Neil Keeble (London, 1995); *Lucy Hutchinson's Translation of Lucretius: 'De Rerum Natura'*, ed. Hugh de Quehen (London, 1996); *Order and Disorder*, ed. David Norbrook (Oxford, 2001).

HYDE, EDWARD, FIRST EARL OF CLARENDON (1609–74) Adviser to Charles I during the Civil War, and to Charles II during the Interregnum; Lord Chancellor 1660–7; fled abroad to avoid impeachment, and died in exile.
   Editions: History of the Rebellion, ed. W. D. Macray, 6 vols. (Oxford, 1888); *Life*, 2 vols. (Oxford, 1857); *Selections from Clarendon*, ed. G. Huehns (London, 1955). *Biography:* B. H. G. Wormald, *Clarendon: Politics, History, and Religion 1640–1660* (Cambridge, 1951).

JAMES, ROBERT (fl. 1684) Author of three unpublished poems in Leeds University Library, Brotherton Collection, MS Lt 18.

KILLIGREW, THOMAS (1612–83) Playwright and manager of the King's Company.

LANGHORNE, RICHARD (1654–79) Catholic executed for his supposed part in the Popish Plot.

MAINWARING, ARTHUR (1668–1714) Wit and gentleman of leisure; at first a Jacobite, later a supporter of William III.

MARVELL, ANDREW (1621–78) Tutor in the family of the Parliamentarian general Sir Thomas Fairfax; served with Milton in the Protectorate's Office for Foreign Tongues, and wrote panegyrics to Cromwell; MP for Hull from 1659 to his death; pamphleteer for the Whigs and against Catholicism. His lyric poems, and some of his political poems, were published posthumously in his *Miscellaneous Poems* (1681).
   Editions: Poems and Letters, ed. H. M. Margoliouth *et al.*, 3rd edn. (Oxford, 1971); *Complete Poems*, ed. Elizabeth Story Donno (Harmondsworth, 1972). *Biography:* Hilton Kelliher, *Andrew Marvell: Poet and*

Politician (London, 1978) [exhibition catalogue]; Pierre Legouis, *Andrew Marvell: Poet, Puritan, Patriot* (Oxford, 1965); *Criticism:* Warren Chernaik and Martin Dzelzainis (eds.), *Marvell and Liberty* (Basingstoke, 1999); Elizabeth Story Donno (ed.), *Andrew Marvell: The Critical Heritage* (London, 1978); Thomas Healy (ed.), *Andrew Marvell* (London, 1998); C. A. Patrides (ed.), *Andrew Marvell: The York Tercentenary Lectures* (London, 1978); Robert Wilcher, *Andrew Marvell* (Cambridge, 1985).

MILTON, JOHN (1608–74) Prominent in the 1640s as the writer of tracts against episcopacy, on education, for divorce, and against pre-publication censorship; after the execution of Charles I, wrote in defence of the regicide and the new republic. Secretary for Foreign Tongues in Cromwell's government. Escaped execution at the Restoration, partly due to Marvell's intervention, and thereafter avoided public life, devoting himself mainly to poetry. Author of *A Masque [Comus]* (1637), *Lycidas* (1638), *Paradise Lost* (1667), *Paradise Regained* and *Samson Agonistes* (1671).

Editions: Paradise Lost, ed. Alastair Fowler, 2nd edn. (London, 1998); *Shorter Poems*, ed. John Carey, 2nd edn. (London, 1997); *Complete Prose Works*, ed. Don M. Wolfe *et al.*, 8 vols. (New Haven, 1953–82). *Biography:* W. R. Parker, *Milton: A Life*, 2nd edn. rev. Gordon Campbell, 2 vols. (Oxford, 1996); Barbara K. Lewalski, *The Life of John Milton* (Oxford, 2000). *Criticism:* Christopher Hill, *Milton and the English Revolution* (London, 1977); G. K. Hunter, *'Paradise Lost'* (London, 1980); David Loewenstein, *Milton: Paradise Lost* (Cambridge, 1993); C. A. Patrides, *Milton and the Christian Tradition* (Oxford, 1966); Christopher Ricks, *Milton's Grand Style* (Oxford, 1963).

OLDHAM, JOHN (1653–83) Briefly schoolmaster and private tutor; on the fringe of the Rochester circle; author of the polemical *Satyrs upon the Jesuits* (1681), and of *Some New Pieces* (1681) and *Poems, and Translations* (1683) which include fine robust satires and translations.

Edition: Poems, ed. Harold F. Brooks and Raman Selden (Oxford, 1987). *Criticism:* Paul Hammond, *John Oldham and the Renewal of Classical Culture* (Cambridge, 1983).

OTWAY, THOMAS (1652–85) Poet and dramatist, author of various plays including *Venice Preserv'd* (1682).

Edition: Works, ed. J. C. Ghosh, 2 vols. (Oxford, 1932). *Biography*: Roswell Gray Ham, *Otway and Lee* (New Haven, 1931).

PEPYS, SAMUEL (1633–1703) Clerk of the Acts to the Navy Board 1660–79, Secretary for Admiralty Affairs 1684–9; diarist 1660–9.

Edition: Diary, ed. R. C. Latham and W. Matthews, 11 vols. (London, 1970–83), including substantial companion volume. *Biography:* Richard Ollard, *Pepys: A Biography* (London, 1974).

PHILIPS, KATHERINE (1632–64) Known as 'Orinda'; poet and translator. During her lifetime her works circulated in manuscript amongst a coterie of friends, who are often themselves the subjects of her verses. Her poems appeared in an unauthorized edition in 1664, and authorized posthumous editions from 1667.

Edition: Works, ed. Patrick Thomas *et al.*, 3 vols. (Stump Cross, 1990–3).

ROCHESTER, JOHN WILMOT, SECOND EARL OF, see WILMOT

SHADWELL, THOMAS (1642–92) Playwright; succeeded Dryden as Poet Laureate in 1689.

Edition: Complete Works, ed. Montague Summers, 5 vols. (London, 1927).

SPRAT, THOMAS (1635–1713) Educated at Wadham College, Oxford, which under the influence of John Wilkins in the 1650s was home to the group of scientists who would found the Royal Society; Bishop of Rochester; editor of Cowley's posthumous works.

Edition: History of the Royal Society, facsimile edition with notes by Jackson I. Cope and Harold Whitmore Jones (St Louis, 1958).

TRAHERNE, THOMAS (1637–74) Anglican priest; writer of devotional and mystical poems and prose meditations which were left in manuscript at his death, and rediscovered piecemeal in the twentieth century; some are still unpublished.

Editions: Centuries, Poems, and Thanksgivings, ed. H. M. Margoliouth, 2 vols. (Oxford, 1958); *Selected Poems and Prose*, ed. Alan Bradford (Harmondsworth, 1991); *Select Meditations*, ed. Julia Smith (Manchester, 1997).

WHARTON, ANNE (1659–85) Poet, niece of the Earl of Rochester.

Edition: The Surviving Works, ed. G. Greer and S. Hastings (Stump Cross, 1997).

WILMOT, JOHN, SECOND EARL OF ROCHESTER (1647–80) Courtier and rake, notorious for his escapades and his alleged deathbed repentance. His lyric, erotic, and satirical poetry circulated mostly in manuscript in his lifetime; some satires were printed separately, and a collection called

Poems on Several Occasions (with many pieces wrongly attributed to him) appeared posthumously in 1680.

    Editions: Works, ed. Harold Love (Oxford, 1999); *Selected Poems*, ed. Paul Hammond (Bristol, 1982); *Letters*, ed. Jeremy Treglown (Oxford, 1980), with biographical introduction. *Criticism:* David Farley-Hills (ed.), *Rochester: The Critical Heritage* (London, 1972); Nicholas Fisher (ed.), *That Second Bottle* (Manchester, 2000); Marianne Thormählen, *Rochester: The Poems in Context* (Cambridge, 1993); Jeremy Treglown (ed.), *Spirit of Wit* (Oxford, 1982).

WODEHOUSE, SIR PHILIP (1608–81) Norfolk MP, author of unpublished poems and translations in Leeds University Library, Brotherton Collection, MS Lt 40.

WYCHERLEY, WILLIAM (1641–1716) Author of four comedies (*Love in a Wood*, *The Gentleman Dancing-Master*, *The Country Wife*, and *The Plain Dealer*), all performed in the 1670s, and some poems.

    Editions: Plays, ed. Arthur Friedman (Oxford, 1979), and in Oxford World's Classics ed. Peter Dixon (Oxford, 1996).

GLOSSARY

The figure in brackets preceding the gloss refers to the number of the item where the word occurs in this sense.

abbethdin (8) presiding judge in a Jewish court

abroad (21, 28) out in the open; (65) out and about

abuse (11) cheat, mystify

accent (45) pronunciation

address (2, 69) dexterity

adjure (51) request solemnly

admiral (6) flagship

admiration (70) wonder; *admire* (72) wonder; *admiring* (41, 70) wondering

adventurer (16) speculator who invested in trading voyages

affect (22, 86) seek, aim at

afford (78) provide [examples of]

affront (19) confront defiantly

agone (20) ago

agreeable to (20) consistent with

à la mode [French] (adj.) (16) in fashion; (noun) (19) man of fashion

alarms (51) skirmishes

alchemy (1) brass [i.e. imitation gold]

alley (38) walk in a garden bordered with trees or bushes; avenue

allowed (8) acknowledged to be valid

alongst (82) by the side of

amain (66) violently; at once

amaze (26, 69) perplex, baffle

amour (46) love affair

angel (8) a gold coin

annoy (noun) (86) trouble, mental pain; (verb) (13) affect adversely

answerable (71) corresponding

antic (adj.) (16) grotesque

apostate (76) one who renounces their religious faith

appease (27) pacify, make peaceful

append (82) hang, attach

apprehension (69, 72) understanding

arbitrary (8, 66) ruling without regard to law or parliament

arboret (13) shrub

arrant (16) thorough, genuine

arras (28, 51) tapestry

arrogating (41) claiming without justification

assistant (51) bystander

astride (16) instead of using a side-saddle as women usually did

auspice (22) propitious influence

averse (66) opposing, hostile

award (29) arbitration

awful (1) respectful; (8) filled with awe; (12, 22, 44i, 63) awe-inspiring

Bacchus (28) god of wine; *Bacchanals* (28) songs in honour of Bacchus

bag (63) scrotum

balked (40) made unsuccessful, thwarted

ball (41) orb

band (83) linen neck-band worn by clergy and academics

banquet (44d) course or light meal of sweetmeats, fruit, and wine

bare (3) bare-headed

basilisk (14) mythical creature whose glance is fatal

basset (10) a card game

bays (16, 32) the poet's crown

beast (44d) a card game

beau garçon [French] (15) handsome youth

Bedlam (16, 32, 83) the lunatic asylum; *bedlams* (20) madmen, inmates of Bedlam behind (45, 66) yet to appear

behoof (11) responsibility

belighted (25) opposite of *benighted*: overtaken by the arrival of daylight

bellman (15) night watchman who called out the hours

bend (verb) (51) aim

bent (noun) (8, 66) direction of motion or inclination

bespeak (52) order

betake (44h) betake themselves, go

betime[s] (35, 72) early

betray (45) exhibit, disclose [without breach of trust]; (66) put in the power of an enemy

big (22, 27, 41) pregnant

bilked (41) cheated, unpaid

bill (29) weekly list of deaths from various causes; (81) charge, indictment

billet-doux [French] (44j) love-letter

birding (6) taking aim

bisson (39c) blinding

black (65) with dark hair

blade (34) convivial companion

bladders (83) animal bladders inflated to provide buoyancy

blast (75) puff of air from the mouth

blind (adj.) (65, 66) out of the way, private

blind (verb) (22) conceal, make difficult to trace

blood: see *s'blood*

blow (verb) (75) flower, blossom; attain perfection

blur (3) blemish

bob (verb) (40) strike, buffet [here, verbally]

bob (noun) (34): see *dry bob*

bob-tail (9a) horse's tail cut short [with sexual innuendo here?]; also, a ruffian

boisterous (66) stiff, unyielding

bolt (8) shot, venture

boom (19) rush headlong like a ship in full sail

boot (15) be advantageous

brake (51, 66, 83) thicket of woodland

brave (noun) (8, 44b) warrior, bully, hired assassin; (adj.) (3, 21) fine, enjoyable; (45) magnificent

bravo (19) boast

bray (40) crush

breathed: see *well-breathed*

breviary (45) brief statement, summary

brewed (8) diluted

brickbat (15) piece of brick

brief (15) official notice requesting charitable donations

brimmer (81) brimming cup

brisk (40, 44e, 44f, 44g) lively, sharp-witted

Bristol-stone (39c) rock crystal

brown (51) dark

bubble (75) [figuratively] something fragile and insubstantial; (83) dupe, victim of a cheat

bud (14) used as a term of endearment for children

bugbear (81) object of needless [esp. superstitious] terror

bulk (15) stall projecting into the street from shop fronts; *bulk-ridden* (15) one who has sexual intercourse on such stalls [*ride* = have sex]

bully-rock (40) ruffian, thug

bush (19) bushy head of hair

business (41) the duties of office; sexual intercourse

buskin (39c, 41) boot worn by actors in Greek tragedy; hence, tragedy itself

but (22, 75) only; (66) except

butt (21) cask

butts (28) archery

canister (12, 70) flat basket

canon (3) ornamental roll around the ends of the legs of breeches

cant (11, 44g) use affected [in 11, esp. Puritan] jargon

caparison (51) horse's trappings

careless (28, 32 [l. 54], 72) free from care; (32 [ll. 54, 178]) without effort and art

caress (36) greeting

carriage (20, 39c, 44j, 76) bearing, way of conducting oneself

case (35, 83) outer covering, esp. the body as the covering of the soul

catachresis (39c) incorrect application of a word, abuse of metaphor

cause (29) law suit

cell (49) cave

censor morum [Latin] (19) judge of morals

censure (45) judgement

cerecloth (17) cloth impregnated with wax, used for plasters in surgery and winding sheets in burials

chagrin (32) anxiety, melancholy

champian (29) level open countryside

chancre (61) ulcer occurring in venereal disease

'change (11, 22) financial or commercial exchange; *Change* (65) Royal Exchange, a centre for shopping

chap (69) lip

charge (28) expense; (41) person for whom one is responsible

charity (46) affection

charming (83) magic

chase (noun) (29) hunt

check (20) restrain

chemist (5) alchemist

cherubims (35, 72) heavenly beings who occupy the second rank in the nine orders of the angelic hierarchy [*cherubim* is the correct Hebrew plural form, but *cherubim* was used as a singular form in the AV, and *cherubims* as a plural]

churlish (72) mean, grudging

chymic (22, 80) alchemical, transforming

circumstance (45) formality, ceremony

cit (9, 15, 44j) citizen [often contemptuous]

citron (22) of citrus wood

city (16) the mercantile district of London, as distinct from the fashionable 'town'

clap (44c) applause; (44c, 44d) venereal disease

clench (39a) pun

clew (5) thread, cord

clinch (41): see *clench*

clip (61) clasp

close (verb) (26) come together

close (adj.) (66, 83) secret

closet (21, 47, 65) small private room

clottered (12) clotted, coagulated

cloudy (79) darkened by trouble, frowning

clout (39c) cloth

clown (37) countryman; ignorant, unsophisticated person

coach (3) captain's state room in a ship

coasting (51) skirting

coat (25) rind

cock (44f) strut; cock one's hat

cockatrice (9) basilisk, mythical creature which kills by its glance

cockle (8) a weed which grows in cornfields

coffin (9b) pie crust

coil (18) commotion

cokes (16) simpleton, fool who is easily duped

colewort (70) cabbage

commence (19) graduate

commerce [stressed on the second syllable] (48) relationship, affectionate exchange

commonwealth (2, 8, 9) republic

compass (noun) (28, 40) enclosure, circumference; (31) range, power of implication

compass (verb) (2, 66) contrive, manage

complaisance (6, 69) desire to please

compound (15) pay

concave (noun) (66) hollow, cavity

conceit (32, 72) thought, imagination

concluded (20) decided upon

conduct (32, 51) management

confess (8) acknowledge

conflagrant (71) burning together

confound (85) destroy

confusion (63) agitation caused by reversal of expectations

congee (19) ceremonious bow

connubial (46) married

conscious (51, 66) knowing [human] secrets; (81) guilty

considerable (40) notable

consort (24) harmony

constrained (22) constricted, contracted

contemn (19, 69) scorn

control (8) challenge, find fault with

conveniencies (44h) opportunities

convenient (noun) (44i) mistress

convex (noun) (1) vault

cope (72) vault

cordial (16) nourishing to the heart

cornel (70) fruit of the cornus tree

corpse (72) [living] body

corrupt (intransitive verb) (86) grow corrupt

cot (70) cottage

countenance (40) acceptance

counterfeit (69) represent

country (51) country's [the noun is frequently used attributively]

course: of course (15) customary

courser (51) horse

coxcomb (16, 32, 34, 83) simpleton; one who pretends to knowledge or accomplishments which he does not have

cozenage (80) cheat, deceit; *cozened* (5, 16) cheated, deceived

crazy (58) shaky, frail

crew (24) company

crop-sick (18) sick in the stomach; completely sick

crotch (70) prop

crown (verb) (24, 28 [l. 762]) bless; (28 [l. 771]) fill to the brim

crude (8) raw, uncooked

cry out of (21) complain about

cully (7, 32) dupe, simpleton

cumber (72) something unwieldy, a hindrance

curiosity (69) object of elaborate workmanship

curious (26, 72) exquisite, delicate; (51) elaborate, carefully worked

cutting (44b) swaggering

daggled (44h) splashed with mud

damp (41) fog

dared (24) dazed, paralysed

darkling (30) in the dark

darling (11) favourite

dart (51) spear

dashed (8) mingled

date (51, 71, 81) duration, term of life

dazzling (83) dazzled

deaf (66) muffled

debate (41) deliberate, consider with oneself; (79) fight, quarrel; *debated* (81) fought over

debauch (63) spoil; dissipate, squander

deepest-mouthed (8) with the deepest or loudest voices [used of dogs]

deeply (32) solemnly

defy (19) refuse; (82) take no notice of

degree (24, 25, 66) social status; (83) place in the natural order of things

dejected (69) lowly, humble

demesne (51) domain

democracy (8, 9b) mob rule

deplore (22, 35, 70, 86) lament, weep over

descent (28) sudden attack

descried (51) perceived

desperate in (45) beyond hope of

detract (76) remove, take off

dial (21, 26) sundial

die (29) singular of *dice*

diet (3) food, provisions

digestive (5) tending to methodize and reduce to order

dire (22) boding ill

discharged (24) unburdened

discoursive (45) conversational

discover (63, 69, 76, 78 [ll. 1–2]) uncover, reveal

discreet (76) sensible, judicious; *discreetly* (16) discerningly, judiciously; *discretion* (16) discernment, discrimination

disdain (51) anger

dishonest (8) hideous

dispatch (84) speed

dispose (noun) (20) decision

dispossess (32) exorcize, free someone from the evil spirit which is possessing them

disquiet (31) upset, spoil

dissettle (72) unsettle

distained (12) stained

distemper (32, 76) disorder or disease of body or mind; *distempered* (5) immoderate, intemperate

distraction (21) disorder, civil conflict

documents (14) instruction, teaching

dome (8) church

doom (22, 81) verdict, decision; *general doom* (22) Last Judgement

doter (32) foolish man; *doting* (19, 83) foolish, senile

doubt (22) suspect; *doubtful* (51, ll. 259, 289) indistinct; (51, l. 259) causing apprehension

dress (21) prepare food, cook

droll (noun) (3) wag, joker

drugget (41) woollen cloth

dry bob (34) sexual intercourse without ejaculation

dull (65) depressed, melancholy

dumpishness (45) melancholy disposition

dusk (adj.) (32) dark, shadowy

duty (76) religious observance, attendance at services

economy (82) management, government

ecstasy (5) trance

ecumenical (69) [probably intended for *economical*] domestic

effeminacy (39c) devotion to women

effluence (30) effulgence, radiance

elaborate (38, 39a) produced by labour

election (66) choice

elocution (37) use of language, capacity to put ideas into words

eloquence (45) rhetoric

emblazonry (1) heraldic devices

empire (8, 41, 44h, 71) government, rule

enchase (28) decorate

engine (6) device, contrivance; (8, 15, 78, 83) machine

enow (1) enough

en ridicule [French] (44g) in a ridiculous fashion

enthusiastic (8) claiming to be inspired directly by God

entrench (59) encroach

enveloped (82) enshrouded, darkened

envy (41, 51) desire to equal someone else's achievement

epoches [three syllables] (5) dates of historical events

equal (31, 47) even, unruffled; (31) adequate to the challenge; (51) adequate, appropriate

essay (69) attempt

even (noun) (30) evening

event (8, 29, 51, 66) outcome

evidence (15) witness

exaction (72) demanding payment or service [perhaps here seen as the labour consequent upon sin]

exequies (66) funeral ceremonies

explode (39c) drive away, banish ignominiously

express (30, 49) represent poetically or symbolically; (66) demonstrate

exquisite (66) refined

extravagance (45) absurdly exaggerated language; *extravagancies* (37) mental wanderings

fabric (41) frame

fabulous (32, 64) of fable or legend

fact (51) deed

factor (5) deputy

faggotted (42) bundled up

falchion (12) sword

fame (66 [l. 408]) reputation

fancy (32, 37, 39c) creative imagination

fantastic (56) creating extravagant fancies, capricious

fare (5) happen

fashion (21) social standing

fat (25) abundant, plentiful

fate (12, 66, 81) death

fear (8 [l. 937], 70, 71) reverence

feeble (noun) (32, 44g) foible, weakness

fellies (39c) curved pieces of wood forming the rim of a wheel

fiddle (16) mirth-maker, jester

fill out (62) pour out

fillet (28) headband

fine (15) pay to avoid serving in an office

firmamental (22) of the heavens

firstling (29) first offspring

fit (verb) (44a) punish suitably

fit (noun) (79) short period

fitch (25) vetch

fixed (66) resolute, determined

flambeau (15) torch

Fleet (32) the Fleet prison near the Fleet [sewer running into the Thames by Fleet Street]

float (8) undulate

floated (70) flooded

flood (22) river; (51) stream

flourish (45) elaborate ornamentation

flout (15) mock

fogue (5) fury, passion

foiled (43) outdone, surpassed

fold (verb) (24) shut up; (noun) (29) sheep pen

fond (16) eager; (26) loving; (26, 32, 52, 66 [l. 329], 81) foolish; *fondness* (16) affection; foolishness

foot-post (14) letter-carrier who travels on foot

fop (16, 32 [ll. 161, 240], 34, 36, 40, 44a, 44h [l. 40], 44i, 83) fool, simpleton; (16, 32 [l. 240], 34, 44h [l. 43], 44j) one who is absurdly attentive to his appearance or manners; hence *foppery* (44g); *fop-corner* (44b) part of the pit where fops chattered during performances

forbid (77) make impossible

forelaid (51) waylaid

forgot (66) omitted

formal (83) grave

forswore (65) denied strongly

forward (5, 11) ready, prompt [perhaps *too* eager]; (40) self-promoting

fount (29) source

frame (83) body

frantic (83) mad

freak (8) whim; *freakish* (32) full of capricious, whimsical ideas

freight (66) weight

fricassee (9b) stew

friend (66) lover; *friends* (76) relations, family

frieze (15, 44d) coarse woollen cloth; *frieze campaign* (15) campaign coat of coarse wool

frisk (34) move briskly, stir up

frolic (34) merry, sportive

froppish (14) fretful, peevish

fruition (46) sexual intercourse

fry (79) suffer intense heat, burn

fume (22) smoke

funeral (22) corpse

fustian (34) bombastic, inflated

gain (44c) serve

gallantry (3, 69) elegant appearance
generosity (69) nobility; *generous*
(5, 33, 79) rich, strong (of wine);
(8, 16, 25, 29, 69, 83) noble;
(33) abundant
genial (11) life-giving; (66,
70) pertaining to marriage and
procreation
genius (22) guardian god or spirit of a
particular person or place; (25, 39b,
41, 45) characteristic inclination;
(32, 39b) skill
gentle (25) noble
genuine (41) natural, not acquired
get (52) beget
gewgaw (67, 72) gaudy toy
ghostly (32) spiritual
gill-flirt (14) flirtatious young
woman
give a loose: see *loose*
give on (22) assault
given over (57) ceased
glass (24, 44g, 72) mirror; (65) coach
window
glimpse (77) momentary shining,
flash
globe (1) compact body [e.g. of
soldiers]
gloat (44i) cast amorous glances at
glory (6, 19, 41, 69) halo
go (72) walk
goblin (81) demon, devil
goodly (41) of good appearance; of
great size
gossiping (83) christening
got (51) begot
government (70) area ruled by a
governor
gown (36) clergy
grain (39b) the smallest English
weight, 1/7000 lb.
grateful (70, 79) pleasing
grave (verb) (51) engrave
griping (24) clutching, grasping
gross (noun) (22) body, mass
grot (28, 66) cave

grudge (verb) (66) begrudge; *grudging*
(65) grumbling, nursing resentment
grum (14, 40) morose, surly
guilty of (20) deserving, liable to the
punishment of
gullery (69) trick, deception
gust (69) taste
gypsy (16) fickle, deceitful, and
promiscuous woman
half-crown (44b) two shillings and
sixpence [the price of admission to
the pit in the theatre; also a
prostitute's charge]
hand (21) servant
handed (46) joined hand in hand
hang an arse (7) hold back, delay
harbour (70) shelter
hardly (5) with difficulty
hautgoût [French] (25) something
which adds relish or strong flavour to
a dish
heady (20) headstrong, violently
passionate
hear (30) be called
heaven (45) sky, climate
hector (noun) (7, 61) swaggering
braggart; (verb) (19) brag, bluster;
(40) intimidate
Hibernian (84) Irish
high-mind[ed] (20) arrogant
hight (41) was called
hit (32) win
hoary (51) venerable, time-honoured
hobgoblin (73) demon, devil
hole (6) hold
honest (66) seemly, decent
honour (41) beauty; *honours*
(79) ornaments
hopeful (41) promising
horn-book (76) sheet of paper
containing the alphabet (and often
numerals and the Lord's Prayer)
covered with a thin layer of horn and
mounted on wood, used for teaching
children
horrent (1) bristling

horrid (51) bristling

huff (verb) (19, 40) bluster, talk big; (noun) (44h) one who brags aggressively

humour (2, 8, 39a, 39b, 76) mood, whim, caprice; fluid in the body thought to determine physical and mental qualities; (37, 39a, 40, 44c) individual characteristics so produced; (39a, 39b, 40) comedy deriving from such psychology

hung (15) endowed with a long tongue, i.e. eloquent

hurry (45) disturbance, tumult

hydra (8, 22) mythical many-headed snake

iambics (41) metre associated with scurrilous subject matter in Greek and Latin poetry

idea (45) representation

idle (22, 54, 59, 72, 81) ineffectual, worthless, useless; (82) lacking purpose; (85) empty, meaningless

ignis fatuus [Latin] (83) a light which misleads travellers

ill-packed (32) [of a pack of cards] shuffled badly, or to the disadvantage of the player who complains

impending (81) hanging threateningly

impertinent (16, 69, 83) absurd, unreasoning, irrelevant

impetuous (79) violent; (81) with violent motion

impudent (69) lewd, immodest

incommode [French] (16) inconvenient, troublesome

inconvenient (72) absurd

increate (30) uncreated

indiscretion (83) lack of judgement or discernment

inditing (44j) composition

indued (43) clothed

infection (66) sympathetic communication of feeling from one person to another

influence (50, 55) the nurturing power of the sun or heavens

inform (41) impress

innovation (8) alteration of what is established [used pejoratively in this period]; revolution, insurrection

insensible (45) indifferent, apathetic

insipid (59) devoid of taste and judgement

institute (66) law

insulted (83) triumphed; *insulting* (6, 22, 43) triumphing; (6, 22) leaping; (43) exulting scornfully

interest (8) self-interest

invade (22) seize, usurp; (51) set upon, assault

inverted (38) diverted

invest (30) cover, wrap

irradiate (30) illuminate, fill with radiance

issue (86) turn

Jack Presbyter (9) name for a Nonconformist clergyman

jack-pudding (15) clown whose act specialized in messy eating

jakes (15) lavatory

jar (verb) (44b) fight; *jarring* (86) warring

jealous (8, 11) suspicious; (31) afraid, uneasy; *jealousies* (8) suspicions, mistrust

jilt (noun) (16, 32, 44g) one who abandons a lover; prostitute; kept mistress

jingles (72) objects which make a jingling sound; so small, worthless objects

jingling (83) playing with words

jointure (15) marriage settlement

jostle (19) have sex with

joy (verb) (86) congratulate

jump (9a) short coat, esp. one worn by Presbyterian ministers

keep (81) guard

kennel (15, 21) drain, gutter

kilderkin (41) cask holding 16 or 18 gallons

kind (noun) (8, 66 [ll. 322, 520]) race; (26, 29, 86) species; (66 [ll. 342, 403]) gender; (66 [l. 483]) nature; *kind* (adj.) (16, 27, 55) sexually available; (55) nurturing; *kind keeping* (9b, 16) keeping mistresses; *kindly* (5, 22) nurturing; *kindness* (47) natural disposition; (61) tenderness, affection, sexual desire

kine (13, 28) cows

knack (44h [with sexual innuendo], 83) toy, trinket; trick; (44h) choice dish

knight of the shire (44f) Member of Parliament for a county

labouring (66) turning over ideas

lac (6) crimson pigment

lade (22) load

laic (84) not ordained, not initiated into sacred mysteries

lake (8) channel of water

lambent (41) playing lightly over the surface

Lares [two syllables] (22) Roman gods of the home and hearth

last (45 [first use]) fullest, most complete; (45 [second use]) final

late (27) lately

laveering (5) tacking

lawn (84) fine linen

lay (11) song

leads (76) roof

leave (15) part with, lose

lee (66) dregs, refuse

leech (5, 29) doctor

Legion (44f) the devil in Mark 5: 9

lenitive (8) soothing medicine

let (20, 22) hinder

level (noun) (66) aim; (70) level ground

lewd (32) worthless, good for nothing

lighter (21) flat-bottomed boat for transferring goods between a ship and a wharf

like (verb) (83) please

like (adv.) (83) likely

likely (21) promising

limber (61) limp

limn (44h) paint

line (84) offspring, descendants

link (42) torch

lion (79) zodiacal sign of Leo

liquid (72) clear, evident

living (noun) (83) vicar's tenure of a parish

living (adj.) (28) refreshing

loathly (19) loth, reluctant

lobe (81) division of the liver

loose (34) inexact; promiscuous, prostituted

loose: give a loose (79) give free rein to

love: see *make love*

lucid interval (41) temporary period of sanity between attacks of lunacy

lumpish (34) without creativity, incapable of creating anything lively and well-formed

lusty (20) merry; pleasing in appearance

luxury (25, 45) abundance

made (5) enlisted, pressed into military service

maggot (9b) whimsy

magnanimous (69) of elevated mind and spirit

magnify (69) praise

main (noun) (5, 41) sea; (25) essential matter; home farm, farm attached to the mansion

make (noun) (17) manufacture; (42) constitution

make love (39a, 44e) engage in courtship

manifest (8) evidently guilty

manufacture (70) handiwork [noun used here attributively]

mark (8, 39c) limit, destination

matrix (36) womb

mawkish (81) nauseating

mean (8, 39b, 66, 69) lowly; *meaner* (55) less exalted

means (76) moderation

meat (25) food

mechanic (adj.) (39a, 39b) [of people] with a manual occupation; (39b) vulgar, low

meditate (66) observe intently

meet (26, 72) suitable

memento mori [Latin] (16) reminder of death

mend (66) supply the deficiencies of

menial (24) household, domestic [not derogatory]

meridies (25) middle point

merit (verb) (34) have merit

metal (8) metal; mettle [originally the same word]

methodize (66) put into order or method

middle region (15) middle region of the air where storms were thought to be generated

midnight-work (42) production of excrement

mien (51, 66) appearance

milch (39c) milk-giving [here, a milk of tears]

mischief (45) evil [stronger than modern usage]; (66) person whose actions are evil or harmful

misdoubting (31) doubting, having misgivings about

miss (44c, 44g) mistress, prostitute; (44e) young lady

moaned (78) wept over

mobbled (39c) with face muffled

mobile (9) mob

mode (19, 31) fashion

mon cher [French] (16) my dear

montero cap (44d) Spanish-style hunting cap

moon-blind (9) suffering from moon-eye, an intermittent blindness in horses

mote (72) speck of dust

mother (9) hysteria

mother-in-law (69) stepmother

move (66) initiate, propose

mould (22) earth; (66) body

mouse (verb) (14) pull a woman about rudely

mouthed: see *well-mouthed*

murmur (50) grumble, express discontent

must (70) grape-juice before fermentation is complete

naked (45 [first use]) unarmed; (45 [second use]) without ornament; *naked bed* (21) bed where one sleeps naked; *nakedness* (16) simplicity

Nantes (36) cheap brandy

native (45) natural

nativity (15, 42) horoscope

natural (noun) (37) person who is naturally simple-minded

naughty (14) wicked [stronger than modern usage]

nave (39c) hub of a wheel

nice (16, 25, 34 [ironic], 69) [too] fastidious; *nicely* (44f) exactly, discerningly

nickname (72) misname, call incorrectly

nightgown (21) dressing-gown

Nilus (38) River Nile

Nokes (16) fool

notices (15) notions, ideas

nuisance (44g) something harmful or obnoxious to the community

number, numbers (31, 33, 41) rhythm, metre; *numbers* (30, 32) lines of verse

oblation (28) offering to a god

obnoxious (11, 22) exposed, vulnerable

occasion (51) opportunity, Fortune; (66) cause; *occasions* (76) business

o'erinformed (8) over-animated

o'erspent (51) worn out, exhausted

offal (81) carrion, dead body

offer (verb) (76) attempt

office (79) duty, function

officious (6, 66, 70) careful, dutiful

ogle (44i) cast amorous glances at

ombre (44d) a card game

operator (15) quack manufacturer of drugs

or . . . or (5, 8, 63, 66, 78) either . . . or

ordinance (76) religious rite

orsons (9) bear cubs [with pun here on 'whoresons'?]

outbrave (19) oppose defiantly

outlandish (20) foreign

overlay (32) cover superfluously, smother

overpoise (29) lack of balance

oversee (66) overlook, disregard

oversold (51) sold at more than the real value

owl (16) solemn fool

own (noun) (24) own resources

own (verb) (66, 70, 83) admit, acknowledge; *owned* (83) open, acknowledged

packed: see *ill-packed*

padder (15) footpad, robber

pair of virginals (21) early form of spinet

pall (81) make wine flat or stale

pantaloon (44c) baggy breeches worn by men

paper (32, 36) folded sheet containing a poem; (34) set of verses

parlous (44e) dangerous, capable of doing mischief or damage

parrallogram (65) pantograph

particoloured (70) multicoloured

parts (2, 16, 66, 69) abilities, talents

pass (86) pass away

passage (81) transition [here, to death]

paste (66) material of which a person is made

pathetic (39c) creating pathos; (83) stirring emotion; passionate, earnest

pease (16) pea; *peason* (25) peas (pl. of *pease*)

peculiar (5, 70) particular, special

pelf (8, 11, 19, 23, 24) money, property

pencil (5, 6) paintbrush

perplexed (31) made too complicated; (66) entangled; *perplexing* (51) entangling

perspective glass (69) telescope or microscope

physic (verb) (8) medicate; (noun) (76) medicine

picking work (42) the work of picking out the good from the bad

pickthank (20) flatterer, tell-tale

pieced (8) pieced together

piercing (79) broaching [of a wine cask]

piety (69) reverence for one's parents [elsewhere it has the modern meaning]

pindaric (34) in the manner of the Greek poet Pindar (b. *c.*518 BCE), using stanzas with lines of irregular length and surprising transitions of subject matter

pinion (8) wing

pious (22, 51) showing duty towards God, country, and family

pit (16, 44e) stalls in the playhouse usually occupied by men of wit and fashion who often commented loudly on the performance

place-house (14) chief residence on an estate

placit (72) opinion, judgement

plat (13) patch of ground

play (16) gambling at cards or dice

pleasant (81) pleasing [stronger than in modern usage]

plight (51) pledge solemnly

plume (verb) (8) pluck the feathers from; (noun) (31) wing

plush (65) imitation velvet

ply (15) carry on a trade

point (noun) (15 [l. 64]) point of the compass; (15 [l. 231], 44c) rich lace; *points* (31) laces; *point Venise* (19), *point Venee* (44h) a form of lace

point (verb) (84) make forceful or poignant

pole (46) sky

policy (4) skill; (84) political skill; *politician* (8) [usually pejorative at this date] schemer, plotter; *politics* (44h) politicians

poorly (3) poor

porridge (8) soup made from stewed meat or vegetables

port (15, 66) appearance

portion (43) attribute allotted by destiny

posed (72) puzzled

positive (40) arrogantly assertive

post (22) post-haste

postboy (17) boy who rode alongside travellers as a guide

postern (21, 66) side gate

poverty (24) state of having just the necessities of life [not destitution]

powers (28, 47, 70) gods

practised (8) performed the duties of

prate (32, 40, 44h) speak foolishly

prefer (70) put forward; *preferment* (20, 42) promotion to an office; *preferred* (15, 66) promoted

prerogative (8, 29) right of a king to act without Parliament's approval; (45) natural or God-given advantage

presently (15, 20, 21, 65, 76) immediately

pretence (8, 15, 41, 49, 54) claim; (83) purpose; *pretend* (31, 40, 66, 78) claim; (69) cover, set forth; *pretending* (69, 83) laying claim to [in 83, to reason and authority]

preternatural (72) unnatural

prevail (8) avail; (44h) win favour

prevent (5, 8, 11, 27, 28, 81) anticipate [elsewhere it has the modern meaning]

prime (8) lunar cycle of nineteen years

primitive (45, 72, 84) original and uncorrupted

privilege (29) rights of Members of Parliament

proceed (43) progress, advance further

prodigal (43) lavish

prodigious (22) ominous, portentous

profess (70) openly acknowledge; *profession* (69) public declaration of [Puritan] Christian beliefs; *professor* (69) one who professes [Puritan] Christianity

projected (51) protruding

proper (16, 20) own; (21, 32) apt, suitable; (45) intrinsic, characteristic

propriety (46, 72) proprietorship, exclusive possession

prove (8) test; (16, 56, 62) experience

provoke (28) call out

pudder (39c) commotion

pug (16) monkey; (44i) small demon

pulvilio (15) perfumed powder

punctual (66) precise, point by point

punk (15, 18, 41, 44b, 44e) prostitute

purblind (34) partially blind

purple (46) bright, shining

qualified (8) moderated, calmed

quality (21, 25, 37, 40) social rank

quarrel (32) complain, find fault

quicken (72) enliven; *quickness* (33) liveliness; sharpness of taste

quit (81) give up, let go of

rabbins (8) rabbis

rabblement (20) rabble

rag (44j) scrap, tiny piece

rage (8) prophetic inspiration; (35) poetic inspiration; (63, 66) passion

raiment (20) clothes [biblical word]

raise (43) elevate mentally or morally

rankness (43) excessive strength; coarseness

rare (30) unusual, rarely undertaken

rate (23) estimated value, worth

rear (24) rouse [a boar] from its hiding place

reasonable (69) rational

receiving (32) receiving holy communion

receipt (5) recipe, prescription

recorded (41) rendered in song, warbled [used mainly of birds]

recreant (61) traitor

recruits (67) supplies; (32, 50) new supplies

regorge (66) make to flow back again

rehearse (48) repeat, tell

relics (25) remains, leftovers

relish (70) add relish to

remains (43) literary works left at an author's death

remitted (66) handed back

rent-charge (43) someone maintained by a rent charged on land which he does not own

repair (noun) (22) dwelling

repair (verb) (44h) resort to; (46) replenish

repeat (22) encounter again

repine (63, 69, 78, 81) complain

require (22, 79) seek for

resentment (63) anger or indignation at an injury

respiration (71) breathing space, rest

retire (transitive verb) (22) remove

return (noun) (66) reply

revolve (81) turn back again

revolution (8) alteration

rheum (39c) tears

rhymes (34) verses, poems

righted (83) cleared from aspersions; rightly defined

rind (70) bark

riot (verb) (66) revel, indulge fully in pleasure; (noun) (69) revelry [to excess]

roar (44i) be boisterously merry

roll (8) parchment roll recording genealogies

Romanize (39a) give a Latin colouring to

rook (16, 32) swindler, sharper

room (44c) vacant place

rude (5, 23, 25, 26, 27, 28, 32, 35, 43, 69, 72) rough, uncivilized; (32, 69) shapeless

ruffle (61) attack violently

ruin (31) reduce

runagate (20) renegade, apostate

running (80) flow of liquor [here, wine]

sack (19) sweet wine

sadly (76) heavily, vigorously

saint (8, 69) term used by Puritans to denote true believers; used sarcastically of Puritanical Nonconformists by others

sallow (70) willow

sanguine (12) bloody; (51) blood-red

sapient (13) wise

sate (22, 41, 51) sat

saturnine (39a) gloomy

satyr (34) in Greek myth a creature half-man, half-goat, proverbially lustful [the association of *satyr* with *satire* had been shown to be erroneous by scholars, but was still common]

savage (51) wild [here, spoils from hunting wild beasts]

saving share (32) a result in gambling where one recovers one's stake, but neither wins nor loses money

savoury (79) appetizing

s'blood (36) God's blood [an oath]

scanted (8) inadequately supplied, restricted

school (72, 83) university, faculty

science (29) knowledge

score (8) count

scorn (45) refusal

scourer (15) violent drunken lout roaming the streets

screw (83) strain, force

scrivener (15, 24) money-lender

scrub (noun) (20) person of no importance or of poor appearance

scrutoire (15) writing desk

seat (66) residence

secrecy to (32) secret from

secure (verb) (83) resolve; *secure* (adj.) (66 [l. 183]) careless, unaware of danger; (66 [l. 626]) resolute; *securely* (51) carelessly, without apprehension; (66 [l. 709]) resolutely; *security* (67) lack of a sense of danger

seed (81, 86) atom

seek: be to seek (37) be at a loss

seether (70) utensil for boiling

seminal (82) pertaining to seeds [here, atoms]

sennight (10) week

sense (81) consciousness

sensible (2, 44g, 66, 69) aware, understanding

serpent (42) firework which burns with serpentine motion or flame [symbol of malice]

servant (52) lover

set (15) occupy; (19) set oneself up as; *set up* (44j) set up shop

several, severed (1, 16, 20, 28, 37, 45, 69) separate, individual

shade (noun) (84) darkness

shade (verb) (43) protect

shard (24) chard beet

share (51) ploughshare

share: for my own share (83) for my part, as far as concerns me

sharp (44d) eager

sharper (9) swindler

shed (70) cottage

shelf (24) sandbank, submerged rock

shift (21) change one's clothes

shog (44f) shake, jerk

shore (15) sewer

show (22) appear

shrieve (15) sheriff; *shrieval* (8) pertaining to a sheriff

shrifted (32) having made confession

side (6) part of a ship between the gunwale and waterline

sign (70) approve, authorize

silly (72) insignificant, trifling

simples (66) plants with medicinal qualities

simplicity (37) simple-mindedness

sincere (66) pure; *sincerely* (8) completely, purely

sinister (41) left

Sion (30) the house of God [from one of the hills on which Jerusalem is built]

Sirian star (79) Sirius the dog star [associated with sultry weather]

sirrah (20) term of address used in contempt or reprimand

sit upon (20) sit in judgement or inquiry

sithes (65) sighs

slattern (34) untidy, slovenly woman; (44a) sexually promiscuous woman

sliddering (12) sliding

sliding (26) flowing

smart (83) stinging, cutting

smoke (noun) (24) steam; (verb) (81) move rapidly; *smoking* (28) steaming

snake (44f) tail attached to a wig

sneak (15) cringe, be servile

sock (41) low shoe worn by actors in Greek comedy

socket (22) part of a candlestick into which the candle is placed

Sol (27) the sun

sorry (65) worthless

sot (32, 83) fool

sounding (39c) resounding

source (35) spring [of water]

spark (16, 44e) one affecting smartness in dress and manners; (44h) plural form of the same word, perhaps as a collective noun

sped (39b) succeeded

spell (31) read or write laboriously letter by letter

spend (18, 61) ejaculate semen

spirit (32) evil spirit, devil

spleen (66) violent malevolent passion

split (24) wrecked

spreading (37) wide-ranging

springing (51) rising, developing

sprite (44a) spirit

sprung (61) made to rise from cover [like a bird being hunted]

spurning (51) kicking

squab (34) inexperienced unfledged person

square: upon the square (83) honestly

stagger (8, 82) begin to doubt or waver

staid (38) steady, free from extravagance or caprice

standard (8) principle, means of judgement; (45) example of perfection

standing (45) providing an example by which others may be measured

start (35) shy away from

state (72) splendour [in decoration, furniture, etc.]

states (11) estates of the realm

stationer (41) publisher

stay (83) stop, pause

stead (28) bedstead

steepy (8) precipitous

stews (sing. and pl.) (8, 61) brothel(s)

stick (45) hesitate

still (26, 76) always

stock (8) block of wood

stop (35) block up

straight (adv.) (32, 84) straight away, immediately

straitened (78) tightened

strangury (32, 61) disease of the urinary organs causing the slow and painful emission of urine

strict (66) close, tight

stripes (81) lashes from a whip

stuff (38) cloth

stum (32) raise a new fermentation in wine by adding stum or must to it, thus producing a false sparkle

Stygian (1, 30) of the river Styx in the classical underworld

suborn (66, 86) procure secretly

subscribe (44g) submit, yield

subsidy (16) tax

subtle (24) of fine texture

suburb ware (15) prostitutes

succeed (22) give success to

success (22) outcome

suffer (5) allow; (40, 66, 69) tolerate

suffrage (43) vote

suffusion (30) cataract over the eyes

sullen (5) threateningly quiet; (39a, 40) solemn, serious, stubborn; (66) gloomy, menacing; *sullenness* (45) gloomy seriousness

supple (65) compliant, yielding to persuasion

support (63) that which supplies the means of life [here, the penis]

suppose (8) imply, presuppose

sustain (86) endure

sward (25) rind

sweet (noun) (33, 46) pleasure

swive (17, 61) have sexual intercourse with

sword-knot (44f) ribbon or tassel tied to the hilt of a sword

sylvan (29) of the woods; *Sylvans* (28, 79) spirits of the wood

tag (verb) (31) attach decorative metal ends to laces

take (44c, 44e) please

take up (16) borrow

taking (noun) passion, excited state

talent (51) Greek and Roman weight, approx. 80 lb.

tampering (8) scheming, plotting; meddling

tares (25) vetches, corn-weeds

tawdry (15, 16, 36, 83) showy, gaudy [and implicitly cheap]

taxed (39a) called to account; *taxing* (38) criticizing

tearing (34) loud and boisterous

tease (44g) annoy, irritate

tedded (13) spread out to dry

temper (45 [first use]) restraint; (45 [second use]) character

tempt (51) attempt

tend (22) approach

terms (20) language of a particular kind [here, offensive language]

texture (66) constitution, nature, temperament

thoughtless (66) unsuspecting

Three-One (47) the Holy Trinity

threshing (41) beating violently as with a flail

thrum (38) loose thread

tickled (32) pleasantly excited

tiring room (44c) actors' changing room

toil (noun) (26, 51) labour; snare, trap

tomrig (40) prostitute

took the word (51) began speaking

topped (11) imposed

toss (44f) toss of the head

touse (14) pull a woman about rudely

toy (noun) (9, 32, 67, 83) trifle, thing of no value; (44h [l. 18], 66) amorous sport; small ornamental article, trinket; (verb) (19) trifle, play

traffic (11, 20) trade, commerce

train (28) group

transitum [Latin] (22) transition

transprose (42) turn verse into prose [the term gained currency from Buckingham's *The Rehearsal*, where Dryden is said to transprose or transverse other writers' work]

transvest (19) dress in other clothes; travesty

travel (70) travail; journeying

traverse (8) move from side to side, dodge

tried (51) proven

trim (44h) cut hair; modify one's political opinions to suit others or gain advantage

trine (22) alignment of planets at 120°, considered propitious in astrology

triumph (4) triumphal procession

trivet (70) three-footed

tun (41) cask holding 210 gallons of wine or beer [describing Falstaff in *1 Henry IV*, II. iv. 442]

tune (44e) music played between the Acts of a play

tympany (41) swelling, tumour; [figuratively:] pretentious, empty style

type (41) person in the Old Testament taken to prefigure another person fully revealed in the New Testament [e.g. Adam is a *type* or prefiguration of Christ]

Tyrian (28) from Tyre [in modern Lebanon], the source of an expensive purple dye

ugly (21) awkward, uncomfortable

unbearing (24) unfruitful

unbespoken (8) not arranged, spontaneous

uncased (44i) removed from its clothing [here, the body of Oates which it had inhabited]

uncouth (19, 72) strange; unseemly

unction (41) oil used to anoint the king in the coronation ceremony

undertake (38) take it upon oneself

under-world (50) earth, the world underneath the sun

undistinguished (32, 84) without separate identity

undone (32) lost

unequal (5) of lower social status; (8) unjust, unfair; (34) uneven

unessential (1) without substance or being

ungrateful (8, 43) not responding to cultivation

unknowing (86) unconscious

unlade (15, 22) unload

unlicked (42) without form [the bear was supposed to lick her formless cubs into shape]

unprofitableness (72) desolation [stronger than *OED* suggests; cf. *Hamlet* I. ii. 133]

unsincere (22) impure, not unmixed; (81) unsound [in one's opinions]

untack (6) detach

urn (22) poetic and artistic image for the source of a river

use (verb) (2, 32, 45, 66) usually do, are accustomed

usually (37) according to a person's normal behaviour

usurped on (66) wrongly exercised over or inflicted on

utter (30) outer

uxorious (69) subservient to one's wife

vain (6, 31, 32, 34, 44i, 45, 77) futile, ineffectual, empty; *vainly* (26) in vain; arrogantly

vale [two syllables; Latin] (40) farewell

vanity (72, 74) empty, worthless thing(s)

vapour (83) mist; foolish idea; *vapouring* (44h) bragging, boasting

vare (8) staff carried as a symbol of office

vaulting bout (15) sexual intercourse

verged (26) stretching

verified (81) made true

vest (26, 51) clothing; *vests* (28) coverings

vicissitude (79, 82, 86) change, alternation

vindicate (22, 29) defend against encroachment

virginals: see *pair of virginals*

virtue (86) power

virtuoso (19) amateur scientist and connoisseur of the arts [at this date often used sarcastically]

vital (30, 66) life-giving

vizard (5) mask; *vizard mask* (44b, 44g) woman wearing a mask, usually a prostitute

void (verb) excrete; (adj.) (30) empty of matter; *void of* (24, 51) free from

voluntary (adj.) (83) willed, deliberate; (adv.) (30) of their own accord

voluble (13) gliding with undulating movement; glib, fluent

votary (47) servant of a god

vulgar (noun) (5, 8) common people; (adj.) (39c, 66, 69, 72) common, ordinary [pejorative in 66, 69, 72, not in 39c]

wain (11) coach, carriage

wainscot (76) wooden panelling

wallow (44f) rolling walk

wandering fire (77) the *ignis fatuus*, a light which misleads travellers

want (verb) (*passim*) lack, be without; (noun) (48) lack

wanton (noun) (32) promiscuous woman, prostitute; (adj.) (25) luxuriating; (6, 28) gambolling; *wantonly* (25) casually; *wantonness* (83) caprice

wanton (verb) (27) luxuriate

ween (46) think, believe

well-breathed (29) well exercised, in good wind

well-mouthed (24) capable of baying loudly

whet (26) preen

whilom (41) once

whimsy (83, 85) fantastic, freakish idea

whiter (5) more innocent, more fortunate

wights (82) men

wilderness (38) part of a garden laid out as a maze or labyrinth

winged with (77) driven swiftly by

wink (15, 75, 78) close one's eyes; *winking* (66) flickering wit (*passim*) sharp intelligence; ideas sharply expressed; (8, 34, 39a, 44b, 45) man of intelligence, esp. a writer; (15, 44b, 44f, 44j, 83) man who thinks himself witty

witness (verb) (6) make evident

wont (44d) be accustomed; *wonted* (22, 48, 66) accustomed, familiar

word: see *took the word*

yard (9a) penis

yeaning (28) giving birth

yeomen (44i) guardsmen

zeal (44i) religious enthusiasm [esp. used of Nonconformist Protestant sects]

zone (62) region; girdle, belt

The Oxford World's Classics Website

www.worldsclassics.co.uk

- Information about new titles
- Explore the full range of Oxford World's Classics
- Links to other literary sites and the main OUP webpage
- Imaginative competitions, with bookish prizes
- Peruse *Compass*, the Oxford World's Classics magazine
- Articles by editors
- Extracts from Introductions
- A forum for discussion and feedback on the series
- Special information for teachers and lecturers

www.worldsclassics.co.uk

American Literature

British and Irish Literature

Children's Literature

Classics and Ancient Literature

Colonial Literature

Eastern Literature

European Literature

History

Medieval Literature

Oxford English Drama

Poetry

Philosophy

Politics

Religion

The Oxford Shakespeare

A complete list of Oxford Paperbacks, including Oxford World's Classics, OPUS, Past Masters, Oxford Authors, Oxford Shakespeare, Oxford Drama, and Oxford Paperback Reference, is available in the UK from the Academic Division Publicity Department, Oxford University Press, Great Clarendon Street, Oxford OX2 6DP.

In the USA, complete lists are available from the Paperbacks Marketing Manager, Oxford University Press, 198 Madison Avenue, New York, NY 10016.

Oxford Paperbacks are available from all good bookshops. In case of difficulty, customers in the UK can order direct from Oxford University Press Bookshop, Freepost, 116 High Street, Oxford OX1 4BR, enclosing full payment. Please add 10 per cent of published price for postage and packing.